QUARKXPRESS for WINDOWS

QuarkXPress
for Windows

Suzanne Sayegh Thomas

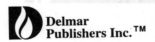

Delmar
Publishers Inc.™

I(T)P™

011

NOTICE TO THE READER

Cover design by Rob Clancy/Spiral Design

All screen shots from QuarkXPress for Windows 3.1. Copyright © 1991 by Quark, Inc. All rights reserved.

Delmar Staff:

Publisher: Michael McDermott
Administrative Editor: John Anderson
Development Editor: Sheila Davitt
Project Editor: Barbara Riedell
Production Coordinator: Larry Main
Design Coordinator: Lisa Bower

For information, address Delmar Publishers Inc.
3 Columbia Circle, Box 15-015
Albany, New York 12212-5015

Printed in the United States of America
Published simultaneously in Canada
by Nelson Canada,
a division of the Thomson Corporation

1 2 3 4 5 6 7 8 9 10 XXX 00 99 98 97 96 95 94

Library of Congress Cataloging-in-Publication data
Thomas, Suzanne Sayegh.
    QuarkXPress for Windows / Suzanne Sayegh Thomas.
        p.   cm.
    Includes index.
ISBN 0-8273-6447-4
    1. QuarkXPress for Windows   2. Desktop publishing I. Title.
Z253.532. Q375T48   1994
686.2′ 2544536—dc20   93-33975
                                                                              CIP

DEDICATION

For my daughters, Elizabeth and Katherine,

whose generosity of spirit and fondness for take-out food

make it possible for me to do all the things I love.

In loving them, I have it all.

CONTENTS

PREFACE

This textbook is written primarily for teachers, trainers, and students of QuarkXPress for Windows. The nature of the material is such that it can be easily used by teachers and students at the secondary and post-secondary levels as well as by trainers in a corporate environment. It is written with an understanding that there is more than one way to achieve a desired effect in QuarkXPress. A person's background in art, graphic design, or type, in book, magazine, or promotional piece production will influence the skills he or she brings to a page layout program and each user should feel free to experiment with the program's many functions.

The book is organized around the basic commands in QuarkXPress, some of which overlap. Type attributes, for example, can be applied from both the Style menu and Measurements palette. In learning to use the Measurements palette, one can also pull down the Style menu and notice how the values applied in the Measurements palette are reflected in the menu.

Since all the functions covered in the text are explained whenever they are used, you can either move sequentially from one lesson to the next or jump from lesson to lesson and section to section. You may, for example, want to skim the section on word processing and move directly to typography. Or, you may choose to concentrate on working with master page elements and leave type for later.

The text is comprised of the explanation for a command or function followed by an exercise based on that function. You can always change the values given in the exercises to create many more exercises which will reinforce your learning—and sometimes produce exciting results!

Those of you who are new to the PC/Windows environment should install Windows; then Lesson 1 will take you through the simple steps of launching QuarkXPress. Macintosh users of QuarkXPress will be immediately comfortable in the Windows version, an elegant translation of the Macintosh application. You will find a different Document Layout palette, and occasionally a different command, but substituting the Control and Alt keys for the Command and Option keys will get you around the program as easily as you navigated on the Macintosh.

The author wishes to extend her gratitude to a number of people who were helpful in putting this material together. The Windows Beta team at Quark Inc. kept me updated with the latest Windows version of QuarkXPress and provided knowledgeable and gracious technical support. They are truly some of the great people behind a great company. Thanks also to Leon Bruno, my Macintosh/PC friend who helped me set up the PC/Windows system and patiently allowed me to complain about DOS being an instrument of the devil!

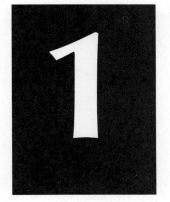

Introduction

to

QuarkXPress

for Windows

WELCOME TO QUARKXPRESS FOR WINDOWS

QuarkXPress for Windows is a powerful page layout program which allows you to combine text and graphics, and, in many ways, replaces conventional page production methods. XPress gives you the freedom to create materials in the program itself and/or import text and graphic files from other programs. Most images, for example, like complex Encapsulated PostScript drawings created in Adobe Illustrator™, CorelDRAW, and Harvard Graphics; bitmapped graphics from programs like Windows Paint and Paintbrush; and PICT files, as well as scanned color and grayscale photographs, can be brought into XPress and manipulated in astonishing ways.

WHY USE QUARKXPRESS?

This powerful and versatile program is used by students who are learning to set type and incorporate text and graphics in single and multiple-page documents on an MS-DOS personal computer running under Windows. Graphic designers who are looking for economical and flexible ways of manipulating design elements will also find QuarkXPress for Windows both fast and friendly. Print shops and desktop publishers will also find that they can manipulate text and graphics easily and quickly in QuarkXPress. Anyone who is working in color knows that QuarkXPress contains the most comprehensive and accurate controls available on the desktop.

WHAT THIS BOOK COVERS

This book is designed to teach you how to create pages; how to use the tool box and floating palettes; how to flow and format text; how to import and manipulate text and graphics; how to draw objects; how to apply color; and how to print your documents.

WORKING IN THE WINDOWS ENVIRONMENT

Windows are just that—windows in which applications and documents are displayed. Each window has its own controls and can be manipulated independently of other open windows. You will need to know how to use the mouse to click and drag for drawing and for dragging down menus. If you are familiar with the Macintosh version of QuarkXPress, you will be immediately comfortable with the Windows version.

USING THE MENUS

When you first launch QuarkXPress for Windows, you are presented with a Menu Bar (Figure 1.1) and the Tool palette. You can access commands from the Menu Bar before creating a new document as well as when working with a document. Place the mouse pointer over a menu title and click the mouse button to reveal that menu item's drop-down menu. To close the menu, either choose a command by clicking on a command to select it or click anywhere else in the window. You can also press the Escape key (Esc) to close the menu while keeping the Menu Bar active. Press the Alt or F10 keys to close the menu and return to the application window.

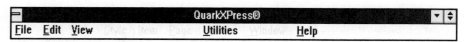

Figure 1.1—The Menu Bar in a QuarkXPress document. This Menu Bar is displayed once the application is launched and before any documents are opened or created.

MENU SYMBOLS

Three symbols can appear before and after commands in the drop-down menus: a check mark, a right-pointing arrow, and an ellipse. Some commands will toggle between Show and Hide. For example, if you choose Show Document Layout from the View menu, the next time you display the View menu commands, Hide Document Layout will be displayed. Other commands, like Fit in Window and Snap to Guides, will display a check mark before the name when that command has been selected.

A right-pointing arrow signals a submenu (Figure 1.2). Click on the command to display the submenu, then drag across to choose a command from the submenu. If you change your mind, drag off both the main and submenus and click anywhere on the screen.

Commands followed by an ellipse (...) indicate that selecting the command will display a dialog box (Figure 1.2) where you can select one or more options. To leave a dialog box without making a selection, click on Cancel.

The check mark next to Snap to Guides indicates that the option is turned on or active. If you select Snap to Guides now, the check mark will not be displayed the next time you pull down the menu.

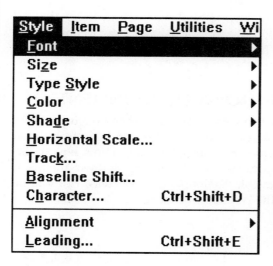

Figure 1.2—Displays a drop-down menu with right-pointing arrows indicating submenus and ellipses which tell you that selecting that command will display a dialog box.

NAVIGATING DIALOG BOXES

Dialog boxes contain buttons, check boxes, text boxes, and drop-down list indicators (Figure 1.3). Click in a button or on its label to select it. Click on it again to deselect it. Click in a check box to select the option; click on it again to deselect the option. Click inside a text box and type a value; drag to select the value and press the Backspace key to delete the text. Clicking on the drop-down list indicator displays a drop-down list of options. Click on an option to select it. Click on the same option to deselect it.

You can also make selections from check boxes and buttons by clicking on the label for that check box or button. Likewise, pressing the Alt key while typing the letter that is underscored in the label also allows you to make selections.

Another way of moving through a dialog box is to press the Tab key, which moves you from one label to another in the dialog box. Then use the arrow keys to highlight an entry.

Leading:	auto
Space Before:	0"
Space After:	0"

Pressing Alt+L highlights the Leading field.

Paragraph Formats

Left Indent:	0"	Leading:	auto
First Line:	0"	Space Before:	0"
Right Indent:	0"	Space After:	0"

☐ Lock to Baseline Grid   ☐ Keep with Next ¶

☐ Drop Caps   ☐ Keep Lines Together

Character Count   ○ All Lines in ¶

Line Count   ○ Start: End:

Alignment: Left ▼   [Apply]

H&J: Standard ▼   [OK]   [Cancel]

Figure 1.3—The Paragraph Formats dialog box displays different selection options: buttons (Keep with Next ¶ field); check boxes (Drop Caps field); drop-down lists (Alignment and H&J fields); and text boxes (Indent fields).

COMMAND BUTTONS IN DIALOG BOXES

Command buttons in a dialog box, like OK and Cancel, allow you to execute the options you just selected (OK) or to cancel them (Cancel) and return to the document exactly as it was before you opened the dialog box. The currently selected command button is outlined with a dark border and can be activated either by clicking on it or pressing the Enter key. If a command has an underscored letter, press the Alt key while typing the underscored letter to highlight the field, or to select the checkbox or button.

A command followed by an ellipse indicates that another dialog box will be displayed if you select the command.

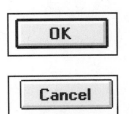

Because the OK button has a border around it, pressing Enter will activate the OK command.

FYI

Some dialog boxes also contain scroll bars, which operate the same way as they do in the document windows.

Control menu

WARNING!

You might not be able to see a Minimized icon if it is covered by the active window. Click and drag the corners of the active window to reduce its size and reveal the Minimized icon.

USING KEYBOARD SHORTCUTS

To work more efficiently in XPress, learn to use the keyboard equivalents for the menu items—you will find your productivity increase significantly. Open a menu *title* from the Menu Bar by pressing the Alt key and the first letter of the menu title. For example, pressing Alt+F opens the File menu.

You can also use keyboard commands to select a menu *command* by typing the underscored letter in the command. For example, when the File menu is displayed, typing the letter *n* (uppercase or lowercase) will display the New (document) dialog box.

The fastest and easiest way to move around in XPress is to use the keyboard equivalents built into QuarkXPress itself. Most of these commands require you to press the Ctrl key plus another key. Ctrl+P, for example, will display the Print dialog box. Ctrl+Alt+M displays the Measurements palette.

QUARK DOES WINDOWS

You may notice that when you launch Windows, the Program Manager displays programs as icons in windows on the screen. To open one of these windows, click on the icon to select it and choose File/Open. You can also double-click on the icon to launch the application.

To close the window under the Program Manager, choose Close from the Control menu which appears when you click on the Control menu box in the upper left corner of the window. Double-clicking on the Control menu box or choosing File/Close will also close the window.

You can open the Control menu on the application window from the keyboard by pressing Alt+Spacebar. To open the Control menu in a document from the keyboard, press Alt+ - [hyphen].

MOVING AND RESIZING WINDOWS

Moving a window on the screen is as easy as dragging the Title Bar. Choosing Move from the Control menu and using the arrow keys also allows you to move the window. Regardless of where a window is on the screen, you can always use the horizontal and vertical scroll bars to move the page in the window. Click on the up or down arrows (at the top and bottom of the gray bar) to move the view in small increments. Click on the gray bar itself to move to different parts of the document in larger increments. You can also drag the scroll box up and down to display any area of the document window (Figure 1.4).

Position the mouse pointer on any border or corner of the window and notice that it changes to a double-pointing arrow. Use this arrow to resize the window by pressing the mouse button and dragging to enlarge or reduce the size of the window. To automatically enlarge a window so that it fills the screen, click on the Control menu to open it and then click on the Maximize button, which displays an up arrow in the window's top left corner. If the window has already been Maximized, click on the Restore button to restore the window to the size it was before it was Maximized. Double-clicking on the Title Bar also restores a Maximized window to its previous size.

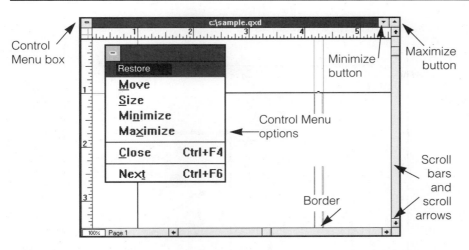

Figure 1.4—A QuarkXPress document window displays several controls. Click and drag the Title Bar to move the document window around the screen. Click on the Maximize button to enlarge the document window to its maximum size. Click on the Minimize button to shrink the document window to an icon. Use the scroll bars and arrows to position the page within the document window.

If you want a file open but do not want to work with it, click on the Minimize box in the upper right corner of the window. This will reduce the window to an icon and place it at the bottom of the screen. Double-clicking on that icon will open the window again.

The important thing to remember about a window is that it must be active before you can work with it. Clicking on a window activates that window. To cycle through different open *application* windows, press the Alt+Esc keys. To cycle through different open *document* windows, press the Ctrl+F6 keys or Ctrl+Tab keys.

HOW TO USE THIS TEXT

This text has been designed so you can easily lay it flat next to your computer and work directly from it. Each lesson ends with a Review which will help you to pull together the different kinds of material covered in the lesson. You will also find multiple choice questions at the end of each lesson which will reinforce what you learned in the lesson.

To help you keep track of the various kinds of information you are working with, the sidebar of each page has become a "pasteboard" for the text. In XPress the pasteboard is the non-printing area that surrounds the margin guides. In this text, it's the narrow column on each page where you will find much helpful information on using the features in QuarkXPress for Windows.

A QuarkXPress document consists of a page with one or all of the following elements: text boxes which contain text, picture boxes which contain pictures like Encapsulated PostScript and bitmapped files, and lines (Figure 1.5). These elements are manipulated by various tools as well as by commands from the Main Menu.

FYI

An application is a program that creates documents or files. Microsoft Word for Windows is an application; QuarkXPress is an application. The files created in those programs are called documents.

Figure 1.5—This is a page created in QuarkXPress for Windows. It contains two text boxes ❶ and ❷, a rectangular picture box ❸, a round picture box ❹, a polygon picture box ❺, a line with an arrow-head ❻, and a dashed line ❼. Elements can overlap one another, as with the dashed line ❼ and the rectangular picture box ❸. Both text boxes and picture boxes can be framed ❷, ❹, and ❺. Text boxes, picture boxes, and lines are called items and can be moved and resized. The handles appearing around the items indicate that those items are selected. Moving these handles resizes the item.

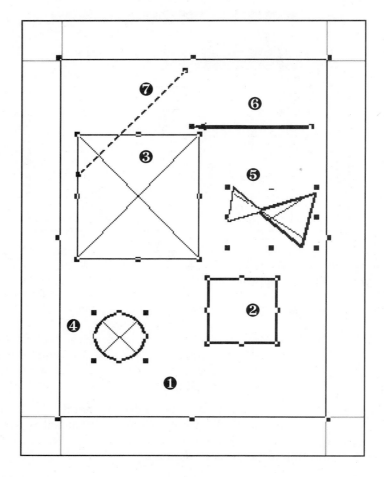

Remember

When you are told to "Choose File/Open," you should drag your cursor to the Menu Bar and click on File. Then drag down and highlight (select) Open before releasing the mouse button.

To select a file, click on it to *highlight* it.

Menu commands and their keyboard equivalents are listed in the sidebar. You may even find some menu commands that have not been taught in that lesson. Don't be afraid to pull the menus down and try things yourself. You can't break the program! Most of the menu commands are self-explanatory, and using them early will make you more proficient in dealing with the more complex parts of the program.

You will also find explanations and diagrams on the sidebar. These will help to make the information in the text clearer as well as separate one piece of information from a larger group. The different elements in the Tool Palette, for instance, are separated and identified in the sidebar.

Look for the How to do it and Design Tip features, also in the sidebar. These are explanations of how some element on the page, text, graphic, special effect, etc. was generated. The Design Tip will give you a method of creating an optically interesting effect on a page. Try recreating the same effect yourself. You may even find that you have a faster and better way of getting the same result. There are several ways to do the same thing in XPress and everything you do teaches you something.

Most sections include Exercises to reinforce what you just learned. After completing the exercises, redo them, changing the values and dimensions given in the text. Use different graphic files and change their position and dimensions. This will help you to see the various design and formatting possibilities available in XPress as well as make you more comfortable with the tools, menu commands, and keyboard equivalents.

When you are given material to type in, that material will be printed with quotation marks. Type only the words, not the quotation marks.

WHAT YOU WILL NEED

QuarkXPress for Windows 3.1 requires an MS-DOS personal computer with at least an 80386 (or higher) processor, MS-DOS® version 3.1 or later, and Microsoft Windows version 3.0 or higher. You should have at least 4 MB of memory and 6 MB of free space on a hard disk drive. You will also need a VGA (or better) graphics card and a mouse that can run under Windows.

If the material on the current page calls for text or graphic files, you will be told what you need at the top of the sidebar. Having a folder with some dummy text files and a few graphic files in different formats will make it easier for you to work. You should have at least one bitmapped file from a Paint program, a TIFF file generated by a scanning program, and one EPS (Encapsulated PostScript) formatted file available. When you work with graphics in XPress, you will learn how to apply different effects to the various file formats.

Since QuarkXPress allows you so much typographical control, you should have a PostScript laser printer which will print text in various sizes (especially smaller sizes) and styles as well as provide the resolution, or measure of the sharpness of the edges of printed text and graphics, needed to produce camera ready materials.

TYPEFACES

In working with XPress, you will most likely be using Type 1 PostScript fonts, TrueType fonts, or Type 3 PostScript fonts. Regardless of the type of font you use, it must be installed in the system. Otherwise, it will not appear under the Style menu in XPress and you will not be able to apply it to text.

When you are asked to use a typeface like Times Roman or MS Sans Serif, feel free to substitute other fonts that are installed in your system. You might have to adjust the font size to make the text fit, but you will most likely attain the same results as if you had used the recommended fonts.

IMPORTING TEXT FILES

You can import many kinds of text files into QuarkXPress. Text generated by PC word processing programs like Microsoft Word 4.0 for DOS, Microsoft Word for Windows, Microsoft Write, WordPerfect 5.1, WordPerfect for Windows, Ami Pro 2.0, and XyWrite III Plus can all be imported with the Get Text command. Unformatted text like ASCII files from any word processor, data that has been saved in ASCII format from a database or spreadsheet, and text that has been transmitted via modem and received as ASCII text can all be brought into XPress and formatted.

FYI

Further information on working with fonts in QuarkXPress for Windows appears at the end of Lesson 10.

FYI

A list of graphic file types which QuarkXPress for Windows imports is found on page 114.

ASCII (American Standard Code Information Interface) text, however, is unformatted text. To import both the text and its formatting, as well as to export it from XPress, you must have the Import/Export filters supplied by Quark present in the same directory as the QuarkXPress for Windows application. Quark provides filters for the Microsoft Word for Windows, Windows Write, WordPerfect for Windows, Ami Pro 2.0, and XyWrite III Plus word processors.

When you import a text file that contains more information than will fit in a text box, an Overflow Indicator box will appear on the screen in the lower right hand corner of the text box. This is a small box with an X in it. You can remove it by either formatting the text so that it fits in the text box, enlarging the text box to accommodate the text, or linking the text box with the Overflow Indicator to another text box. To change the formatting, however, use Edit/Select All (Ctrl+A) so that the new formatting will be applied to all the text, even the hidden text.

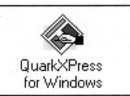

The Overflow Indicator appears in the lower right corner of a text box which is too small to contain all the text which has been flowed or typed into it.

THINKING IN BOXES

QuarkXPress uses both a pasteboard metaphor and a box metaphor. The pasteboard metaphor allows you to move items around on a page, between pages, and onto the non-printing area itself. The box metaphor gives you the control to place any item at a precise point on a page. All text in XPress is either typed in or imported into text boxes. All graphics are imported into picture boxes. If you find yourself typing, for instance, and nothing appears on the screen, that's because you are not typing in a text box. Create one with the Text Box tool or create a document with the Automatic Text Box option which will put a text box on every page of your document. Use the Picture Box tool to create a picture box into which you will import graphics created in other programs.

LAUNCHING THE QUARKXPRESS APPLICATION

To launch QuarkXPress for Windows, open the QuarkXPress window in the Windows Program Manager (Figure 1.6). Then double-click on the program icon. If you did not set up a program icon in the Program Manager, you can choose File/Run from the Program Manager or File Manager's File menu. This will display the Run dialog box where you can type the path and program name. If you enjoy clicking through directories, do so under the File Manager until you locate the Xpress.exe file. Double-click on the file name or on the name of a QuarkXPress document.

The QuarkXPress for Windows application icon. Double-click on this icon in the Finder to launch QuarkXPress for Windows.

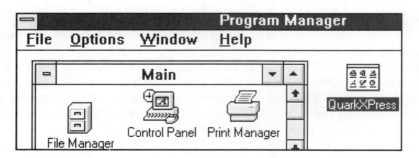

Figure 1.6—Locate the QuarkXPress window in the Windows Program Manager. Double-clicking on the icon will display the application icon. Double-click on the

SAVING FILES

Once you have created a document, you will want to save that file so that you can open it at another time. To save a file, move the cursor to the Menu Bar, click on File, and highlight Save from the pull-down menu. Type a name for your file in the File Name field (Figure 1.7) and drag through the directories to locate another directory or drive where your file will be saved. Click on Save.

FYI

Windows applies the QXD extension automatically to a QuarkXPress document when you first save it. Double-click on this icon to simultaneously launch the application and open the file.

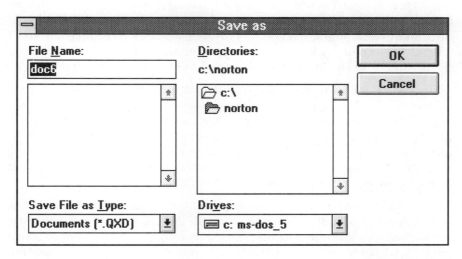

Figure 1.7—Displays the Save as dialog box which appears when you choose Save as (Ctrl+Alt+S) from the File menu.

OPENING FILES

Any file that has been previously created and saved by choosing File/Save or File/Save as can be opened. (Save as allows you to change the name of your file while leaving the original file unchanged.) To open a file you have saved, choose File/Open (Figure 1.8). Place your cursor over the file name you wish to open to select (highlight) it and click on Open. You can also open a file by double-clicking on the name of the file itself under the File Manager.

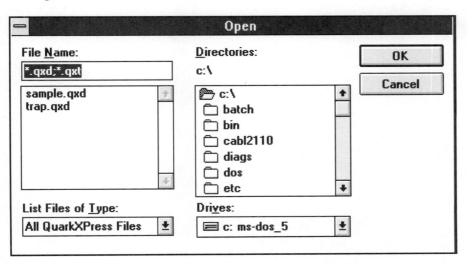

Figure 1.8—The Open dialog box is where you locate the document (file) to be opened by dragging through the List Files of Type, Directories, and Drives scroll boxes.

MOVING ON...

If it seems like you just started and now you're being told to move on, you're right! Once you complete the next lesson, you will be familiar with many features in XPress and can begin creating pages immediately. But to do that well, you have to train your eye by looking at other materials. When you see a flyer or advertisement that catches your eye, ask "Why? What is it about its design, color, typography, that intrigues me?" Then ask, "How would I do this in XPress? Would I use text boxes? Picture boxes? Both? Would I start with an automatic text box or build the whole document from scratch? Which typefaces would I use? In what size? Should I use color?" These may be hypothetical questions, but answering them—and learning the answers to them—will teach you a great deal.

Make a habit, too, of reproducing materials you get in the mail. If you get a flyer or brochure that looks like a nursery school project, redo it correctly. Think about the changes you're making and why what you're doing is making the material a better piece of communication. That's the bottom line, of course. If your pages don't communicate a message, no matter how intricate and interesting they are, they fail. So always keep in mind that printed materials must communicate information.

QuarkXPress for Windows is a complex and powerful tool. But that's all it is. It will never be able to provide you with the vision and understanding to manipulate color, type, texture, and dimension so as to create effective pages. It will only give you the tools to do that. You yourself must take the first steps in studying typography, design, and communications. Read widely among the many excellent books currently available on type and computer-generated art. Learn how to use a pica ruler and to read an E-gauge. You will find editors, designers, and printers much easier to deal with if you speak their language. Once you have an understanding of how to proceed visually, XPress will give you the tools to move from the realm of the imaginary to the real so that your pages will 'e both mechanically correct and aesthetically beautiful.

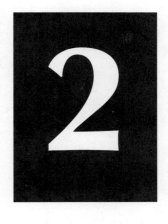

LESSON

2

Document

Construction

OVERVIEW

In this lesson you will learn how to create a new document with specific margin settings, how to use the rulers and ruler guides and how to draw text boxes, picture boxes, circles, squares, and lines. Further information on saving and opening files is also covered. You will also be introduced to the Tool palette and learn how to use eleven of the program's tools. Because it is easier and faster to use keyboard shortcuts, you will practice accessing menu items from the keyboard. As a review, you will create and modify text and graphic boxes.

TOPICS

Creating a new document
Rulers and ruler guides
Zero point
Setting General Preferences
Setting Application Preferences
Saving files
Opening files
Tool palette
How the tools work
Review Exercise
Review Questions

TERMS

auto page insertion
automatic text box
Content tool
default setting
Document Layout
    palette
facing pages
framing
greeking
gutter width
Item coordinates
item tool

Library palette
Line tool
margin guides
master page items
Measurements palette
Menu Bar
Open
Orthogonal Line tool
pasteboard
Polygon Picture Box
    tool
Rectangle Picture Box
    tool

Rotation tool
ruler guides
rulers
Save
Snap to Guides
template
Text Box tool
Tool palette
zero point
Zoom tool

Ctrl+N File/New

CREATING A NEW DOCUMENT

Before you can begin working in XPress, you must launch the program, then either create a new document or open an existing document. When you launch QuarkXPress, you are presented with the Menu Bar and the Tool palette. The Menu Bar, which runs across the top of the screen, allows you to choose all the commands available in XPress. The Tool palette which appears on the left side of the screen, allows you to select the tools needed to create and manipulate items in the program.

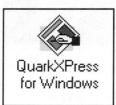

The QuarkXPress icon found in the QuarkXPress window.

EXERCISE A

1. Enter Windows and launch QuarkXPress for Windows by double-clicking on the QuarkXPress icon in the QuarkXPress window.

2. When the Menu Bar and Tool palette appear, click on the word File in the Menu Bar and drag down to highlight (select) New. When you release the mouse button, the screen displays the New (document) dialog box (Figure 2.1).

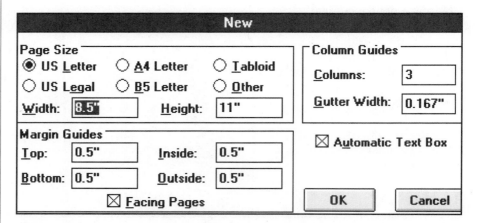

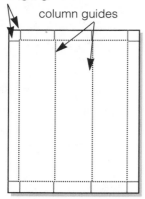

margin guides

column guides

Figure 2.1—When you create a new document, this is the screen which appears. Make margin and column selections from the dialog boxes.

The program defaults to US, Letter, which is 8.5 X 11 inches. A default setting is the setting which is in effect until you change it. Not only does QuarkXPress default to letter-size pages, it also defaults to: half-inch (.5-inch) margins for those pages; facing pages with one column; a gutter width of 0.167 inches; and creating an automatic text box. Let's examine some of these default settings.

The margin guides are four non-printing guides which appear around the page and define the printing area.

This is what a page in the 3-column document you just created should look like.

3. Format the document with ¾-inch margins by typing 0.75 in the Top, Bottom, Inside, and Outside fields.

4. *Deselect* the Facing Pages option by clicking in the Facing Pages check box, and notice that Inside and Outside change to Left and Right. You would leave Facing Pages checked to produce a document that will be printed on two sides of the paper.

5.   In the Column Guides area on the right side of the New dialog box, locate the Columns field and type 3 for the number of columns which will appear on each page of the document. The gutter width, or white space between columns, defaults to 0.167 inches, but you can change that to another number. XPress calculates the width of each column based on the number of columns and width between columns which you specify in this dialog box.

The area outside of the margin guides is called the pasteboard. It is used for storing text and graphics that you don't want printed on the finished page but that you want available to drag on or off the page.

6.   When the Automatic Text Box option is selected, XPress will flow text automatically from one page to another (anywhere in the document) and from one text box to another. You can always manually link boxes (you'll learn about linking in Lesson 6), but if you are flowing text from one page directly to the next, it's better to select the Automatic Text Box option.

7.   Once you have defined your page specifications in the New dialog box, click on OK. A document page based on the specifications you just set appears on the screen.

RULERS AND RULER GUIDES

Rulers are displayed above and to the left of the page. The ruler above the page is called the horizontal ruler; the ruler to the left of the page is called the vertical ruler. These rulers are "storage bins" for ruler guides, nonprinting guides which help you to accurately position items on a page.

EXERCISE B

1.   Display the rulers by choosing View/Show Rulers (Ctrl+R).

2.   To determine ruler measurement display (inches, picas, etc.), choose Edit/Preferences/General (Ctrl+Y). When the General Preferences dialog box appears (Figure 2.2), use the drop-down list to select inches as the unit of measure. Click on OK.

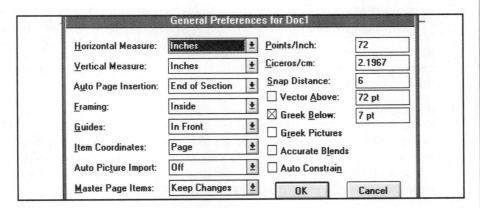

Figure 2.2—The General Preferences dialog box.

Ctrl+R View/Show Rulers
Ctrl+Y Edit/Preferences/
        General

When you click on a ruler guide, the cursor temporarily changes to the Ruler Guide cursor.

FYI

You move a ruler guide by clicking on it anywhere on the page with the Item tool and dragging it to a new location. To remove a ruler guide, click on it and drag it up or across back to the ruler it came from.

You can also Alt-click on the horizontal or vertical rulers to remove all the horizontal and vertical rulers on the page.

Your page should look like Figure 2.3, which shows the margin guides and rulers. Notice that the rulers are displayed in inches, the magnification is at 46.7%, and the document page is Page 1.

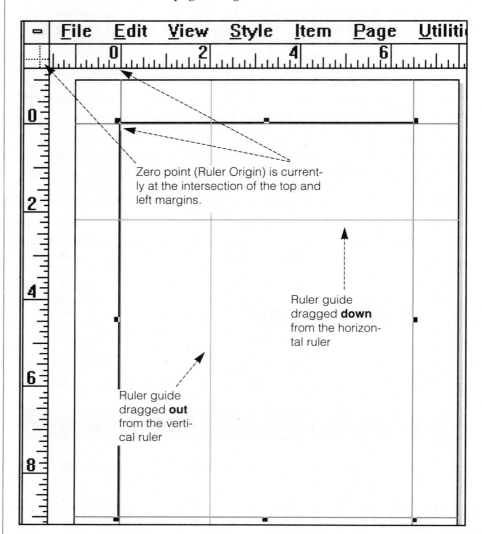

The zero point (ruler origin) is in the upper left corner of the document window where the two dotted lines intersect. Drag it to reset the zero point anywhere on the page.

Figure 2.3—Notice the arrow at the zero point.

3. Move your cursor up to the horizontal ruler and drag a ruler guide down onto the page to the 2-inch mark on the vertical ruler. Drag another ruler guide out of the vertical ruler to the 1.5-inch position on the horizontal ruler.

4. Ruler guides are helpful in accurately aligning elements. If you choose the Snap to Guides option by choosing View/Snap to Guides, any boxes or lines you create near these guides will automatically snap to or rest against these ruler guides. You can specify the distance from which an object will snap to the ruler guides by choosing Edit/Preferences/Application and typing a value in the Snap to Guide field.

ZERO POINT

When you choose View/Show Rulers (Ctrl+R), the zero point becomes visible. The ruler origin, where the horizontal ruler and vertical ruler intersect, can be adjusted by moving the zero point. This is the intersection of two dotted lines in the upper left corner beneath the Close box.

Moving the zero point lets you indicate the starting position of an item like a box or line and measure its height, width, or length accurately.

Look at the page of your document and notice the left margin line visible at the 0-inch mark. The zero point of this document is currently at the left edge of the page.

Ctrl+R View/Show Rulers
Ctrl+B Item/Frame

EXERCISE C

1. To change the zero point, place your cursor on the point and drag it down onto the page so that the zero point of intersection is directly over the point on the page where the top and left margins meet. Notice now that the ruler's 0 origin is at that point, as displayed in Figure 2.3. Moving the zero point of the ruler allows you to set the 0 to 1-inch mark (or any unit of measure) anywhere on the page.

2. Reset the ruler point of origin (zero point) back to the left margin by clicking once on the zero point.

SETTING GENERAL PREFERENCES

Figure 2.2 displays the General Preferences dialog box, where drop-down menus allow you to choose how the program behaves. Here, the document is set to display units of measure in picas, to insert pages at the end of each section, to frame boxes on the inside, and to display ruler guides in front of the boxes. Greek Below means that all text below 7 points will be displayed in gray lines called greeking. The text is still there at its proper size, but is only displayed as gray bars, which allows for faster screen redraw. The Auto Page Insertion option tells XPress where in the document to insert additional pages automatically. Here it is set for the end of a section; it could also be set for the end of the document, the end of the story, or turned off completely so that new pages would have to be inserted manually.

Framing, or putting borders around text boxes and picture boxes, is set to appear on the inside of the box. You access the Frame dialog box by choosing Item/Frame (Ctrl+B) and selecting a style of frame and its weight.

Ruler guides, the non-printing horizontal and vertical guidelines, are set to appear behind all objects on a page. They are virtually useless there, though, since you can only see the top and bottom of each guide and you need to see the entire ruler guide if you are going to snap boxes and lines against it. For most purposes, you will find it easier if you select the In Front option for Guides.

Design Hint

A *spread* is a group of adjacent pages that spread across the fold in a document. Spreading a graphic over three pages, as seen here in the three-page spread, makes the picture a prominent design element and subordinates the text to the graphic.

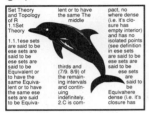

Click on the Content tool in the Tool palette to select it.

When you have the Content tool selected, hold down the Alt key to turn the cursor into the Grabber Hand. Use the Grabber Hand to move the page around the screen.

Item Coordinates will be based on a single page, which means that the ruler's point of origin will be at the same position on every page. If you use the drop-down list to select Spread, the ruler will appear at the same position on every spread where the ruler extends over all adjacent pages. Auto Picture Import—automatic updating of images (graphic files that you create in a drawing program) that you changed since you last saved the document—is turned off, and changes made to Master Page Items (text and graphics you placed on the master pages and which repeat on every document page) will not override changes which you make to those items on the document pages.

SETTING APPLICATION PREFERENCES

The Application Preferences dialog box is where you can set preferences about how the program itself behaves.

EXERCISE D

1. Choose Edit/Preferences/Application to display the Application Preferences dialog box (Figure 2.4).

2. If you are working with a color monitor, you can designate colors for the margins, ruler guides, and grid colors by double-clicking on each button. This will display the Color Wheel and allow you to select a color.

3. Click in the Live Scroll check box to watch the screen move as you scroll so you can see where you're going on the screen when you click and drag the scroll bars.

4. Click in the Page Grabber Hand check box. With this option selected, when you hold down the Alt key, the cursor will change to the Grabber Hand and allow you to click and then drag the page across the screen.

5. Click in the Auto Library Save check box, which tells XPress to automatically save a library each time you add an item to the library.

6. Click on the Scroll Speed scroll bar and drag it to determine how fast or slowly you can scroll through the document.

7. Once you have set the preferences, click on OK. Use the vertical scroll bar to scroll through the document. Choose Edit/Preferences/Application to change the Scroll Speed value.

8. With the Content Tool selected (see sidebar), hold down the Alt key and use the Page Grabber Hand to move the page around the screen.

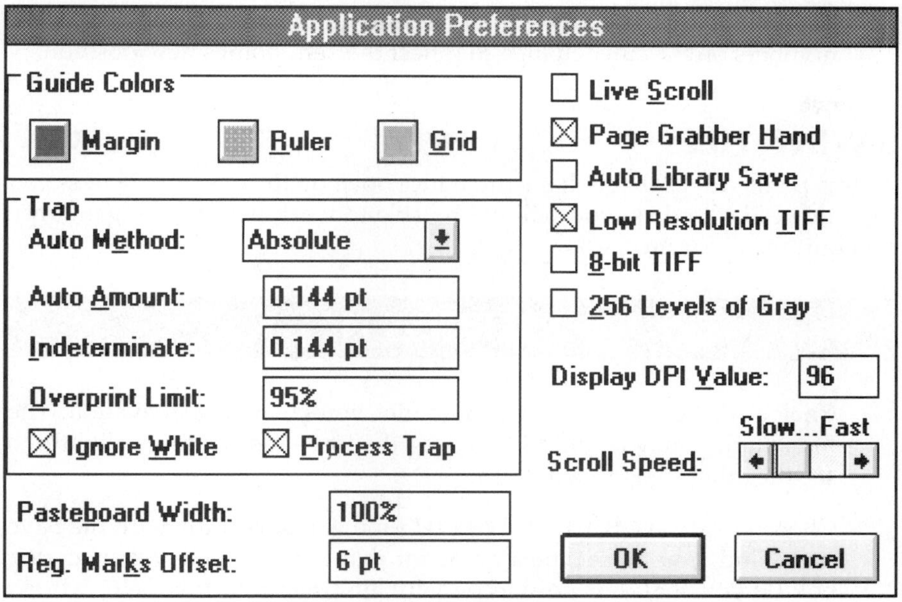

Application Preferences

Guide Colors
■ **M**argin   ▨ **R**uler   ▨ **G**rid

Trap
Auto **M**ethod: Absolute ▼
Auto **A**mount: 0.144 pt
Indeterminate: 0.144 pt
Overprint Limit: 95%
☒ **I**gnore **W**hite   ☒ **P**rocess Trap

Paste**b**oard Width: 100%
Reg. Mar**k**s Offset: 6 pt

☐ Live **S**croll
☒ Page Grabber **H**and
☐ Auto **L**ibrary Save
☒ Low Resolution **T**IFF
☐ **8**-bit TIFF
☐ **2**56 Levels of Gray

Display DPI **V**alue: 96

Slow...Fast
Scroll Spee**d**: ← ▮ →

OK   Cancel

Figure 2.4—The Application Preferences dialog box is displayed when you choose Edit/Preferences/Application. It allows you to tell XPress how you want some of the program functions to operate.

EXERCISE E

1. Create a new document (File/New) with 1-inch margins all around. Select the Facing Pages and Automatic Text Box options by making sure there is an X displayed in their check boxes. If not, click in the check box to display the X and activate the option.

2. Display the units of measure in inches with ruler guides placed behind the boxes. Click on OK.

EXERCISE F

1. Create a new document (File/New) without facing pages which has top and bottom margins of 6 picas and left and right margins of 4 picas.

2. Choose Edit/Preferences/Application and change the Guide colors by double-clicking on each colored rectangle to access the Color Wheel; deselect the Page Grabber Hand option; and set the Scroll speed to Fast. Click on OK to return to the document.

EXERCISE G

1. Create a new document (File/New) using inches as the unit of measure and guides to be placed in front of the box. Pull down a ruler guide to the 4-inch mark on the vertical ruler and another guide to the 5-inch mark on the horizontal ruler.

FYI

When typing a name for a file you are saving, you must observe the DOS conventions for naming files. This can be more complicated than using QuarkXPress itself. Files can have names which combine up to eight letters and numbers (not including the file name extension which XPress will apply). Don't use punctuation marks (except before the extension). Don't use special characters. Avoid using symbols because many of them are not acceptable. Got that?

Figure 2.5—Displays the Save as dialog box where you can save a file under another name or name it the first time you save it. In this example a file is being saved to the hard (c) drive.

The number in the name (doc6) indicates the number of new documents you've opened since you launched QuarkXPress.

2. Then move the zero point to the vertical guideline and notice how the numbers on the ruler change to reflect the zero point's new position.

SAVING FILES

At this point you probably have three files open on the desktop. Unless you save these files to disk, you will not be able to work with them again once you quit the program.

EXERCISE H

1. Click anywhere in one of the new files you created to activate it. The file window may be hidden, so drag the top window down slightly to see the other two file windows.

2. Choose File/Save (Ctrl+S). The first time you save a file with the Save command, you must type a name for that file in the File Name dialog box (Figure 2.5). For now, type your first name in this field. XPress will save the file as a fully editable document or, if you choose Template from the Save File as Type field, as a template. A template is a document which contains items you will be using frequently. A newsletter, for instance, will usually have the same column structure, placement of the masthead, and page numbering style. This template could be used as the basis for a new edition of the newsletter and then saved under a new name. The template would remain unchanged, available to receive the next issue's new text and graphics.

3. Now that you have named the file, choose a directory on the current drive or another directory on another of the displayed drives. When you have located the folder and/or drive and they are displayed in the dialog box, click on the Save button. You will be returned to the document you just saved.

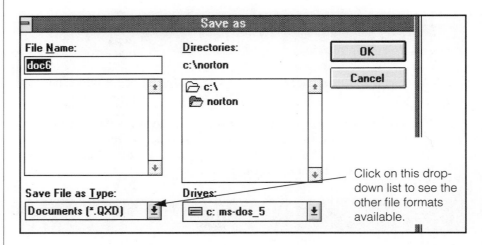

4. Repeat this procedure with the other files you created, assigning them different names.

OPENING FILES

Any file that has been saved as a document can also be opened, changed, and saved again.

EXERCISE I

1. Choose File/Open (Ctrl+O). Scroll through the drives and directories on the drives where you saved the document under your first name.

2. Locate the file and move your cursor over it to highlight it. Click on the Open button. You could also open the file by double-clicking on the file name. The file is now open on your screen and available for editing.

FYI

Any file saved as a template can be opened and edited; however, it must be saved under a different name.

THE TOOL PALETTE

The Tool palette, which is displayed whenever you create a new file or open an existing file, allows you to select tools to create and manipulate items like boxes, lines, and text material. Figure 2.6 displays the Tool palette. Now try using some of these tools.

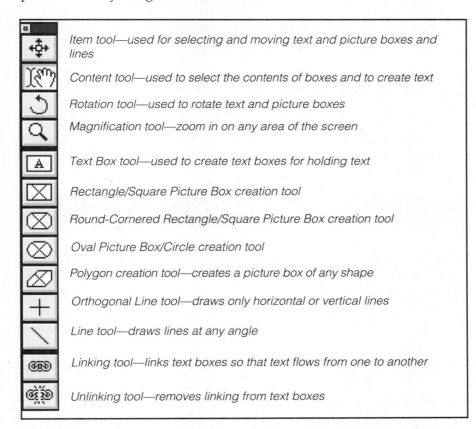

Item tool—used for selecting and moving text and picture boxes and lines

Content tool—used to select the contents of boxes and to create text

Rotation tool—used to rotate text and picture boxes

Magnification tool—zoom in on any area of the screen

Text Box tool—used to create text boxes for holding text

Rectangle/Square Picture Box creation tool

Round-Cornered Rectangle/Square Picture Box creation tool

Oval Picture Box/Circle creation tool

Polygon creation tool—creates a picture box of any shape

Orthogonal Line tool—draws only horizontal or vertical lines

Line tool—draws lines at any angle

Linking tool—links text boxes so that text flows from one to another

Unlinking tool—removes linking from text boxes

FYI

The four tools above the first bar in the Tool palette are used to position and view items. The tools in the middle section between the bars are used to create items, and the last two tools are used to establish text flow in a document.

Figure 2.6—The QuarkXPress Tool palette displays tools for creating and manipulating elements in a document.

Ctrl+N File/New
Ctrl+Y Edit/Preferences/
General
Ctrl+E File/Get Picture

 Item tool moves items.

 Content tool makes changes to the contents of boxes.

 Text Box tool creates text boxes.

 Rectangle Picture Box tool draws rectangular and square picture boxes.

 Hold down the Shift key to create squares and circles with the Rectangle or Oval Picture Box tools.

 The Pointer Finger is used to resize items.

EXERCISE J

1. Choose File/New (Ctrl+N) to create a new document with 1-inch margins, facing pages, and an automatic text box. Choose Edit/Preferences/General (Ctrl+Y) to display the General Preferences dialog box. Use the drop-down list to select Inches as the unit of measure. Click on OK.

2. Click once on the Text Box tool to select it. Your cursor will change into a crosshair. Drag the cursor down and to the right to create a text box that is about 2 inches wide and 3 inches high. Release your mouse button. Notice that the Content tool has automatically been selected and a blinking text cursor appears in the newly created text box. Type: "Use the Content tool to make changes to the contents of boxes."

3. Next, click once on the Rectangle Picture Box tool to select it and drag the crosshair to create a picture box that is about 3 inches wide and 2 inches high. The large X in the box tells you that this is a picture box.

4. Click on the Content tool and choose File/Get Picture (Ctrl+E). Locate a graphic on your hard drive, click on it to select it, and notice that a thumbnail view of that picture appears in the Preview window.

5. Click on Open and the picture will appear in the picture box you just created. You'll learn more about resizing graphics in Lesson 8.

HOW THE TOOLS WORK

The Item tool is used to move items—boxes, lines, and grouped items—on a page. When you select the Item tool, the cursor becomes a pointer but changes to a four-pointed mover pointer once you position it over a box or line. It will change to a resizing pointing finger if you position it over the handle of any active item (see sidebar).

EXERCISE K

1. Click once on the Item tool; then click on the text box to select it; then click and drag to move the box around on the page.

2. Do the same with the picture box. Notice that if you place your cursor on one of the handles of any box, the cursor changes into a pointing finger. Use this finger to click and drag a handle to resize each box, making it larger and smaller.

3. To create a square, hold down the Shift key while dragging with the Rectangle Picture Box tool. To create a circle, hold down the Shift key while dragging with the Oval Picture Box tool.

4. Select either the Item tool or the Content tool and click on the text box you just created to select it. Position the cursor on any handle of the text box and use the Finger pointer to make it larger or smaller. Now repeat this procedure with the picture box, making it larger and smaller.

The Rotation tool will freely rotate any item—text box, picture box, or line—in any increment.

EXERCISE L

Rotation tool rotates an item.

1. Click on the Item tool and choose Edit/Select All (Ctrl+A) to select all the items on the page.

2. Press the Backspace key to delete all the items on the page.

3. Click on the Text Box tool to select it and drag to create a text box that is about 3 inches wide and 1 inch high. Type your name and address in the box, pressing Enter after each line.

When you click on an item with the Rotation tool, the cursor changes into the Rotation cursor. The longer the handle you draw out with this cursor, the more control you have over rotating the item.

4. Click on the Rotation tool to select it. With the text box still selected and with the Rotation tool selected, click on the upper right hand corner of the text box. The cursor changes into a crosshair in a circle.

5. Drag that cursor to the right to draw a line out of the text box. (The longer the line, the easier it is to rotate the item.) When the line is about 3 inches long, move it up and down to rotate the text box. Then release your mouse button.

6. Click on the Zoom tool to enlarge the text box; then click on the text box you just rotated to enlarge your view by 25%. Continue to click to enlarge the view in 25% increments. Alt-click to reduce your view in 25% increments.

The Polygon Picture Box tool is used to create picture boxes of at least three straight sides in any shape.

EXERCISE M

Polygon Picture Box tool will create picture boxes of any shape. If you find that you've lost control of the tool (it happens!) and you can't deselect it, double-click to close the polygon picture box.

1. Choose Edit/Select All (Ctrl+A) to select all the items on the page. Then press Backspace to clear your page.

2. Click once on the Polygon tool to select it and place the crosshair cursor in the center of the page.

Zoom tool
Click to enlarge view by 25%. Alt+click to reduce view by 25%. Hold down the Control key to temporarily change your cursor into the Zoom tool. You can also draw a marquee around an item with the Zoom tool to enlarge that item at the center of the screen.

3. Click once and release the mouse button to set the first vertex (point). Then click once again and drag down and to the right to create a line that is about 2 inches long. Release the mouse button. Drag to the left to create the base of a triangle. Release the mouse button.

4. Click and drag up to complete the triangle. When your last vertex is over the first vertex, the cursor becomes a round-cornered rectangle. Click once to complete and close the box. You can always double-click at any time to complete and close a shape. Notice that because a polygon box is a picture box, it displays a large X after it is created and before a picture is imported into it.

Ctrl+E File/Get Picture

Orthogonal Line tool draws either horizontal or vertical lines.

Line tool draws lines at any angle. Hold down the Shift key while drawing to constrain the line's angle to 45° increments.

Get the picture

To place a picture in a document, first create a picture box and keep it selected. Choose File/Get Picture (Ctrl+E) and scroll through the directories to find a graphic file. Highlight the name of the graphic file in the File Name dialog box and click on Open.

The Orthogonal Line tool draws only horizontal or vertical lines.

EXERCISE N

1. Click once on the Text Box tool to select it and drag to create a text box 4 inches wide.

2. Click once on the Orthogonal Line tool to select it. The cursor turns into a crosshair. Click once in the text box and drag to the right to draw a horizontal line about 3 inches long. Release your mouse button.

3. Click once on the Orthogonal Line tool again to select it and click in the text box. Drag to draw a vertical line about 2 inches long. You will learn more about modifying lines with the Style menu in Lesson 14.

The Line tool draws lines at any angle—horizontal, vertical, or diagonal. If you hold down the Shift key while drawing with the line tool, you will constrain the line to 45° angles.

EXERCISE O

1. Click on the Line tool to select it and draw a diagonal line next to the vertical line.

2. Click on the Line tool again and draw another line on the page.

REVIEW EXERCISE

In this review you will use the Tool palette to create and manipulate items.

1. Click on the Text Box tool to select it and drag to create a text box approximately 3 inches wide by 2 inches high.

2. Type a few words in the box and click on the Rotation tool to select it.

3. With the text box still selected, click on one of the handles and draw out a line from the handle to rotate the box.

4. Use the Line tool to draw a diagonal line from the upper left corner to the lower right corner of the box. Your box should resemble Figure 2.7.

5. Use the Rectangle Picture Box tool and hold down the Shift key while dragging to create a square picture box approximately 4 x 4 inches.

6. Import a picture into the box by choosing File/Get Picture (Ctrl+E). Use the resizing Pointer Finger cursor to make the picture box smaller. Then use the Item tool to move the picture box directly under the text box.

7. Use the Polygon Picture Box tool to create a picture box with 5 sides. Import a picture into it by choosing File/Get Picture (Ctrl+E). Your picture box should look something like Figure 2.8.

8. Use the Text Box tool and hold down the Shift key while dragging to create a square text box about 1 inch x 1 inch. Type some text in the box.

9. Use the Orthogonal Line tool to draw a line under the first line of text.

10. Then use the Zoom tool to click and drag a marquee around one word in the box to enlarge the text.

11. Now create other text boxes and picture boxes. Use the Rotation tool to rotate and resize them. Be sure to select an item before manipulating it.

Ctrl+E File/Get Picture

Use the Zoom tool to enlarge an area of the page. Alt-click with the Zoom tool to *decrease* magnification.

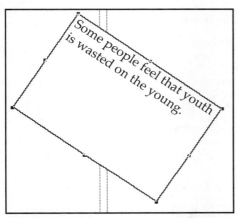

Figure 2.7—A rotated text box. You can still edit text in a rotated box. Use the Content tool to click inside the box and edit the text.

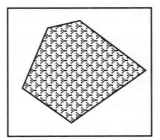

Figure 2.8—A five-sided picture box created by clicking and dragging with the Polygon tool. A rectangle with a patterned fill was created in a drawing program and exported from the drawing program as an EPS file. When that EPS rectangle was imported into XPress, it assumed the dimensions of the polygon box.

REVIEW QUESTIONS

Read the following questions and select the answer which best completes the statement.

1. In QuarkXPress, you choose a unit of measure in the _____.
   a. Application Preferences dialog box
   b. Tool palette
   c. General Preferences dialog box
   d. New (document) dialog box

2. The origin at which the horizontal and vertical rulers meet is called _____.
   a. a palette
   b. the rule
   c. the zero point
   d. a ruler guide

3. Margin guides are _____.
   a. always horizontal
   b. always vertical
   c. resized in the Application Preferences dialog boxes
   d. non-printing guides

4. Text and pictures can be placed only _____.
   a. in boxes
   b. when the rulers are displayed
   c. through dialog boxes
   d. on a page with an automatic text box

5. The Polygon Picture Box tool _____.
   a. creates text boxes
   b. creates picture boxes with at least three sides
   c. is accessed from a dialog box
   d. is available only when a text box is active

6. To save a file under a new name, choose _____.
   a. File/Save
   b. Edit/Preferences
   c. File/New
   d. File/Save as

7. When you select the Text Box tool, the cursor _____.
   a. changes to a crosshair
   b. disappears
   c. changes to a box
   d. remains the same

8. All the commands and functions in QuarkXPress are available _____.
   a. in the Tool palette
   b. from the Menu Bar
   c. under the File menu
   d. in a Preferences dialog box

9. Clicking to display an X in a check box _____.
   a. turns off the function
   b. activates the function
   c. displays a dialog box
   d. executes the command immediately

10. You would select the Facing Pages option if you were going to print a document _____.
    a. to a laser or Linotronic printer
    b. with many graphic files
    c. on both sides of the paper
    d. with color elements

Answers: 1. c; 2. c; 3. d; 4. a; 5. b; 6. d; 7. a; 8. b; 9. b; 10. c

3

Using

Palettes

OVERVIEW

In this lesson you will be introduced to the Measurements palette for text boxes and the Measurements palette for picture boxes. You will learn how to use these palettes to execute formatting controls without resorting to the drop-down menus. Because it is easier and faster to use keyboard shortcuts, you will practice accessing menu items from the keyboard. As a review, you will create text boxes and picture boxes and manipulate them and their contents to create a letterhead.

TOPICS

Measurements palette for text boxes
Using the Measurements palette
Kerning and tracking with the Measurements palette
Type styles in the Measurements palette
Measurements palette for picture boxes
Importing pictures
Picture scaling
Corner Radius
Picture Offset
Picture Rotation and Picture Skewing
Review Exercises
Review Questions

TERMS

horizontal and vertical offset
kerning
leading
Measurements palette
picture box coordinates
picture skew
text box coordinates
tracking

Ctrl+Alt+M View/Show
Measurements

FYI

Double-click on a value in
the Measurements palette
to select it before typing
in a new value.

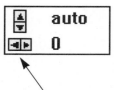

Leading, the white space
between lines of type, is
measured in points. First
select a line or lines. Then
type in an absolute value
like 12 or click on the
arrows to increase (up
arrow) or decrease (down
arrow) leading in 1-point
increments.

Text Alignment icons:
Left, center, right, and
justified. Click on an icon
to activate it.

MEASUREMENTS PALETTE FOR TEXT BOXES

The Measurements palette for text boxes (Figure 3.1) allows you to modify the origin and size of boxes, their angle, and the number of columns in a text box, as well as the typeface, size, style, paragraph alignment, leading, tracking, and kerning—all from the keyboard. Learning to use this palette will save you thousands of trips to the Menu Bar and give you more immediate and visible control over your document. If necessary, access the Measurements palette by choosing View/Show Measurements (Ctrl+Alt+M).

USING THE MEASUREMENTS PALETTE

To use the Measurements palette, simply highlight the text you want to format and, in the Measurements palette, type the size and formatting changes you wish to make. Changing the X value in the Measurements palette in Figure 3.1, for example, will move the text box to the right or left of the left page margin. Changing the Y value will move the text box up or down on the page from the top page margin. Press Enter when you have finished to accept the changes.

Placing the cursor and clicking on the black triangles to the left of MS Serif and 12pt (Figure 3.1) will display pop-up menus with other typefaces and type sizes. To change the typeface, highlight the text you want to format and click on the black triangle to the left of the current typeface. This will display the pop-up menu of all the typefaces currently installed in your system. Highlight the one you want and release the mouse button. Do the same to change the size of the selected text.

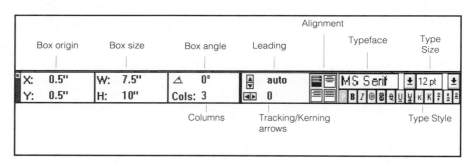

Figure 3.1— Measurements palette for a text box.

To apply leading changes, click on the up and down leading arrows to increase or decrease the leading. You can also select a displayed value (like auto or 13) and type in an absolute leading value. Remember to press Enter after typing in any value in the Measurements palette. However, when you click on an arrow or on an icon, the change takes place without your having to press Enter.

To change a paragraph's alignment, click with the Content tool anywhere in that paragraph; then click on the appropriate icon in the Measurements palette. The change takes place immediately.

EXERCISE A

1. Choose File/New (Ctrl+N) and create a new document with an automatic text box. Click on OK.

2. When the page appears, type a few lines. If the Measurements palette is not displayed, choose View/Show Measurements (Ctrl+Alt+M) to display it. (You can move the Measurements palette around the screen the same way you move any active window around.)

3. Drag to select the text and place your cursor on the black triangle to the left of the current typeface on the Measurements palette. Click to display the pop-up menu and drag to highlight another typeface.

4. Do the same with the black triangle to the left of the type size and then drag to highlight another type size.

5. Type a few lines and press Enter to indicate the end of a paragraph.

6. With the Content tool selected, click on the paragraph and then click on one of the alignment icons in the Measurements palette. Click on another icon to view the change in the paragraph's alignment.

7. If "auto" is displayed to the right of the leading arrows, select it with the Content tool and type in 12.

8. Then click on the up arrow to increase the space between lines; click on the down arrow to reduce the space between the lines of text (leading).

KERNING AND TRACKING WITH THE MEASUREMENTS PALETTE

Kerning is adding or deleting white space between two letters. To add space, click once on the Content tool and insert the Text Insertion bar between the two letters you want to kern. Click on the forward arrow in the Leading field to *increase* spacing by 10 units; click on the back arrow to *decrease* spacing by 10 units. Alt-clicking on the arrows increases and decreases spacing in 1-unit increments.

Tracking applies letter spacing to a range of characters. Highlight a group of letters and click or Alt-click on the arrows to increase or decrease space evenly throughout the whole selection. You can also type a value directly in the tracking/kerning fields on the Measurements palette. Highlight the 0 and type the value you want.

TYPE STYLES IN THE MEASUREMENTS PALETTE

Type styles such as Plain (P), Boldface (**B**), Italic (*I*), Outline (Ⓞ), and Shadow (S) are also available from the Measurements palette.

Highlight the text you wish to format and click the appropriate icon along the bottom right side of the Measurements palette to apply the style.

You can also apply other styles from the Measurements palette. These are discussed in Lesson 9.

Ctrl+N File/New
Ctrl+Alt+M View/Show
   Measurements

Who cares?

QuarkXPress allows you to kern to 1/20,000-em space. If you can't decipher that value, don't worry about it. Tracking and kerning are used to make type *visually* appealing, so use these functions to make type behave. You don't have to understand em-spaces to do that; use your eyes.

Tracking (adding or removing white space between a selected range of letters and words) and kerning (adding or removing white space between two adjacent characters) can be adjusted in +10-unit increments by clicking on the right tracking arrow or in −10-unit increments by clicking on the left arrow. Alt-clicking on the arrows increases or decreases space between letters (kerning) in 1/200-em increments.

EXERCISE B

1. With the Content tool selected, place the insertion point between two letters in the paragraph you just created or type another short paragraph.

2. Click on the forward kerning arrow and notice that the space between the two letters has increased by 10 units. With the insertion point still between the same letters, hold down the Alt key and click on the back kerning arrow. The space between the letters has been *reduced* by 1 unit.

3. Try typing and kerning other letters by increasing and decreasing the space between them in 1-unit and 10-unit increments until you are comfortable with the kerning arrows.

4. Type in a few lines of text and triple click on a line to select the whole line. Then click on the back tracking arrow to reduce the space between letters and words in increments of ¹⁰⁄₂₀₀ths of an em-space. Alt-click on the arrows to change tracking in increments of ½₀₀ths of an em-space.

MEASUREMENTS PALETTE FOR A PICTURE BOX

The Measurements palette for a picture box (Figure 3.2) is displayed whenever a picture box is selected. It includes not only fields for typing the box's origin, dimensions, and angle, but also fields for typing in the angle of the box corner radius, the horizontal and vertical scaling factors, and the horizontal and vertical offset of the picture itself.

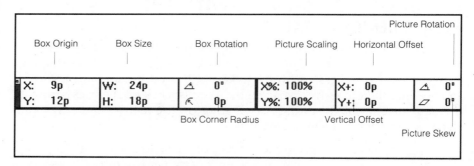

Figure 3.2—Measurements palette for a picture box.

The X and Y coordinates allow you to place a box at a precise point on the page. The X coordinate is the item's distance from the left margin. In Figure 3.2, X: 9p means that the item is positioned horizontally 9 picas from the left margin. A negative X value would put the picture box to the left of the left margin. The value Y: 12p means that the same item is positioned 12 picas down from the top margin.

The W and H values allow you to make the box a precise width and height. The picture box defined by the Measurements palette in Figure 3.2 is 24 picas wide by 10 picas high. You can rotate the box (and the picture) a full 360° in 1-point increments by typing a value in the Box Rotation dialog box.

IMPORTING PICTURES

Ctrl+E File/Get Picture

To import a picture into an active picture box, first make sure the Content tool is active. Then click on the File menu and select Get Picture (Ctrl+E). When the Get Picture dialog box appears, scroll through the directories on your drive(s) and click on a graphic file to select it. Click on the Open button. You can also open the graphic file by double-clicking on the name of the file in the dialog box.

PICTURE SCALING

When a picture box is active and the Content tool is selected, the X% and Y% values are displayed in the Measurements palette. These values apply to the picture, not the box. If you increase the X% value from 100% to 125%, the picture's horizontal scale is enlarged by 25%. If you increase or decrease the Y% value, the picture's vertical scale is increased or decreased accordingly. To scale a picture proportionally, the X% and Y% must be the same value.

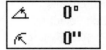

The angle of rotation (top) allows you to freely rotate a picture box. The picture also rotates with the box.

To specify a corner radius for an active rectangle or for a round-corner picture box, type in a value between 0 and 2 in the corner radius field (bottom).

CORNER RADIUS

To specify a corner radius for an active rectangle (Figure 3.3) or rounded corner picture box, type in a value between 0–2 in the Corner Radius field (below the Box Rotation field). Figure 3.3 displays a picture box (W=2; H=1) that was modified by typing 10 in the Angle of Rotation field and .7 in the Corner Radius field.

X%: 50%
Y%: 50%

Modify the horizontal scale of a graphic in an active picture box by entering different values in the X% and Y% fields. To keep the picture proportionally shaped, however, both the X% and Y% must be the same number.

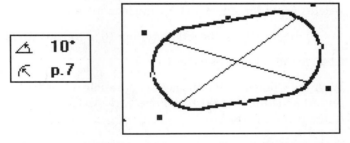

Figure 3.3—A picture box that has been rotated 10° to the left and whose corners have been assigned a Corner Radius value of .7.

PICTURE OFFSET

You can modify the horizontal offset (the distance a picture is from the side of the picture box) and vertical offset (the distance a picture is from the top edges of the picture box) in 1-point increments by clicking on the arrows in these fields. Alt-clicking on the horizontal offset or vertical offset values modifies the picture's offset in ⅒-point increments. As always, when working with pictures (box contents), the Content tool must be selected.

PICTURE ROTATION AND PICTURE SKEWING

Type a value in the Picture Rotation field to rotate the *picture*, but not the picture box. Slant a picture (called skewing) to the right or left by typing a positive (right) or negative (left) number in the Picture Skew box.

X+: -0.01"
Y+: 0.187"

Modify the horizontal and vertical offset (the distance a picture is from the sides and top edges of the box) in 1-point increments by clicking on the arrows in these fields.

What you will need

A graphic file

Ctrl+N File/New
Ctrl+Alt+M View/Show
   Measurements
Ctrl+A Edit/Select All
Ctrl+E File/Get Picture

Box Rotation field

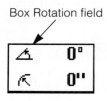

Picture Rotation field

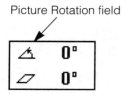

Change your mind?

If you have selected one unit of measure in the General Preferences dialog box (for example, inches) and you want to type a measurement in the Measurements palette in picas, type the value followed by a p. Likewise, to type a value in inches when picas is the unit of measure, type the value followed by the inches mark (").

EXERCISE C

1. Create a new document by choosing File/New (Ctrl+N). Choose Edit/Preferences/General (Ctrl+Y) and select inches as the unit of measure. Display the Measurements palette (Ctrl+Alt+M).

2. Use the Tool palette and Measurements palette to create a text box that is 4 inches wide and 1 inch high. Type in a few sentences.

3. Use the Item tool to place the box at the 1-inch mark on the horizontal ruler (X axis) and at the 2-inch mark on the vertical ruler (Y axis).

4. Rotate the box 25° to the left by typing 25 in the Box Rotation field on the Measurements palette.

5. Assign it 3 columns by typing 3 in the Cols field. Your screen should resemble Figure 3.4 after the box is rotated.

6. Choose Edit/Select All (Ctrl+A) and when all the items have been selected, press Backspace to remove them from the page.

7. Use the Tool palette and Measurements palette to create a picture box that is a 3-inch square. (Hold down the Shift key when drawing a box with the Picture Box tool to change the rectangle into a square.)

8. Place the picture box at the 4-inch mark on the X axis and at the 2-inch mark on the Y axis by typing those numbers in the Measurements palette. (You don't have to type the inch marks.)

9. Rotate the box 10° to the left by typing 10 in the Box Rotation field.

10. Change the corner radius to .4.

11. With the Content Tool selected, choose File/Get Picture (Ctrl+E) and import a picture into the box. Press Ctrl+Alt+Shift+F to proportionally fit the picture in the box.

12. Scale the picture horizontally and vertically to 80% of its original size by typing 80 in the X% and Y% Picture Scaling fields on the Measurements Palette.

13. Use the arrows in the Horizontal Offset area to move the picture 1 inch from the left side of the box and down 1 inch from the top of the picture box.

14. Rotate the *picture* 10° to the left by typing 10 in the Picture Rotation field.

15. Skew the picture 15° to the left by typing 15 in the Picture Skew area.

Figure 3.5 shows what the graphic looked like when it was imported into the 3-inch square picture box and made to fit in the box with the Ctrl+Alt+Shift+F command. Figure 3.6 displays the graphic and picture box as it looks with all the modifications made through the Measurements palette.

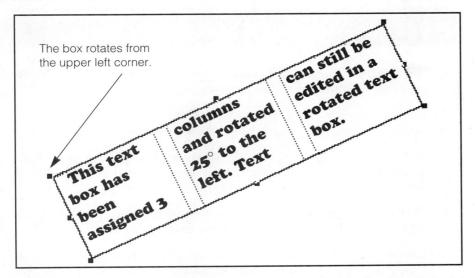

The box rotates from the upper left corner.

This text box has been assigned 3 columns and rotated 25° to the left. Text can still be edited in a rotated text box.

Figure 3.4—Displays the text box after it was rotated. Notice that the box rotates to the left from the upper left corner.

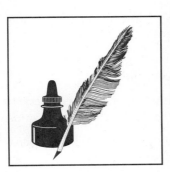

X%: 63.7%	X+: 1p.557
Y%: 63.7%	Y+: -p5

Figure 3.5—The picture box and picture before scaling and rotation. The Ctrl+Alt+Shift–F command was applied to make the graphic fit in the middle of the picture box. Notice that it was proportionally scaled to 63.7% of its original size and offset about 1 pica from the side of the picture box and less than a point from the top of the picture box.

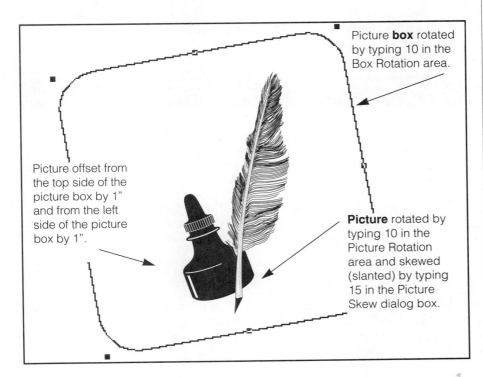

Picture **box** rotated by typing 10 in the Box Rotation area.

Picture offset from the top side of the picture box by 1" and from the left side of the picture box by 1".

Picture rotated by typing 10 in the Picture Rotation area and skewed (slanted) by typing 15 in the Picture Skew dialog box.

Design Tip

Skewing (slanting) pictures is a way of achieving different visual effects. For instance, the Porsche in the first picture is displayed just as it was imported—without applying any skewing value. The Porsche below it looks like it's moving because a value of 40 was typed in the Picture Skew field in the Measurements palette.

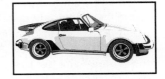

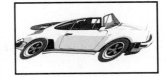

Figure 3.6—The picture as it is imported into the picture box (Figure 3.5) and the same picture after scaling, rotating, skewing, and modifying the horizontal and vertical offsets.

Ctrl+N File/New
Ctrl+Alt+M View/Show
   Measurements
Ctrl+A Edit/Select All
Ctrl+E File/Get Picture

WARNING!

When you want to type a value in picas, always type the number followed by a p (10p); otherwise, the value will be displayed in points (p10).

REVIEW EXERCISE #1

1. Create a new document by choosing File/New (Ctrl+N) with inches as the unit of measure and an automatic text box.

2. Use the Text Box tool to create two text boxes. Activate the Measurements palette by choosing View/Show Measurements (Ctrl+Alt+M).

3. Use the X point of origin in the Measurements palette to align the boxes at the same point along the left margin, one above the other, as in Figure 3.7.

4. With the Content tool selected, type some text in each box and choose Edit/Select All (Ctrl+A) to select all the text in one box.

5. Use the right side of the Measurements palette to change the text to Helvetica, the type size to 9 points, and the style to bold. Double click on "auto" in the leading area and type 10 to change the leading to 10 points.

6. In the Measurements palette, change the W(idth) value to 2 inches and the H(eight) value to 1 inch. Be sure to press the Enter key to accept the changes.

7. Double-click on the Columns value and change it to 2.

8. Type some text in the lower text box. Use the Measurements palette to change its W value to 4 inches and its H value to 2 inches.

9. Choose File/Select All (Ctrl+A) to select all the text and use the Measurements palette to change it to 10 point Times New Roman. Change the type style to Italics by clicking on the *I* icon in the Measurements palette. Use the leading arrows (click once, then Alt-click five times) to change the leading to 15 points. Assign the box 3 columns. Your screen should resemble Figure 3.7.

REVIEW EXERCISE #2

1. Choose File/New (Ctrl+N) to create a new document with picas as the unit of measure and an automatic text box. Activate the Measurements palette by choosing View/Show Measurements (Ctrl+Alt+M).

2. With the Picture Box tool selected, draw a picture box any place on the page. Use the Measurements palette to position the box at the 5p point on the horizontal (X) axis and at the 32p point on the vertical (Y) axis.

3. Make the picture box 15 picas wide and 13 picas high by typing 15p in the W field and 13p in the H field.

4. With the Content tool selected, select the first picture box and choose File/Get Picture (Ctrl+E) and import a graphic file into the picture box. Use the Measurements palette to scale the picture down to 70% of

its original size (type 70 in the scaling fields) or to any size that will fit the graphic into the box. Press Enter to accept the changes. Center the graphic in the picture box with the Grabber Hand.

5. Rotate the picture box (and the picture) 25° to the left by typing 25 in the Box Rotation field. Rotate the *picture* by typing 10 in the Picture Angle field. Give the corner radius of the box a value of 5p (5 picas).

6. Skew the picture 20° . Your screen should resemble Figure 3.8.

Box Rotation field

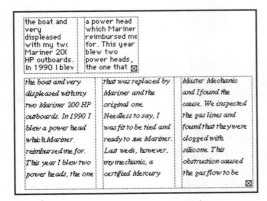

Figure 3.7—Use the Measurements palette to change the formatting of a text box as well as the text itself. Both of these boxes have the same X value, that is, their upper left corners are at the same point on the horizontal ruler or the same distance from the zero point.

Picture Angle field

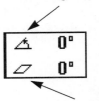

Picture Skew field

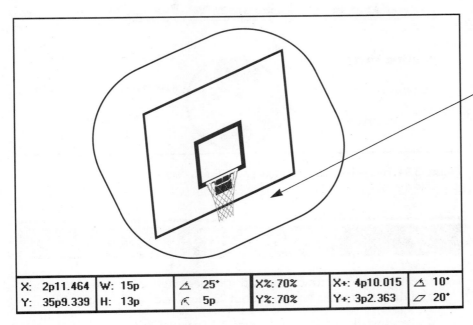

| X: | 2p11.464 | W: | 15p | ⊿ | 25° | X%: 70% | X+: 4p10.015 | ⊿ | 10° |
| Y: | 35p9.339 | H: | 13p | ⨼ | 5p | Y%: 70% | Y+: 3p2.363 | ⟋ | 20° |

Figure 3.8—A picture box containing a graphic. The Measurements palette displays the values for the box and the graphic. This picture box is a little more than 2 picas from the left margin and a little more than 35 picas down from the top margin. It is 15 picas wide and 13 picas high. The picture of the basketball hoop has been scaled both horizontally and vertically to 70% of its original size, The picture is offset 4p10.015 picas from the left edge of the picture box and 3p2.363 from the top edge of the picture box. The picture has also been rotated 10° to the left and skewed 20° to the left.

Ctrl+N File/New
Ctrl+Alt+M View/Show
    Measurements
Ctrl+B Item/Frame
Ctrl+A Edit/Select All
Ctrl+P File/Print

REVIEW EXERCISE #3

1. Choose File/New (Ctrl+N) to create a new document with picas as the unit of measure and an automatic text box.

2. Activate the Measurements palette by choosing View/Show Measurements (Ctrl+Alt+M). Use the Picture Box tools, Text Box tool, and the line tools to create a letterhead.

3. Use the Picture Box tools and the frame Ctrl (Ctrl+B) to create graphics for the letterhead.

4. Try applying different horizontal scaling values to text to achieve different graphics effects. You can copy the one in Figure 3.9 or you can create your own, using graphics from another program or generating all of the artwork in XPress.

5. Feel free to try different typefaces, type sizes, type styles, and alignments for the text. Experiment with scaling the graphics up and down and with rotating the text and graphic boxes.

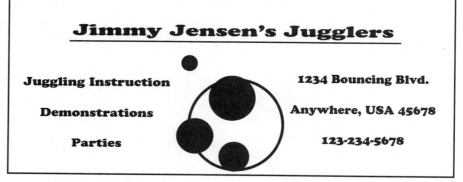

Figure 3.9—This letterhead was created in XPress using the Oval Picture Box tool to create the logo.

REVIEW EXERCISE #4

1. Create a new document or add another page to an open document and drag to create a text box about 30 picas wide and 4 picas high.

2. Type your first name and print the page (Ctrl+P). Select the text (Ctrl+A). Format it in any typeface at 60 points. Double-click in the percentage view window next to the page number and type 400 to enlarge your view 400%.

3. Place the cursor between any two letters and click on the left kerning arrow in the Measurements palette to reduce the space between the letters. Print the page (Ctrl+P) and notice how much better the text looks.

REVIEW QUESTIONS

Read the following questions and select the best answer which completes the statement:

1. The Measurements palette is available from the _____.
    a. File menu
    b. Edit menu
    c. Style menu
    d. View menu

2. The Measurements palette for text boxes does not display values for _____.
    a. tabs
    b. type size
    c. typeface
    d. alignment

3. Leading is _____.
    a. lengthening lines
    b. shortening lines
    c. increasing space between words
    d. increasing or decreasing space between lines

4. The leading arrows in the Measurements palette are active when _____.
    a. text is selected
    b. an absolute value is entered in the leading field
    c. no text is selected
    d. a picture box is not active

5. When changing a paragraph's alignment from Centered to Justified by clicking on the Alignment icon, _____.
    a. the entire paragraph must be selected
    b. at least one line must be selected
    c. click with the Content tool anywhere in the paragraph
    d. select the paragraph with the Content tool

6. Kerning is _____.
    a. adding and deleting space between two characters
    b. adding space between all letters in a line of text
    c. deleting space between all letters in a line of text
    d. adjusting spacing between lines of text

7. Adjusting the space between letters *and* words is called _____.
    a. leading
    b. kerning
    c. tracking
    d. scaling

8. To change the size of a picture in a picture box from the Measurements palette, _____.
    a. drag the corner of the picture box
    b. click on the offset arrows in the Measurements palette
    c. adjust the X% and Y% fields
    d. modify the X and Y fields in the Measurements palette

9. When a picture has been imported into a picture box, _____.
   a. only the picture can be resized from the Measurements palette
   b. only the picture box can be resized from the Measurements palette
   c. both picture and picture box can be resized from the Measurements palette
   d. neither the picture nor the picture box can be scaled from the Measurements palette

10. The X and Y axes in both Measurements palettes _____.
    a. are always the same
    b. reflect the position of the box relative to the top and left page margins
    c. are modified differently
    d. reflect the position of the box's contents from the top and left sides of the box

Answers: 1. d; 2. a; 3. d; 4. b; 5. c; 6. c; 7. a; 8. c; 9. c; 10. b

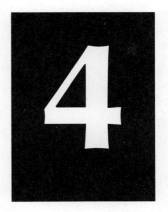

LESSON

4

Using

More

Palettes

OVERVIEW

In this lesson you will be introduced to the Document Layout palette and the Library palette. You will learn how to insert and delete document pages using the Document Layout palette and how to recognize the different kinds of pages in a document from their icons on the Document Layout palette. You will work with the Library palette, dragging, labeling, and removing items from the Library you create. As a review, you will use all the palettes to create and format two one-page flyers.

TOPICS

The Document Layout palette
Master page icons
Document page icons
Master Pages
The Library palette
Creating and opening a Library palette
Moving items into and out of the Library
Naming Library entries
Review Exercises
Review Questions

TERMS

Auto Library Save
Document Layout palette
document page icon
drag-copying
Labels menu
Library entry
Library palette
Master Page
master page icon
Overflow Indicator

THE DOCUMENT LAYOUT PALETTE

The Document Layout palette (Figure 4.1) is a palette that can be displayed in front of any open document. To display it, choose View/Show Document Layout.

The Document Layout palette contains a menu bar. Pulling down the Document menu allows you to access, add, and delete document and master pages. Pull down the Apply menu to apply blank or master page formats to existing pages.

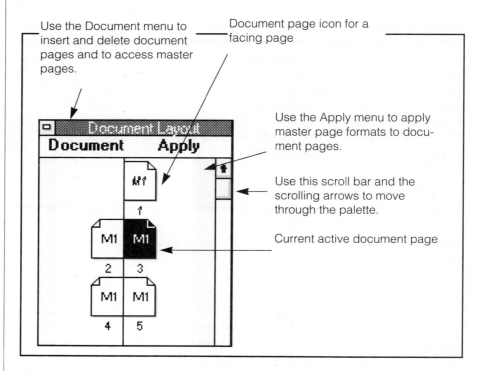

Use the Document menu to insert and delete document pages and to access master pages.

Document page icon for a facing page

Use the Apply menu to apply master page formats to document pages.

Use this scroll bar and the scrolling arrows to move through the palette.

Current active document page

Figure 4.1—The Document Layout palette displaying one master page, M1.

MASTER PAGE ICONS

Whenever you create a new document, XPress automatically creates master page M1-Master 1 and one document page based on that master page.

Access the master pages from the Document Layout palette by choosing Document/Show Master Pages. Then double-click on the master page icon to get to that master page.

DOCUMENT PAGE ICONS

The Document Layout palette also displays icons representing a document's pages. In Figure 4.1 the number below the icon refers to the page's position in the document, not to its actual page number. You'll learn more about assigning page numbers in Lesson 6.

The label "M1" in the document page icon refers to the master page on which those pages are based—in this case, 1-Master 1. This document contains only one master page and five document pages. The "dog ears" on the icons indicate that this document was created with the Facing Pages option

Facing master page icon

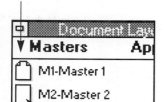

Non-facing master page icon

in the New dialog box. Notice the bold italic M1 on the page 1 icon and the bold italic 1 below the page 1 icon. This bold italic formatting indicates that page 1 is the active page, that is, an item on that page has been selected.

MASTER PAGES

Use the Document pull-down menu and highlight Show Master Pages to display the M-1 master page icon. You can add document pages based on the master page by choosing Document/Insert and choosing either blank document pages or pages containing master page formats. After highlighting your choice, the cursor changes to one of the Page Insertion pointers and the page outline will snap into position when you place the page on the document page area of the Document Layout palette by releasing the mouse button.

If you double-click on a document page icon, that page will be displayed on the screen.

EXERCISE A

1. Create a new document by choosing File/New (Ctrl+N) without facing pages. If necessary, click in the Automatic Text Box check box to deselect it.

2. Choose View/Show Document Layout to activate the Document Layout palette.

3. Choose View/Fit in Window (Ctrl+0) [zero]) to make the page visible on the screen.

4. Pull down the Document menu on the palette and choose Show Master Pages. Double-click on the 1-Master 1 icon. This brings you to the master pages and allows you to place text and graphic items on them. Scroll to the left hand master page.

5. Click on the Text Box tool to select it and drag on the page to draw a text box on the master page. Type your name in the text box.

6. Choose Masters/Show Document Pages. Then choose Document/Insert and drag to select M1-Master 1. When you release the mouse button and the cursor changes to the Page Insertion pointer, move the pointer over the document page area of the palette and place it under the Page 1 icon. Release the mouse button.

7. Repeat this process three more times until you have five pages in the document. Your screen should resemble Figure 4.2.

8. Double-click on the document page 3 icon. Notice that the text box you created on the right hand master page M-1 Master 1 appears on page 3 and on every right hand page in the document.

9. Choose File/Save as (Ctrl+Alt+S) and save this file as "MPdoc."

Ctrl+N File/New
Ctrl+0 [zero] View/Fit in Window
Ctrl + Alt+S File/Save as

Page M1 is the first page in the document, but is also page number 35, as seen in the page number area in the lower right portion of the screen.

The asterisk next to the number 1 indicates that this page is the first page in a new section.

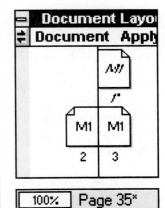

The Control Menu box allows you to move, close, or change the size of an active document window.

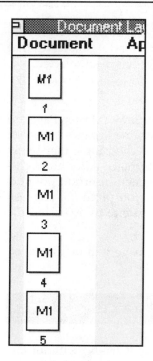

Figure 4.2—The Document Layout palette for a 5-page document based on M1 Master 1. The absence of "dog ears" on the document pages and the vertical position of the pages indicate that this document was created without using the Facing Pages option in the New dialog box.

How to do it

To open a Library in Document B that you created previously in Document A, choose Utilities/Library. Locate the Library you created in Document A and click on Open. The Library is now available in Document B. Any items you add, delete, or modify will remain as such when you open this same library in Document A again or in any other document.

Auto Library Save

If you check Auto Library Save in the Applications Preferences dialog box (Edit/Preferences/Application), XPress will automatically save the library each time you add an item to the library.

LIBRARY PALETTE

The Library palette (Figure 4.3) is a "storage bin" for the text and graphics you are using in your document. You can move items with the Item tool from your page to the Library palette and you can also move items from the Library palette back onto your page. When you move items to and from the Library palette, you move copies of the item, not the item itself. This is called drag-copying.

If you check Auto Library Save in the Application Preferences dialog box (Edit/Preferences/Application), XPress will automatically save the Library each time you add an item to the Library.

CREATING AND OPENING A LIBRARY PALETTE

You can create a new Library or open a previously created Library from the Utilities menu. You can also have more than one Library open in a document at one time.

EXERCISE B

1. In the 5-page document you just created, choose Utilities/Library. Click on Create, and when the Library dialog box appears, type "mylib" in the File Name dialog box. XPress automatically assigns a new library the extension ".qxl." Tell XPress in which directory to store the Library by clicking on the appropriate Directories and/or Drives. Click on Create. The Library palette will appear on your screen.

2. Click in the Menu Control box on the Library palette (Figure 4.4) and click on Close (Alt+F+4). The Library palette disappears but is saved on the disk.

3. To open the library you just created, choose Utilities/Library.

4. In the Library dialog box, scroll through the directories to find the name of the library you just created. Click on it to highlight it. Click on Open or double-click on the library's name. The palette reappears on your screen.

MOVING ITEMS INTO AND OUT OF THE LIBRARY

You move items to and from the Library palette with the Item tool. To move an item into the Library, click on the Item tool to select it. Then click on the item, either a text box, picture box, or line, and drag it onto the Library palette. As you drag the item into the Library, the cursor changes from the 4-pointed Mover pointer to the Library pointer, which looks like a pair of eyeglasses.

Moving items to and from the Library palette is another example of drag-copying. Only thumbnail *copies* of an item are placed in the Library. The original stays on the page as well as in the Library. If you make changes to an item in the document, you must remember to either move the new item to the Library and delete the old item by choosing Edit/Cut (Ctrl+X) from the Edit menu in the Library palette, or update the item already in the Library by dragging it out of the Library and onto the page. You cannot edit Library items while they are in the Library.

The cursor changes into the Library cursor as you drag an item into a library.

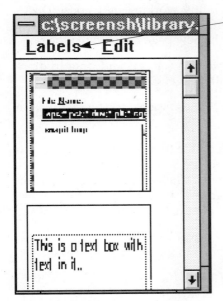

Figure 4.3—The Library palette displays a Labels menu and several items.

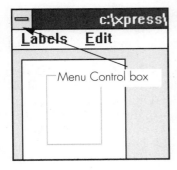

Figure 4.4—The Library palette. Click on the Menu Control box to remove the Library palette from the screen. The Library is saved when you close it. Use the Labels pull-down menu to display the Library Entry dialog box where you can type a label (name) for the library item.

What you will need

A graphic file

Ctrl+E File/Get Picture

Ctrl+Shift+F Fits a picture
    in a picture box

NAMING LIBRARY ENTRIES

You can scroll through the items in the Library palette, and you can drag the palette anywhere on the screen. It's a good idea to label items in the Library so you can access them easily from the pull-down Labels menu (Figure 4.5) located on the palette under the Library's name.

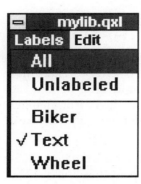

Figure 4.5.—Pull-down Labels menu under the Library's title bar displays the titles you assigned to the items dragged into the Library.

EXERCISE C

1. Display the Document Layout palette (View/Show Document Layout) for the document you are currently working in. Choose Document/Insert and insert a Blank Single page on the document page area of the palette. Double-click on the new page to get to that page.

2. Click on the Rectangle Picture Box tool to select it and drag to draw two picture boxes on the newly created page.

3. Click on the Text Box tool to select it and drag to draw a text box on the screen.

4. With the Content tool selected, click on the first picture box to select it and choose File/Get Picture (Ctrl+E). Scroll through the drives and/or directories to find a graphic file. Click on it to highlight it and click on Open. The picture will appear in the picture box. Press Ctrl+Shift+F to fit the picture in the picture box or click on one of the picture box handles and resize the box.

5. Repeat this process to import a picture into the second picture box.

6. Click on the text box and type some text in the text box. You now have two picture boxes and one text box displayed.

7. Create a new Library by choosing Utilities/Library and type a name for your library. Click on Create. Click on the Item tool and drag the three items you just created, one by one, into the Library.

8. Double-click on the first item in the Library. When the Library Entry dialog box (Figure 4.6) appears, type a name for that entry in the Label field of the Library Entry dialog box. Click on OK. Repeat this process to apply labels (names) to the other two items in the library.

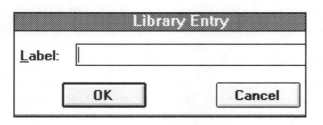

Figure 4.6.—Type a name for a library entry in the Library Entry dialog box.

9. Close the library by choosing Close from the Menu Control box in the upper left corner of the Library palette.

10. Now open that same library by choosing Utilities/Library. Pull down the Labels menu located below the title bar (Figure 4.5) and click on an item to highlight it.

11. When the item appears alone in the Library, click on it and drag it out of the library and onto the page. Notice that the box remains in the library even though it appears on the document page.

12. Do the same with the other two items in the Library.

REVIEW EXERCISE #1

Now that you've been introduced to and experimented with the tools, palettes, and several of the menu items, use them to create a one-page flyer based on the following specs:

Page size	U.S. letter	*Margins*	1 inch all around
Columns	1	*Unit of measure*	inches
Facing pages	no	*Automatic text box*	no

1. Choose File/New (Ctrl+N) to create a new document using the specifications given above. When the blank page appears, make the rulers visible by choosing View/Show Rulers (Ctrl+R). Then change your view to Fit in Window by choosing View/Fit in Window (Ctrl+0 [zero]).

2. Create a text box: X=1; Y=2; W=6; H=1. Type (no quotes), in all caps, "PETAL POWER!" Select all the text by choosing Edit/Select All (Ctrl+A).

3. If necessary, display the Measurements palette by choosing View/Show Measurements (Ctrl+Alt-M). Use the Measurements palette to change the typeface to Times New Roman and the type size to 60 points. Click on the Center Alignment icon in the Measurements palette to center the text in the text box.

4. Create a picture box: X=2; Y=4; W=3.5; H=2. With the Content tool selected, choose File/Get Picture (Ctrl+E) and import any kind of graphic into the box. Use the Grabber Hand to position the graphic in the center of the box. You can also type Ctrl+Shift+M to center it.

5. With the Item tool selected, select the picture box and use the Measurements palette to rotate the picture box 10° to the left by typing 10 in the Box Rotation area.

What you will need

A text file
Any kind of graphic file

Ctrl+N File/New
Ctrl+R View/Show Rulers
Ctrl+A Edit/Select All
Ctrl+Shift+M Center a
    picture in a picture box
Ctrl+E File/Get Text/
    Picture

Design Tip

When creating several picture boxes with captions in a document, be consistent in leaving the same amount of space between the picture box and the text box which holds the caption. One way to do this is to draw a narrow picture box below the picture box which holds the graphic. This narrow picture box acts as a buffer between the graphic and the caption. Then draw the text box which holds the caption below that narrow picture box.

Typing a value in the Box Rotation field will rotate both the picture box and the picture.

Ctrl+E File/Get Text
Ctrl+A Edit/Select All
Ctrl+B Item/Frame

FYI

Scroll in the Frame Speci-fications dialog box to select a frame style, then choose a width for the frame, as well as a color and a shade of that color.

If you select an ornate frame style, you have to make it wide enough so that it will display and print properly.

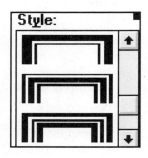

The Overflow Indicator appears in a text box when the text box is too small to hold all the text imported or typed into it.

Figure 4.7—This page has two text boxes and one picture box. Notice the Overflow Indicator in the lower right corner of the bottom text box. This tells you that there isn't enough room in the text box to hold all the text in the file. You'll learn how to link text boxes in Lesson 6.

6. Select the Content Tool and scale the graphic proportionally down to 50% of its current size by typing 50 in the X% and Y% percentage fields of the Measurements palette. Center the graphic again in the picture box with the Grabber Hand.

7. Use the Text Box tool to create another text box: X=1.5; Y=8; W=5.5; H=1.5. Assign it two columns by typing 2 in the Cols field of the Mea-surements palette.

8. With the Content tool selected, choose File/Get Text (Ctrl+E) and import a text file into the box. Choose Edit/Select All (Ctrl+A) and use the Measurements palette to change its typeface to Times; its type size to 9 points; and its type style to italics.

9. As a finishing touch, with either the Item tool or Content tool selected, click on the text box to select it. Choose Item/Frame (Ctrl+B) to dis-play the Frame Specifications dialog box. Scroll down the Style win-dow on the left and highlight a frame to select it. Press the Tab key to get to the Width field and type 4 to create a frame around the box that is 4 points wide. Click on OK to close the dialog box. Choose View/Hide Guides to stop displaying the guidelines and admire your flyer! Your screen should resemble Figure 4.7.

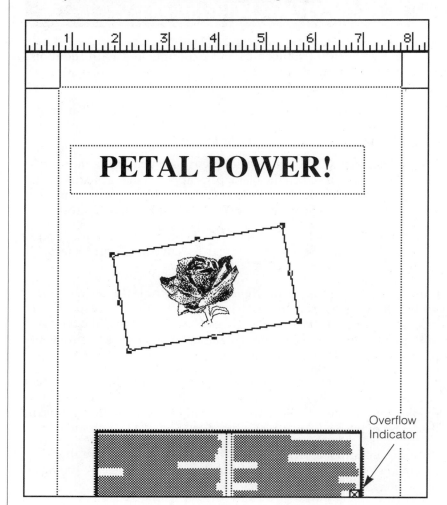

REVIEW EXERCISE #2

Choose File/New (Ctrl+N) to create a new document based on the following specs:

Page size	U.S. letter	*Margins*	1.25 inches
Columns	1	*Unit of measure*	picas
Facing pages	no	*Automatic text box*	no

1. When the empty page appears, choose View/Fit in Window (Ctrl+0 [zero]) to make it fit in the window. Place your cursor on the zero point and move it down and to the right until the two dotted lines sit directly on top of the margin lines.

2. Drag a horizontal ruler guide down to the 12-pica mark on the vertical ruler. Drag a vertical ruler across to the 36-pica mark on the horizontal ruler.

3. Select the Text Box tool and drag to create a text box from the point where the ruler guides meet over to the right margin and down to the bottom margin.

4. Use the Measurements palette to make sure your box has the following dimensions: X=24p1.089, Y=11p9.572; W=11 p; H=39 p.

5. With the Content tool selected, choose File/Get Text (Ctrl+E) to import a text file; then use the Measurements palette to change its typeface to Times New Roman and its type size to 9 points. Click on the Right Align icon, the first icon in the second row of the Measurements palette, to align the text to the right side of the text box.

6. Select the Oval Picture Box tool and hold down the Shift key to create a circle that is about 12 picas wide. Move the circle on top of the horizontal ruler guide and, with the Content tool selected, import a picture into the box by choosing File/Get Picture (Ctrl+E).

7. Choose Item/Frame (Ctrl+B) and select a frame style by scrolling through the frame window on the left. In the box at the right, type 12 to give the frame a weight of 12 points.

8. Create another picture box: X=2p; Y=17p; W=20p; H=30p. Be sure to type the letter p after the number or XPress will display the box in point sizes, not picas. Import a graphic, center it, and frame the box.

9. Select the Orthogonal Line tool and draw a vertical line directly on top of the vertical ruler guide from the top margin down to the bottom margin.

10. Choose Utilities/Library and click New to create a new Library. Type (no quotes) "Revilib" in the dialog box and click on the Create button.

What you will need

A text file
Any kind of graphic file

Ctrl+N File/New
Ctrl+0 [zero] View/Fit in Window
Ctrl+E File/Get Text
Ctrl+B Item/Frame

11. When the Library palette appears, select the Item tool and drag both picture boxes and the text box into the Library. Double-click on each Library item and type a name for it. Finally, choose View/Hide Guides and admire your work! Your screen should resemble Figure 4.8.

FYI

Choosing Hide Guides from the View menu allows you to see exactly how your page will print without the box outlines, ruler guides, and margin guides cluttering up your view. You can always work with items when the guides are invisible; you just won't be able to see their boundaries.

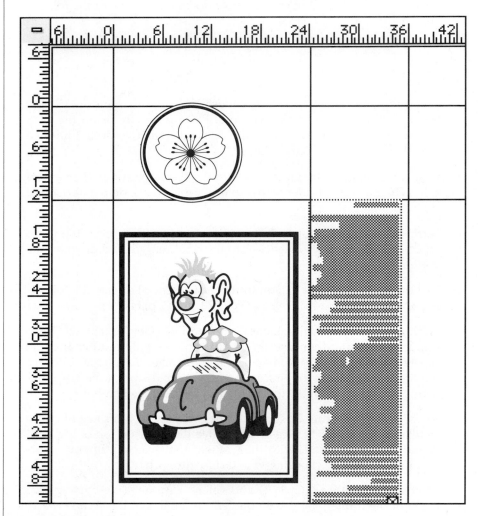

Figure 4.8—Your finished page should look something like this.

REVIEW QUESTIONS

Read the following questions and choose the answer which best completes the statement.

1. The Document Layout palette displays _____.
   a. master page and document page icons
   b. master page icons
   c. document page icons
   d. page items

2. The Document Layout palette is accessed from the _____.
   a. Utilities menu
   b. Item menu
   c. View menu
   d. File menu

3. M1-Master 1 is created _____.
   a. by double-clicking on the master page icon
   b. by dragging the icon down on the palette
   c. when the document is created
   d. through a dialog box

4. Master pages are accessed in the Document Layout palette by _____.
   a. highlighting the master page icon
   b. clicking on the scrolling arrows
   c. double-clicking on the palette
   d. double-clicking on the master page icon

5. Items placed on master pages _____.
   a. cannot be edited
   b. appear on every document page based on that master page
   c. do not include graphic elements
   d. are visible on the Document Layout palette

6. The Library function is accessed from the _____.
   a. File menu
   b. View menu
   c. Item menu
   d. Utilities menu

7. An item that is drag-copied _____.
   a. is duplicated while remaining in its original position
   b. is moved horizontally across the page to the Library
   c. replaces another item in the Library or in the document
   d. is replaced by another item from an open Library

8. Library items are named via the _____.
   a. Library palette
   b. Library Entry dialog box
   c. Labels menu
   d. Utilities menu

9. Items stored in a Library _____.
   a. can be edited
   b. can be accessed
   c. can be deleted
   d. b and c

10. Pictures stored in a Library are _____.
    a. kept in their picture boxes
    b. removed from their picture boxes
    c. imported via the Get Picture dialog box
    d. able to be edited in the Library

Answers: 1. a; 2. c; 3. c; 4. d; 5. b; 6. d; 7. a; 8. b; 9. c; 10. a

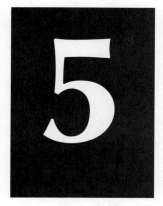

LESSON

5

Working with Master Pages

OVERVIEW

In this lesson you will learn how to create documents with single and multiple master pages. You will insert document pages based on master pages as well as on blank pages. You will learn how to rename master pages and change documents from non-facing page documents to facing page documents. You will continue to use menu commands and keyboard equivalents. As a review, you will create a booklet using multiple master pages.

TOPICS

Master pages
Master page icons
Naming master pages
Accessing master pages
Master Page contents
Adding items to a master page
Creating new master pages
Inserting document pages based on master pages
Deleting master pages and document pages
Changing documents from non-facing pages to facing pages
Applying master pages to previously created document pages
Changing master page items
Review Exercises
Review Questions

TERMS

automatic text box
delete pages
facing master page icon
facing pages
intact link icon
keep changes
master guides
master pages
non-facing master page icon
unlinking

MASTER PAGES

Master pages are pages which contain text and graphic elements to be used on every page in the document based on that master page. Text boxes that contain headers and footers like chapter titles and page numbers usually occur on every page. A logo might appear on every left hand page; a line could appear across the bottom of the page. Elements like these which are used consistently throughout a document should be placed on master pages. You can always edit material on master pages so that what you add to or remove from the master page will be added to or removed from every document page based on that master page.

MASTER PAGE ICONS

The master page icon under Masters in the Document Layout palette (Document/Show Master Pages in Figure 5.1) identifies it as Master Page M1-Master 1. This is a facing page master page icon, as indicated by the "dog ears." You can create master pages based on both facing pages and on non-facing pages. Place items on the master page to create document pages which contain the same text and graphic elements you placed on M1-Master 1. XPress creates Master Page 1 and Document Page 1 called M1 automatically at the same time you create your document with the New (document) command.

Keep Changes/ Delete Changes

If you select Keep Changes in the General Preferences dialog box, any changes you make to master page items on the document page will be kept if you trash the master page or add or delete items from that master page. If you select Delete Changes in the General Preferences dialog box, changes you make to master page items on the document pages will be deleted if you trash the master page or if you add or delete items from the master pages.

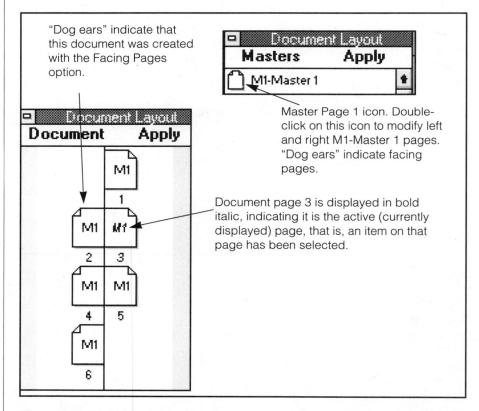

"Dog ears" indicate that this document was created with the Facing Pages option.

Master Page 1 icon. Double-click on this icon to modify left and right M1-Master 1 pages. "Dog ears" indicate facing pages.

Document page 3 is displayed in bold italic, indicating it is the active (currently displayed) page, that is, an item on that page has been selected.

Figure 5.1—Document Layout palette showing a six-page facing pages document based on one master page (M1).

NAMING MASTER PAGES

You can name a master page icon by choosing Document/Show Master Pages on the Document Layout palette. Click on the master page icon and when its current name is highlighted, type the new name for that or for any other master page icon which you select. In a document for a book, for example, one master page might be called "Front Matter" and another master page might be named "Index."

The master page's name has two parts separated by a hyphen. The first part is restricted to the characters which appear on the document page icons in the Document Layout palette, like M1, M2, etc. The actual *name* of the master page, like Master 1 or Index, appears after the hyphen. When you change the name of a master page, the prefix indicating the master page number always appears followed by a hyphen, and then the name you assigned to that master page.

ACCESSING MASTER PAGES

You access master pages either through the Document Layout palette or by choosing Page/Display/M1-Master 1 (or any other master page) from the Menu Bar. To use the Document Layout palette, choose Document/Show Master Pages and double-click on the master page icon. Figure 5.1 displays the Document Layout palette for a document that contains one master page (M1) and 6 document pages. The "dog ears" around the document pages indicate that the Facing Pages option was checked in the New dialog box.

MASTER PAGE CONTENTS

Every master page contains master guides (margin and column guides) and an automatic text link icon (the miniature chain links in the upper left corner of every master page created with an automatic text box). The text link feature in XPress allows you to control the flow of text from one text box to another anywhere in the document. The automatic text link box, a text box that is created if you select the Automatic Text Box option in the New (document) dialog box, will also be displayed on the master page.

ADDING ITEMS TO A MASTER PAGE

You can add text boxes (with or without text), picture boxes (with or without graphics), rules, and ruler guides to the master pages. You can also change the master guides by choosing Page/Master Guides *only when you are viewing the master pages*. Each element you place on a master page will appear on every document page unless you change either the master page or the document page. You may not, however, import or type text in the automatic text box on a master page.

To modify a master page from the Document Layout palette, choose View/Show Document Layout to display the Document Layout palette. Then choose Document/Show Master Pages. Double-click on the icon of the master page you wish to modify to display that master page in the document window. You may have to scroll through the palette to view the master page. If your master page is a facing page, scroll to view both the left and right master pages.

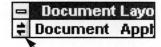

Click on these arrows in the Document Layout palette to move quickly from the document pages to the master pages without pulling down the Document or Masters menus.

The automatic text link icon appears on the master pages when you select Automatic Text Box in the New (document) dialog box.

Ctrl+N File/New

Ctrl+Y Edit/Preferences/
    General

Ctrl+R View/Show Rulers

Ctrl+Alt+M View/Show
    Measurements

Ctrl+B Item/Frame

Ctrl+Alt+S File/Save as

Check it out

When a check mark appears before a menu item, that item is selected. To keep the item selected, scroll off the menu. To deselect the item, highlight it and release the mouse button.

Facing page master page icon

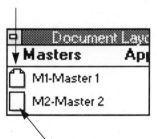

Non-facing page master page icon

Make room for rulers

You can move the palettes around the page by clicking and dragging on the title bar of the palette and moving it to a new location. This will allow you to see the rulers more easily.

EXERCISE A

1. Create a new document (Ctrl+N) with 1-inch margins, facing pages, an automatic text box, and 2 columns.

2. Display the Document Layout palette (View/Show Document Layout) and choose Document/Show Master Pages. Double-click on the M-1 Master 1 icon to access the master page itself.

3. Display the General Preferences dialog box by choosing Edit/Preferences/General (Ctrl+Y) and make sure that the unit of measure is inches, the margin guides are displayed in front of the page, and the Keep Changes option is selected. Click on OK.

4. Scroll to the left hand master page. Make sure the Snap to Guides option is checked (View/Snap to Guides) and display the Rulers by choosing View/Show Rulers (Ctrl+R). Drag a ruler guide down from the horizontal ruler to the 2-inch mark on the vertical ruler; drag a vertical ruler guide across to the 1.5-inch mark on the horizontal ruler.

5. Select the Picture Box tool, click on the page, and drag to create a picture box at the point below where the two ruler guides intersect. Then activate the Measurements palette (Ctrl+Alt+M) and make sure that X=1.5 inches; Y=2 inches; W=1 inch; H=2 inches. Press Enter to accept the changes.

6. With the picture box still selected, choose Item/Frame (Ctrl+B) and type 2 in the Width field on the right to give the picture box a frame that is 2 points wide. Your page should look like Figure 5.2.

7. Repeat this process on the right master page, placing the picture box on the right side of the page.

8. Choose Masters/Show Document Pages in the Document Layout palette and double-click on document page M1, which will take you from the master page to the first document page. Notice that page 1, a right hand page, contains exactly the same elements as the master page.

9. Now save this one-page document by choosing File/Save as (Ctrl+Alt+S). When the Save as dialog box appears, select a drive and directory, then type (no quotes) "MPfile" and click on OK.

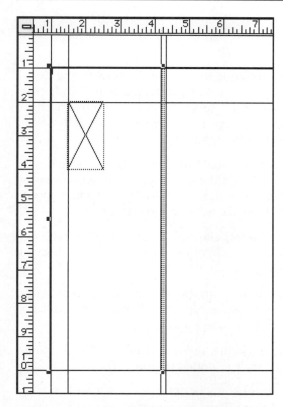

Figure 5.2—Left Master Page M1 displays 2 columns, ruler guides, and a picture box.

Besides adding boxes to master pages, you can also add lines. These will appear on every document page based on the master page on which you drew the lines.

EXERCISE B

1. Create a new document (Ctrl+N) with an automatic text box and 3 columns. If necessary, *deselect* the Facing Pages option to create a non-facing master page.

2. Choose Edit/Preferences/General (Ctrl+Y) and select inches as the unit of measure.

3. Display the Document Layout palette by choosing View/Show Document Layout (Ctrl+Alt+M) and choose Document/Show Master Pages. Double-click on the M1-Master 1 icon to display the master pages. Because you *deselected* the Facing Pages option in the New (document) dialog box, the M1-Master 1 icon is a non-facing page and does not display "dog ears."

4. Select the Orthogonal Line tool and click at the top of the gutter space between the columns. (It's easier if you turn off Snap to Guides by choosing View/Snap to Guides). When the cursor turns into a crosshair, drag to draw a vertical line from the top to the bottom margin between the columns.

Ctrl+N File/New
Ctrl+Y Edit/General/
        Preferences
Ctrl+Alt+M View/Show
        Measurements

Safety first

Because pages which are deleted via the Document Layout palette cannot be retrieved, always save your document before dragging pages to the trash icon. This way, you can choose File/Revert to Saved to retrieve them.

FYI

To **deselect** a checkbox, click in it to remove the x. To **select** a checkbox, click in it to display the x.

Orthogonal Line tool

How to do it

When drawing several horizontal or vertical lines, draw the first one and position it correctly. Then activate the Measurements palette and with the original line selected, double-click on its X or Y measurement and copy that number (Ctrl+C). Select the other lines, highlight their X or Y measurements in the Measurements palette, and paste in the dimension of the first line (Ctrl+V).

When you're setting lines between columns, turn off the Snap to Guides option (View/Snap to Guides) so you can move the line more easily to position it.

Ctrl+Alt+S File/Save as

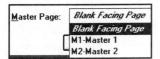

If you have created different master pages in a document, you can select the master page on which you want your document pages based by pulling down the Master Page pop-up menu in the Insert Pages dialog box.

The check mark next to a Chapter 1 master page indicates that the newly inserted page(s) will be based on Master Page A which you have named Chapter 1.

FYI

If you delete a page from the Document Layout palette and the Overflow Indicator appears at the bottom of the page, new pages will be added to accommodate that text if Auto Page Insertion is turned on in the General Preferences dialog box.

5. Use the Measurements palette to change the line's width to 12 points by typing 12 in the W(idth) field. Draw a similar line in the second gutter on that same page (Figure 5.3).

6. Now choose Page/Display/Document. You will return to the document page, although the Document Layout palette will still display the master page. Then choose Page/Insert. Type 2 in the Insert Pages dialog box. Insert 2 pages after page 1 by clicking on the After Page button, selecting the number in the After field, and typing 1.

7. Use the Master Page pull-down menu in the Insert Pages dialog box to select M1-Master 1, which will add those two pages based on master page M1 to the document. Click on OK. Choose Page/Display/Document from the Menu Bar to view the lines on those pages.

8. In the Document Layout palette, choose Document/Show Master Pages if it is not already displayed. Double-click on the M1-Master 1 icon to get to the master pages.

9. Select the Orthogonal Line tool again and draw a horizontal line 1 inch down from the top margin at the 2-inch mark on the vertical ruler and across the 3 columns on the master page.

10. Select the horizontal line and use the Measurements palette to change its width to 12 points and its style to dotted (Figure 5.4).

11. Then choose View/Hide Guides. In the Document Layout palette, choose Masters/Show Document Pages to view the lines.

12. Choose File/Save as (Ctrl+Alt+S) and in the Save as dialog box, type (no quotes) "NonFP " (for non-facing pages). Drag to find the directory where you want this file saved. Click on Save. You will use this file for the next exercise.

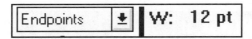

Figure 5.3—When a line drawn with the Orthogonal Line tool is selected, the Measurements Palette displays a Width (W) field. Type in the weight of the line.

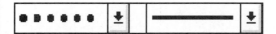

Figure 5.4—Displays a dotted line for the selected line's Style and no arrowheads for its endpoints. When a line drawn with the Orthogonal Line tool is selected, the Measurements palette also displays a pop-up menu for line styles and a pop-up menu for line endpoints.

CREATING NEW MASTER PAGES

A publication like a magazine might have several kinds of pages. Some would be for articles and stories; some for advertising; some for editorial content. Each of these pages might use a different kind of master page. In a book, the introduction, the body, and the index might all have different page attributes and therefore require different master pages.

To create another master page, open the "NonFP" file, if necessary. Display the Document Layout palette (View/Show Document Layout) and choose Document/Show Master Pages. Choose Masters/Insert/Blank Single Master (Figure 5.5). When you release the mouse button, the cursor changes to the Single-page Insertion pointer. Place that pointer below the first master page icon and release the mouse button. The M2-Master 2 master page icon is displayed. However, unlike document page 1, which was automatically created when M1-Master 1 was created, there are no document pages based on a second, third, etc. master page until you insert them manually.

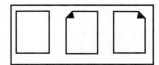

The cursor changes to a Page Icon pointer (blank, left facing, and right facing) to indicate the type of document page being inserted.

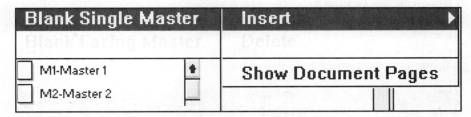

Figure 5.5—To add a master page to a document, Choose Document/Show Master Pages. Then choose Insert from the Masters menu. To insert a document page, choose Document/Insert and select either a Blank Single or Blank Facing document page.

INSERTING DOCUMENT PAGES BASED ON MASTER PAGES

Inserting document pages based on a master page is very easy. Display the Document Layout palette (View/Show Document Layout). Make sure Document is displayed at the left side of the menu. Choose Document/Insert and select either Blank Single Page, which will insert a non-facing page, or Blank Facing Page to insert a facing page, or select one of the available master pages. Then click on the palette where you want the new document page to appear. The arrow pointer changes to one of three page pointers that indicate what kind of a page is being placed (non-facing, left facing, or right facing page). Release the mouse button to place the page.

To place a new document page between two existing document pages, release the mouse button when the Force Down pointer is displayed between the two original pages.

You can also insert pages based on the master page by choosing Page/Insert from the Menu Bar and typing in the number of pages you want, where you want those pages placed, and whether you want Blank Facing document pages, Blank Single document pages, or document pages based on a master page.

DELETING MASTER PAGES AND DOCUMENT PAGES

To delete a master page from the Document Layout palette, choose Document/Show Master Pages. Click on the master page icon for the master page you want to delete and choose Masters/Delete. When the alert box appears, click on OK. To delete a document page from the Document Layout palette, make sure that Document is active on the palette. Then click on the page you want to delete. Choose Document/Delete and when the alert box appears, click on OK.

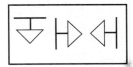

The Force Down, Force Right, and Force Left page pointers appear to indicate where the new document page will be inserted relative to another page in the document—beneath it, to its right, or to its left.

CHANGING DOCUMENTS FROM NON-FACING TO FACING PAGES

You can change a document created with non-facing pages to a document with facing pages by first going to the Document section of the palette (if you're in the master page section), and choosing Masters/Show Document Pages. Then choose File/Document Setup. Click in the Facing Pages check box. Once you do this, the Blank Facing Page option will be available from the Insert menu in the Document Layout palette as well as from the Page menu. You can change a facing page document to a non-facing page document only if the blank facing page master page was not applied to any document pages. This is a little more complicated than clicking in the Document Setup dialog box, and it's usually easier to create a new non-facing page document from scratch.

EXERCISE C

1. If necessary, open the file (Ctrl+O) you named "NonFP." This document has 1 master page and 3 non-facing document pages based on M1-Master 1. Display the Document Layout palette (View/Show Document Layout). Choose View/Show Guides and make sure that you are in the Document area of the palette.

2. Choose File/Document Setup. In the Document Setup dialog box, click on the Facing Pages check box to change this document to a facing pages document. Click on OK. Notice that document pages 2 and 3 are now positioned as facing pages. However, the "dog ears" do not appear on these or any pages created prior to the change made in the Printer Setup dialog box.

3. Create a new master page with facing pages from the Document Layout palette by choosing Document/Show Master Pages. Choose Insert/Blank Facing Master. Click under the M1-Master 1 icon to place the facing pages master page, M2-Master 2. The facing page M2-Master 2 icon is now active and can be used to create facing pages document pages.

4. In the Document Layout palette, create another master page, M3-Master 3 by choosing Document/Show Master Pages. Choose Masters/Insert/Blank Facing Master and then click on the palette below M1-Master 2 to place the new master page, M3-Master 3.

5. Click on the M1-Master 1 icon and change its name to Editorial. Click on the M2-Master 2 icon and change its name to Advertising. Click on the M3-Master 3 icon and change its name to Fiction.

6. Double-click on the Advertising icon to get to the master page. Select the Oval Picture Box tool and, holding down the Shift key, draw a circle about 2 inches wide on the left master page M2-Advertising.

7. With the circle still selected, choose Item/Modify (Ctrl+M), and in the lower right hand corner of the Picture Box Specifications dialog box, change the Background color from 0% Black to 100% Red (or any other color) by clicking on the down arrow to the right of the Shade menu. You'll learn more about using the Item/Modify command in Lesson 7. Click on OK to return to the document where the circle is still selected.

8. Duplicate the circle by choosing Item/Duplicate (Ctrl+D). Use the Item/Modify command (Ctrl+M) to change its color. Use the Item tool to move the new circle to the center of the right master page.

9. In the Document Layout palette choose Masters/Show Document Pages. Choose Document/Insert/M2-Advertising to insert one document page based on M2-Advertising. Click on the palette below page 2 to insert the page.

10. Repeat this process to place a second document page based on M2-Advertising. You should now have 5 pages in this document. Document page 4 should have a red circle; document page 5 should have a blue circle (or any colors you applied on the master pages). They should look like Figure 5.6.

What you will need

A text file of about 500 words

Ctrl+Alt-M View/Show Measurements
Ctrl+D Item/Frame

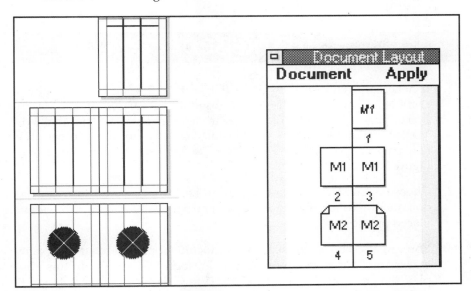

Figure 5.6—Document with master pages M1 and M2 and 6 document pages. Pages 1, 2, and 3 reflect the lines drawn on M1-Master 1. Document pages 4 and 5 reflect the circles drawn on M2-Master 2.

You can also insert pages based on the master page by choosing Page/Insert from the Menu Bar and typing in the number of pages you want, where you want those pages placed, and what kind of pages they should be.

Figure 5.7 displays the Insert Pages dialog box. Type the number of pages you want to insert in the Insert field. Click in the appropriate box on the right side of the dialog box to place the new page(s) where you want them. If your document was created with an automatic text box, the Link to Current Text Chain box will be active. Clicking in this box will link the new

A text file

Ctrl+O File/Open
Ctrl+0 [zero] View/Fit in
    Window

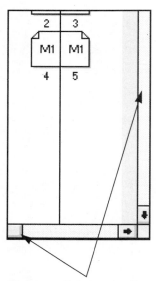

The scroll bars in the Document Layout palette work the same way as the ones in the document window. Use them to scroll through the palette to display all the document pages.

FYI

You can change the position of a master page icon by clicking on it and moving it to another position in the Document Layout palette.

pages to the ones already in the document and text will flow from the existing pages to the newly inserted pages. The Master Page pull-down menu allows you to select a master page on which to base the new pages or to select a blank single or a blank facing page.

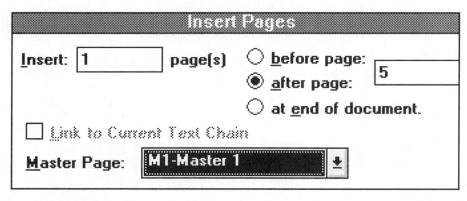

Figure 5.7—The Insert Pages dialog box is used to indicate how many pages you want and where you want them inserted. If you created your document with an automatic text box and that text box is active (selected), you can choose to link the new pages to the existing text chain.

EXERCISE D

1. If necessary, choose File/Open (Ctrl+O) and open the file named "MPfile." Choose Page/Insert and insert 4 pages based on M1-Master 1 after page 1 for a total of 5 pages in the document. Be sure that M1-Master 1 is highlighted in the Master Page pop-up menu to base the new pages on M1-Master 1. Click on OK. Your screen should resemble Figure 5.8.

2. Choose View/Fit in Window (Ctrl+0 [zero]) and scroll through the document. Notice that each document page contains every element placed on the master page.

3. You can also choose to insert blank document pages, document pages that are not based on any master page specifications. To do this, display the Document Layout palette (View/Show Document Layout) and choose Document/Insert/Blank Single Page.

4. Click the Blank-Single-Insertion pointer beneath page 4 and release the mouse button to display document page 6. Notice that it does not display an M, indicating that it is not based on a master page. It also does not display "dog ears," because it is not a facing page.

5. Create a second master page in this document by choosing Document/Show Master Pages in the Document Layout palette. Choose Masters/Insert/Blank Facing Master. Click below the M1-Master icon to create master page M2-Master 2.

6. Repeat this process to create a third master page, M3-Master 3.

Ctrl+B Item/Frame

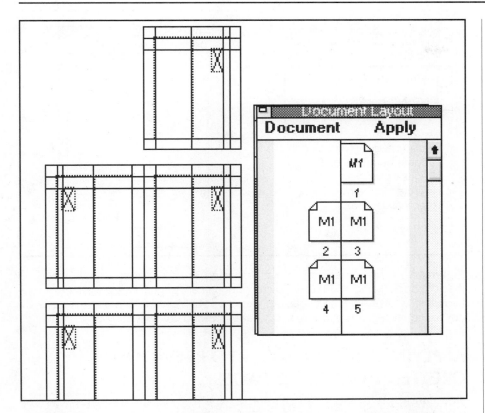

Figure 5.8—A document of five pages based on M1-Master 1. The Document Layout palette indicates that all the pages in the document are based on M1-Master 1. Notice that every page in the document contains all the elements placed on the left and right master pages.

7. Double-click on the M3-Master 3 icon to get to the master page itself. Scroll until you are on the left master page. Select the Rectangle Picture Box tool and drag to create a picture box. Use the Measurements palette to make the box 4 inches wide and 2 inches high.

8. With the picture box still selected, choose Item/Frame (Ctrl+B) and scroll down the Style window in the Frame dialog box. Click on an ornate frame and in the Width box on the right. Then use the arrow pull-down menu to the right of the Width field to give it a width of 12 points. Click on OK.

9. Choose Masters/Show Document Pages. Choose Document/Insert and select M3-Master 3. Click to the right of document page 6 to insert one page based on M3-Master 3 in the document, for a total of 7 document pages. Your screen should resemble Figure 5.9.

Ctrl+M Item/Modify
Ctrl+D Item/Duplicate

Use the Item tool to select picture boxes. If you have the Content tool selected, hold down the Ctrl key to temporarily turn the Content tool into the Item tool. The cursor will return to the Content tool when you release the Ctrl key.

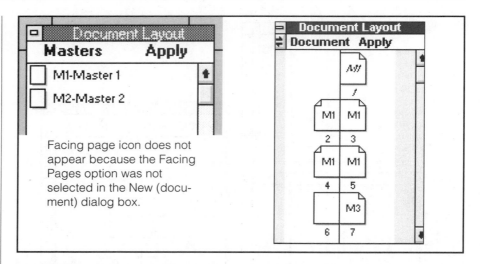

Figure 5.9—A seven-page document containing 3 master pages, with only two master pages (M1 and M3) used to create document pages. Five pages are based on M1-Master 1; no pages are based on M2-Master 2; one blank page is not based on any master page; and 1 page is based on M3-Master 3.

APPLYING MASTER PAGES TO PREVIOUSLY CREATED DOCUMENT PAGES

You can apply a master page's items to a document page that was not based on a master page. This is done by using the Apply command in the Document Layout palette.

EXERCISE E

1. Create a new document (Ctrl+N) with 1-inch margins, an automatic text box, and facing pages. If necessary, display the Document Layout palette by choosing View/Show Document Layout.

2. Choose Edit/Preferences/General (Ctrl+Y) and select inches as the unit of measure. Make sure that the Keep Changes option is selected.

3. In the Document Layout palette, choose Document/Show Master Pages. Click once on the M1-Master 1 icon to highlight it. Change the name of the master page to Glossary by typing "Glossary" and pressing Enter. Then double-click on the M1-Glossary icon to access the master page.

4. Choose View/Fit in Window (Ctrl+0 [zero]). Click on the Text Box tool to select it and click and drag on the left master page to draw a text box about 1 inch high. If necessary, display the Measurements palette by choosing View/Show Measurements (Ctrl+Alt+M). Select the first four fields and make sure that X=1, Y=1, W=6.5, and H=1. Press Enter to accept the values.

5. Click inside the new text box and type (no quotes), "LEFT MASTER PAGE" in all caps. Select all the text by choosing Edit/Select All (Ctrl+A) and use the arrows in the Measurements palette to assign it a typeface of Times New Roman and a type size of 36 points.

6 With the text still selected, click on the Center Align icon and on the B(old) icon in the Measurements palette.

7. With the text box still selected, click on the Item tool to select it and choose Item/Duplicate (Ctrl+D). Use the Item tool to move the duplicate text box from the left master page to the right master page. Select the Content tool and double-click on "Left" and type "RIGHT."

8. Click on the Rectangle Picture Box tool to select it. Drag on the left master page to draw a rectangle that is 4 inches wide and 2 inches high. Use the Measurements palette to input the correct values. Then, with the picture box still selected, choose Item/Modify (Ctrl+M). Use the Color pull-down arrow to select Red. Use the Shade pull-down arrow to select 100%. Click on OK. Your screen should resemble Figure 5.10.

9. Choose Masters/Show Document Pages to return to the document page 1 which is based on M1-Master 1. Because the red box was placed on the left master page, it is not displayed on the right document page. Choose Document/Insert/Blank Facing Page. Click below and to the left of the M1 page to place the new page. Notice that this page does not have an M on it because it was not based on any master page.

10. Double-click on the page 2 icon to get to the page. Notice that the M1-Glossary items do not appear on this document page. To apply the master page items to the blank page, first click on the page to highlight it. Then, in the Document Layout palette, choose Apply/M1-Glossary. The master page items now appear on the formerly blank page because it is now based on the master page, M1-Glossary. Notice also that the M1 prefix appears on the icon for document page 2.

11. Choose File/Save (Ctrl+S) and save this file as Apply. You will use it for the next exercise.

Ctrl+A Edit/Select All
Ctrl+D Item/Duplicate
Ctrl+M Item/Modify
Ctrl+S File/Save

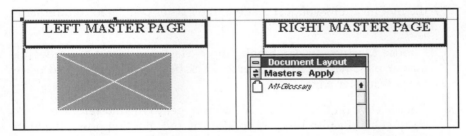

Figure 5.10—Displays the left and right master pages with a colored picture box on the left master page. Notice that the name of the master page has been changed to Glossary. That name appears in italics because the page is selected.

Ctrl+Y Edit/Preferences/
  General
Ctrl+M Item/Modify
Ctrl+B Item/Frame

Back to square one

Alt-click on the ruler origin
to restore the zero point to
its original setting.

CHANGING MASTER PAGE ITEMS

Thus far you have placed items on the master page and seen them appear on the document pages. Now see what happens on a document page when you *change* a master page item.

Choose Edit/Preferences/General (Ctrl+Y) and notice the Master Page Items field at the bottom of the left column in the dialog box. To be really helpful, this field should read, "Keep changes to master page items which have been altered on document pages if and when a master page is deleted *or* if and when a new master page format is applied to the document page." Naturally, all of this can't fit in a dialog box, but what it means is that if you manually change (how else can you?) a master page item on a document page, like the colored picture box in the Apply file, should you delete the master page on which that document page is based, Keep Changes will make sure that that modified colored box—a master page *item*, stays on the page. Likewise, if Keep Changes is selected and you apply another master page to a document page based on a master page, that modified picture box would remain, regardless of what text and graphics items were applied via the new master page.

EXERCISE F

1. If necessary, open the file saved as Apply. Display the Document Layout palette and double-click on the icon for page 2, a left facing page which contains a text box and a colored picture box.

2. On the *document* page, select the picture box and choose Item/Modify (Ctrl+M). Change the background color of the box and click on OK.

3. With the picture box still selected, choose Item/Frame (Ctrl+B) and apply a 12-point frame to the box. Click on OK.

4. Using the Item tool, drag the box down to the middle of the page. You have now modified a master page item on a document page. In the Document Layout palette, choose Document/Show Master Pages. Notice that the left master page is still the same and does not display the modifications you just made to the master page items on the *document* page.

5. Choose Masters/Insert/Blank Single Master to insert a non-facing master page named M2-Master 2. Click below M1-Glossary to place the new master page.

6. Double click on the M2-Master 2 icon to get to the master page. Click on the Oval Picture Box tool to select it and, holding down the Shift key, drag on the master page to draw a large circle. Choose Item/Modify (Ctrl+M) and assign it a background color. Click on OK.

7. Choose Item/Frame (Ctrl+B) and assign it a 36-point frame. Click on OK to return to the master page.

8. Choose Masters/Show Document pages to return to the document page area of the Document Layout palette. Click once on document

page 2, the left facing page based on M1-Glossary. Choose Apply/M2-Master 2.

Ctrl+N File/New
Ctrl+Y Edit/Preferences/
General

9. Notice that not only has the new master page format been applied to page 1 (the framed circle), but also that the modified item on the page is still there. This is because you told XPress to keep any changed item (the picture box) if you applied a new master page. Your screen should resemble Figure 5.11.

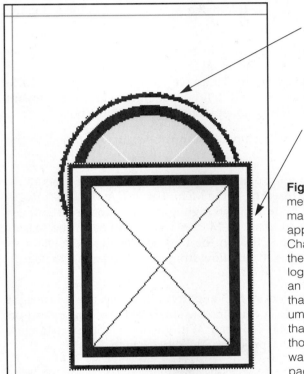

Circle appears when the new master page is applied.

Rectangle remains because the Keep Changes option is selected.

Figure 5.11—Displays document page 2 when a new master page has been applied to it and the Keep Changes option is selected in the General Preferences dialog box. Since the rectangle is an M1-Glossary master item that was modified on the document page, it was kept on that document page even though a new master page was applied to that document page.

REVIEW EXERCISE #1

In this exercise you will create an eight-page booklet.

1. Create a new file by choosing File/New (Ctrl+N). When the New dialog box appears select US Letter; assign the document top, bottom, and inside margins of 1.5 inches and an outside margin of 1 inch; 1 column; and select the Automatic Text Box and Facing Pages options. Click on OK.

2. Choose Edit/Preferences/General (Ctrl+Y) and use the pull-down menus to select picas as the horizontal and vertical units of measure; Auto Page Insertion off; Framing inside; and Guides in front. Select Keep Changes to master page items. Click on OK.

64 Lesson 5

Ctrl+Alt+M View/Show
     Measurements
Ctrl+A Edit/Select All
Ctrl+E File/Get Text
Ctrl+C Edit/Copy
Ctrl+V Edit/Paste

3. Double click on the M1-Master 1 icon (Document/Show Master Pages), and drag the zero point (ruler origin) over to the right hand page so that the dotted lines lie on top of the top and left margins, making the intersection of those margins 0 on the horizontal and vertical rulers.

4. Select the Text Box tool and drag to create a text box on the right hand page that is about 30 picas wide and 5 picas high. Activate the Measurements palette, if necessary, by choosing View/Show Measurements (Ctrl+Alt+M) and use it to make sure the box has the following values: X=0p; Y=0p; W=36p; H=4p6.

5. Use the Content tool to type in that box "Who We Are" and choose Edit/Select All (Ctrl+A) to select all the text. Use the Measurements palette to change its typeface to Times New Roman, its type size to 48 points, and its style to bold and italic. Click on the Center Alignment icon in the Measurements palette to center the text in the box.

6. Choose Page/Display/Document from the Menu Bar to get to the document pages.

7. In the Document Layout palette, choose Masters/Show Document Pages. Choose Page/Insert from the Menu Bar. When the Insert Pages dialog box appears, type 2 in the highlighted box to insert 2 pages after page 1. Make sure that M1-Master 1 is displayed in the Master Pages pull-down menu. Click on the Link to Current Text chain so that your text will automatically flow from page 1 to page 2 to page 3. Click on OK.

8. Double-click on document page 3 and notice that because it is a right hand page (like page 1), it contains the small text box you placed on the right hand page of M1-Master 1. With the Item tool selected, click on that small text box and press the Backspace key to delete it.

9. Click on the Content tool to select it, and double-click inside the large text box on page 1. Choose File/Get Text (Ctrl+E) and open a text file. If it doesn't fill all three pages, select it (Ctrl+A) and then Copy (Ctrl+C) and Paste it (Ctrl+V) until the three document pages are just about filled. Your pages should resemble Figure 5.12.

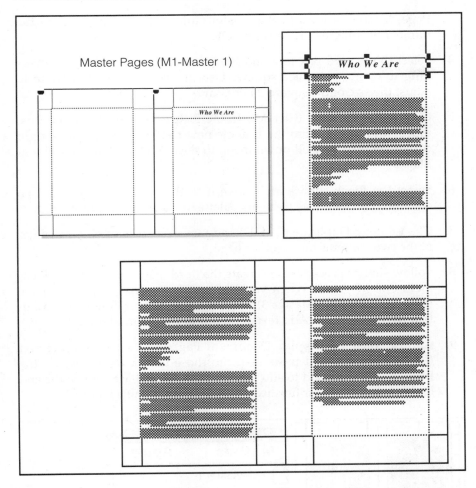

Figure 5.12—Three pages based on M1-Master 1. The small text box placed on the right master page was deleted from document page 3.

REVIEW EXERCISE #2

Now that the document and the first master page with the document pages based on it have been formatted, create two more master pages.

1. In the Document Layout palette, choose Document/Show Master Pages. Choose Masters/Insert/Blank Facing Master. Click below the M1-Master 1 icon to place M2-Master 2.

2. Double-click on the M2-Master 2 icon to get to the master page. Select the Text Box tool and drag to create a text box on both the left and right master pages. Use the Measurements palette to give the box the following values: X=-3p; Y=0p; W=39p; H=48p.

3. Choose Page/Insert and add 2 more pages based on M2-Master 2 at the end of the document. There are now 5 facing pages in the document. Choose Document/Show Master Pages and double-click on the M2-Master 2 icon. When the master pages are visible, choose

Ctrl+M Item/Modify
Ctrl+D Item/Duplicate
Ctrl+E File/Get Text

Page/Master Guides. In the Master Guides dialog box, change the number of columns to 2. Click on OK.

4. Select the Picture Box tool and hold down the Shift key while dragging to create a 10-pica square. Use the Measurements palette to adjust the size of the square if necessary.

5. Choose Item Modify (Ctrl+M). In the Picture Box Specifications box, move your mouse onto the triangle next to Shade in the lower right corner and use the pull-down menu to select 100%. Leave the Color at Black.

6. Select the Black square and move it to the intersection of the two columns. Use the Measurements palette to place it at X=11p5; Y=0p.

7. Choose Item/Duplicate (Ctrl+D) and move the duplicate to the center of the two columns on the other page.

8. Follow similar procedures to create the third master page in this document, M3-Master 3. When you have made the master pages visible (Page/Display/M3-Master 3), choose Page/Master Guides to assign that page 3 columns. Add text and graphics to the master page

9. Choose Masters/Display Document Pages and either import text (Ctrl+E) or copy and paste text into those text boxes. Then use the Page/Insert command to add 3 pages based on M3-Master 3 at the end of the document. Your finished pages should resemble Figure 5.13.

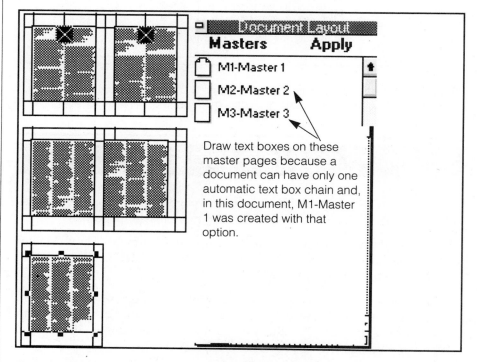

Figure 5.13—Displays document pages formatted in Master Pages M2 and M3.

REVIEW QUESTIONS

Read the following questions and choose the answer which best completes the statement.

1. Master page items _____.
    a. can be edited
    b. appear on document pages based on the master page
    c. include both text boxes and picture boxes
    d. all of the above

2. Master pages are accessed _____.
    a. from a dialog box
    b. from the Page menu
    c. from the Document Layout palette
    d. b and c

3. New master pages are created _____.
    a. in the Document Layout palette
    b. from the Page menu
    c. from the File menu
    d. in the Measurements palette

4. Master page icons include _____.
    a. facing and non-facing page icons
    b. facing page icons
    c. non-facing page icons
    d. duplicate page icons

5. Document pages are inserted _____.
    a. from the Page menu
    b. from the File menu
    c. from the Document Layout palette
    d. a and c

6. To insert a document page not based on a master page, _____.
    a. use the Edit menu
    b. use the Apply command in the Document Layout palette
    c. use the document page icons in the Document Layout palette
    d. use the Insert command from the Menu Bar

7. A document can be changed from a non-facing page document to a facing page document in the _____.
    a. dialog box
    b. Document Layout palette
    c. Document Setup dialog box
    d. Insert Pages dialog box

8. Master pages can be named _____.
    a. in the Document Layout palette
    b. in the Insert Pages dialog box
    c. in the Document Setup dialog box
    d. from the Edit menu

9. Access multiple master pages by _____.
   a. scrolling in the document
   b. choosing Page/Display
   c. scrolling in the Document Layout palette
   d. b and c

10. The Link to Current Text Chain option is active in the Insert Pages dialog box when _____.
   a. the Document Layout palette is displayed
   b. the Automatic Text Box option was checked in the New (document) dialog box
   c. text has been flowed in the document
   d. no text has been flowed in the document

Answers: 1. d; 2. d; 3. a; 4. a; 5. d; 6. b; 7. b; 8. a; 9. d; 10. b

LESSON

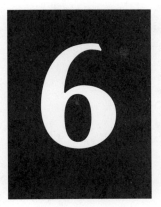

Working with Document Pages

OVERVIEW

In this lesson you will learn how to delete document pages, create headers and footers with page numbers and "jump lines," and link and unlink text boxes. You will also learn how to copy items between pages and between documents and move pages within a document, as well as how to import and export text. You will continue to use menu commands and keyboard equivalents. As a review, you will create two documents using single and multiple master pages, numbered footers, and linked text boxes.

TOPICS

Deleting document pages
Auto Page Insertion
Numbering pages consecutively
Creating document sections
Linking text boxes
Unlinking text boxes
Creating "jump lines"
Copying items between documents
Copying pages between documents
Moving pages
Importing and exporting text files
Review Exercises
Review Questions

TERMS

Broken Chain icon
current page number symbol
delete pages
filters
Intact Chain icon
linking
Section Start
thumbnails
unlinking

Ctrl+N New
Ctrl+Y General/
      Preferences
Ctrl+3 Current page
         number

FYI

When creating a text box for page numbers (folios), make sure that text box runs the entire width of the main text box on the page. This will prevent the text from flowing around or on top of the page number.

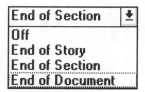

The Auto Page Insertion drop-down list in the General Preferences dialog box lists choices for adding pages to a document.

DELETING DOCUMENT PAGES

Just as you used the Document Layout palette and the Insert Pages dialog box to add pages to a document, you can also use the Document Layout palette and the Delete Pages dialog box to delete pages from a document.

EXERCISE A

1. Choose File/New (Ctrl+N) to create a new document without facing pages and without an automatic text box. Choose View/Show Document Layout to activate the Document Layout palette.

2. Use the Page/Insert command to insert three new document pages based on M1-Master 1.

3. To delete pages using the Delete Pages dialog box (Figure 6.1), choose Page/Delete and type 1 in the first field of the dialog box. Press Tab and type 3 in the next field. Click on OK. You can also type the page number of a single page in the first field and click on OK to delete just that one page.

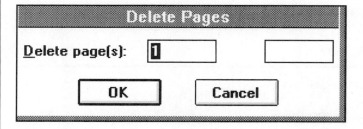

Figure 6.1—The Delete Pages dialog box allows you to delete a single page or a range of pages.

AUTO PAGE INSERTION

If you have turned Auto Page Insertion off in the General Preferences (Ctrl+Y) dialog box, the pages will be deleted and will not be replaced in the document. If you delete pages with Auto Page Insertion set to Off and the deleted pages leave text "homeless," XPress will store the text and display the overflow indicator to tell you that you must manually add (or let XPress automatically add) pages in order to view the overflow text. If Auto Page Insertion is not set to Off, then the pages you delete will automatically be replaced by other pages and the text from the deleted pages will be flowed on to those new pages.

NUMBERING PAGES CONSECUTIVELY

XPress will automatically number pages anywhere in the document if you type Ctrl+3. This, of course, leaves strange numbers running around your document. The best way to number pages is to create a text box on the master page beyond the top or bottom margin of the automatic text box or within the automatic text box if the automatic text box defines the whole printing area. Type Ctrl+3 in that smaller box there and the *symbol* for the current page number (<#>) will be displayed on the master page (Figure 6.2).

The correct page number, however, will appear only on the document page. Format the symbol's type, size, alignment, etc. on the master page. Add a prefix if you wish. Then double-click on any document page to see the page number (Figure 6.3).

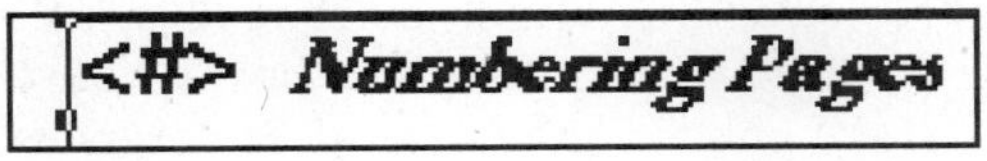

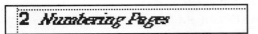

Figure 6.2—The Current Page symbol as it appears formatted on the master page.

Figure 6.3—The page number as it appears formatted on the document page.

CREATING DOCUMENT SECTIONS

You can also number pages using the Section dialog box. Choose Page/Section and click in the Section Start check box. This allows you to number your pages consecutively from any page in the document. The first few pages of a book's introduction could be numbered with Roman numerals; the first chapter would begin from Arabic number 1, while the index of the book might start at Roman numeral i again.

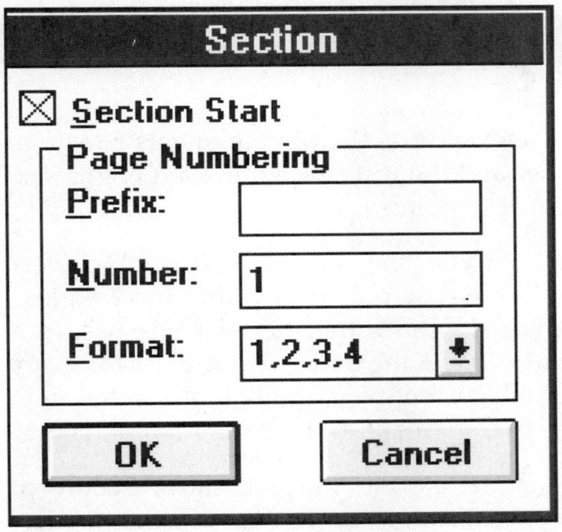

Figure 6.4—Displays the Section dialog box. Regardless of this selected page's position in the document, it will now be page 1, and if a Ctrl+3 command is applied to this page, it will display the number 1.

Ctrl+N New

Tip

To delete a sequence of pages from one page to the end of the document using the Delete Pages dialog box, type the first page to be deleted in the Page(s) field. Then tab to the Thru field and type *end*.

FYI

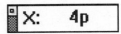

When you select picas as the unit of measure in the General Preferences dialog box, remember to type p after any of the dimension numbers in the Measurements palette. If you typed 4 for the X value above instead of 4p, XPress would have calculated the origin in points and made the origin of the text box 4 points from the zero point (ruler origin) which is a lot closer than 4 picas.

EXERCISE B

1. Choose File/New (Ctrl+N) to create a new document using the Facing Pages and Automatic Text Box options. Display the Document Layout palette (View/Show Document Layout). Choose Document/Show Master Pages. Double-click on the M1-Master 1 icon.

Ctrl+Y Edit/Preferences/
    General
Ctrl+Alt+M View/Show
    Measurements
Ctrl+A Edit/Select All
Ctrl+D Item/Duplicate
Ctrl+C Edit/Copy
Ctrl+V Edit/Paste

2. Place items like picture boxes and rules on the left and right pages of M-1 Master 1. Then use both the Document Layout palette and the Insert Pages dialog box to insert a few pages based on M-1 Master 1 as well as blank pages. Notice the difference between the document pages based on M-1 Master 1 and those based on the blank pages.

3. Create a new document (File/New) with half-inch margins (0.5") all around, 1 column, facing pages, and an automatic text box. Choose Edit/Preferences/General (Ctrl+Y) and, in the General Preferences dialog box, select picas as the unit of measure. Use the Page/Insert command to insert three pages based on M1-Master 1 at the end of the document. You now have four pages in the document.

4. Double-click on page 1 in the Document Layout palette to get to that page. Select the automatic text box on page 1 by clicking anywhere in the box and choose Page/Insert to display the the Insert Pages dialog box. Add 2 additional pages at the end of the document based on M1-Master 1. Click in the Link to Current Text Chain box so text will flow automatically to the new pages. You now have six facing pages in the document.

5. Choose Document/Show Master Pages. Double-click on the M-1 Master 1 icon to get to the master pages. Select the Text Box tool and draw a text box on each page just above the bottom margin. Activate the Measurements palette (Ctrl+Alt+M) and make sure that X=3p; Y=61p7; W=45p; H=1p6.

6. In the box on the left master page, type the current page command (Ctrl+3). Type 2 spaces after the <#> symbol; then type (no quotes) "My Exciting Childhood."

7. Choose Edit/Select All (Ctrl+A) and use the Measurements palette to format both the page number and the text. Assign it a left alignment, any typeface, and a type size of 10 points.

8. Duplicate that text box which you just formatted (Ctrl+D). After selecting the Item tool, move the new box to the other master page. Use the Measurements palette to check that the text box has an X value of 3p, a Y value of 61p7, and the text is right aligned. Copy (Ctrl+C) and Paste (Ctrl+V) the current page symbol <#> on the right hand page so that it appears two spaces after the text.

9. In the Document Layout palette, choose Masters/Show Document Pages. Double-click on the page 2 icon to get to page 2. Scroll to view the footers on pages 2 and 3. Your screen should resemble Figure 6.5.

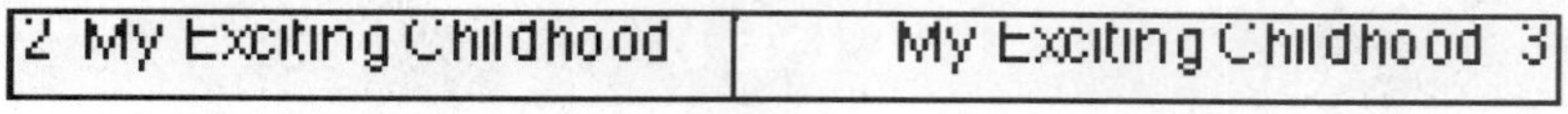

| 2 My Exciting Childhood | My Exciting Childhood 3 |

Figure 6.5—Footers created on the left and right on M1-Master 1 pages using the Current Page command will display the actual page numbers on the document pages. Notice that the page numbers on both the right and left hand pages are at the margin, while the text reads to and from the binding.

EXERCISE C

1. In the same document, use either the Document Layout palette or the Insert Pages dialog box (Page/Insert) to add three additional pages based on M1-Master 1 at the end of the document for a total of nine document pages.

2. Click anywhere on page 5. Choose Page/Section. Click on the Section Start box to select it and type 67 in the Number field of the dialog box. Click on OK. Notice that page 5 on the Document Layout palette displays an asterisk indicating that it is the start of a section.

3. Since document page 5 has now become numbered page 67, document page 6 has become numbered page 68, and so on, you need a new master page with running heads for these pages.

4. Create M2-Master 2 from the Document Layout palette by choosing Document/Show Master Pages. Choose Masters/Insert/Blank Facing Master. Click below M1-Master 1 to place the second master page. Double-click on M2-Master 2 to get to the left and right master pages.

5. Create a text box for the header on both the left and right master pages, just as you did for the footers on M1-Master 1. Use the Measurements palette to give the text box the following values: X=3p; Y=3p; W=45p; H=1p6.

6. Type Ctrl+3 followed by two spaces to produce the Current Page symbol <#> and type (no quotes): "My Boring Adolescence" in each box. Format the left and right headers just as you formatted the left and right footers.

7. Delete page 6 via the Document Layout palette by clicking on it to select it. Then choose Document/Delete. When the alert box appears, click on OK. You now have eight document pages.

8. Get to the document page area of the Document Layout palette (Masters/Show Document Pages). Click once on the page 8 icon to highlight it. Choose Apply/M2-Master 2 to apply the formatting from the master page you just created (M2-Master 2) to page 8.

9. Choose Document/Show Master Pages to get to the master page area of the Document Layout palette.

10. Click once on the M1-Master 1 icon to highlight it. Type (no quotes) "Chapter 1" in the field to the right of the icon. Then highlight the M2-Master 2 icon and type "Chapter 2." View your pages. Your Document Layout palette should look like Figure 6.6.

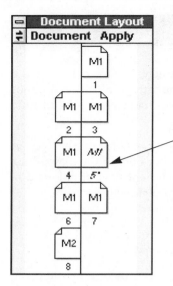

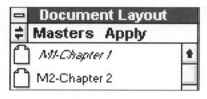

Figure 6.6—A Document Layout palette showing M1-Master 1, which has been applied to seven document pages, and M2-Master 2, which has been applied to page 8. Notice the asterisk next to page number 5, which indicates that a new section starts with that page.

Asterisk indicates that this page starts a new section.

Linking tool

Unlinking tool

The Broken Chain icon, found in the upper left corner of a master page that does not contain an automatic text box.

LINKING TEXT BOXES

Linking text boxes is how you control where text flows in a document. When you set up master pages containing an automatic text link box, those pages are dynamically linked. Text will flow from the text box on the first page to the text box on the next page throughout the document if you have Auto Page Insertion turned on in the General Preferences dialog box. When you add or delete text or graphics, the text will adjust itself within those linked boxes.

You can link the text from one document page to the new ones you create using the Page/Insert command if you selected the Automatic Text Box option in the General Preferences dialog box. Click in the Link to Current Chain check box in the Insert Pages dialog box to link the text on those pages.

If you don't select the Automatic Text Box option in the General Preferences dialog box and you want to create a text box that is linked to the Intact Chain icon in the upper left corner of each master page, do the following. (1) Display the master page (Page/Display/M1-Master 1) and then draw the text box you want to be the automatic text box. (2) Select the Linking tool and click on the Broken Chain icon in the upper left corner of the left master page. Then, with the Linking Tool still selected, click on the text box you just created. An arrow will go from the broken chain to the text box, making that text box an automatic text box (Figure 6.7).

WARNING!

One text box can be linked to another text box only if that second text box is empty. Links cannot be established from one text box to another text box which contains text.

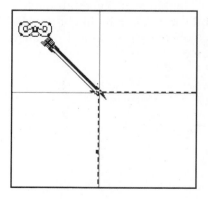

Figure 6.7—When a document is created without an automatic text box and you want to establish an automatic text box link, go to the master page, select the Linking tool and click on the Broken Chain icon. Then click in the text box on the master page. An arrow will appear and the Broken Chain icon will become an Intact Chain icon, indicating that the text boxes on the master pages (and all pages based on those master pages) are now linked.

Notice the sidebars on the pages of this book. The narrow text boxes in which that material was created are not linked to the automatic text boxes in which the body of the text (what you're reading now) was flowed. That text box is linked to the large text box on the next page. Notice the Linking arrows (Figure 6.8) that are displayed when you select the Linking tool and click on a text box. Figure 6.9 displays the linking arrows from page 3 to page 5.

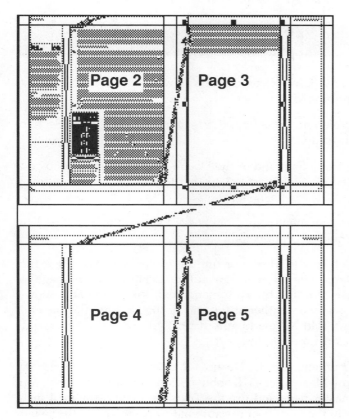

Figure 6.8—The linking arrows appeared when a text box was selected with the Linking tool. Notice the arrows going from page 2 to page 3; from page 4 to page 5, etc. Neither the text boxes on the outside margins nor the text boxes used to hold the page numbers or headers are affected; only the boxes that were linked in the chain (story) will receive the text.

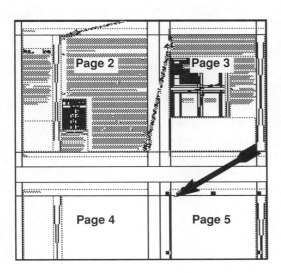

Figure 6.9—The linking arrows indicate that page 3 is linked to page 5. This is done by clicking on page 3 with the Linking Tool and then clicking on page 5—before flowing text into page 5. You cannot link a text box to another text box that already contains text.

Linking boxes on non-sequential pages is called non-sequential linking. It allows you, for example, to start an article on one page and have it flow to another page anywhere in the document.

WARNING!

When you have finished linking text boxes, click *immediately* on another tool so that you don't accidentally continue linking boxes.

FYI

You cannot link a text box to another text box that already contains text. Linking boxes on non-sequential pages is called non-sequential linking. It allows you, for example, to start an article on one page and have it flow to another page anywhere in the document.

FYI

Clicking on the Linking tool alone does not display the linking arrows. You must click on a text box to display the arrows.

What you will need

A text file of about 500 words

Ctrl+N File/New
Ctrl+Y Edit/Preferences/ General
Ctrl+E File/Get Text
Ctrl+Alt+S File/Save as

The Unlinking tool

FYI

You can delete any *text box* in a linked chain by deleting it (Ctrl+K). You can also *disconnect* only one box in a series of linked boxes by pressing the Shift key while you click on the *text box* you want to remove with the Unlinking tool.

Tip

Press the Shift key while dragging with the Text Box tool to constrain the text box to a square.

UNLINKING TEXT BOXES

Any text box that is linked can be unlinked. To unlink text boxes, first select the box from the chain of text boxes that you wish to unlink by clicking on it. Select the Unlinking tool from the Tool palette (the last tool), which will display the Linking arrows. The cursor will also turn into a broken chain. Click on either the arrowhead or the tailfeathers of the arrow you want to delete, and Bingo! The link is severed.

EXERCISE D

1. Choose File/New (Ctrl+N) to create a new document with facing pages and an automatic text block.

2. Choose Edit/Preferences/General (Ctrl+Y) and select End of Section for Auto Page Insertion.

3. Use the Page/Insert command or the Document Layout palette to add two pages based on M-1 Master 1 to the document, for a total of 3 pages.

4. Double-click on document page 1 or choose Page/Go to and type 1 in the Go to Page field to get to page 1.

5. Choose File/Get Text (Ctrl+E). Locate the folder with your text file and click on Open. The file will flow automatically from one page to another, because choosing the Automatic Text Box option and allowing Auto Page Insertion (either at the end of the section or at the end of the document) told XPress to automatically flow the text from the first page in the document to the next.

6. In the same document, use the Document Layout palette and choose Document/Show Master Pages. Double-click on the M1-Master 1 icon to get to that master page and use the Text Box tool to draw a 4-inch square text box in the middle of the automatic text box on both the left and right master pages. (Don't worry about displacing text on the document pages.)

7. Then select the Linking tool and click on the small text box you just created on the left hand page. When the moving dotted marquee appears around it, click on the small empty text box on the right hand page.

8. Choose Masters/Show Document Pages and double-click on the page 1 icon. Click inside the small text box to select it. Choose File/Get Text (Ctrl+E) and import a text file into the small text box. It should flow from box to box on each page, as in Figures 6.10 and 6.11. Choose File/Save as (Ctrl+Alt+S) and save the file under the name "Links."

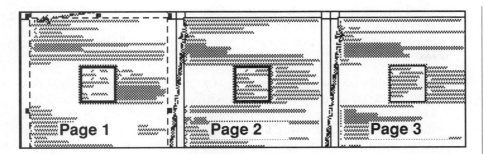

Figure 6.10—Notice the arrows going from page 1 to page 2 to page 3, indicating that these three larger text boxes are linked, not the smaller ones in the center of the pages.

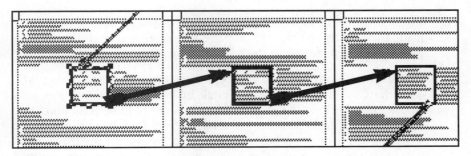

Figure 6.11—Here the smaller text boxes are linked, with the linking arrows going from the small box on page 1 to the small box on page 2 and so on.

CREATING "JUMP LINES"

"Jump lines" like "Continued on page…" and "Continued from page…" occur frequently in newspapers and periodicals. XPress has two other page numbering commands which allow you to "jump" text on one page to a linked text box anyplace else in the document. Typing Ctrl+2 in a text box displays the page number of a text box on a previous page. Typing Ctrl+4 displays the page number of the next text box in a chain.

EXERCISE E

1. Create a new document (Ctrl+N) without facing pages but with an automatic text box. Choose View/Show Document Layout and choose Page/Insert from the Menu Bar. In the Insert Pages dialog box, insert 2 pages at the end of the document based on M1-Master 1.

2. Double-click on the page 1 icon to get to page 1. Click anywhere inside the automatic text box (Box A) and draw another text box about 4 inches high (Box B). Click inside that smaller text box and draw another smaller text box (Box C) inside the second box. It is important that the "jump" text box be positioned inside the larger text box. You now have three text boxes on that page: the largest (automatic) text box (A); the smaller text box inside that one (B); and an even smaller text box (C) (see sidebar).

Ctrl+4 Next Text Box
Ctrl+2 Previous Text Box
Ctrl+N File/New

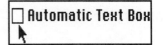

FYI

When you create a new document and do *not* select the Automatic Text Box option in the New dialog box, any text you create or import is not linked to any pages you insert after page 1. You must then manually link the text box which you create on the first page to hold the text with text boxes on any subsequent pages.

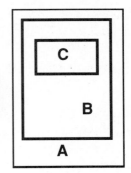

Box A is the automatic text box. Box B is the smaller text box that will be linked to another box on page 3. Box C is the "jump" box which will contain "Continued on" and "Continued from" commands.

Ctrl+4 Next Text Box
Ctrl+2 Previous Text Box
Ctrl+0 [zero] View/Fit in
Window
Ctrl+J Page/Go to
Ctrl+O File/Open

Shortcut

Alt-clicking on a tool keeps that tool selected until you select another tool.

3. Click inside the smallest text box (C) and type "Continued on page" and press Ctrl+4—make it larger if you like. The <None> symbol appears, indicating that the text box (B) is not yet linked to another text box.

4. Double-click on the page 3 icon to get to that page. Select the Text Box tool and draw another text box (B) with a smaller one inside of it (C), just as you did on page 1. Position the smaller text box inside and at the top of the larger one. Click inside that smallest text box and type "Continued from" and press Ctrl+2. The <None> symbol will appear again.

5. Choose View/Fit in Window (Ctrl+0 [zero]). Click on the Linking tool to select it. Click inside the middle text box (B) on page 1. A marquee will appear running around the box.

6. With the Linking tool still active, scroll down to page 3 and click inside the middle text box (B) on page 3. An arrow will appear linking the text box on page 1 with the text box on page 3.

7. Choose Page/Go to (Ctrl+J) and type 1 in the Go to Page dialog box. With the Content tool selected, click inside the large text box and choose File/Get Text (Ctrl+E). Click on a text file to select it and click on Open. If the text file is large enough, it will flow from the text box on page 1 (B) to the text box on page 3 (B), bypassing the three automatic text boxes that were created when the document was created and the new pages inserted.

8. Look at the smallest text box (C) on page 1. It should now read "Continued on page 3." Typing Ctrl+4 told XPress to display the page number on which the next box linked to this one appears. The smallest text box (C) on page 3 should read "Continued from page 1." Typing Ctrl+2 in this text box told XPress to display the page number on which the previous box linked to this one appears. Easy!

COPYING ITEMS BETWEEN DOCUMENTS

You can easily drag-copy a non-linked item from one document to another by opening both documents and resizing them so you can see the page with the item you want to copy as well as the target page in the other document.

EXERCISE F

1. Choose File/Open (Ctrl+O) and open the file saved under your first name. If necessary, open the "Links" file. Click on the small text box in the "Links" file.

2. Select the Item tool and click on the item (box or line) you want to move to select it.

3. Hold down the mouse button and drag the item to any page in the other file. A copy of the item appears in the target document.

COPYING PAGES BETWEEN DOCUMENTS

To copy a page or pages from one document to another, both documents must be open and displayed in Thumbnails view.

Ctrl+O File/Open
Ctrl+N File/New
Ctrl+E File/Get Text

EXERCISE G

1. If necessary, open the "Links" file (Ctrl+O) and then create a new file (Ctrl+N).

2. Click on any page in the "Links" file and choose View/Thumbnails. This will put a miniature version of your document on the screen. You can scroll through the document, but you can't edit the document. Do the same with the other file. You should now have two files open on the desktop, both of them in Thumbnails view.

3. Scroll in both documents so that the pages you want to copy, as well as the position in the target document where you will place these pages, are visible.

4. Select the page or Shift+select the page(s) you want to move from the "Links" file and, holding down the mouse button, drag them over to the target document. Before releasing the mouse button, place them in the appropriate location. You can reposition them later in the target document.

Save File as Type:
ASCII Text [*.TXT]
ASCII Text [*.TXT]
Rich Text Format [
XPress Tags [*.XT
Word for Win 2.0 [

QuarkXPress allows you to export text in several formats.

When you copy pages from one document to another, you also copy the master pages on which they were based. When you choose Document/Show Master Pages for the target document, the new master page icon will appear under the Masters menu.

MOVING PAGES

You can move a single page or a range of pages in a document by choosing Page/Move. In the Move Pages dialog box, type the page number of the page you want to move or type a range of pages. Click in the appropriate box on the right to indicate where you want the page(s) moved.

FYI

When you copy a page (or pages) from one document to another, you copy all the text in a chain of linked text boxes from the original document to the target document.

IMPORTING AND EXPORTING TEXT FILES

Since you have already imported text files into documents, you are familiar with the procedure. Simply choose File/Get Text (Ctrl+E), highlight the file you want, and click on Open. It's important to remember to position the insertion point in the text box where you want the new text to flow *before* you import it. In the Get Text dialog box, check the boxes for converting quotes from typewriter quotes to typeset curly quotes. However, be sure that the filter for any word processor file you are importing is present in the same folder as the QuarkXPress program. Quark supplies many filters with the program.

List Files of Type:
All Text Files
All Text Files
ASCII Text [*.TXT
Rich Text Format
Ami Pro 2.0 [*.SA

QuarkXPress allows you to import various kinds of text files.

Ctrl+N File/New
Ctrl+Y General
Preferences
Ctrl+0 [zero] View/Fit in
Window
Ctrl+M Item/Modify
Ctrl+B Item/Frame
Ctrl+D Item/Duplicate

When moving pages between documents, the cursor changes to a page icon indicating whether it will be a right or left page when it is placed.

FYI

When Item Coordinates is set to Page in the General Preferences dialog box, the ruler will start from the zero point on each page. This allows you to use the same measurements for items appearing on both of the facing pages.

To export text from XPress so you can work with it in a word processor or import it into another (heaven forbid!) page layout program, do the following: Use the Content tool to select a text box which contains the story you want to export. Choose File/Save Text. When the Save Text dialog box appears, enter a name for the file you are exporting. Click on either the Entire Story or Selected Text button and then use the pop-up format menu to choose the format for the exported file.

REVIEW EXERCISE #1

You will first create a four-page newsletter comprised of two master pages and then create a second newsletter. You will also copy items to and from both documents.

1. Choose File/New (Ctrl+N) to create a new document with 2 columns, 1-inch margins all around, facing pages, and an automatic text box.

2. Choose Edit/Preferences/General (Ctrl+Y); select picas as the unit of measure; Guides in Front, Auto Page Insertion set to Off; Item Coordinates set to Page, and Keep Changes. Click on OK. Display the Document Layout palette (View/Show Document Layout).

3. In the Document Layout palette, choose Document/Show Master Pages. Double-click on the M1-Master 1 icon to get to the master pages. Drag the zero point (ruler origin) to the intersection of the two margin guides.

4. Choose View/Fit in Window (Ctrl+0 [zero]). Using the Orthogonal Line tool, draw a 1-point vertical line from the top to the bottom margin between the columns on each master page.

5. Use the Orthogonal Line tool to draw a horizontal line on the top margin line on each master page. Check the Measurements palette to be sure that Endpoints is selected and that the dimensions of both horizontal lines match those in Figure 6.12. Press Enter to accept the values.

6. Draw a text box across the top of the right hand page using the specs in Figure 6.13 and type (no quotes) "Newsletter." Use the Measurements palette to center the text and format it in Times New Roman, all caps, bold, at 60 points with automatic leading. Press Enter to accept the values.

7. With the small text box still selected, choose Item/Modify (Ctrl+M). In the right hand box under Vertical Alignment, use the drop-down list to choose Centered. Click on OK.

8. Choose Item/Frame (Ctrl+B) and assign the box a 4-point frame. Click on OK.

9. Create a text box on the left master page with the specs in Figure 6.14. Press Enter to accept the values. This will put a text box at the bottom of the page to hold the page number.

10. Duplicate the box by selecting it and choosing Item/Duplicate (Ctrl+D). Use the Item tool to move the duplicate onto the right mas-

ter page. In each box type the command for the Current Page (Ctrl+3); skip 2 spaces and type "Desktop Publisher." Use the Measurements palette to format the text in 10-point MS Sans Serif. Click on the Italic icon. Use the Alignment icons to left align the text on the left master page and right align the text on the right master page. Copy (Ctrl+C) and Paste (Ctrl+V) the symbol for the page number so that it appears on the margin on the right master page.

Ctrl+3 Current Text Box
Ctrl+C Edit/Copy
Ctrl+V Edit/Paste
Ctrl+X Edit/Cut
Ctrl+J Page/Go to
Ctrl+S File/Save

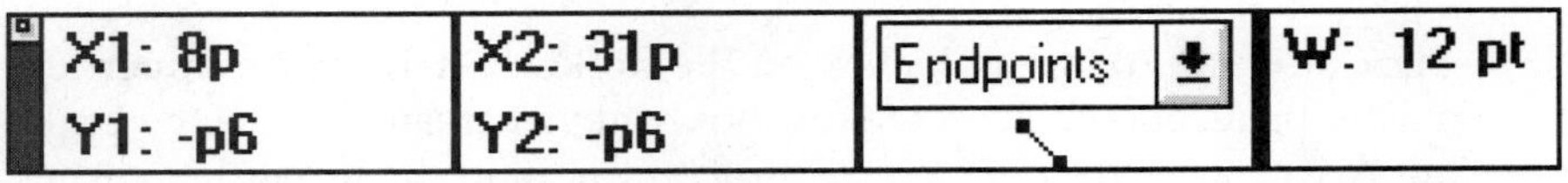

11. Choose Masters/Show Document Pages. Double-click on the page 1 icon. Click inside the large (automatic) text box to select it. Choose Page/Insert to insert 3 more pages based on M1-Master 1 at the end of the document. Click in the Link to Current Text Chain box to select it. Click on OK. You now have a four-page document.

12. Double-click on page 3 and use the Item tool to select the "Newsletter" text box. Choose Edit/Cut (Ctrl+X) to delete that text box.

13. Go to page 1 (Ctrl+J) and use the Item tool to select and delete (Ctrl+X) the horizontal bar over the "Newsletter" box.

14. View your pages. Your screen should resemble Figure 6.15. Save this document (Ctrl+S) as "News."

X1: 8p	X2: 31p	Endpoints ↕	W: 12 pt
Y1: -p6	Y2: -p6		

Figure 6.12—Specs for horizontal lines on master pages.

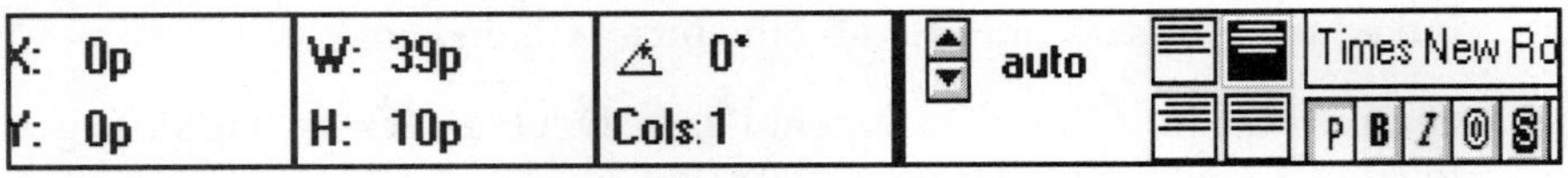

X: 0p	W: 39p	∠ 0°	auto	Times New Ro
Y: 0p	H: 10p	Cols:1		P B I ⓞ Ⓢ

Figure 6.13—Specs for the "News" text box on the right hand master page.

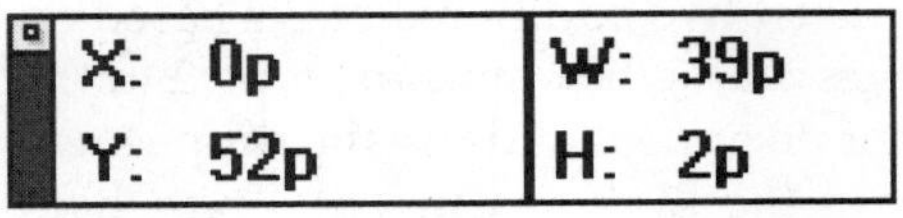

X: 0p	W: 39p
Y: 52p	H: 2p

Figure 6.14—Specs for text box with page numbers.

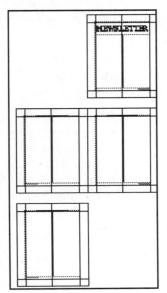

Figure 6.15—The finished "News" document.

A text file

Ctrl+O File/Open
Ctrl+Alt+M View/Show
Measurements

The Broken Chain icon as it appears on the master page of a document created without an automatic text box.

REVIEW EXERCISE #2

If necessary, open the "News" file (Ctrl+O).

1. Use either the Document Layout palette or the Delete Pages (Page/Delete) dialog box to delete document pages 3 and 4. You now have a two-page document.

2. Create a new master page with the same specs as M1-Master 1 by displaying the Document Layout palette (View/Show Document Layout) and choosing Document/Show Master Pages. Choose Masters/Insert/Blank Facing Master. Click below the M1-Master 1 icon to place the M2-Master 2 icon.

3. Double-click on that icon to get to M2-Master 2. Notice the Broken Chain in the upper left corner of each master page. Because there is no automatic text box on these pages, there is no Intact Chain. Notice also that the lower left corner of the screen reads "L-M2-Master 2" for "Left page of M2-Master 2."

4. Use the Measurements palette to create a text box on each master page with the values: X=0p; Y=0p; W=39p; H=54p; 2 columns.

5. Click on the Linking tool, click on the Broken Chain in the upper left master page, and click on the text box you just created. Once the Linking Arrow appears, click on the Broken Chain in the upper left corner of the right master page, and click on the text box. You now have linked the boxes, as indicated by the Intact Chain icon.

6. Choose Masters/Show Document Pages. Double-click on page 4 to get to page 4. Click in the large text box on page 4.

7. Use the Page/Insert command to insert two additional pages based on M2-Master 2. When the Insert Pages dialog box appears, type 2 in the Insert Page(s) field. Click on End of document and use the drop-down list to select M2-Master 2. Click in the Link to Current Text Chain check box. Click on OK. You should now have a total of four document pages. Pages 1 and 2 are based on M1-Master 1 and pages 3 and 4 are based on M2-Master 2.

8. Choose Page/Display/M2-Master 2 from the Menu Bar to get to that master page. Drag a vertical ruler guide over the right margin guide on the left hand page; drag another ruler guide over the right margin guide on the right hand page.

9. Use the Orthogonal Line tool to draw a vertical line from the top to bottom margin over the ruler guide on each page. Select the line and use the drop-down lists on the Measurements palette (Ctrl+Alt+M) to make that line 24 points wide and dashed. Use the drop-down list on the far right of the Measurements palette to give the line on the left master page a top arrow point with tailfeathers and the line on the right master page a bottom arrow point with tailfeathers.

10. Choose Masters/Show Document pages. Double-click in the automatic text box on page 1 with the Content tool and choose File/Get Text (Ctrl+E). When you locate the text file, click on Open to flow the file from page 1 to page 2, where it will stop flowing.

11. Alt-click on the Linking tool to keep it selected. Click on page 2, then click on page 3. Click once more on page 4. The text will now flow from pages 2 to pages 3 and 4. Your document should resemble Figure 6.16. Save your file as "News.1" (File/Save).

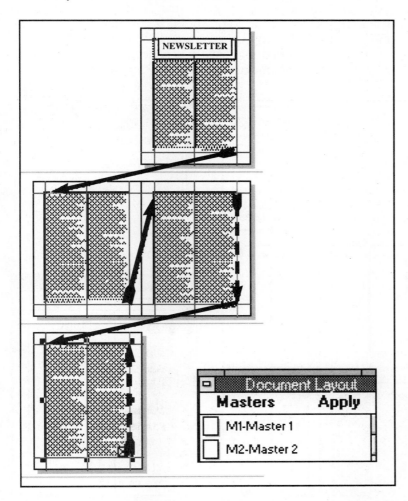

Figure 6.16—The "News.1" file displays 4 pages based on 2 master pages. Notice the linking arrows which were created when the pages based on M2-Master 2 were linked to the ones based on M1-Master 1.

Tip

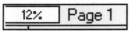

To see the linking arrows for a whole document, type 12 in the percent view field of the document window. Then click on the Linking tool and click on any text box.

12. To copy items and pages from one document to another, both files must be open. If necessary, open both the "News" and "News.1" files. Resize their windows so that you can see all four pages of each document on the screen. Change the view of both files to Thumbnails (View/Thumbnails).

13. Select the Item tool and drag page 4 from the "News.1" file over to the "News" file. Position it before page 4 in the "News" file. As you drag between the files, the cursor will first change to a left facing page icon. You can keep moving the page around the document, letting the page icons tell you where the page would be positioned if you released the mouse button. Because page 2 was based on M-1 Master 1 in the "News" file, it carried that master page icon with it to the new document ("News") and renamed it M2-Master 2, as displayed in Figure 6.17.

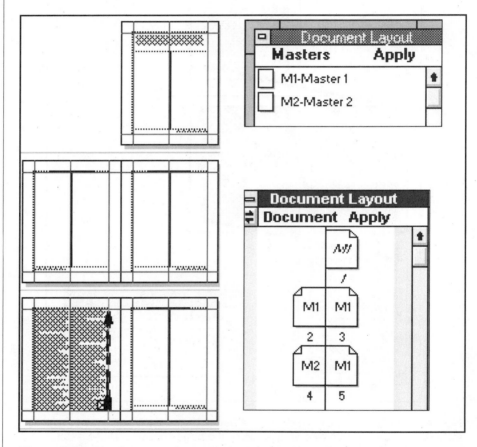

Figure 6.17—The Document Layout palette for the News file after page 4 from the News.1 file was added to it. Notice that the Document Layout palette now displays master pages M1-Master 1 and M2-Master 2. Notice also the Overflow indicator at the bottom of the newly placed page 4. This appears because the entire story was moved to the News document when the single page was moved.

REVIEW QUESTIONS

Read the following questions and choose the answer which best completes the statement.

1. Pages can be deleted from a document _____.
    a. from the File menu and the Edit menu
    b. by choosing Edit/Delete
    c. from the Page menu and the Document Layout palette
    d. from the Edit menu and the Document Layout palette

2. If Auto Insertion is turned off in the General Preferences dialog box, pages that are deleted _____.
    a. are deleted and replaced with blank pages
    b. are replaced with blank pages
    c. are deleted but not replaced with blank pages
    d. will always force the Overflow Indicator to appear

3. To number pages consecutively, type _____.
    a. Ctrl+P on the page
    b. Ctrl+2 in a text box
    c. Ctrl+4 in a "jump" box
    d. Ctrl+3 in a text box

4. When a page number command is typed on a master page, _____.
    a. the appropriate symbol appears
    b. it must be formatted along with the text
    c. the number appears in brackets
    d. nothing appears

5. Documents created with an automatic text box _____.
    a. must have those text boxes linked manually
    b. must have the text boxes unlinked before text will flow in them
    c. contain linked text boxes
    d. do not display the Intact Chain icon on the master pages

6. To unlink text boxes, _____.
    a. choose Page/Unlink
    b. click on the linking arrow with the Unlinking tool
    c. double-click on the linking arrow
    d. double-click with the Unlinking tool

7. Text can be flowed from text box to a previous or next text box by _____.
    a. typing Ctrl+4 and Ctrl+2
    b. choosing Page/Go to
    c. typing Ctrl+2 and Ctrl+4
    d. using the Document Layout palette

8. Ctrl+4 and Ctrl+2 _____.
    a. must always be typed in a text box inside another text box
    b. must never be typed in a text box inside another text box
    c. link boxes that cannot be unlinked
    d. replace the Go to Page command

9. To make a document's linking arrows appear, _____.
   a. choose View/Link
   b. select a text box and click on the Linking tool
   c. double-click on the Linking tool
   d. b and c

10. You can import a text file into XPress from _____.
    a. any word processor
    b. most word processors
    c. only Macintosh word processors
    d. any word processor for which QuarkXPress can access the filter

Answers: 1. c; 2. c; 3. d; 4. a; 5. a; 6. c; 7. b; 8. c; 9. a; 9. b; 10. d

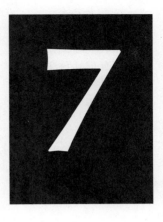
OVERVIEW

In this lesson you will learn how to recognize and work with several new Menu Bar commands. You will learn how to set Preferences, use the Specifications dialog boxes to manipulate text and graphics, and group and ungroup items. You will be introduced to the Runaround command and use it to position text around items. The Duplicate, Space/Align, and Step and Repeat commands are also among those to be covered. So that you can keep track of fonts and graphics in your document, you will learn about the Font Usage and Picture Usage utilities. As a review, you will create a document using many of these commands.

Menu Bar

Commands

TOPICS

File menu
Printing a document
Printing selected pages
Paper source
Printing colors
Printer output
Printing odd and even pages
Registration and crop marks
Edit menu
Undo command
Cut, Copy, and Paste
Paste Special, Paste Link and Links
Delete

Select All
Show Clipboard
Find/Change
Preferences dialog boxes
Typographic preferences
Superscript and subscript values
Superior characters
Hyphenation Method
Auto Leading and Flex Space
Auto Kern
Maintain Leading and Leading Mode

Tools Preferences
View menu
Style menu
Item menu
Grouping and ungrouping items
Text runaround
Layering items
Duplicating items
Space/Align
Constraining and unconstraining items
Locking items
Utilities menu
Windows menu
Review Exercise
Review Questions

TERMS

absolute page
Close
constrain
crop marks
Flex Space
Font Usage
Get Picture
Get Text

New
Open
Picture Usage
Print
registration marks
Revert to Saved
Save
Save as

Save Page as EPS
Save Text
Specifications dialog boxes
text runaround
thumbnails

Ctrl+N File/New
Ctrl+O File/Open
Ctrl+S File/Save
Ctrl+Alt+S File/Save as
Ctrl+E File/Get Text/
   Get Picture
Ctrl+Q File/Exit

FILE MENU

Since you have already used several menu commands and keyboard short-cuts, much of the material in this lesson will be a review. Let's take a look at some of the commands under the File menu. Choose File/...

1. New (Ctrl+N) to create a new document.

2. Open (Ctrl+O) to open a previously created XPress document.

3. Close to close an active document.

4. Save (Ctrl+S) to save an existing document under its current name.

5. Save as (Ctrl+Alt+S) to save a document under a different name, to another drive or directory, or to save it as a template. When the dialog box appears, type the new name for your file in the File Name dialog box. The Save File as Type drag-down menu (Figure 7.1) defaults to {*QXD} extension for "QuarkXPress Document." If you want to save the file as a template, use the drag-down menu to select "Templates {*QXT} for "QuarkXPress Template." This creates a file that cannot be altered and saved under the same name.

6. Revert to Saved to close the current file without saving any of your changes, and open the most recently saved version of that file.

7. You have already used the Get Text command (Ctrl+E) when the Content tool is selected to import a text file or a word processing file into an active text box. When a picture box is selected and the Content tool is active, this command becomes Get Picture (Ctrl+E). The Get Picture dialog box is displayed where you locate and highlight the graphic file you want to open and import into the active picture box.

8. Choosing Save Text opens the Save Text dialog box and allows you to export the text in a story or in the entire document to a text file which can then be imported into another application. This option is available only when a text box is active and the Content tool is selected.

9. Selecting Save Page as EPS allows you to save an active (selected) page in the Encapsulated PostScript format. To save a page in XPress as an EPS file, choose File/Save Page as EPS and give the file a name. Then click on the Color or B&W (black and white) button and adjust the scaling if you wish. If you click on the Include TIFF Preview option, you will be able to view the EPS page on the screen. When you save a page as an EPS page, that page can be imported into any XPress picture box and resized.

10. Document Setup allows you to change the current document's page size from the specifications you selected in the New dialog box.

11. Choosing the Exit command closes all saved documents and returns you to the Program Manager.

Design Tip

If you create a file and set up master pages for a newsletter, saving the file as a template allows you to retrieve it with all the settings when you want to create a new document based on those settings. When you open the template, the columns, masthead, and any other items you will use for each issue are already in place. Just flow the text and change the graphics. Save this new file under another name.

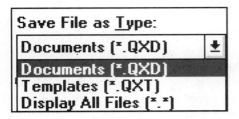

Figure 7.1—Displays the Save File as Type drag-down menu where you can choose to save a file as a document or as a template.

PRINTING A DOCUMENT

Printing a document as camera-ready materials is what desktop publishing is all about. You will most likely be printing to either a 300 dpi (dots per inch) laser printer like the HP LaserJet Series II or to an imagesetter like the Linotype or Afga Compugraphic, which will print from 600 to 2400 dpi. Before you access the Print dialog box by choosing File/Print (Ctrl+P), choose File/Printer Setup (Figure 7.2). Here you can specify commands for printing the document, such as the printer (Specific Printer drag-down menu); orientation; paper size and source (Upper Tray or Manual Feed); image position (horizontal, vertical, or inverted); halftone frequency (lines per inch when printing halftone pictures, shaded items, and shaded text); printer resolution (dots per inch); material (paper or film); and paper width, offset, and page gap, which are available only when an imagesetter is selected in the Specific Printer field. Clicking on the Options button takes you to a Windows Options dialog box where you can select other printer settings and system dialog boxes.

Printer Setup

Printer
- ⦿ Default Printer
  (currently HP LaserJet Series II on LPT1:)
- ○ Specific Printer:
  HP LaserJet Series II on LPT1:

OK
Cancel
Options...

Orientation
A ⦿ Portrait
   ○ Landscape

Paper
Size: Letter 8 1/2 x 11 in
Source: Upper Tray

Image
☐ Flip Horizontal
☐ Flip Vertical
☐ Invert

Halftone Frequency: 60 (lpi)

Material: ○ Paper ○ Film

☐ Use PDF Screen Values

Figure 7.2—The Printer Setup dialog box for a document being printed to a HP LaserJet Series II. The Paper Size defaults to 8.5 x 11 inches. The Orientation defaults to Portrait (Tall).

PRINTING SELECTED PAGES

To print a file, choose File/Print (Ctrl+P) and the Print dialog box appears (Figure 7.3). The Copies option defaults to 1 copy; the Pages option lets you print the entire document (All) or select a range of pages. You can enter an "absolute" location in a document by preceding the page number with the plus sign. If, for instance, your document contains 20 pages beginning with page 15 and you want to print beginning with page 21, you can print From 21 or you can print From + 7, the seventh page in the document. The +7 is an absolute page sequence number and is not related to any page numbers you applied with the Ctrl+3 function.

You can print master pages which are displayed in the document window. However, the All and From/To options are not available in the Print dialog box.

If you check the Blank Pages check box in the Print dialog box, any pages in the page range you select will print. If you deselect this check box, blank pages (pages which contain no printable items) will not print.

Select the Cover Page option to print a page which contains the document's name and the time and date it was printed.

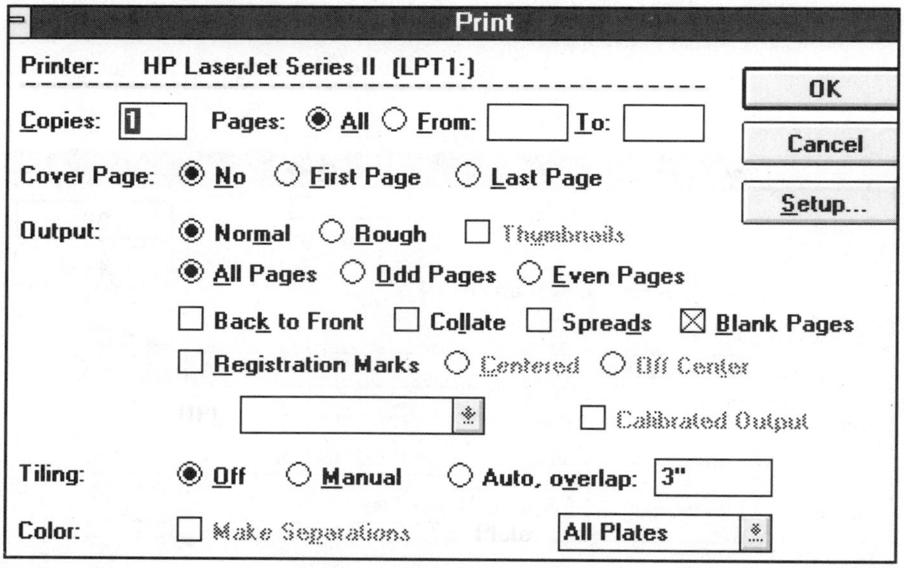

Figure 7.3—The Print dialog box.

FYI

Spreads is an important option to select when printing spreads to an imagesetter. If you check Spreads in the print dialog box and Landscape in the Printer Setup dialog box, the printer will advance the amount of paper or film necessary to print the widest spread in the range of pages to be printed.

OUTPUT

If you keep the **Normal** setting for the Output option, the document will print as it is displayed on the screen. If you select **Rough**, pictures will be replaced with boxed X's and complex frames will be simplified.

Click on **Thumbnails** to print images of your pages which are one-eighth the size of the actual page. This option is available only when a PostScript printer is selected.

If you select the **Collate** option, you can print multiple copies of a document with each copy printed in numerical order. If you select the **Spreads** option,

XPress will print the spread as contiguous output. Otherwise, all pages are printed separately. This means that when you click on the Spreads box, the facing pages or pages you have formatted as spreads (pages with material that runs across the inside margins) will print side-by-side with no break between the pages.

PRINTING COLORS

You can tell XPress to convert each page, even the ones with color pictures and text, to black and white by clicking in the Print Colors as Grays check box at the bottom of the dialog box. This option is available only if you have selected a PostScript printer.

PRINTING ODD AND EVEN PAGES

You can print All pages or only Odd or Even pages. This option allows you to print the Odd pages first, then replace the paper in the printer tray and print the Even pages, which will give you two-sided copy. You can print pages Back to Front so as to collate a single copy in the correct order if you are printing to a laser printer that feeds the printed sheets face up. If you have selected multiple copies in the Copies box, clicking on the Collate button will print one complete set of pages at a time. It's a handy feature, but time-consuming because XPress has to process each page each time for each copy.

REGISTRATION AND CROP MARKS

If you select the Registration Marks option, XPress will place registration marks on your page. These indicate where color plates are to be aligned. Crop marks indicate the outside boundaries of a document page. They are printed just slightly outside of the page corners and indicate where the pages are to be cut or trimmed.

EXERCISE A

1. Create a new document (Ctrl+N) with an automatic text box and Auto Page Insertion set to End of Document. (This is a good time to practice with master pages.)

2. Use the Document Layout palette (View/Show Document Layout) or the Page/Insert Page command to insert a second page in the document. Select the Content tool, click in the automatic text box on document page 1 to set the insertion point, and choose File/Get Text (Ctrl+E) to flow text onto page 1.

3. Create a picture box on the second empty page and, with the Content tool selected, import a graphic into the picture box (File/Get Picture).

4. With the second page active (click anywhere inside the text box on the second page to select it), choose File/Save Page as EPS. When the Save dialog box appears, give it a name and scale it to 50%. Click on Color or B&W depending on the type of graphic you have, and click on Save.

Ctrl+E File/Get Text/
Get Picture
Ctrl+P File/Print
Ctrl+Z Edit/Undo
Ctrl+X Edit/Cut
Ctrl+C Edit/Copy
Ctrl+V Edit/Paste
Ctrl+Alt+Y Edit/
Preferences/
Typographic

When the Item tool is selected, you can Cut or Copy active boxes and lines.

When the Content tool is selected, you can cut or copy selected text or the contents of an active picture box. Generally, the Content tool selects and manipulates the contents of boxes.

5. Insert a third page in your document (Page/Insert) and use the Picture Box tool to draw a picture box about the size of the graphic you just saved. With the Content tool selected, choose File/Get Picture (Ctrl+E) and highlight the name of the EPS page you just saved. Click on Open and position the picture with the Grabber Hand.

6. In the same document, use either the Document Layout palette (View/Show Document Layout) or the Page/Display command to view the master pages.

7. Choose Page/Master Guides and give the document 2-inch margins all around.

8. Choose File/Print (Ctrl+P) and when the Print dialog box appears, click in the Print From button and tab to the next field. Type 2. Tab to the next field and type 3 to print from pages 2 to 3. Click in the Registration Marks check box. Click on OK.

9. When the pages have printed, choose File/Print (Ctrl+P) again and print all the pages as Thumbnails by clicking on the Thumbnails button in the Print dialog box.

EDIT MENU

The Edit menu is where you Undo the most previous action, as well as Cut, Copy, Paste, and Delete text and items. You can also set all your preferences as well as create and edit colors, style sheets, and hyphenation and justification values.

Under the Edit menu are also commands for selecting all text (when the Content tool is active) and all items (when the Item tool is active). You can also use the Find/Replace command to locate and change text and text attributes in a document or story. You will learn to use several of these commands in later lessons.

UNDO COMMAND

The first command (Ctrl+Z) allows you to undo the last action you took, like deleting an item (unless you were warned before deleting it that that action could not be undone), undoing typing, or moving or resizing an item.

CUT, COPY, AND PASTE

The Cut (Ctrl+X), Copy (Ctrl+C), and Paste (Ctrl+V) commands cut or copy selected boxes, lines, and the contents of an active picture box or text box. When you choose Edit/Paste (Ctrl+V), whatever is on the Clipboard is pasted on the pages if the Item tool is selected and a picture box is active. Otherwise, it places any text on the Clipboard at the insertion point if the Content tool is selected and a text box is active.

PASTE SPECIAL, PASTE LINKS, AND LINKS

The Paste Special, Paste Link, and Links commands enable you to work with the Object Linking and Embedding (OLE) functions which are part of Microsoft Windows. These commands let server applications like graphic programs create links to the graphics imported into QuarkXPress from those programs so that you can specify the way that graphic file is updated or not updated when it is imported into XPress after being modified in the graphic program. This feature is available only with Windows applications which support OLE.

DELETE

The Edit/Delete command does not put the deleted text (when the Content tool is active) or the deleted item (when the Item tool is active) on the Clipboard, as do the Edit/Cut (Ctrl+X) and Edit/Copy (Ctrl+C) commands. When you choose Edit/Delete, text or graphics are deleted from the file and cannot be retrieved using the Paste command.

SELECT ALL

Depending on which tool is selected, choosing Edit/Select All (Ctrl+A) will: (1) select all of the text in an active box and the text in all boxes linked to the active box, if the Content tool is selected and the cursor is positioned in a text box; or (2) select all the (unlocked) text boxes, picture boxes, and lines on the active spread, as well as on the adjacent pasteboard section, if the Item tool is selected.

SHOW CLIPBOARD

Choose Edit/Show Clipboard to display a window showing the contents of the Clipboard. Text and items are placed on the Clipboard when you choose Edit/Copy or Edit/Cut. They remain on the Clipboard until you cut or copy another item or text.

FIND/CHANGE

Edit/Find/Change (Ctrl+F) displays the Find/Change dialog box. Deselecting the Ignore Attributes option displays another Find/Change dialog box which allows you to find and change text based on Font, Style, and Size. You will learn more about using the Find/Change command in Lesson 11.

PREFERENCES DIALOG BOXES

You have already worked with the General Preferences and Application dialog boxes. There are two more Preferences dialog boxes available which allow you to set preferences for type and for the way tools behave.

TYPOGRAPHIC PREFERENCES

Choosing Edit/Preferences/Typographic (Ctrl+Alt+Y) displays the Typographic Preferences dialog box (Figure 7.4). Here you can change the program's default settings for superscript, subscript, superior, and small caps characters. The Hyphenation method allows you to choose between Standard and Enhanced Hyphenation.

The Typographic Preferences dialog box is at the heart of QuarkXPress's powerful typographic controls. You can live happily ever after without changing any of the options available here, but if a paragraph or a page doesn't look quite right, chances are that tweaking some of the values in

Ctrl+X Edit/Cut
Ctrl+C Edit/Copy
Ctrl+A Edit/Select All
Ctrl+F Edit/Find/Change
Ctrl+Alt+Y Edit/
    Preferences/
    Typographic

WARNING!

The values in the Typographic Preferences dialog box affect an entire document. Any changes you make to the values in this dialog box affect the whole document, not just a single paragraph.

this dialog box will make your text behave.

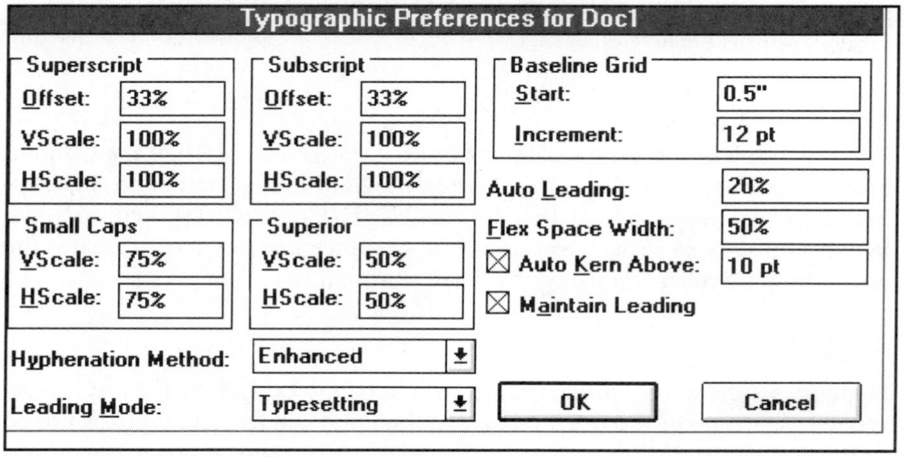

Figure 7.4—The Typographic Preferences dialog box. All changes made in this dialog box affect the entire document, not just the contents of an individual box.

SUPERSCRIPT AND SUBSCRIPT VALUES

The Superscript and Subscript Offset values allow you to determine the superscript or subscript character's distance from the baseline. The 33% default Offset value means that a 12-point superscript or subscript character would move 4 points above or below the baseline. The H(orizontal) and V(ertical) scale values allow you to adjust the height and width of a superscript and/or subscript character. Reduce these values to make superscript and subscript characters less obvious in a paragraph (Figure 7.5).

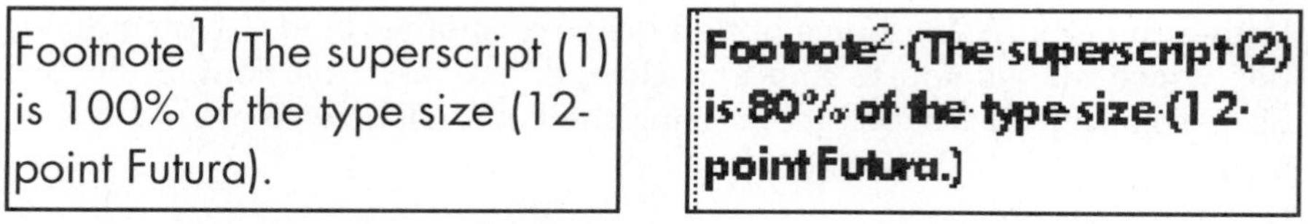

Footnote[1] (The superscript (1) is 100% of the type size (12-point Futura).

Footnote[2] (The superscript (2) is 80% of the type size (12-point Futura.)

Figure 7.5—The text box on the left displays a superscript at the default HScale and VScale value of 100%. The text box on the right displays the superscript with HScale and VScale values of 80%.

SUPERIOR CHARACTERS

Superior characters automatically sit flush with the font's capital letter. Their HScale and VScale values default to 50% (Figure 7.6). You can also adjust the HScale and VScale values of the small caps to achieve different typographic effects.

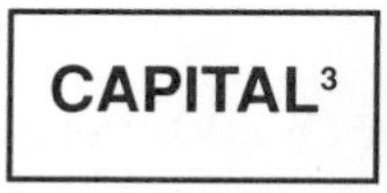

CAPITAL[3]

Figure 7.6—A superior character sits flush with the top of the capital letter.

In the lower and right areas of the Typographic Preferences dialog box, you can select options for Hyphenation Method, Character Widths, and Leading Mode.

Ctrl+N File/New

HYPHENATION METHOD

The Hyphenation Method drop-down menu allows you to choose between Standard (Macintosh Version 3.0) and Enhanced, which includes the more sophisticated hyphenation and justification algorithms of Version 3.1. Choosing Enhanced allows XPress to hyphenate more words than it did in previous versions, as well as to hyphenate them in a more conventional manner. Hyphenation and justification of text is covered in Lesson 12.

AUTO LEADING AND FLEX SPACE

Beneath the Baseline Grid fields are the Auto Leading and Flex Space Width fields. Auto Leading defaults to 20% of a font's type size. Flex Space Width refers to the flex(ible) space you create when you type Ctrl+Shift+5. You can specify how wide this space is in terms of the percentage of an en-space. The default value is 50%. Increasing this value in .1% increments widens the flex space; decreasing the value reduces the width of the flex space.

AUTO KERN

The Auto Kern Above value determines at what point size a font's built-in kerning pairs kick in. The program defaults to 10 points, that is, for whenever text is formatted over 10 points, XPress will use the font's built-in kerning pairs.

MAINTAIN LEADING AND LEADING MODE

The Maintain Leading option determines how text is leaded when it follows a box or line to which a Runaround value has been applied. If you deselect Maintain Leading, the ascenders of text beneath an item with a runaround value will touch the item. If the Maintain Leading option is selected, the XPress will add the specified leading value between the base of the item and the baseline of the first line of text which falls beneath that item.

The Leading Mode drop-down menu allows you to choose between Typesetting and Word Processing modes. If you select Typesetting, XPress will maintain a line's designated leading value even if a picture box or other element intrudes on the line of text. Unless you have a good reason to change this setting, leave it at its default Typesetting mode.

EXERCISE B

1. Create a new document (Ctrl+N) with an automatic text box and type a few lines on the first page.

2. Use the File/Cut, Copy, and Paste commands to add, delete, and move words.

Ctrl+X Edit/Cut
Ctrl+V Edit/Paste
Ctrl+F Edit/Find/Change
Ctrl+N File/New
Ctrl+Alt+Y Edit/
    Preferences/
    Typographic

3. Delete a word with the File/Cut (Ctrl+X) command; then choose Edit/Show Clipboard and notice that the word you just cut is on the Clipboard and available to the Paste command.

4. Choose File/Paste (Ctrl+V) and paste the word back into the text box.

5. Select and delete a word by choosing Edit/Delete. Choose Edit/Show Clipboard and notice that the word is not on the Clipboard.

6. Type "It is better to have loved and lost than never to have loved at all." Place the insertion bar before the I in It.

7. Choose Edit/Find/Change (Ctrl+F). In the Find what dialog box, type "better" (no quotes).

8. Tab to the Change to dialog box and type "much better." Click on the Whole Word option. Click on Find Next. When "better" is highlighted, click on Change. Then close the Find/Replace box by clicking in the Close button on the left.

Now work with the Typographic Preferences dialog box.

EXERCISE C

1. Choose File/New (Ctrl+N) to create a new document with an automatic text box.

2. Type "Typographical Preferences" in the text box. Select both words and format them in 18-point Helvetica. Choose Style/Type Style/Small Caps.

3. Choose Edit/Preferences/Typographic (Ctrl+Alt+Y) and in the Small Caps area, change the VScale value to 50%. Click on OK and notice how the height of the words has changed.

4. Make other changes to the Typographic Preferences dialog box and notice how the text in the document changes.

TOOLS PREFERENCES

Choosing Edit/Preferences/Tools displays the Tools Preferences dialog box, where you can specify how the tools are to function. By clicking on the Modify button, you can specify the percentage of magnification, how boxes are to be framed, the width of lines, how much text runaround should be, and some default specifications for boxes. When you have made your selections, click on Save to apply those changes to the current document only.

If you modify a tool after using it in the document, only items created after you modify the tool will reflect the modifications. Any items created before the modification will not be affected.

Tip

If you are going to be creating many items with consistent attributes, save time and effort by modifying the tools. For example, if every picture box in your document will have a 1-point frame, modify the Picture Box tool in the Tools Preferences dialog box so that every time you draw a picture box it will already be framed.

VIEW MENU

The upper part of the View menu allows you to view your document at various levels of magnification. The middle part of the View menu lets you turn Snap to Guides on and off, view and hide the rulers and guides, display the baseline grid, and view and hide invisibles. The lower part hides and displays the palettes.

Click on the text box in your document (or create a new document with an automatic text box and type a few words on the page), and choose View/Show Invisibles (Ctrl+I). A small dot between words indicates that you pressed the Spacebar; an arrow indicates that you pressed the Tab key; a paragraph symbol indicates that the Enter key was pressed.

The lower part of the View menu controls the display of the six palettes in XPress. Highlight the item to toggle the display on and off. When a function is available or a palette is displayed, a check mark will appear next to the item in the menu.

STYLE MENU

The Style menu displays different commands depending on what is selected: text, a picture, a box, or a line. Many of these commands are also available from the Measurements palette for text, for pictures, and for lines.

If a picture box is active and the Content tool is selected, the Style menu allows you to change the Color, Shade, and Screen values of certain kinds of pictures. If a line is selected, the Style menu's commands allow you to change its Style, Endcaps, Width, Color, and Shade (Figure 7.7). You will learn more about using the commands in the Style menu(s) in later lessons when you are working with text and graphic items.

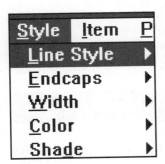

Figure 7.7—The Style menu for lines. The arrows to the right of a listing indicate that the listing includes a drop-down menu with more options.

Ctrl+I View/Show Invisibles

| 100% | Page 1 |

The View Percentage can be seen and changed in the window to the left of the page number.

The paragraph marker is displayed when the Enter key is pressed and View/Show Invisibles is selected. The dots before the paragraph marker are the invisibles displayed each time the Spacebar is pressed.

FYI

Although most of the values displayed with the Item/Modify command are available in the Measurements palette, the advantage of using the Measurements palette is that it will make the changes to text or picture boxes immediately, without having to go through a dialog box. This is a handy feature when you're not quite sure what you want.

What you will need

A graphic file

Ctrl+N File/New
Ctrl+M Item/Modify

Shortcut

Alt-clicking on a tool keeps that tool selected until you select another tool.

ITEM MENU

Unlike the Style menu, which controls the contents of boxes, the Item menu controls changes to the box itself (Figure 7.8). When you click on a text box, on a picture box, or on a line and choose Item/Modify (Ctrl+M), the Specifications dialog box for that item appears.

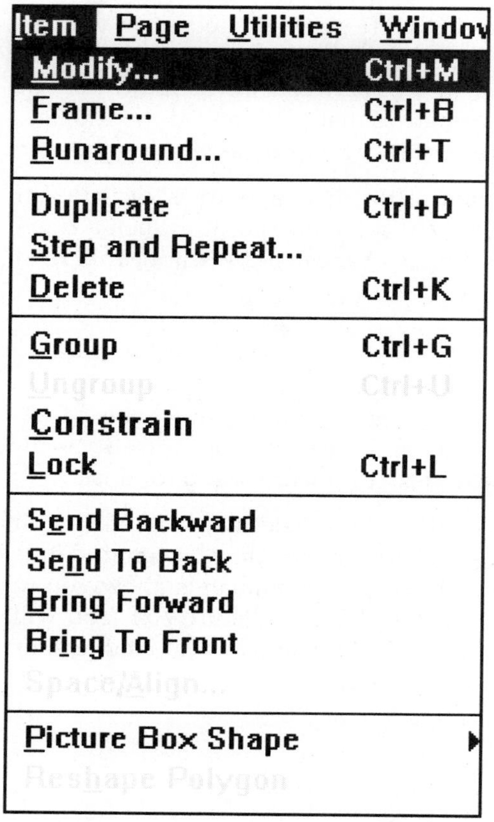

Item	Page	Utilities	Window
Modify...			Ctrl+M
Frame...			Ctrl+B
Runaround...			Ctrl+T
Duplicate			Ctrl+D
Step and Repeat...			
Delete			Ctrl+K
Group			Ctrl+G
Ungroup			Ctrl+U
Constrain			
Lock			Ctrl+L
Send Backward			
Send To Back			
Bring Forward			
Bring To Front			
Space/Align...			
Picture Box Shape			▶
Reshape Polygon			

Figure 7.8—The Item menu for text boxes and picture boxes. Some of the options (Ungroup and Reshape Polygon) are dimmed.

EXERCISE D

1. Create a New file (Ctrl+N) with inches as the unit of measure and draw a text box on the document page.

2. Activate the Measurements palette (View/Show Measurements) and give the box the following values: X=1; Y=2; W=2; H=1.5.

3. Choose Item/Modify (Ctrl+M) to display the Text Box Specifications dialog box (Figure 7.9) and *change* the Origin, Width, Height, Box Angle, Columns, and Background values in the appropriate fields to match those in Figure 7.9. Tab from one field to the next. Then click on OK to see the changes on your screen.

4. Use the Rectangle Picture Box tool to create a picture box below the text box.

5. With the picture box and Content tool selected, choose File/Get Picture (Ctrl+E).

6. Position the picture in the box; then choose Item/Modify (Ctrl+M) and tab through the Picture Box Specifications dialog box to give the picture box these values: Origin Across=1; Origin Down=5.3; Width=3.5; Height=2.5; *Picture* Angle=25 (on the right side of the dialog box).

7. Click on OK. Select the text box and choose Item/Frame (Ctrl+B). Type 2 in the Width field and click on OK.

8. Select the picture box and choose Item/Frame (Ctrl+B). Type 6 in the Width field and click on OK. Your screen should resemble Figure 7.10.

Ctrl+E File/Get Picture
Ctrl+M Item/Modify

Text Box Specifications

Origin **A**cross:	1.5
Origin **D**own:	4
Width:	3
Height:	2
Box Angle:	45°
Col**u**mns:	1
Gutter:	0.167"
Text I**n**set:	1 pt

☐ **S**uppress Printout

First Baseline
Offset: 0"
Minimum: Ascent ⬍

Vertical Alignment
Type: Top ⬍

Background
Color: White ⬍

[OK]   [Cancel]

Figure 7.9—The Text Box Specifications dialog box is displayed when a text box is selected and you choose Item/Modify.

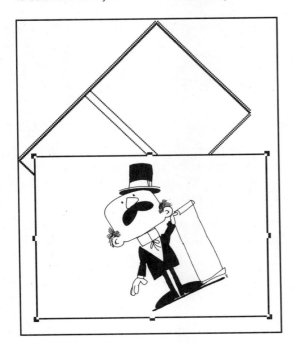

Figure 7.10—A text box and picture box modified with the Item/Modify command. Both the text box and the picture inside the picture box (but not the picture box itself) have been rotated.

What you will need

A text file

Ctrl+G Item/Duplicate
Ctrl+M Item/Modify
Ctrl+U Item/Ungroup

Be a groupie!

The Group command is a powerful one because it allows you to manipulate items without disturbing the spatial relationship between those items. In the document for this book, each figure was grouped with its caption box so that when the figure was moved to accommodate text, the caption box moved with it and stayed in the same position. Likewise, all the arrows used in the figures were grouped with the figure.

FYI

To delete a group, select it with the Item tool and press the Backspace key or choose Edit/Cut (Ctrl+X). When the alert box appears, click on OK.

If you use the Cut command to delete the group, that group stays on the Clipboard and can be pasted back anywhere in the document with the Item tool.

GROUPING AND UNGROUPING ITEMS

Not only can you use the Item menu to move, rotate, and frame boxes, but you can also use it to group items. Grouping items allows you to move many items—text boxes, picture boxes, and rules—all together.

You can also group groups. Shift-select more than one item and group it. Shift-select another few items and group them. Then, with the Item tool, select the first group and Shift-select the second group and group both groups into a third group (Ctrl+G). When you ungroup this third group, you will ungroup it in layers: that, is your first Ungroup command (Ctrl+U) will ungroup the two groups; the second Ungroup command will ungroup the second set of items; and the third Ungroup command will ungroup the first group of items.

Even though items are grouped with the Item tool, they can be edited with the Content tool. If you select a grouped text box with the Content tool, you can make changes to the box and text without ungrouping the box. Likewise, if you select a grouped picture box or line with the Content tool, you can make changes to those items without ungrouping them. Use the Content tool to change the picture, but instead of selecting the Item tool to change the box, hold down the Ctrl key while the Content tool is active to change the Content tool to a temporary Item tool. When you release the Ctrl key, you are returned to the Content tool.

EXERCISE E

1. Use the Text Box tool to create a text box and use a Picture Box tool to create a picture box.

2. With the Item tool, Shift-select both boxes and choose Item/Group (Ctrl+G). Notice the bounding box that appears around both items (boxes).

3. With the Item tool still selected, click anywhere on the group and move it around the page. (If you select the Content tool, you will activate only the selected box.)

4. Select the Content tool and click inside the text box. Type a few lines of text.

5. Choose Item/Modify (Ctrl+M) and change the box angle (on the right side of the dialog box) to 45°.

6. Click on the Item tool and move the group around the page. Notice that even though you made changes to an item in the group with the Content tool, both items remained grouped.

7. To ungroup these items, click on the group with the Item tool and choose Item/Ungroup (Ctrl+U). Click anywhere on the page to deselect the items.

TEXT RUNAROUND

Under the Item menu, the Runaround command (Ctrl+T) allows you to add space between an item and the text that is flowing around that item. You will learn more about working with the Runaround command in Lesson 15.

What you will need

A text file

Ctrl+T Item/Runaround
Ctrl+X Item/Cut
Ctrl+K Item/Delete
Ctrl+M Item/Modify
Ctrl+E 103
File/Get Text

EXERCISE F

1. In your document, delete the text box with either the Item tool (Ctrl+X or Ctrl+K) or with the Content tool (Ctrl+K).

2. Use the Item tool to move the picture box to the left margin of the one-column page. If necessary, create another picture box and move it to the left margin of the page.

3. Use either the Measurements palette or the Item/Modify command (Ctrl+M) to change the picture box angle to 0 (zero).

4. With the Content tool and the automatic text box selected, choose File/Get Text (Ctrl+E) and import a text file which will run around the graphic (item) on three sides.

5. Select the picture box and choose Item/Runaround (Ctrl+T) to display the Runaround Specifications dialog box (Figure 7.11).

6. Leave the Mode set to Item. In the dialog box, type 10 to insert 10 points of white space between the sides of the picture box and the text flowing around it.

7. Click on OK. Your screen should resemble Figure 7.12.

FYI

On a page consisting of only one column, when you flow text around an item or around a picture, the text will flow on only one side of that item or picture. If you want text to flow on both sides of a box or picture, you must designate more than one column.

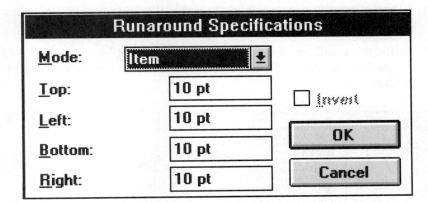

Figure 7.11—The Runaround Specifications dialog box for the picture in Figure 7.12. Notice that although 10 points of space was applied in the Left field, that space was not applied to the left side of the box, because that box was against the margin.

Ctrl+E File/Get Text
Ctrl+M Item/Modify
Ctrl+T Item/Runaround
Ctrl+B Item/Frame

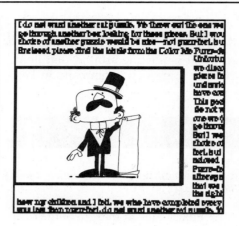

Figure 7.12—A picture box with 10 points of runaround space applied to the picture box. The extra amount of space above and below the picture box appears because of the leading value applied to the text.

EXERCISE G

1. In the current document (or create a new document with an automatic text box), choose Page/Insert to insert one page based on M1-Master 1 at the end of the document.

2. Select the automatic text box and, with the Content tool selected, choose File/Get Text (Ctrl+E).

3. Use the Text Box tool to create a text box about 2 inches wide and 3 inches high.

4. Choose Item/Modify (Ctrl+M) and assign the following values in the Text Box Specifications dialog box: Origin Across: 0"; Origin Down: 1"; Width: 2"; Height: 3". Click on OK.

5. Choose Item/Runaround (Ctrl+T) and in the Runaround Specifications dialog box type 15 in the Top, Bottom, and Right fields. Click on OK.

6. With the small text box still selected, choose Item/Frame (Ctrl+B). Type 1 in the Width field. Click on OK. Your screen should resemble Figure 7.13.

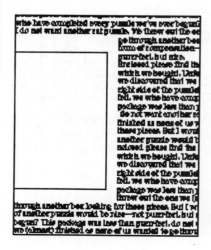

Figure 7.13—Text box with 15 points of Runaround white space.

LAYERING ITEMS

When more than one item, like boxes or a box and a rule, overlap each other even a little bit, you are layering items. The first item you create appears on the first layer. The second item you create appears on the layer in front of that first layer. Choosing Send to Back sends the selected item to the last layer which exists behind the automatic text box (if there is one) or behind the bottom item on the page. Bringing an item to the front puts it on top of the most recently created item on the page. Sending an item Backward sends it behind the item it is currently in front of.

If you send an item to the back and can't find it to select it because it has become invisible, select the Item tool and press the Ctrl+Alt+Shift keys simultaneously while clicking in the location of the invisible item. Once it becomes selected, choose Item/Bring to Front to display and reposition the item.

DUPLICATING ITEMS

To duplicate an item, choose Item/Duplicate (Ctrl+D). This will place a duplicate of a text box, picture box, or line 1/4-inch to the right and down from the original item.

The Step and Repeat command (Ctrl+Alt+D) allows you to to duplicate one or more selected items with specific horizontal and vertical offsets as many times as you wish.

EXERCISE H

1   Select the Orthogonal line tool and draw a horizontal line about 2" long.

2.   While the line is selected, choose Item/Step and Repeat (Ctrl+Alt+D) .

3.   In the Step and Repeat dialog box (Figure 7.14), type 5 in the Repeat Count field to duplicate the original line 5 times; type 0 in the Horizontal Offset field to constrain the duplicated lines from moving to the right or to the left; type .25 in the Vertical Offset box to duplicate the lines ¼ inch above the original (selected) line.

4.   Click on OK. Your screen should resemble Figure 7.15.

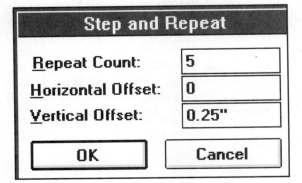

Figure 7.14—The Step and Repeat dialog box for Figure 7.15.

Ctrl+B Item/Frame
Ctrl+Alt+D Item/Step and
    Repeat
Ctrl+D Item/Duplicate

Lost?

If you "lose" an item behind several other items and can't see it to select it, select the Item tool and press the Ctrl+Alt+Shift keys together er while clicking in the general vicinity of the invisible item. Eventually you'll select it. When the selection handles appear (which is all you will see), choose Item/Bring to Front.

Design Tip

The Step and Repeat function is good to use when creating forms. Create one narrow text box; use Step and Repeat to generate many boxes, and then add text and apply shading to selected text boxes.

Ctrl+D Item/Duplicate
Ctrl+Alt+D Item/
    Step and Repeat

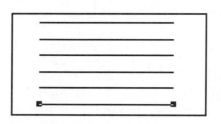

Figure 7.15—The bottom (selected) line has been duplicated 5 times for a total of 6 lines.

If you type a negative number in the Horizontal or Vertical Offset boxes, the items are duplicated horizontally to the right and vertically up.

EXERCISE I

1. Select the Text Box tool and Shift-drag to draw a text box that is 1 inch square.

2. Choose Item/Frame (Ctrl+B) and type 1 in the Width box to give the text box a 1-point frame.

3. Choose Item/Step and Repeat (Ctrl+Alt+D) and type 4 in the Repeat Count field; 1 in the Horizontal Offset field; and 0 in the Vertical Offset field.

4. Click on OK. Your screen should look like Figure 7.16.

5. Repeat the exercise above by drawing a circle and using negative Horizontal and Vertical Offset values.

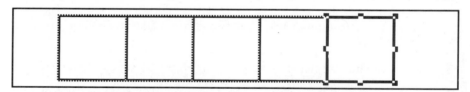

Figure 7.16—A 1-inch square (on the right) duplicated 4 times to the left with the Step and Repeat command using a Horizontal Offset of 1 inch.

WARNING!

Before invoking the Space/Align command, at least two items must be Shift-selected with the Item tool.

SPACE/ALIGN

There are probably only a handful of people in the world who understand how the complicated Space/Align function in XPress works, but there isn't anything you can do with the Space/Align command that you can't do from the Measurements palette. One thing to remember about Space/Align is that every time you input values and click Apply in the Space/Align dialog box, changes are made to the selected items based on the last change you made to those items. So, if you select two or more items, choose Item/Space/Align, input Horizontal and/or Vertical values, and click on Apply, if you want to change those values before clicking on Apply again, the second set of values will be applied to the items as they were arranged via the first set of values. It's usually easier to click on Cancel and start again from the items' original position.

The Space/Align command allows you to apply space between selected items and/or to align them horizontally or vertically. When aligning items horizontally, the Space/Align function moves all the selected items except the item furthest to the left (Figure 7.17). The other items move up or down to match their position to the leftmost item. When aligning items vertically, all items except the topmost item are moved. The other items match their vertical alignment to the position of the topmost item (Figure 7.18).

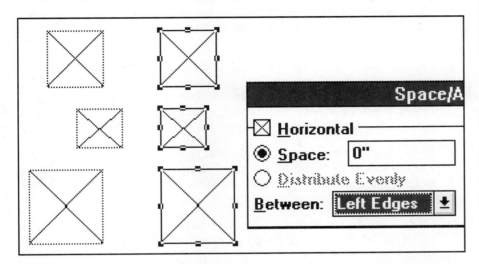

Figure 7.17—When the Horizontal Space/Align command was applied to the original three boxes (left), the two top boxes moved to the same horizontal position as the bottom box because the bottom box was the furthest to the left.

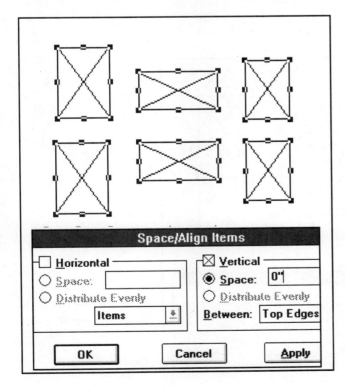

Figure 7.18—The three boxes (top) were selected and the Space/Align command applied vertical spacing, which resulted in their new position (bottom). The two boxes on the right moved up to match their new position to the existing position of the topmost box on the left.

Ctrl+D Item/Duplicate

EXERCISE J

1. Use the Picture Box tool to create three different-sized boxes. Position them somewhat as they appear on the top row in Figure 7.19.

2. Use the Item tool to Shift-select all three boxes. Choose Item/Duplicate (Ctrl+D) to duplicate the set of three boxes. While all three boxes are still selected, use the Item tool to drag the duplicates to the pasteboard.

3. Choose Item/Space/Align to display the Space/Align dialog box.

4. Click on Vertical and use the Between drop-down menu to select Top Edges. Click on Apply. The boxes should resemble the lower set of boxes in Figure 7.19 with their top edges aligned. Click on OK.

5. To both align the edges vertically and space the three items equally, use the Item tool to Shift-select and drag the duplicate of the three boxes back onto the page. With the three boxes still selected, choose Item/Space/Align.

6. Click in the Horizontal check box and click the Distribute Evenly button. Use the Between drop-down menu under Horizontal to select Items.

7. Click in the Vertical check box and click the Distribute Evenly button. Use the Between drop-down menu to select Top Edges. Click on Apply. Notice that the boxes are not only aligned vertically along their top edges, but they are also spaced equidistantly apart. Click on OK. Your screen should resemble Figure 7.19.

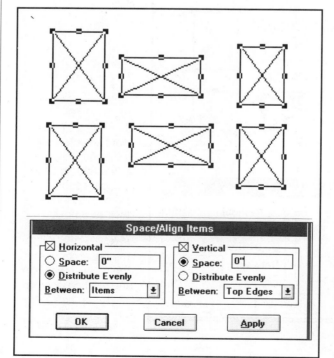

Figure 7.19—The three boxes (top) were selected, then aligned horizontally and evenly between the three boxes and vertically between the top edges.

CONSTRAINING AND UNCONSTRAINING ITEMS

Ctrl+Y Edit/Preferences/
General

Constraining items restricts items created entirely within a box and *grouped with that box* from being moved and/or resized beyond the boundaries of the box. This is a helpful feature when generating forms and tables, but under most circumstances, using the Group command will keep items where you want them. If you check the Auto Constrain check box in the General Preferences dialog box (Ctrl+Y), items placed inside and grouped with other items will be automatically constrained.

EXERCISE K

1. Use a Picture Box tool to draw a picture box.

2. Use the Orthogonal Line tool to draw a 12-point line that fits entirely inside the picture box.

3. Use the Item tool to Shift-select the picture box and the line. Choose Item/Group.

4. With the group still selected, choose Item/Constrain.

5. Select the Content tool and click on the line. Try to resize it beyond the dimensions of the picture box. Because you applied the Constrain command, that line is constrained to the dimensions of the box in which it was created.

6. To unconstrain the line, select the group with the Item tool and choose Item/Unconstrain. The line can now be resized and moved anywhere on the page.

LOCKING ITEMS

When you lock an item you prevent it from being moved or resized. To lock an item, select it with either the Content tool or the Item tool and choose Item/Lock. The cursor changes to a padlock when you select that locked item. To unlock a selected item, choose Item/Unlock.

When you lock an item and then select it, the cursor changes to a padlock at the resizing handle until you unlock the item.

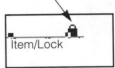

Item/Lock

UTILITIES MENU

The Utilities menu contains commands for checking the spelling of a word, a story, or an entire document. It allows you to create or open an auxiliary dictionary where you can use the Keep command in the spell checker to store words in a text file that are not found in the XPress Dictionary. Choosing Edit Auxiliary lets you edit that Auxiliary Dictionary file.

Highlighting Utilities/Font Usage when a text box is active displays a list of all the screen (bitmapped) fonts used in that file (Figure 7.20). You can use this dialog box to find and replace typefaces in a document.

Choosing Utilities/Picture Usage displays a list of all the graphic files used in that document. You can use this dialog box to search for missing pictures and update pictures that have been modified. This is a critical feature because XPress does not store the actual high resolution graphic in the document, only a low resolution version of that picture. If you want your file

WARNING!

High resolution files— EPS, TIFF, and RIFF files—which are imported into XPress with the Get Picture command will not print at the higher resolution unless XPress can access the original high resolution file.

to print using the higher resolution picture, then you must have that picture file accessible to the program. You will learn more about using these commands in later lessons.

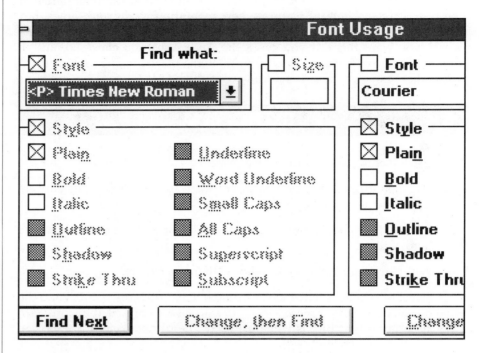

Figure 7.20—The Font Usage dialog box. Use the Font drop-down menu to list all of the fonts used in a document.

WINDOWS MENU

The Windows menu lists commands which make QuarkXPress function in the Microsoft Windows environment. Use them to size and arrange all the open document windows so that they either butt up against each other or are layered on the screen

The Arrange Icons command aligns the document icon windows that were minimized and made to appear at the bottom of the screen. The Close All command closes all the open documents after giving you a chance to save changes to those documents.

The Windows command lists all the open documents, allowing you to activate one instead of clicking on its window (in case you can't find it).

REVIEW EXERCISE

What you will need

A text file of about 500 words

Ctrl+M Item/Modify
Ctrl+E File/Get Text/
        Picture
Ctrl+Alt+S File/Save as
Ctrl+J Go to
Ctrl+Alt+D Step and
        Repeat

Create a new document with picas as the unit of measure, facing pages, an automatic text box, and 2 columns. Assign it the following margins: Top=1.5 inches; Bottom= 2 inches; Inside=1.5 inches; Outside = 1 inch.

1. Use the Document Layout palette (View/Show Document Layout) or the Page/Display command to get to the master page. Use the Rectangle Picture Box tool to create a picture box 10 picas wide and 11 picas high on both the left and right hand pages. Choose Item/Modify (Ctrl+M) and type 20p in the Origin Down field.

2. Choose File/Get Picture (Ctrl+E) and load a picture into the box on the right hand page. Leave the other picture box empty.

3. Double-click on the page 1 icon to get to page 1. Choose File/Save Page as EPS, and when the Save Page dialog box appears, type "EPS Page" and select 50% scaling. Click on B&W or color, depending on the file you imported. Click on Save.

4. Use the Document Layout Palette (View/Show Document Layout) or the Page/Display command to make the first document page visible. On page 1, select the automatic text box and choose File/Get Text (Ctrl+E) to flow the text file onto the page. Then select the picture box and choose Item/Runaround (Ctrl+T) and assign each field 8 points, which will leave 8 points of white space between the picture box and the text. Your screen should resemble Figure 7.21.

5. Choose File/Save as (Ctrl+Alt+S) and save the file under your last name.

6. If necessary, use the Document Layout palette (View/Show Document Layout) or the Page/Insert command to insert a third page in the document. Go to page 2 (Ctrl+J) and select the empty picture box. Choose File/Get Picture (Ctrl+E) and locate the file named "EPS Page." Click on Open to load it into the picture box. Use the Grabber Hand to place it in the center of the box.

7. Go to page 3 (Ctrl+J). Use the Oval Picture Box tool while pressing the Shift key to draw a circle about 2 picas in diameter in the left column. Use the Item Modify command (Ctrl+M) and in the Picture Box Specifications dialog box type 5p in the Width and Height fields. On the right side of the box give it a Shade of 100% Black. Click on OK.

8. With the circle selected, choose Item/Step and Repeat (Ctrl+Alt+D). In the Step and Repeat dialog box, type 5 in the Repeat Count box; –6 in the Horizontal Offset box; and –2 in the Vertical Offset box. Click on OK.

9. Shift-select the six circles and choose Item/Group (Ctrl+G) to group them. Use the Item tool to move the group to the lower right corner of the page. Then choose Item/Duplicate (Ctrl+D). With the duplicate selected, choose Item/Modify (Ctrl+M) and type 45 in the Box Angle field in the Picture Box Specifications dialog box. Use the Item tool to

move the duplicate to the upper right corner of the page. Using the Item tool, delete (Ctrl+X) the square picture box in the center of the screen. Your screen should resemble Figure 7.22.

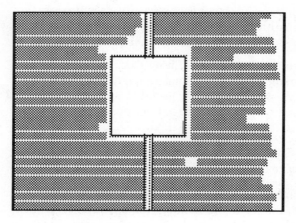

Figure 7.21—A picture box centered on a 2-column page with 8 points of runaround white space.

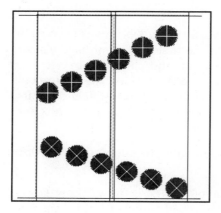

Figure 7.22—Picture boxes duplicated using the Step and Repeat command.

REVIEW QUESTIONS

Read the following questions and choose the answer which best completes the statement.

1. The difference between the Edit/Cut (Ctrl+X) and Item/Delete (Ctrl+K) commands is that _____.
   a. Ctrl+X deletes only text
   b. Ctrl+K does not copy the item to the Clipboard
   c. Ctrl+X does not copy the item to the Clipboard
   d. there isn't any difference

2. Changes made in the Typographic Preferences dialog box _____.
   a. become the program's default values
   b. are made from the Style menu
   c. cannot be changed
   d. affect the entire document

3. In QuarkXPress, thumbnails are _____.
   a. grouped items
   b. body parts
   c. miniature pages
   d. Specifications dialog boxes

4. A file that is saved so it cannot be modified is called _____.
   a. an EPS file
   b. an ASCII file
   c. a template
   d. a thumbnail

5. The Style menu _____.
   a. changes with the selected item
   b. is the primary vehicle for editing text
   c. duplicates all the commands in the Measurements palette
   d. does not access dialog boxes

6. To keep selected items together, use the _____.
   a. Utilities menu
   b. Group command
   c. File menu
   d. Lock command

7. Display tab marks and paragraph returns by choosing _____.
   a. Style/Character
   b. View/Show Guides
   c. Page/Display
   d. View/Show Invisibles

8. Layering items _____.
   a. brings all items to the front
   b. is done through the Utilities menu
   c. can make some items invisible
   d. sends all selected items to the back

9. Before an item can be constrained, it must be _____.
   a. grouped
   b. locked
   c. duplicated
   d. brought forward

10. Text Runaround _____.
   a. aligns items at equal distances
   b. applies white space between items and text
   c. is accessed from the Style menu
   d. always requires multiple columns

Answers: 1. b; 2. d; 3. c; 4. c; 5. a; 6. b; 7. d; 8. c; 9. a; 10. b

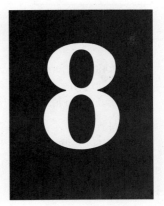

LESSON

8

Working
with
Picture
Boxes and
Pictures

OVERVIEW

In this lesson you will learn how to create, resize, and rotate picture boxes. You will also import, scale, and rotate pictures. Fine tuning and printing grayscale images will also be covered. Finally, you will learn how to list and update the graphics in your document. As a review, you will create a one-page flyer incorporating different graphic file formats.

TOPICS

Resizing picture boxes
Scaling pictures
Rotating picture boxes
Rotating pictures
Skewing pictures
Halftone screens
Picture screening specifications
Listing and updating pictures
Review Exercises
Review Questions

TERMS

aspect ratio
contrast
file formats QuarkXPress imports
halftones
line screens
reverse type
scale
Shift-dragging
skew

What you will need

For this lesson you will need several graphic files in various formats like bitmapped, halftone TIFF, and EPS images. You will also need some text files.

Ctrl+N File/New
Ctrl+Y Edit/Preferences/
   General
Ctrl+E File/Get Picture

Wait a sec!

If you pause for a half second after clicking on an item (box or line) before rotating, resizing, or dragging it, you will be able to view the actual item rather than an outline of it. If you click and drag immediately, only the outline of the item is displayed.

RESIZING PICTURE BOXES

When working with graphics in XPress, it's important to remember that XPress treats picture boxes differently from pictures. What you do to a box in terms of scaling and positioning does not always affect what happens to the picture in that box. When working with a picture *box,* use the Item tool; when working with the *picture* in the box, use the Content tool.

Among the many graphic file formats you can import into XPress with the Get Picture command, you will probably most frequently be importing bitmapped files (.BMP, .DIB, .GIF, .PCX, .RLE); Metafiles (.CGM, .DRW, .PCT, .PLT, .WMF); Encapsulated PostScript files (.EPS); and TIFF files (.CT, .TIF). All of these formats allow you to resize the picture in XPress; some allow you to color them and adjust their grayscale.

EXERCISE A

1. Create a new document by choosing File/New (Ctrl+N) and in the General Preferences dialog box (Ctrl+Y) select inches as the unit of measure.

2. Use the Rectangle Picture Box tool to create a picture box.

3. With the picture box active and the Content tool selected, choose File/Get Picture (Ctrl+E). Scroll through the File Name and Directories fields to locate a graphic file. Highlight the file and click on Open to import the file.

4. When the Content tool is selected and a picture is imported into the picture box, the cursor turns into a Grabber Hand which you can use to position the picture (Figure 8.1).

5. To resize the *box* randomly, click and drag any of the handles. This action may obscure the picture, but it does not affect its size (Figure 8.2).

6. Hold down the Shift key and drag on one of the box's handles. Notice that although the picture box was constrained to a square, the picture was not resized (Figure 8.3).

7. Click and drag to change the box to a long rectangle. Alt+Shift+click and drag a handle. Notice that now the box maintains the same aspect ratio (it is proportionally resized) and the picture is still unchanged (Figure 8.4).

8. Use the Grabber Hand to move part of the picture to the upper right corner. Click on the picture box handles and resize the box so that only the section you want displayed is visible.

9. Press the Alt key while you drag to enlarge the box. Notice that only the cropped portion of the picture is enlarged with the box.

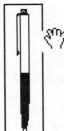

Figure 8.1—Use the Grabber Hand to move the picture randomly within the picture box.

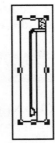

Figure 8.2—Part of the picture is obscured when the box is randomly resized by dragging one of its handles.

Ctrl+Shift+F Fits a picture into the picture box
Ctrl+Z Edit/Undo
Ctrl+Alt+Shift < Reduces the picture size in 5% increments
Ctrl+Alt+Shift > Increases the picture size in 5% increments

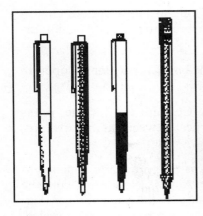

Figure 8.3—Shift+dragging the same picture box in Figure 8.2 constrained it to a square. The additional size reveals more of the picture which was not resized.

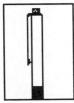

Figure 8.4—Alt+Shift dragging resized the box proportionally but did not affect the picture size.

SCALING PICTURES

So much for the picture box. Now scale (resize) the picture without resizing the picture box.

EXERCISE B

1. Select the picture box and press Ctrl+Shift+F. Notice that the picture is non-proportionally scaled to fit within the box and the box size hasn't changed.

2. Choose Edit/Undo once more (Ctrl+Z). Press Ctrl+Alt+Shift+F and notice that now not only does the picture fit in the box, but it has maintained its aspect ratio, that is, it was proportionally scaled to fit in the box.

3. Display the Measurements palette (View/Show Measurements). With the picture box still selected, press Ctrl+Alt+Shift+< to scale the picture *down* in 5% increments.

4. Press Ctrl+Alt+Shift+> to scale the picture *up* in 5% increments.

What you will need

A graphic file

Ctrl+N File/New
Ctrl+E File/Get Picture
Ctrl+D Item/Duplicate
Ctrl+Alt+M View/Show
    Measurements
Ctrl+Alt+Shift+F
    Proportionally fits a
    picture in the box
Ctrl+Alt+Shift > Increases
    the picture size in 5%
    increments
Ctrl+Alt+Shift < Reduces
    the picture size in
    5% increments
Ctrl+Alt+S File/Save as

About space

If you fit a picture in a box
with the Ctrl+Shift+F or
with the Ctrl+Alt+Shift+F
commands and a lot of
white space appears
around the picture, that is
because the picture was
saved or exported with
that white space. XPress
reads all the information
in a file, even the sur-
rounding space informa-
tion, as part of the picture.

When resizing picture boxes and pictures, remember to select the appropriate tool—the Item tool for boxes and the Content tool for pictures.

EXERCISE C

1. Create a new document (Ctrl+N) with inches as the unit of measure. With the Rectangle Picture Box tool, drag to create a picture box about 3 inches wide and 4 inches high.

2. With the picture box active and the Content tool selected, choose File/Get Picture (Ctrl+E) to import a picture into the box. Position the picture with the Grabber Hand.

3. Press Ctrl+Shift+F to fit the picture in the box. Choose Item/Duplicate (Ctrl+D) to duplicate the picture box.

4. With the duplicate selected and the Content tool active, press Ctrl+Alt+Shift+F and notice the difference between the two pictures (Figure 8.5).

5. Select the last duplicate, the one that was proportionally scaled, and activate the Measurements palette (Ctrl+Alt+M). Notice that both the X% and Y% in the Picture Scaling field display the same number (Figure 8.6). This means that the picture has been proportionally scaled, both horizontally and vertically.

6. Now press Ctrl+Alt Shift+> and notice that the 5% increase to the picture size is reflected in those percentages. Press Ctrl+Alt+ Shift+> again.

7. Proportionally reduce the size of the picture in 5% increments by pressing Ctrl+Alt+Shift+<. Choose File/Save as (Ctrl+Alt+S) and save this document under the name "picfile."

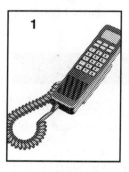 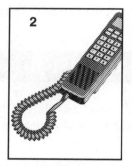 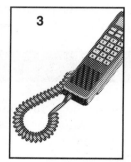

Figure 8.5—A picture imported into XPress and (1) positioned with the Grabber Hand; (2) with the Ctrl+Shift+F command applied; and (3) with the Ctrl+Alt+Shift+F command applied.

X: 5.556"	W: 1.597"	△ 0°	X%: 70%
Y: 3.583"	H: 2.056"	⋲ 0"	Y%: 70%

Figure 8.6—The Measurements palette displays the same X% and Y% values for a picture that has been proportionally scaled, in this case, to 70% of its original size.

ROTATING PICTURE BOXES

Rotating picture boxes is accomplished in one of three ways: using the Rotation tool in the Tool palette; typing a value in the Box Angle field in the Picture Box Specifications dialog box; and typing a value in the Box Rotation field in the Measurements palette.

When typing numbers in the Angle field in the dialog box or in the Box Rotation field in the Measurements palette, typing a positive number will rotate the box or picture from its center to the left. If you type a negative number, the box or picture will rotate from its center to the right.

EXERCISE D

1. If necessary, open the file you saved as "picfile" (File/Open) and insert a new page based on M1-Master 1. Then activate the Measurements palette (Ctrl+Alt+M).

2. Use the Round Corner Picture Box tool to create a picture box about 2 inches wide and 4 inches high. Choose File/Get Picture (Ctrl+E) to import a picture into the box. Apply a 1-point frame (Ctrl+B).

3. Duplicate that picture box twice (Ctrl+D) and arrange the three boxes on the screen so you can conveniently work with them.

4. Select the first box and then select the Rotation tool from the Tool palette. Click on the handle of the box, drag the rotation handle out about 2 inches, and rotate the box about 45° to the left. You can see how far you've moved the box by checking the Box Rotation field in the Measurements palette.

5. Select the second box and choose Item/Modify (Ctrl+M). In the Picture Box Specifications dialog box, type 12 in the Box Angle field on the left side of the dialog box. Click on OK.

6. Select the third picture box and type –20 in the Box Rotation field on the Measurements palette. Press Enter to accept the change. Your screen should resemble Figure 8.7.

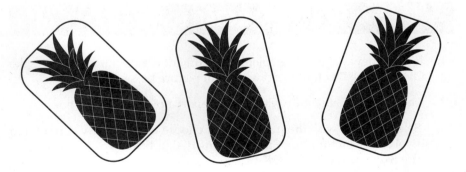

Figure 8.7—Picture boxes rotated at various angles using the Rotation tool, Picture Box Specifications dialog box, and the Measurements palette. Boxes are rotated *from their centers* to the right (negative number) or to the left.

What you will need

A graphic file

Ctrl+O File/Open
Ctrl+Alt+M View/Show
    Measurements
Ctrl+E File/Get Picture
Ctrl+B Item/Frame
Ctrl+D Item/Duplicate
Ctrl+M Item/Modify

Rotation tool

Box Angle field as it appears in the Measurements palette.

A graphic file

Ctrl+M Item/Modify
Ctrl+E File/Get Picture
Ctrl+Alt+M View/Show
    Measurements

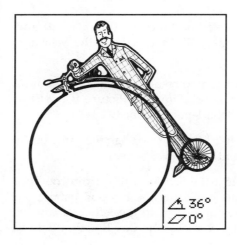

Picture Rotation field (top)
and Picture Skew field
(bottom) on the Measure-
ments palette when a pic-
ture box is active.

ROTATING PICTURES

Notice that when you rotate a picture box, the picture is rotated with it. The only way to restore the picture to its original position is to select the picture box with the Content Tool and choose Item/Modify (Ctrl+M). In the Picture Angle field on the right, type the reverse value of the box rotation. If, for instance, you rotated the picture box 45°, type –45 in the Picture Angle field in either the dialog box or on the Measurements palette. This will rotate the picture, but not the box (Figure 8.8).

To rotate a picture, then, select the picture box with the Content tool and choose Item/Modify (Ctrl+M). Type a positive or negative value in the Picture Angle box on the right, or type a value in the Picture Rotation field in the Measurements palette.

Figure 8.8—Displays a *picture* rotated 36°, as seen in the Picture Rotation field in the Measurements palette. The picture box is not rotated.

SKEWING PICTURES

To skew or slant a picture (you can't skew a box in XPress), select the Picture box with the Item tool and choose Item/Modify (Ctrl+M). Type a positive or negative value in the Picture Skew box on the right. You could also type a value in the Picture Skew field in the Measurements palette. Notice that only the picture, not the picture box, is skewed.

EXERCISE E

1. Insert a new page in the "picfile" document (Page/Insert) and use the Oval Picture Box tool to draw an oval picture box.

2. Choose File/Get Picture (Ctrl+E) to import a picture into the box.

3. Select the box with the Item tool and choose Item/Modify (Ctrl+M) to display the Picture Box Specifications dialog box. Type 10 in the Picture Skew box. Click on OK.

4. Activate the Measurements palette (Ctrl+Alt+M) and select the picture box with the Content tool. Type –50 in the Picture Skew field in the Measurements palette. Press Enter to accept your changes. Figure 8.9 displays some examples of skewing pictures.

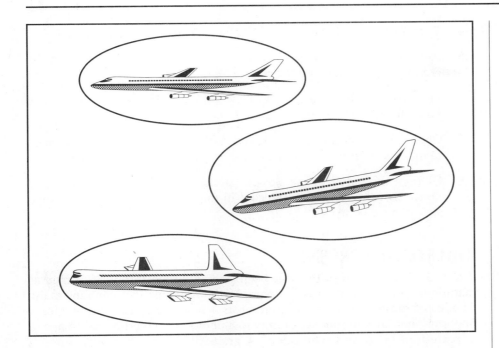

Ctrl+E File/Get Picture
Ctrl+Shift+F Fit a picture
in the picture box
Ctrl+M Item/Modify

Figure 8.9—Displays a picture without skewing (top); skewed 10° to the left (center); and skewed 20° to the right (bottom).

You can also skew a picture by entering a value in the Picture Skew field of the Picture Specifications dialog box (Figure 8.10).

Picture Box Specifications

33p	Sc**a**le Across:	50
13p	S**c**ale Down:	50
10p9	**O**ffset Across:	-1p
5p10	O**f**fset Down:	1p6
0	Picture **A**ngle:	0°
0"	Picture S**k**ew:	-50

┌─ Background ──────

Figure 8.10—The Picture Box Specifications dialog box displays a value of –50 in the Picture Skew field.

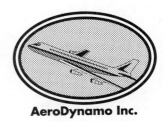

AeroDynamo Inc.

Design Tip

Use the Rotation and Skew tool to create interesting designs for logos. In the picture above, the picture was rotated –20° to the right and skewed –10° to the right. The picture box was given a Background Shade of 20% Black.

EXERCISE F

1. Insert a new page in the "picfile" document and use one of the Picture Box creation tools to create a picture box.

2. Import a picture into the box (Ctrl+E) and press Ctrl+Shift+F to fit it in the picture box.

3. Choose Item/Modify (Ctrl+M) and type 15 in the Picture Skew field of the Picture Box Specifications dialog box.

4. Type 45 in the Box Angle field. Click on OK to view your changes.

5. Activate the Measurements palette (Ctrl+Alt+M) and type 25 in the Picture Rotation field on the right.

6. Below that, change the Picture Skew value to –45. Press Enter to view your changes.

7. Choose Item/Modify (Ctrl+M) and notice that the changes you made in the Measurements palette are also displayed in the dialog box.

8. Change the value in the Box Angle field to –90. Click on OK and notice that the change is reflected in the Box Angle field of the Measurements palette.

HALFTONE SCREENS

Printers refer to artwork that has been photographed through a screen as halftones. When you scan a photograph or any image that contains many shades of gray, you can scan it either as a halftone or as a grayscale. A halftone simulates the shades of gray in a photo by converting the image to a pattern of black and white dots. A grayscale image, however, doesn't convert the image into a pattern; it saves the various parts of that image in different shades of gray.

In XPress, the halftone settings allow you to specify the number of lines per inch (lpi), their angle, and their dot shape, which will define the pattern of dots in the halftone screen that you print from bitmap-based line art, grayscale, or color images.

When you use the Content tool to select a picture box that contains a bitmapped, metafile, or TIFF (Tag Image File Format) grayscale image, the Style menu displays four predefined settings for the picture color, shade, and contrast, as well as the most common lines per inch and angle settings (Figure 8.11). The Color command allows you to change all the black dots in a picture to colors from the Color palette. With the Shade command you can adjust the saturation level of a color in a picture. Choosing Negative produces a negative image of the picture.

When an image that has been scanned as a grayscale is selected, the Contrast values are available (Figure 8.12). The Normal Contrast settings will display and print a picture with its original contrast between black, various shades of gray, and white. High Contrast changes the image to black and white. With this setting, any gray shade below 50% becomes white. Any gray shade above 50% becomes black. The Posterized option changes the image so it has only six levels of gray, which include 80% black, 60%, 40%, and 20% gray, and white. Selecting Other Contrast will display the Picture Contrast Specifications dialog box (Figure 8.13). Here you can use the various tools to adjust the contrast curve in a photograph scanned as a grayscale image.

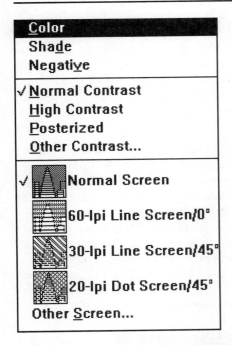

Figure 8.11—The Style menu for pictures.

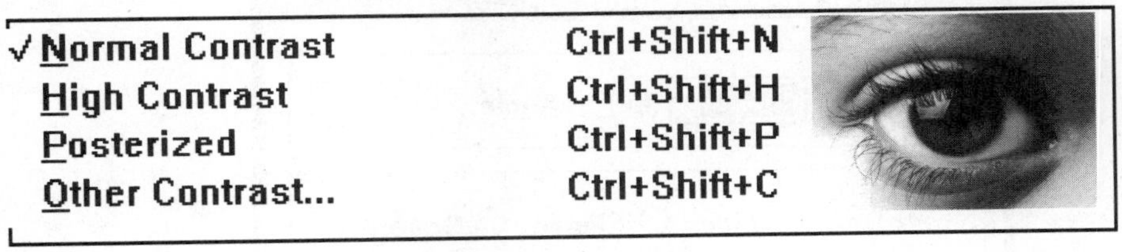

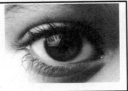

√ **Normal Contrast**	Ctrl+Shift+N
High Contrast	Ctrl+Shift+H
Posterized	Ctrl+Shift+P
Other Contrast...	Ctrl+Shift+C

Figure 8.12—You can adjust the contrast of a photograph scanned as a grayscale image.

Hand tool drags the entire curve around the chart.

Pencil tool creates spikes or drags a point on the chart to reshape the curve in the path.

Line tool reshapes the curve in straight lines. Use the Shift key to constrain lines to 45° angles.

Posterizer tool creates handles between the 10% incremental marks on the curve. The Spike tool creates handles on the curve.

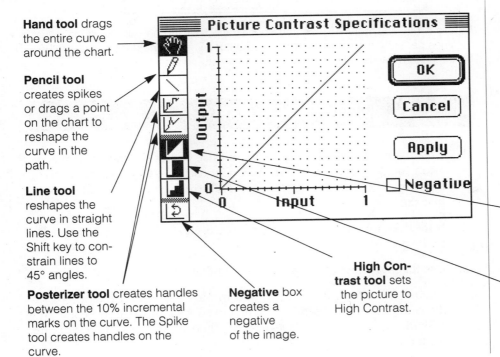

Negative box creates a negative of the image.

High Contrast tool sets the picture to High Contrast.

Figure 8.13—Choosing Other Contrast displays the Picture Contrast Specifications dialog box. Use these tools to adjust the contrast of a grayscale image.

Normal Contrast tool sets the picture back to its original contrast.

Posterized Contrast tool sets the picture to Posterized Contrast.

A graphic file

Ctrl+N File/New
Ctrl+E File/Get Picture
Ctrl+M Item/Modify
Ctrl+P File/Print

PICTURE SCREENING SPECIFICATIONS

The commands in the lower part of the Style menu for pictures affect an image's line screen. The default is Normal Screen, which is determined by the value you entered in the Halftone Frequency field in the Printer Setup dialog box. This value defaults to 60 lpi. You can also choose from a 60-line screen at no angle; a coarser 30-line screen at a 45° angle, or an even coarser 20-line dot screen at 45°.

To define a custom setting, choose Style/Other Screen (Ctrl+Shift+S) to display the Picture Screening Specifications dialog box (Figure 8.14). Here you can enter a value from 15 to 400 lines per inch in the Screen field. (A 300 dpi printer like the HP LaserJet, however, won't accurately reproduce screens finer than 75 lpi.) Change the Angle value (of the screen, not the image), and the Pattern to achieve optimal or special effects when printing a halftone. Selecting the Ordered Dither option will optimize printing to a low resolution laser printer and should not be selected when printing to an imagesetter like the Linotronic. Click in the Display Halftoning check box to see the effects of the settings you have chosen, but be aware that this option slows down the screen redraw considerably.

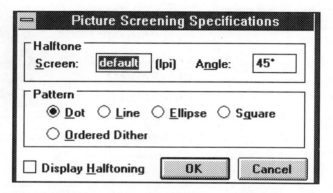

Figure 8.14—The Picture Screening Specifications dialog box allows you to adjust the lines per inch, angle, and pattern of a halftone image. The default value in the Screen field defaults to the value in the Printer setup dialog box.

EXERCISE G

1. Create a new document (Ctrl+N) and use one of the Picture Box Creation tools to draw a picture box. Choose File/Get Picture (Ctrl+E) and import a bitmap, metafile, or TIFF (line art or grayscale) image into the box.

2. With the Content tool selected, choose Style/Color and assign a color to the picture.

3. Use the Style menu to apply a shade of that color to the picture.

4. Choose Item/Modify (Ctrl+M) and in the Background dialog box on the right, use the drop-down menus to select a Background color and a Shade of that color. Click on OK. Choose File/Print (Ctrl+P) and print the page.

5. Choose File/Printer Setup and make sure the Halftone Screen value is set to 60 lpi (lines per inch). This will assign 60 lines per inch to the picture. Choose Style/Normal Screen (Ctrl+Shift+N). Choose File/Print (Ctrl+P) and print the page.

6. Choose File/Printer Setup and change the Halftone Screen value to 75. Print the page and see if you can notice any difference. Depending on the type of graphic you used, you may not see much difference at all. You would, however, see a difference if the file was printed at 2400 dpi on a Linotronic imagesetter.

7. Assign different screen lines from the Style menu as well as from the Picture Screening Specifications dialog box (Ctrl+Shift+S) and print them out to see the difference in output.

EXERCISE H

1. Select all the items on the page and delete them. Draw another picture box and import a photograph saved as a TIFF grayscale image into the box (Ctrl+E). Use the Item tool, choose Item/Duplicate (Ctrl+D), and make a few duplicates of that picture.

2. With the Content tool selected, choose Style/High Contrast (Ctrl+Shift+H) and notice how the picture changed. Select one of the duplicates and Choose Style/Posterized (Ctrl+Shift+P); then select Style/Normal Contrast (Ctrl+Shift+N) to return the picture to its normal setting.

3. Choose Other Contrast (Ctrl+Shift+C) and use the tools to change the contrast levels of the photograph. Click on the Apply button to see your changes without leaving the dialog box. Use the Normal Contrast tool to return the picture to its original contrast.

4. After applying different contrast settings to the duplicate pictures, print out the page (Ctrl+P) and notice the difference in the output. Click on the picture and check its Contrast settings to see how you achieved that effect.

LISTING AND UPDATING PICTURES

When you import a high resolution graphic like an EPS or TIFF file into an XPress document, only a low resolution version of that graphic is displayed on the screen. XPress links that low resolution graphic to the high resolution graphic on your hard disk or floppy disk. In order to print the high resolution picture, however, XPress must be able to locate it. If you modify the graphic in another program or if you move it from its original position on the disk, XPress will display a dialog box (Figure 8.15) which will allow you either to Cancel the Print command or to list and update the picture. This dialog box is also available from the Utilities menu by choosing Utilities/Picture Usage. If you want XPress to re-import all the graphics that have been modified since you last opened the document, choose Edit/Preferences/General (Ctrl+Y) and set Auto Picture Import to On.

Ctrl+Shift+N Style/Normal Screen
Ctrl+P File/Print
Ctrl+Shift+S Style/Other Screen
Ctrl+Shift+H Style/High Contrast
Ctrl+Shift+P Style/Posterized
Ctrl+E File/Get Picture
Ctrl+D Item/Duplicate
Ctrl+Shift+C Style/Other Contrast

Tip

It's a good idea to label each picture so you will know which contrast setting you applied to each one.

The Normal Contrast tool returns the image to its original setting.

Auto Picture Import:
On
Off
On
On (verify)

Use the Auto Picture Import drop-down menu in the General Preferences dialog box to select On.

What you will need

A halftone grayscale image

Ctrl+M Item/Modify
Ctrl+N File/New
Ctrl+Y Edit/Preferences/
    General

FYI

If you select the Suppress Picture Printout option in the Picture Box Specifications dialog box, then XPress will print only the frame or background color specified for that picture box.

If you select the Suppress Printout option, neither the box's frame nor its background color (if any) will print.

If you click on OK, the Picture Usage dialog box appears (Figure 8.16). This lists all of the pictures in your document and their status.

Click on the picture labeled as Missing. Next, clicking on Show Me will select the picture on the screen so you can connect the picture with a name in the Picture Usage dialog box

To locate a picture flagged as "Missing" in the Picture Usage dialog box, click once on the name of the picture and click on Update. A dialog box will be displayed through which you can direct XPress to the missing or modified picture by scrolling through directories and drives.

If your files are very large and you want to save time when printing drafts, choose Item/Modify (Ctrl+M) and check the Suppress Picture Printout box on the left. This will suppress the picture printout and leave the picture box blank when you print the document.

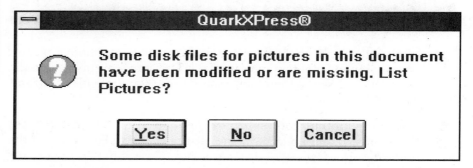

Figure 8.15—XPress displays this warning if high resolution files are missing or have been modified since you last opened the document.

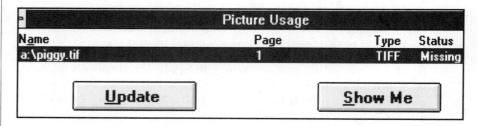

Figure 8.16—Use the Picture Usage dialog box to locate missing or modified pictures in a document.

REVIEW EXERCISE #1

For this Review Exercise you will create a one-page flyer which incorporates text, a high resolution EPS file, a TIFF file saved as a grayscale image, and a bitmap or metafile.

1. Begin by creating a new document (File/New) with 2 columns. Choose Edit/Preferences/General (Ctrl+Y) and select picas as the unit of measure, Auto Page Insertion set to Off, Guides set to In Front, and Auto Picture Import set to Off. Click on OK.

2. Click on the zero point (ruler origin) and drag it on top of the point where the top and left margin guides meet. This will put the zero point at the intersection of those two guides.

3. Choose File/Get Text (Ctrl+E) and place the text file so that it fills or almost fills the two columns.

4. Create a text box 45 picas wide and 6 picas high. Position it across the middle of the page. Type (no quotes) "College Connections—1993."

5. Choose Select All (Ctrl+A) and use the Measurements palette to format the text in 36-point Times bold, all caps. Use the alignment icons to give it a center alignment.

6. Center it vertically in the text box by choosing Item/Modify. In the Vertical Alignment box on the right, use the drop-down menu to select Centered. This will center the text vertically as well as horizontally in the text box. Click on OK.

7. With the text still selected, choose Style/Color and choose White.

8. Choose Item/Modify (Ctrl+M) again. In the Background box on the right, use the drop-down menu to give the box a background color of Black and a Shade value of 100%. Click on OK. You have now created reverse type—white type on a black background.

9. With the text box still selected, click on the Rotation tool, click on one of the text box's handles, and rotate the text box towards the left about 90 degrees.

10. Choose Item/Modify (Ctrl+M) and make sure 90° is in the Box Angle field. Click on OK. Position it so that it's centered on the left margin line.

11. Use the Measurements palette to make sure that X= –3p (minus 3 because the box's X coordinate is outside of the left margin); Y=45p; W=45p; H=6p; Box Angle=90.

12. Now select the 2-column text box and use either the Text Box Specifications dialog box or the Measurements palette to change its Origin Across value to 3p5, or use the Measurements palette to change its X value to 3p5, so that none of the text will be hidden by the rotated text box. Your screen should resemble Figure 8.17.

13. Use the Rectangle Picture Box tool to create a picture box. Choose File/Get Picture and import an EPS file into the box.

14. Choose Item/Modify (Ctrl+M) and in the Picture Box Specifications dialog box, type 10 in the Width field and 14 in the Height field. Click on OK.

15. With the picture box still selected, choose Item/Runaround (Ctrl+T). Type 6 in the Top, Left, and Bottom fields. Click on OK.

16. With the Content tool selected, reduce and enlarge the picture in 5% increments by pressing Ctrl+Alt+Shift+> and Ctrl+Alt+Shift+< until you are pleased with the way the picture looks.

Ctrl+E File/Get Text
Ctrl+A Edit/Select All
Ctrl+M Item/Modify
Ctrl+E File/Get Picture
Ctrl+T Item/Runaround

FYI

You can create an em dash (—) by pressing Alt+Shift+Hyphen instead of typing two hyphens whenever you are typesetting. Likewise, use an en dash (–) by pressing Alt+Hyphen instead of a hyphen when typesetting time or number spans like 1893–1940 and 7–10.

The index for this text was typed using the hyphen between page numbers. Then the Find/Change command was used to substitute the en dash for the hyphen.

Ctrl+Alt+Shift > Increases the picture size in 5% increments

Ctrl+Alt+Shift < Reduces the picture size in 5% increments

Ctrl+E File/Get Picture

Ctrl+M Item/Modify

Ctrl+T Item/Runaround

Ctrl+Shift+T Style/Tabs

Ctrl+Shift+C Style/Other Contrast

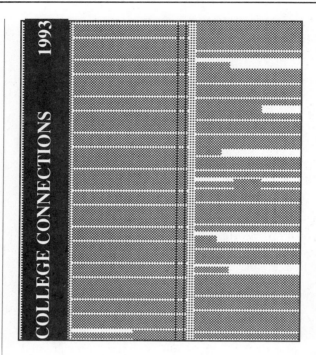

Figure 8.17—Displays a 2-column page with a rotated text box. Notice that the rotated text box is centered on the left margin guides.

REVIEW EXERCISE #2

1. In the same document, create another picture box and import a bitmap file into it (Ctrl+E). Use the Picture Box Specifications dialog box (Ctrl+M) to give the picture box the following values: Origin Across=26p; Origin Down=0p; Width=9p; Height=8p; Box Angle=–10.

2. Type 50% in the Scale Across field and 50% in the Scale Down field to proportionally reduce the picture to half of its original size. Then click on OK.

3. With the picture box still selected, choose Item/Runaround (Ctrl+T). Type 5 in the Left, Bottom, and Right fields. Click on OK.

4. Create a third picture box 9 picas wide by 8 picas high. Use the Measurements palette to give it the following values: X=30p; Y=28p7; W=6p; H=8p.

5. Import the grayscale image saved as a TIFF file. Choose Style/Color and apply a color to the image.

6. Choose Style/Other Contrast (Ctrl+Shift+C) and use the various tools to apply different Contrast values to the image. Click on the Apply button to see how the changes you made affect the image. When you are pleased with the image, click on OK.

7. With the picture box still selected, choose Item/Runaround (Ctrl+T). Type 6 in the Top, Left, and Bottom fields. Click on OK. Your screen should resemble Figure 8.18. Print your page using different line screen values and see if you can notice any difference in the output.

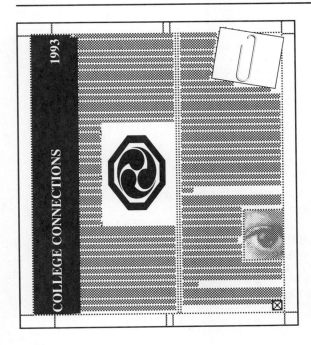

Figure 8.18—The finished flyer!

REVIEW QUESTIONS

Read the following questions and choose the answer which best completes the statement.

1. Picture boxes can be resized from _____.
    a. the Measurements palette
    b. a dialog box
    c. with the Pointer tool
    d. all of the above

2. Scaling a picture _____.
    a. changes it and its box
    b. slants it
    c. resizes only the picture
    d. resizes the picture box

3. Pictures can be resized _____.
    a. from the keyboard
    b. from the Measurements palette
    c. from a dialog box
    d.   all of the above

4. When a picture box is rotated, _____.
    a. the picture rotates with it
    b. the picture doesn't rotate with it
    c. the angle of rotation is defined from the Measurements palette
    d. values must be applied in the Picture Box Specifications dialog box

5. When resizing pictures, _____.
   a. use the Item tool
   b. use the Rotation tool
   c. select the picture with the Content tool
   d. select the picture box with the Item tool

6. Skewing a picture _____.
   a. rotates it
   b. resizes it
   c. scales it
   d. slants it

7. Once a picture has been rotated, subsequent rotation values are _____.
   a. applied to the current position
   b. applied from 0°
   c. applied only from the Picture Box Specifications dialog box
   d. applied only from the Measurements palette

8. To adjust a picture's contrast, that picture must be _____.
   a. scanned as a grayscale image and saved as a TIFF file
   b. an EPS file exported from a drawing program
   c. a color TIFF file
   d. a color bitmap file

9. High resolution images imported into XPress are _____.
   a. embedded in the document
   b. displayed as EPS images
   c. locked to the picture box
   d. linked to the low resolution display

10. You can get a list of the pictures used in a document from the _____.
    a. File menu
    b. Edit menu
    c. View menu
    d. Utilities menu

Answers: 1. d; 2. c; 3. d; 4. a; 5. d; 6. c; 7. a; 8. a; 9. d; 10. d

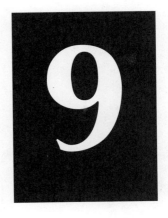
OVERVIEW

In this lesson you will continue to work with the Picture Box Specifications dialog box by modifying picture boxes and determining a corner radius for rectangles. You will also learn how to create many-sided picture boxes, as well as how to resize and reshape these polygon picture boxes. You will use the Color Wheel to add colors to the Color palette and to apply colors to a picture box's background. As a review, you will create a masthead for a newsletter incorporating text boxes and different kinds of picture boxes.

Modifying Picture Boxes

TOPICS

Picture Box Specifications dialog box
Origin Across and Origin Down fields
Width and Height fields
Corner Radius field
Scale Across and Scale Down fields
Offset Across and Offset Down fields
Picture Angle Field
Skewing pictures
Suppress Printout
Background field
Picture Box Shape
Polygon Picture Box tool
Review Exercise
Review Questions

TERMS

background
bounding box
corner radius
horizontal offset
origin across
origin down
picture angle
picture skew
reshape polygon
shade
vertex
vertical offset

Ctrl+M Item/Modify

PICTURE BOX SPECIFICATIONS DIALOG BOX

Since you have already worked with the Picture Box Specifications dialog box (Figure 9.1), there are only a few fields in that box to be covered. The fields in the left column of the dialog box govern the position (origin) and shape of picture *boxes;* the fields in the second column govern the scale, offset, angle, and skew values of the *pictures* themselves. Access the Picture Box Specifications dialog box by choosing Item/Modify (Ctrl+M).

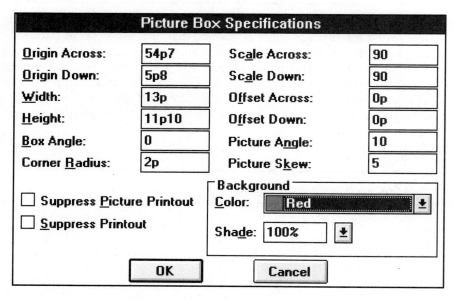

Figure 9.1—The Picture Box Specifications dialog box showing that both the picture box (left column) and picture (right column) have been modified. The fields on the left side of the box affect picture boxes; the fields on the right side of the box affect pictures. The Background box allows you to apply color to the picture box.

ORIGIN ACROSS AND ORIGIN DOWN FIELDS

You will recall that the Origin Across field refers to the upper left corner of the picture box as it is positioned in relation to the zero point on the horizontal ruler. A picture box that is placed 1 inch from the zero point *on the horizontal ruler* would have an Origin Across value (or X value in the Measurements palette) of 1 inch or, if the unit of measure is set to picas, an X value of 1 pica. The Origin Down field refers to the upper left corner of the picture box as it relates to the zero point on the vertical ruler. If a picture box were placed 2 inches down from the zero point *on the vertical ruler*, it would have an Origin Down value (or Y value in the Measurements palette) of 2 inches. Just remember that those X and Y (Origin Across and Origin Down) values always refer to the upper left corner of the box.

WIDTH AND HEIGHT FIELDS

The Width and Height fields (W and H in the Measurements palette) allow you to input the width and the height of the picture box. The Box Angle field is where you type the degree of rotation for a picture box. This field defaults to 0 degrees.

CORNER RADIUS FIELD

The Corner Radius field is available whenever a rectangle or round-cornered picture box is selected. Type a number between 0 and 12 inches or picas, etc. in this field to round the corner of the picture box (Figure 9.2).

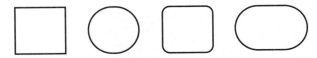

Figure 9.2—The first rectangle displays a corner radius value of 0; the second of 2 picas; and the third of 10 points. The last rectangle was drawn with the Round-Corner Rectangle tool and defaults to a corner radius of .25" or 1 pica and 6 points (1p6).

The Corner Radius field in the Measurements palette when a picture box is active.

SCALE ACROSS AND SCALE DOWN FIELDS

In the second column, the Scale Across and Scale down values (X% and Y% values in the Measurements palette) allow you to make the picture larger or smaller. If the same value appears in both fields, the picture is proportionally scaled; otherwise, it is distorted.

OFFSET ACROSS AND OFFSET DOWN FIELDS

The Offset Across and Offset Down values (X+ and Y+ values in the Measurements palette) affect the distance a picture is positioned from the left and top edges of the picture box. When a picture box is selected and the Content tool is active, you can enter positioning values in the Measurements palette. To offset the picture to the left or upwards, type a negative value in the Offset fields (Figure 9.3). To offset a picture to the right of or down from the edge of the picture box, type a positive number.

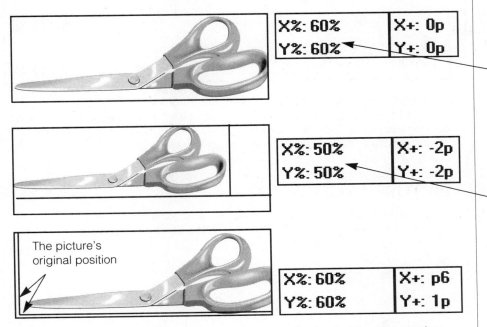

The top picture was imported, positioned in the picture box, and scaled down to 60% of its size. The 0p values indicate that it is not offset from the top, bottom, or sides of the picture box.

This picture was imported, scaled to 50% of its original size, and offset (moved) to the left 2 picas (X+:–2p) and up (Y+:–2p). The horizontal and vertical lines indicate the picture's original position.

Figure 9.3—The same picture is imported into equally-sized picture boxes, then scaled and offset differently.

What you will need

A graphic file

Ctrl+N File/New
Ctrl+Y Edit/Preferences/
    General
Ctrl+B Item/Frame
Ctrl+E File/Get Picture
Ctrl+Shift+M Centers a
    picture in the picture
    box
Ctrl+M Item/Modify
Ctrl+Alt+M View/Show
    Measurements

80%	X+: p6
80%	Y+: 1p

FYI

When you move a picture with the Grabber Hand, the picture's position is reflected in the X+ and Y+ fields in the Measurements palette.

Don't bother

You don't have to type the percent symbol (%) or the degree symbol (°) in the Measurements palette. Just type the number and XPress will add the appropriate symbol.

EXERCISE A

1. Create a new document (Ctrl+N) with 1 column. Press Ctrl+Y and, in the General Preferences dialog box, select picas as the unit of measure.

2. Use the Square Corner Rectangle tool to draw a rectangle 28 picas wide and 6 picas high. Assign it a 1-point frame (Ctrl+B). Import a picture into the box (Ctrl+E). Press Ctrl+Shift+M to center the picture in the picture box. Keep the picture box selected.

3. Choose Item/Modify (Ctrl+M). In the Picture Box Specifications dialog box, change the picture's horizontal and vertical scale to 80% of its original size by typing 80 in the Scale Across and Scale Down fields on the right side of the dialog box. Because both the horizontal and vertical scales are the same number, the picture has been *proportionally* scaled.

4. Now change its Horizontal Offset value (Offset Across), so that the picture is 6 points to the right of the left side of the picture box, by typing p6 in the Offset Across field. Offset the picture 1½ picas down from the top side of the picture box by typing 1p6 in the Offset Down field. Click on OK. Your screen should resemble Figure 9.4.

5. Activate the Measurements palette (Ctrl+Alt+M). In the Measurements palette, change the Scale values (X% and Y%) back to 100 and the Offset Across and Offset Down (X+ and Y+) values back to 0p to restore the picture to its original values.

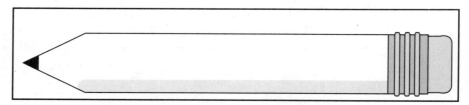

Figure 9.4—This picture was scaled down to 80% of its original size and moved 6 points (p6) to the right (X+ value) and 1½ points (1p6) down (Y+ value) from the left and top sides of the picture box. Keep in mind that XPress treats the white space around a picture that is imported with the picture as part of the picture.

PICTURE ANGLE FIELD

The Picture Angle field in the dialog box and Measurements palette allows you to rotate the picture *from its center* to the left by typing a positive number. To rotate the picture from its center to the right, type a negative number.

SKEWING PICTURES

Skew (slant) a picture to the left by typing a positive number in the Picture Skew field; type a negative number to skew the picture to the right.

SUPPRESS PRINTOUT

If you want a picture visible on your screen but don't want to print it, click in the Suppress Picture Printout check box. Only the background and simple frame (if any) of the box will print; the picture itself will not print. If you want to prevent the active picture box as well as its background and frame from printing, click in the Suppress Printout check box below.

BACKGROUND FIELD

The Background (color) field on the right allows you to specify a color and shade of that color for the picture box—not the picture. Use the Color pull-down menu to select a color. Use the Shade pull-down menu to select a shade (tint) of that color.

What you will need

A graphic file

Ctrl+E File/Get Picture
Ctrl+M Item/Modify

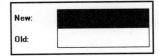

FYI

As you make changes to the duplicate color, those changes are reflected in the upper bar (New) of the swatch box in the Edit Color dialog box.

EXERCISE B

1. Use any Picture Box tool to create a picture box.

2. To add a color to the Color menu, choose Edit/Colors and click on New. When the Color Wheel appears, click on a color and type a name for it in the Name field. Click on OK and click on Save.

3. Select the rectangle and choose Item/Modify (Ctrl+M). In the Color field on the right, use the pull-down menu to select the color you just added to the color palette. Use the Shade pull-down menu to select a tint of that color. Click on OK.

PICTURE BOX SHAPE

Finally, you can change the shape of the picture box by choosing Item/Picture Box Shape. Select a new shape for an active picture box from the drag-up menu.

EXERCISE C

1. Add a new page to your document (Page/Insert) and use the Oval Picture Box tool while pressing the Shift key to draw a circle with a diameter of 10 picas (W=10p). Import a picture (Ctrl+E) into the box.

2. Choose Edit/Colors and click on New in the dialog box. When the Color Wheel appears, click on a color and type its name in the Name box. Click on OK and click on Save.

3. Select the picture and choose Item/Modify (Ctrl+M). Use the Background Color pull-down menu on the right to assign the box the new color you just created. Click on OK.

What you will need

A text file
A graphic file

Ctrl+E File/Get Text
Ctrl+T Item/Runaround

EXERCISE D

1. Use the Text Box tool to create a text box 20 picas wide by 10 picas high. Activate the Measurements palette (Ctrl+Alt+M) and assign the text box 2 columns.

2. Import a text file into the box (Ctrl+E).

3. Use the Item tool to drag the picture you just created into the new text box and position it between the two columns.

4. With the picture box selected, choose Item/Runaround (Ctrl+T) and use the Mode pull-down menu to select Item. Type 7 in the Text Outset box to leave 7 points of space between the text and picture. Click on OK. Your screen should resemble Figure 9.5.

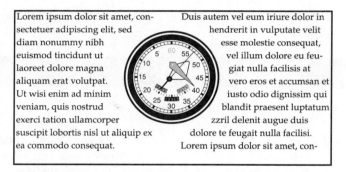

Figure 9.5—Displays a text box with a picture box to which a newly created color was applied. The picture box was assigned a text outset of 7 points in the Picture Box Specifications dialog box.

POLYGON PICTURE BOX TOOL

The Polygon Picture Box tool

So far you have modified picture boxes created with the Rectangle tool, Round-Cornered Rectangle tool, and Oval Picture Box tool. Let's take a look now at the powerful Polygon Picture Box tool located on the Tool palette below the Oval Picture Box tool. The Polygon Picture Box tool creates picture boxes composed of at least three straight sides. A polygon picture box is surrounded by a bounding box with eight handles which are used to resize the picture box (Figure 9.6).

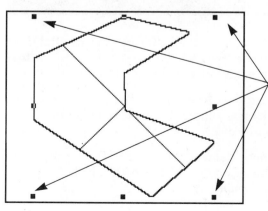

Figure 9.6—An eight-sided polygon displays only the eight handles of its bounding box when selected and Reshape Polygon under the Item menu is not checked. The handles are used to *resize* the polygon.

When the Reshape Polygon option (Item/Reshape Polygon) is checked, each line segment on the polygon box has its own handles or points which can be moved to reshape the polygon (Figure 9.7). Handles can also be added and deleted to reshape the polygon. When the Reshape Polygon item is not checked, only the eight handles on the bounding box can be used to resize, but not reshape, the polygon.

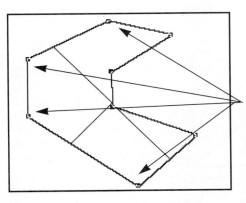

Figure 9.7—An eight-sided polygon displays points on every line segment when selected and Reshape Polygon under the Item menu is checked. These points are manipulated to *reshape* the polygon.

Sometimes drawing a polygon picture box is like riding a wild horse—you can't stop the lines from dragging all over the screen. If you can't find the first point (vertex) to click on and thus close the polygon, double click anywhere on the screen and the polygon will (sometimes) close automatically. It will also create the third line segment and close automatically if you double-click after drawing only two line segments.

To delete a polygon picture box, click on it with the Item tool and choose Edit/Cut (Ctrl+X) or click on it with the Content tool and choose Item/Delete (Ctrl+K).

EXERCISE E

1. Insert a new page in the same document (Page/Insert). Select the Polygon Picture Box tool and click anywhere on the screen. Release the mouse button.

2. To draw a triangle, move the mouse about 3 inches to the right of the first point and click again to create both a line and another corner (vertex).

3. Move the mouse to drag another line about 3 inches above that corner and click once more.

4. Then, without clicking, drag the mouse down until the cursor is on top of the first point you created. The crosshair cursor changes to the Handle Creation pointer. Then double-click on the first point to close the picture box and create a triangle. The crossed black lines inside the picture box tell you that you have created a picture box.

5. With the polygon picture box active and the Content tool selected, choose File/Get Picture (Ctrl+E) and load a picture into that box. Press Ctrl+Alt+Shift+F to proportionally resize and fit the picture into the picture box.

What you will need

A graphic file

Ctrl+E File/Get Picture
Ctrl+X Edit/Cut
Ctrl+K Item/Delete
Ctrl+Alt+Shift+F Proportionally fits a picture in the box

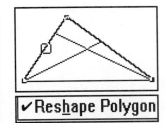

✔ **Reshape Polygon**

When Reshape Polygon is checked, the cursor changes to the Handle Creation Pointer and allows you to add a point to the polygon's line segment.

Important info

Should you find the Polygon Picture Box tool running wild, try pressing the Ctrl+. (period) keys. If the moon is in a certain phase and the creek don't rise, it works. It's things like this that give QuarkXPress its nickname, "Quirky Quark!"

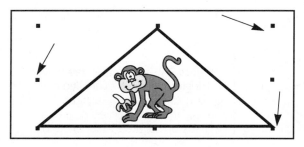

The Line Segment Pointer appears when a polygon picture box is selected and Item/Reshape Polygon is also selected.

6. Use the Item tool to move the polygon picture box around the screen just as you would move any other picture box.

7. Pull down the Item menu and notice that the last item in the menu, Reshape Polygon, is not checked. This means that only the polygon's bounding box handles are displayed (Figure 9.8). The bounding box is a rectangle with eight handles which surround the polygon. Use these handles to resize the active polygon by dragging the bounding box handles with the Resizing Pointer.

Figure 9.8—A polygon picture box with a picture. The eight points of the bounding box indicate that the Reshape Polygon option is not checked and the polygon can only be *resized.*

8. To resize the polygon picture box proportionally, hold down the Alt and Shift keys while dragging a bounding box handle. This will proportionally resize the polygon picture box but not the picture. To proportionally resize the picture while proportionally resizing the box, hold down the Ctrl, Alt, and Shift keys while dragging to resize the polygon picture box.

The crosshair changes to the Handle Creation Pointer to close the polygon when it is placed over the first point of a polygon picture box.

9. Use the Item tool to select the polygon picture box and choose Item/Reshape Polygon from the Menu Bar. Notice that now you have only 3 handles at each corner (vertex) of the triangle (Figure 9.9). You can now reposition, add, and delete polygon handles. You can also reposition the polygon's line segments.

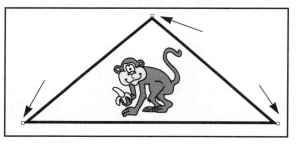

Figure 9.9—A polygon picture box with a picture. The three points on each side of the polygon indicate that the Reshape Polygon option is checked and the polygon can be *reshaped.*

The Resizing Pointer always appears when a polygon picture box is selected and allows you to resize the polygon by moving the eight handles of the bounding box. If Reshape Polygon is checked, the Resizing Pointer allows you to reshape the polygon by manipulating the polygon's points.

10. Click on one of the triangle's three handles. When the cursor changes to the Resizing Pointer, drag the handle outward and release the mouse button. Hold down the Shift key while dragging to constrain that movement to 0°, 45°, or 90°.

11. To add a new handle to one of the line segments in a polygon picture box, hold down the Ctrl key and move the pointer over the segment. The cursor turns into the Handle Creation Pointer. Click on the line segment where you want to add a handle. Drag the new handle to a new location (Figure 9.10).

12.   To delete a handle from a line segment, hold down the Ctrl key and move the cursor over the handle you want to delete. The cursor changes to the Handle Deletion Pointer. Click to remove the handle. Since every polygon picture box must have at least 3 handles, you cannot delete a handle on a polygon picture box that has only three handles.

13.   To move or reposition a line segment on a polygon picture box, move the cursor over the line segment you want to reposition. The cursor changes into the Line Segment Pointer. Click and drag the line segment to a new position, as seen in Figure 9.10. Hold down the Shift key to constrain that movement to 0°, 45°, or 90°.

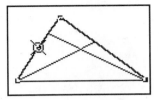

When Reshape Polygon is checked, the cursor changes to the Handle Deletion Pointer and allows you to delete a point from a polygon's line segment.

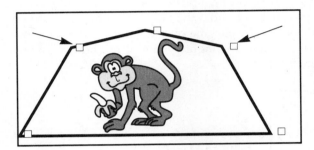

Figure 9.10—A three-sided polygon that has been reshaped by adding two more points to create two additional line segments.

EXERCISE F

1.   In the same document, create a few more polygon picture boxes, each with a different number of line segments (sides). Make sure that Reshape Polygon is not checked and resize the polygons using the bounding box handles. Hold down the Alt and Shift keys to resize them proportionally.

2.   Choose Item/Reshape Polygon and use the Ctrl key (hold down the Ctrl key while clicking on the segment where you want to add the handle) to add a new handle to a line segment. Pull out the new handle to reshape the the polygon. Then click on the new handle while holding down the Ctrl key to delete that same handle. Reshape each polygon using the original handles.

3.   To convert that polygon picture box into a standard picture box shape, select the picture box and choose Item/Picture Box Shape. Use the pull-down menu and select the inverted-rounded corner rectangle. The polygon picture box is now sized according to the dimensions of its bounding box.

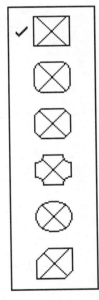

When a rectangle is selected, use the Item menu to select a different picture box shape. A check mark appears in front of the currently selected shape.

REVIEW EXERCISE

You will now create a masthead for a newsletter. Begin by using the Text Box tool to draw a text box about 30 picas wide by 10 picas high where you will place all the text and graphics for the masthead.

1. Either create a new document (File/New) or insert a new page in an existing document (Page/Insert). Assign picas as the unit of measure.

2. Select the Polygon Picture Box tool and click and drag to create a many-sided picture box which (to anyone but an architect) resembles a city skyline. Since you are creating a picture box, you do not have to draw a rectangular picture box to hold the polygon picture box. When you have closed the polygon by clicking over the first point you created, only the rough figure and the eight points of the bounding box will be visible (Figure 9.11).

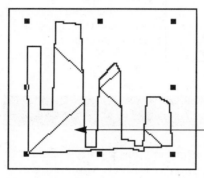

Figure 9.11—Select the Polygon Picture Box tool and click at point 1; then click and drag to create a rough outline of a city skyline. The crossed black lines indicate that a picture box has been created. The bounding box handles indicate that the Reshape Polygon option under the Item menu has not been selected.

3. Choose Item/Reshape Polygon. Notice that every line segment displays handles at each vertex (Figure 9.12). Be sure that Snap to Guides is selected (View/Snap to Guides). Place horizontal and vertical ruler guides on the horizontal and vertical lines of the rough skyline. Then click on a line segment to make the Line Segment Pointer appear.

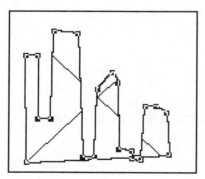

Figure 9.12—When a polygon picture box is selected and Item/Reshape Polygon is checked, handles appear at each vertex (corner) of the polygon picture box's line segments.

4. Reposition the line segments with the Pointer Finger until the polygon picture box more clearly resembles a skyline. Be sure that Reshape Polygon is checked (Item/Reshape Polygon). Then select the Rectangle tool and draw some small squares (hold down the Shift key while drawing) and a few rectangles to be placed as windows on top of the skyline picture box.

5. Select a rectangle and choose Item/Modify (Ctrl+M) and assign it a different background color. Then choose Edit/Colors and create some gold and amber colors and add them to the color palette under the Background field in the Picture Box Specifications dialog box. Assign these new colors to the small rectangles you just created.

6. When you are satisfied with the way the skyline picture box looks, make sure it's selected and choose Item/Frame (Ctrl+B) and type 1 in the Width field.

7. Then use the Item tool to select the skyline picture box and all of the windows. Choose Item/Group (Ctrl+G) to group them together. Frame each window in a narrow contrasting line or import an appropriate graphic into the skyline picture box or into the windows for an even more striking effect.

8. Place the grouped skyline graphic on the left side of the text box you created earlier.

9. Then draw another text box 20 picas wide and 4 picas high in the upper right corner of the original text box. Use the Content tool to type (no quotes) "CITY TIMES." Select all the text by choosing Edit/Select All (Ctrl+A). Use the Measurements palette (Ctrl+Alt+M) to format it in 36- point Times bold italic.

10. Choose Item/Modify (Ctrl+M) and use the pull-down menu in the Vertical Alignment field to select Centered. Click on OK.

11. Draw another text box below CITY TIMES and type in a city and state of publication, as well as a publication date.

12. Select the Orthogonal Line tool and draw a 2-point line between the two smaller text boxes. Your screen should resemble Figure 9.13.

Ctrl+M Item/Modify
Ctrl+B Item/Frame
Ctrl+G Item/Group
Ctrl+A Edit/Select All
Ctrl+Alt+M View/Show Measurements

Tip

To frame each window separately, first select each grouped item with the Content tool before applying the Frame command (Ctrl+B).

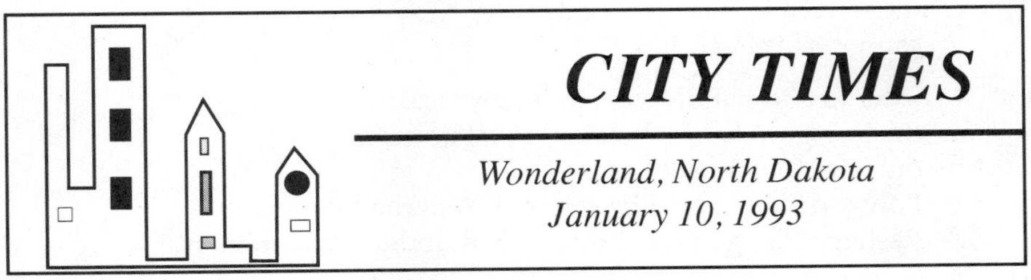

CITY TIMES

Wonderland, North Dakota
January 10, 1993

Figure 9.13—The finished masthead includes a polygon picture box without a picture.

REVIEW QUESTIONS

Read the following questions and choose the answer which best completes the statement.

1. The Origin Across value refers to _____.
   a. the upper left corner of a box
   b. the lower right corner of a box
   c. a picture's distance from the left corner of the picture box
   d. a picture's distance from the right corner of the picture box

2. The Corner Radius can be changed _____.
    a. on a text box
    b. on a polygon picture box
    c. on a frame
    d. on a rectangle or round-cornered picture box

3. The Scale fields in the Picture Box Specifications dialog box _____.
    a. refer to the picture box
    b. refer to the outside text box
    c. use values based on the size of the picture box
    d. are applied to a picture

4. The Offset values in the Measurements palette for picture boxes _____.
    a. reflect a picture's distance from the edges of the picture box
    b. are not reflected in the Picture Box Specifications dialog box
    c. reflect the picture box's distance from the page margins
    d. reflect the picture's distance from the page margins

5. Clicking on the Suppress Picture Printout button in the Picture Box Specifications dialog box _____.
    a. leaves the picture visible on the screen
    b. does not print the picture
    c. does not print the picture box's background
    d. a and b

6. The shape of a picture box can be changed from the _____.
    a. Picture Box Specifications dialog box
    b. Item menu
    c. Style menu
    d. Measurements palette

7. A polygon picture box _____.
    a. can have any shape
    b. is created with the Round-Cornered Picture Box tool
    c. must have at least three sides
    d. cannot be framed

8. In order to add handles to a polygon picture box, _____.
    a. the Polygon Picture Box tool must be active
    b. the Item tool must be active
    c. Polygon Shape must be selected from the Item menu
    d. Reshape Polygon must be checked under the Item menu

9. The Handle Creation Pointer is displayed when you _____.
    a. create the polygon
    b. close the polygon
    c. resize the polygon
    d. delete a polygon's handle

10. When Reshape Polygon is not checked, _____.
    a. the polygon cannot be resized
    b. the polygon can be resized using the bounding box handles
    c. the polygon can be reshaped but not resized
    d. the Item tool must be used to resize the polygon

Answers: 1. a; 2. d; 3. d; 4. a; 5. d; 6. b; 7. c; 8. d; 9. b; 10. b

OVERVIEW

In this lesson you will learn how to format text by applying different typefaces, type styles, and color to text. You will also learn how to create columns using different tab alignment icons. The commands available from the Paragraph Formats dialog box will also be touched on. Finally, you will learn how to align text vertically within a text box. All of this material will be reinforced by creating a menu incorporating text formatting, tabs, text inset, and alignment commands.

TOPICS

Formatting text
Applying color to text
Setting tabs
Clearing tabs
Paragraph formats
Paragraph indents
Leading values
Space Before and Space After
Keep With Next ¶ (Paragraph)
Keep Lines Together
Paragraph alignment

Hyphenation and justification
Lock to Baseline Grid
Drop caps
Text inset
Establishing leading
Setting paragraph alignment
Vertical alignment
Font handling in QuarkXPress for
    Windows
Review Exercise
Review Questions

TERMS

alignment
baseline
copy
drop cap
Fill Character
First Line indent
leading
Left indent
paste

Right indent
shade
tab stop
text inset
type size
type style
vertical alignment
widow

What you will need

A text file

Ctrl+N File/New
Ctrl+Y Edit/Preferences/
    General
Ctrl+E File/Get Text
Ctrl+X Edit/Cut
Ctrl+V Edit/Paste
Ctrl+Alt+M View/Show
    Measurements

Clickity click...

To select one word, double-click on the word. To select a line of text, triple-click anywhere in the line; to select a paragraph, quadruple-click anywhere in the paragraph; to select an entire story, click five times anywhere in the story.

FORMATTING TEXT

Once text has either been imported into or created in XPress, it is cut, copied, and pasted just as it would be in most word processors. Remember: Before text can be manipulated in any way, it must first be selected (highlighted).

EXERCISE A

1. Create a new document (Ctrl+N) without facing pages, with an automatic text box, and with 1 column. Then choose Edit/Preferences/ General (Ctrl+Y) and select picas as the unit of measure and Auto Page Insertion set to End of Document.

2. Choose File/Get (Ctrl+E) text and import any text file. Once it has been placed, quadruple-click (click four times) on the first paragraph to select it and choose Edit/Cut (Ctrl+X). Although it is no longer on the page, it is still on the Clipboard and available for pasting.

3. Press Enter after the third paragraph and choose Edit/Paste (Ctrl+V) to paste the first paragraph you cut after the third paragraph.

4. Select the second paragraph either by dragging the cursor from the first to the last word in the paragraph or by quadruple-clicking on it. Choose Edit/Delete. This removes the selected text from the page but does not save it to the Clipboard. Click after the first paragraph to place the Insertion Bar there and choose Edit/Paste (Ctrl+V). If you cut or copied text before you cleared this paragraph and that item was still on the Clipboard, that item would be pasted, not the paragraph you just cleared. To keep removed text in memory, use either the Cut or Copy commands. To both cut text and remove it from the Clipboard, use the Edit/Delete command.

Aside from the commands for moving and deleting text available under the Edit menu, XPress also allows you to perform sophisticated formatting functions from both the Style menu (Figure 10.1) and the Measurements palette (Ctrl+Alt+M).

To apply these formats to text, first select (highlight) the text, then pull down the Style menu and use the pop-up menus to apply the desired character formatting.

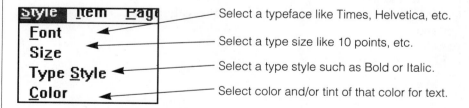

Select a typeface like Times, Helvetica, etc.

Select a type size like 10 points, etc.

Select a type style such as Bold or Italic.

Select color and/or tint of that color for text.

Figure 10.1—The Style menu for text is available whenever a text box is selected.

EXERCISE B

1. Use the Document Layout Palette in the document you just created to add another page to your document (Document/Insert/M1-Master 1). Then choose Document/Show Master Pages and double-click on the M1-Master 1 icon to get to the master page. Use the Text Box tool to draw a text box 39 picas wide and 2 picas high.

2. Use the Item tool to position this text box below the top margin guide on the left hand master page. Notice that as soon as you draw a text box, the Content tool is automatically selected and you can now begin to type.

3. Type "Chapter One" (no quotes). Then select both words by either dragging across them or choosing Edit/Select All (Ctrl+A). Use the Style menu to select Font and slide the cursor over and down to select Times New Roman. With the words still selected, choose Style/ Size/12 pt. You could also choose Style/Size/Other (Ctrl+Shift+\). This will bring up the Font Size dialog box where you can type a font size in the highlighted field before clicking on OK.

4. Once again with the text selected, choose Style/Type Style and select Bold (Ctrl+Shift+B). Then choose Type/Style again and select Italic (Ctrl+Shift+I). Select Style/Type Style once more and choose ALL CAPS (Ctrl+Shift+K) from the drop-down menu.

5. Duplicate that text box (Ctrl+D) and drag it to the same position on the right hand master page. Select all the text by choosing Edit/Select All (Ctrl+A). Type "My Travels in Burma." Choose Style/Alignment to select Right. Then choose Masters/Show Document Pages and double-click on the page 1 icon to get to that document page.

6. With the Insertion Point placed in the large (automatic) text box, choose File/Get Text (Ctrl+E) to import a text file into the document. Quadruple-click on the first paragraph to select it and choose Style/Font/Helvetica. Choose Style/Size/10 pt. Then select just the first word of that first paragraph and choose Style/Type Style/ALL CAPS (Ctrl+Shift+H). Choose Style/Type Style/Bold (Ctrl+Shift+B).

7. Double-click on the last word in the first paragraph to select it and choose Style/Type Style/Small Caps. (Ctrl+Shift+H). Then select two other words in the paragraph and choose Style/Type Style/Word Underline (Ctrl+Shift+W). Your screen should resemble Figure 10.2.

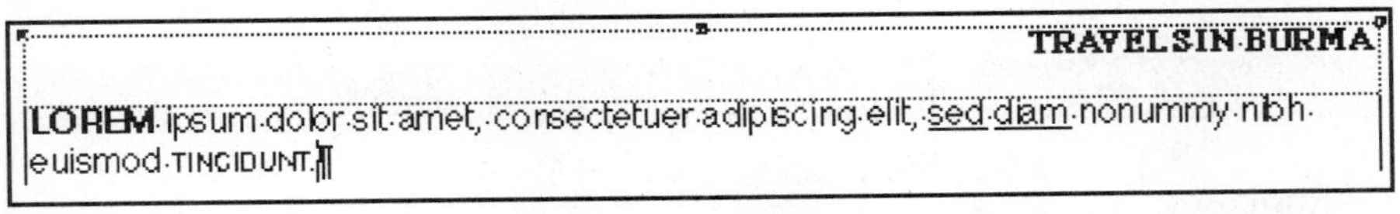

Figure 10.2—The right hand page displays the master page item at the top and the formatted text in the automatic text box below.

What you will need

A text file

Ctrl+A Edit/Select All
Ctrl+Shift+\
    Style/Font/Other Size
Ctrl+Shift+B Style/Type
    Style/Bold
Ctrl+Shift+I Style/Type
    Style/Italic
Ctrl+D Item/Duplicate
Ctrl+E File/Get Text
Ctrl+Shift+K Style/Type
    Style/All Caps
Ctrl+Shift+H Type/Type
    Style/Small Caps

Tip

It's a good idea to use Select All (Ctrl+A) whenever you are selecting all the contents of a text box, even if it's just one letter.

APPLYING COLOR TO TEXT

Applying color to text in XPress is simply a matter of selecting the text and choosing Style/Color (Figure 10.3). Use the drop-down menu to select a color or choose Edit/Colors and create another color using the Color Wheel, as you did in the last lesson.

Select Style/Shade to apply a shade or tint (a percentage of the selected color) to selected text. Remember that if you assign certain colors and/or light tints of those colors, they will print as lighter shades of gray on a black and white printer like the LaserJet, but will print in the correct tints on a color printer or on the color separation plates.

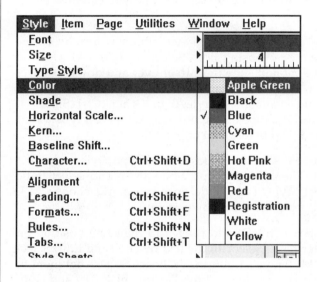

Figure 10.3—The drop-down Color menu allows you to apply a color to selected text. The colors Apple Green and Hot Pink were added by accessing the Color Wheel from the Style/Colors menu.

SETTING TABS

A tab stop is just that—a stop. In XPress tabs default to every half inch. Each time you press the Tab key, the Insertion Bar moves to the next tab stop. XPress sets tab stops every half inch, but you can override these default settings.

To set custom tabs, select the paragraph(s) to which you want to apply the tabs and choose Style/Tabs (Ctrl+Shift+T). This displays the Paragraph Tabs dialog box (Figure 10.4), where you set any of six kinds of tab stops: a left tab aligns text to the left; a right tab aligns text to the right; a center tab centers the text at the tab stop; decimal tabs center numerical text at the decimal point; the Align On tab stop aligns tabs on any character you type in the Align On field. The Right Align tab is discussed below.

Figure 10.4—Displays the Paragraph Tabs dialog box. Use the Alignment drop-down menu to select a tab alignment. Then click in the appropriate spot on the ruler *at the bottom of the Paragraph Tabs dialog box* where you are applying the tabs. Click on the Apply button or on OK to set each tab.

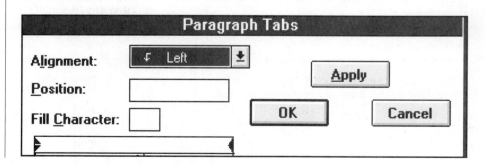

EXERCISE C

Ctrl+I View/Show Invisibles
Ctrl+A Edit/Select All
Ctrl+Shift+T Style/Tabs

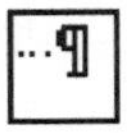

1. Use the Page/Insert command to add another page to your document. Then use the Text Box tool to draw a text box 30 picas wide and 10 picas high.

2. Choose View/Show Invisibles (Ctrl+I) to display the non-printing characters embedded in the text.

3. Type the following material in that text box, pressing only the Tab key and the Enter key between items, not the Spacebar. Choose Edit/Select All (Ctrl+A) and use the Style menu to make the text 12-point Helvetica.

Product (Tab) Catalog Item (Tab) Price (Tab) Shipped (Enter)
Telephone (Tab) Yes (Tab) $72.99 (Tab) 10/02/93 (Enter)
Lamp (Tab) No (Tab) $15.99 (Tab) 9/19/93 (Enter)
Chair (Tab) Yes (Tab) $39.95 (Tab) 11/18/93 (Enter)

4. With the Invisibles displayed, take a look at the symbols for certain formatting keystrokes like pressing the Tab and Enter keys. Notice the arrows which appear between the items where you pressed the Tab key and the paragraph marker symbol at the end of each line where you pressed the Enter key.

5. With the text still selected, choose Style/Tabs (Ctrl+Shift+T). When you invoke the Tabs command, a ruler appears at the bottom on the Paragraph Tabs dialog box (Figure 10.5).

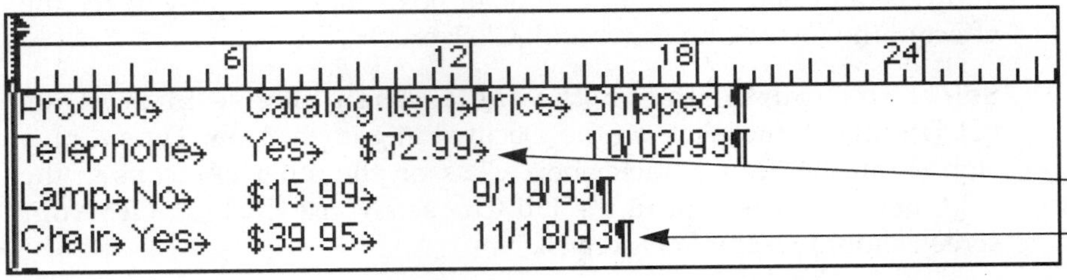

The paragraph marker is displayed when View/Show Invisibles is checked. The dots before the paragraph marker are the invisibles displayed each time the Spacebar is pressed.

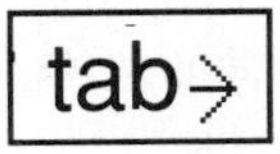

The little arrow indicates that the Tab key was pressed.

Figure 10.5—Use the ruler that appears in the Paragraph Tabs dialog box when you invoke the Tabs command to position tab alignment icons. This ruler displays picas as the unit of measure.

Indicates that the Tab key was pressed at this point and the Enter key was pressed at this point.

In Version 3.1 two additional tab options are available. The first is the Right Indent Tab. If you hold down the Shift key while pressing the Tab key, the line will tab flush right with the right indent. The second Tab stop is the Align on Tab. When you select Align On from the drop-down menu in the Paragraph Tabs dialog box, you can align the tab stop on any character. Type any character in the highlighted field (it defaults to a period) and type a value in the Position window. Then click on Apply or on OK. This function allows you, for example, to set a tab stop under a dollar sign or under a parenthesis.

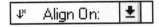

The Align On tab option allows you to align the tab stop on any character.

Ctrl+I View/Show Invisibles
Ctrl+Shift+T Style/Tabs
Ctrl+Shift+B Style/Type
Style/Bold

Tip

Because tabs are paragraph-based, you don't need to select the whole paragraph when applying tabs. Just click anywhere in the paragraph before choosing Style/Tabs.

FYI

Use the black arrows on either side of the ruler in the Paragraph Tabs dialog box to scroll through the ruler. You may not be able to see all of the tab icons, especially a right aligned tab icon, unless you scroll through the ruler.

EXERCISE D

1. Drag to select the four lines you just typed. Make sure that View/Show Invisibles (Ctrl+I) is displayed and choose Style/Tabs (Ctrl+Shift+T). When the Paragraph Tabs dialog box appears, select Center from the Alignment field.

2. Click in the Position box and type 10p to set the tab at the 10-pica mark. Click on the Apply button to set the tab stop. This places a Center aligned tab at the 10-pica mark on the ruler and centers the entire Catalog Item column at the 10-pica position.

3. With the four lines still selected and the Paragraph Tabs dialog box still displayed (if you clicked on OK after setting the center tab, select the four lines again and choose Style/Tabs again), click on the Decimal tab icon in the Alignment field and type 19p7 in the Position box. Click on Apply.

4. Click on the Right alignment icon and type 29p in the Position box. Click on Apply to set the tab stop. Click on OK. Drag or triple click on the first line to select it and choose Style/Type Style Bold (Ctrl+Shift+B). Your screen should resemble Figure 10.6.

5. To add a fill character between tabs (also called a tab leader), first click in the second line of the table, or drag across the second line). Choose Style/Tabs (Ctrl+Shift+T) and when the Paragraph Tabs dialog box appears, click once on the Center align tab icon in the ruler at the bottom of the dialog box. Then click in the Fill Character box to select it and type a period in the Fill Character box. Click on Apply to see the effect of the formatting command. Click on OK.

6. Select the fourth line in the table. Then choose Style/Tabs (Ctrl+Shift+T) and click on the Decimal alignment icon. Type a plus sign (+) in the Fill Character box. Click on the other tab icons in the ruler and type a + sign in the Fill Character box. Click on OK. Your screen should resemble Figure 10.7.

Product	Catalog Item	Price	Shipped
Telephone	Yes	$72.99	10/02/93
Lamp	No	$15.99	9/19/93
Chair	Yes	$39.95	11/18/93

Figure 10.6—A four-column table created with three different tab alignments.

Product	Catalog Item	Price	Shipped
Telephone ....Yes		$72.99	10/02/93
Lamp	No	$15.99	9/19/93
Chair +++++++++++Yes +++++++++++$39.95++++11/18/93			

Figure 10.7—A table created displaying a period (.) as the fill character in the second line and a plus sign (+) as the fill character in the fourth line.

To remove a Fill Character, highlight the line(s) with the Fill Character. Choose Style/Tabs (Ctrl+Shift+T). In the ruler in the Paragraph Tabs dialog box, click on the tab icon which contains the Fill Character. This displays and highlights a character in the Fill Character field. Press the Backspace key to delete it.

Ctrl+Shift+T Style/Tabs

CLEARING TABS

To delete all the tab stops in a single paragraph or in several paragraphs simultaneously, select the paragraph(s), choose Style/Tabs (Ctrl+Shift+T), and hold down the Ctrl key while you click on the ruler displayed at the bottom of the dialog box.

PARAGRAPH FORMATS

The Paragraph Formats dialog box (Figure 10.8) controls many of the text settings in XPress. In Lesson 11 you will learn how to create style sheets, a combination of many formatting commands assigned to one keystroke. Since styles are applied on a paragraph basis, familiarity with the Paragraph Formats dialog box is important.

When working with paragraphs, remember that a paragraph is selected when the cursor (Insertion Bar) is blinking anywhere in that paragraph. To be selected, words must be highlighted, but paragraphs do not have to be highlighted.

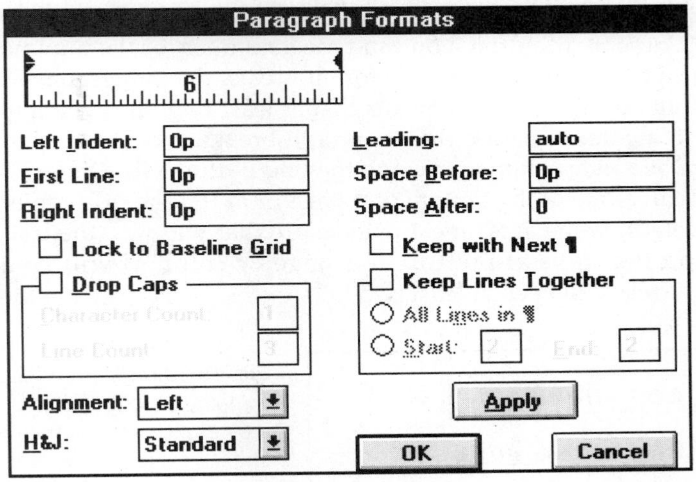

Design Tip

Select an entire story (click five times) and assign it a First Line value so that every paragraph will automatically be indented the same amount of space. This consistency will make your document more visually appealing. It also saves you the trouble of pressing the Tab key to indent every paragraph.

Figure 10.8—The Paragraph Formats dialog box controls many of the text settings, including the tab settings as set in the Paragraph Tabs dialog box for the selected paragraph.

Another Tip

When creating documents with many paragraphs that are not indented, first select all the paragraphs. Then choose Style/Formats and apply a Space After value. This will put the same amount of space between each paragraph in the document.

PARAGRAPH INDENTS

The Left Indent field allows you to type a value for the left indent or the distance of the text in a paragraph from the left edge of the text box. The Right Indent field allows you to set the distance of the text from the right edge of the text box. The First Line field allows you to set the indent of the first line in the paragraph. For example, instead of pressing the Tab key to indent the paragraph, you could assign each paragraph a First Line indent value and every paragraph would be consistently indented at that point.

LEADING VALUES

Typing a value in the Leading field will apply that leading to a selected paragraph. This allows you to change the leading (white space between lines of type) in one (or selected) paragraphs without affecting the rest of the document.

SPACE BEFORE AND SPACE AFTER

The Space Before and Space After fields allow you to add blank space before and after a paragraph. For example, applying a Space After value of 3p will place 3 picas or ½ inch of space after the paragraph.

KEEP WITH NEXT ¶ (PARAGRAPH)

Clicking in this check box tells XPress to keep the selected paragraph on the same page or in the same column with the next paragraph. This is a nifty feature when you want to keep heads and subheads or heads and body copy together.

KEEP LINES TOGETHER

The Keep Lines Together command tells XPress to keep a certain number of lines in a paragraph together on a page or in the same column. When you click on the Keep Lines Together check box, the Paragraph Formats dialog box expands (Figure 10.9). The default value is to keep all the lines in a paragraph together on a page or in a column.

If you click the Start button, you can type a number for the minimum number of lines that XPress requires before it breaks the paragraph. The dialog box defaults to 2 (lines). This means that at least two lines will appear on a page or in a column before the paragraph breaks and moves the text to a new page or a new column. Clicking the End button tells XPress how many lines can fall alone at the bottom of a page or at the top of a column. Leaving the default value at 2 (lines) will ensure that widows (the last line of a paragraph that falls at the top of a page or column) will be avoided, because XPress will keep at least two lines of the paragraph together.

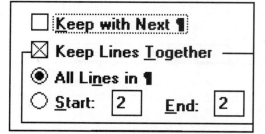

Figure 10.9—When Keep Lines Together is checked, you can indicate the minimum number of lines in a paragraph that must be kept together at the start of the paragraph (Start) and the minimum number of lines in that paragraph which can begin a new page or new column (End).

PARAGRAPH ALIGNMENT

The Alignment drop-down menu allows you to select horizontal alignment for a paragraph—either Left aligned, Right aligned, Centered, or Justified. These are the same alignment options available with the Alignment icons in the Measurements palette.

HYPHENATION AND JUSTIFICATION

H&J refers to Hyphenation (of words) and Justification (of text). You will learn more about setting H&J values in Lesson 12. The H&J styles that you set can be accessed from the H&J drop-down menu in the Paragraph Formats dialog box.

LOCK TO BASELINE GRID

The baseline is an invisible line on which a line of text sits. The distance between baselines is determined by the Increment value set in the Baseline Grid field in the Typographic Preferences dialog box (Figure 10.10). You will learn how to set the Baseline Grid in Lesson 12.

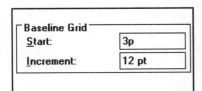

Figure 10.10—The Baseline Grid fields in the Typographic Preferences dialog box is where you determine the first baseline's distance from the *top of the page*—not from the top of the text box (Start)—and the increments between baselines (Increment).

DROP CAPS

This paragraph displays a drop cap—an initial cap that drops below the first baseline in a paragraph and occupies more than one line of vertical space in a paragraph. Drop caps are also covered later in Lesson 12. Clicking on the Drop Cap check box in the Paragraph Formats dialog box displays another dialog box where you can indicate the number of letters to be dropped, as well as the number of lines they should be dropped. In this paragraph, one character is dropped three lines.

TEXT INSET

Every text box defaults to a 1-point inset for text. This means that the left margin of text in that text box is 1 point from the left side of the text box. You can change this default for the entire text box by using either the Text Box Specifications dialog box (Figure 10.11) or by making the change on a paragraph level using the Indent fields in the Paragraph Formats dialog box (Figure 10.8).

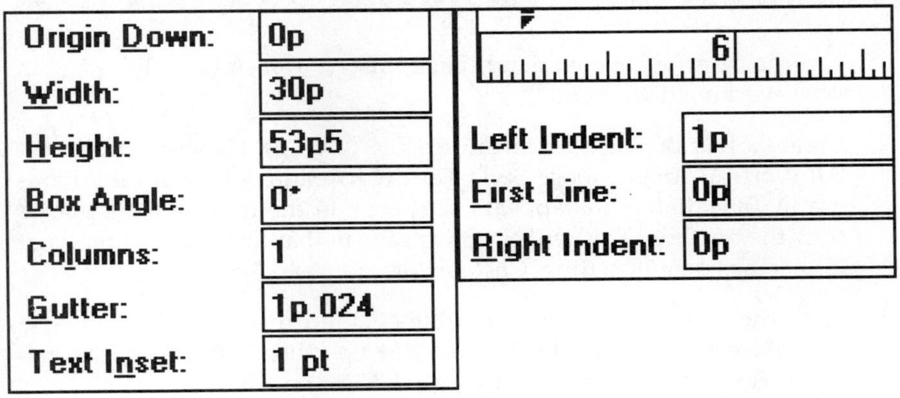

Origin Down:	0p
Width:	30p
Height:	53p5
Box Angle:	0°
Columns:	1
Gutter:	1p.024
Text Inset:	1 pt

	6
Left Indent:	1p
First Line:	0p
Right Indent:	0p

Sorry!

You cannot apply a drop cap to a paragraph that begins with a tab stop.

Figure 10.11—The Text Inset field in the Text Box Specifications dialog box (left) defaults to 1 point. Change this to 0 [zero] when setting a value in the Left Indent field of the Paragraph Formats dialog box, because the Left Indent value does not override the Text Inset value. Rather, it *adds* the Text Inset value to the Left Indent value.

What you will need

A text file

Ctrl+I View/Show Invisibles
Ctrl+M Item/Modify
Ctrl+Shift+F Style/Formats
Ctrl+A Edit/Select All
Ctrl+Shift+T Style/Tabs
Ctrl+E File/Get Text

WARNING!

Text Inset values affect the distance between text and all *four sides* of the text box.

EXERCISE E

1. Insert a new page in your document (Page/Insert) and create a text box about 20 picas wide and 10 picas high. Type a few lines of text, then press the Enter key. Choose View/Show Invisibles (Ctrl+I) and notice the paragraph marker after the last word in the paragraph.

2. With the text box still active (selected), choose Item/Modify (Ctrl+M). Double-click in the Text Inset box in the lower right corner and type 0 [zero]. It's a good idea to do this whenever you're going to change a paragraph's left indent, because any changes you make in the Left Indent field do not override the text inset value, which defaults to 1 point. If you want to indent a paragraph 6 points from the left side of the text box, you must either type 5 in the Left Indent field of the Paragraph Formats box (5 points + the 1 point default text inset = 6 points) or change the Text Inset field in the Text Box Specifications dialog box to 0 [zero] and specify 6 points in the Left Indent field.

3. Choose Style/Formats (Ctrl+Shift+F) and type 0p6 (6 points) in the Left Indent field. Press Tab twice and type 0p6 in the Right Indent field. Click on Apply. This will move the text 6 points from the left side of the text box and 6 points from the right side of the text box. Click on OK.

4. With the text box still active, click to place the Insertion Bar at the beginning of the paragraph. Press the Tab key and notice that the first line indents ½ inch, the default setting. Choose Style/Formats (Ctrl+Shift+F) and double-click in the First Line field to select the 0 [zero] and type 1p (1 pica). Click on OK and then delete the tab marker. Notice how the tab space moved to the left and is located 1 pica from the left margin.

5. Type another line under the last line of the original paragraph and notice how, without pressing the Tab key, the first line automatically indented 1 pica. Press Enter to end that paragraph.

EXERCISE F

1. Use the Insert Page command (Page/Insert) to insert another page in your working document.

2. Create a text box and import a text file (Ctrl+E). Choose Edit/Select All (Ctrl+A), then choose Style Tabs (Ctrl+Shift+T). When the Paragraph Tabs dialog box appears, Ctrl-click in the ruler which appears over the text box. This will clear any tabs in that text box and return it to the Tabs default setting. Click on OK.

3. With the Item tool selected, double-click on the text box or choose Item/Modify (Ctrl+M). In the Text Box Specifications dialog box, tab to the Text Inset field and type 0 [zero]. Click on OK.

4. Place the Insertion Bar anywhere in the first paragraph and choose Style/Formats (Ctrl+Shift+F). Type 2p in the Left Indent field; 2p in the Right Indent field; and 0p6 in the First Line field to indent the first line 6 points from the newly defined left margin. Click on Apply to view the formatting changes. Click on OK. Your screen should resemble Figure 10.12.

5. With the same text box selected, choose Edit/Select All (Ctrl+A). Choose Style/Formats (Ctrl+Shift+F) and change the Right Indent and Left Indent to p8 (8 points). Change the First Line Indent to 0p63 (3 points). Click on OK. Your screen should resemble Figure 10.13.

Ctrl+Shift+F Style/Formats
Ctrl+A Edit/Select All
Ctrl+Shift+T Style/Tabs
Ctrl+Alt+M View/Show
Measurements

> Create a text box and import a text file. Choose Edit/Select All then choose Style Tabs. When the Paragraph Tabs dialog box appears, Ctrl-click in the ruler which appears over the text box. This will clear any tabs in that text box and return it to the Tabs default setting. Click on OK.

Figure 10.12—A text box with a Right and Left indent of 2 picas and a First Line indent of 6 points.

> Create a text box and import a text file. Choose Edit/Select All then choose Style Tabs. When the Paragraph Tabs dialog box appears, Ctrl-click in the ruler which appears over the text box. This will clear any tabs in that text box and return it to the Tabs default setting. Click on OK.

Figure 10.13—A text box with a Right and Left indent of 8 picas and a First Line indent of 3 points.

EXERCISE G

1. Insert a new page in your working document (Page/Insert). Make sure Invisibles are displayed (Ctrl+I). Draw a text box 30 picas wide and 10 picas high. Type the following text, pressing the Tab key between the first and second items, between the second and third items, between the third and fourth items, and the Enter key after the fourth item, the date, as displayed in Figure 10.14.

Name→	Amount·Due→	Paid→	Date·Submitted¶
Sarah→	12.15→	Yes→	January,·1990¶
Mike→	115.18→	No→	March,·1991¶
Jack→	1.10→	No→	November,·1992¶
Kate→	2,690.12→	Yes→	February,·1993¶

Figure 10.14—Use different alignment tabs to create columns in tables.

Ctrl+Shift+T Style/Tabs
Ctrl+Shift+B Style/Type
Style/Bold
Ctrl+Shift+W Style/Type
Style/Word Underline

Tip

Press Ctrl+Shift+: (colon) to change "auto" to the absolute value it represents.

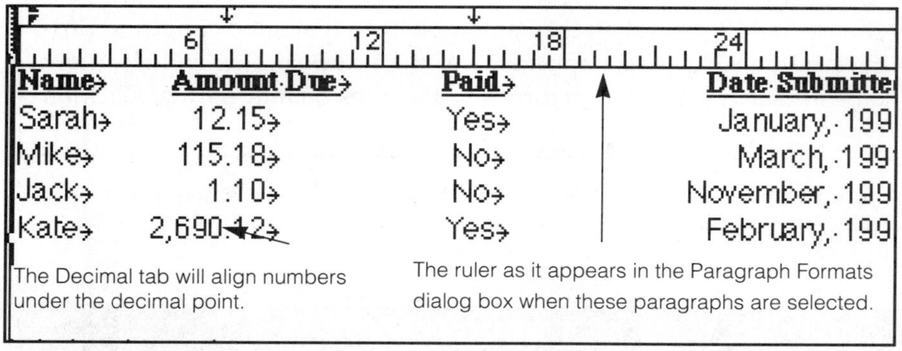

2. Choose Edit/Select All (Ctrl+A) to select all five lines in the text box and use the Measurements palette (Ctrl+Alt+M) to format the text in 12-point Helvetica. Then choose Style/Tabs (Ctrl+Shift+T). In the Paragraph Tabs dialog box, click first on the Decimal alignment icon, then type 6p10 in the Position box and click on Apply to set the tab stop at the 6 picas/10 points mark. Then click on the Center alignment icon and type 15p in the Position box; click on Apply. Finally, click on the Right alignment icon and type 29p5 in the Position box and click on Apply. View the formatting and click on OK.

3. Triple-click or drag to select the first line (the headings) and choose Style/Tabs (Ctrl+Shift+T). In the Paragraph Tabs dialog box, Shift-click on the ruler in the Paragraph Tabs dialog box to clear all the tabs. Click on the Center align tab and type 7p10 in the Position box to center "Amount" over the rest of the decimal aligned column. Click on Apply. Click on OK.

4. With the first line of headings still selected, choose Style/Font/Times New Roman. Choose Style/Type Style and select Bold (Ctrl+Shift+B). Choose Style/Type Style again and then select Word Underline (Ctrl+Shift+W) to underline only the headings and not the space between them. Your screen should resemble Figure 10.15.

Figure 10.15—Use different alignment tabs to create columns in tables.

ESTABLISHING LEADING

Leading (rhymes with "heading") is the white space between lines of type. It is measured in points from the baseline of one line to the baseline of the line above it. XPress allows you to set (1) absolute leading, that is, a leading value that remains constant regardless of the type size or type face in a paragraph, and also (2) relative leading, which is based on a percentage of a type size. You can set leading values from both the Paragraph Formats dialog box and from the Measurements palette.

EXERCISE H

1. Create a new document (File/New) with an automatic text box. Use the General Preferences dialog box (Ctrl+Y) to select picas as the unit of measure. Import a text file (Ctrl+E) and select all the text (Ctrl+A).

2. Use the Measurements palette to change its font to Helvetica and its size to 12 point. Leave the leading arrows set at auto.

3. Choose Edit/Preferences/Typographic (Ctrl+Alt+Y) and notice that the Auto Leading field on the right is set to 20%. XPress defaults to leading that is 20% of any type size used in the document. This means that your 12-point Helvetica is set on 2.4 points of leading or 12/14.4. Click on OK.

4. Now select that text again (Ctrl+A) and double-click on Auto in the Leading field of the Measurements palette. Type 14.4. Press the Enter key. There is no change in the leading. Select the 14.4, change it to 20, and press the Enter key. Your screen should resemble Figure 10.16.

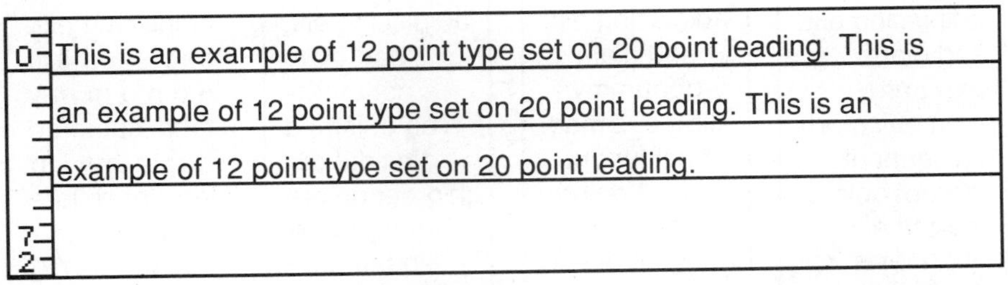

0	This is an example of 12 point type set on 20 point leading. This is
	an example of 12 point type set on 20 point leading. This is an
	example of 12 point type set on 20 point leading.
7 2	

Figure 10.16—The vertical ruler displays points as the unit of measure and indicates that there are 20 points of white space between each baseline of the three lines of text. The ruler on the left displays points as the unit of measure.

Figure 10.16 displays the document's vertical ruler, which is set to points as the unit of measure. The distance between the baseline of the second line up to the baseline of the first line is 20 points.

You adjust the leading in XPress in one of three ways. (1) Choose Style/Leading (Ctrl+Shift+E) and type a value in the Leading dialog box. (2) Type a value in the Leading field of the Measurements palette. You can also use the up and down leading arrows to increase and decrease leading, provided "auto" has been replaced with a number. (3) Set the leading value in the Leading field of the Paragraph Formats dialog box or choose (Ctrl+Shift+F) to access the Leading field.

SETTING PARAGRAPH ALIGNMENT

Alignment determines where the text lines up relative to the four sides of the text box. If you have specified a left indent and/or a right indent, the text alignment is relative to the indent specification. You can use the Alignment icons in the Measurements palette to change the alignment of selected text, or you can choose Style/Alignment and choose from Left, Centered, Right, and Justified alignment from the pop-up menu. Alignment is paragraph-specific, so be sure to either select the text you want to align or simply place the cursor in the paragraph itself.

✓ **Left**	Ctrl+S
Centered	Ctrl+S
Right	Ctrl+S
Justified	Ctrl+S

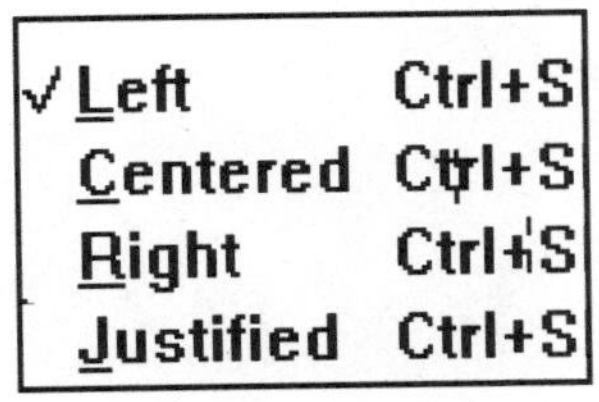

The Alignment drop-down menu under Style is available when the Content tool is selected. Use the keyboard shortcuts to quickly align any paragraph. Remember: Because this is a paragraph command, you don't have to select the entire paragraph. Just click anywhere inside the paragraph before applying the formatting command.

Ctrl+Shift+L Style/
    Alignment/Left
Ctrl+Shift+C Style/
    Alignment/Centered
Ctrl+Shift+R Style/
    Alignment/Right
Ctrl+Shift+J Style/
    Alignment/Justified

EXERCISE I

1. In your working document, draw a text box about 30 picas wide and type a paragraph in it. Place the cursor somewhere in the paragraph and click on the Left Alignment icon in the Measurements palette. The text is flush left to the left side of the text box.

2. Now click on the Centered Alignment icon in the Measurements palette. Notice how each line is centered in the middle of the text box.

3. Click on the Right Alignment icon and notice how the text is aligned to the right side of the text box. Click on the Justified icon and the text begins at the left side of the text box and wraps exactly at the right side of the text box (Figure 10.17).

Lorem ipsum dolor sit amet, consectetuer adipiscing elit, sed diam nonummy nibh euismod tincidunt ut laoreet dolore magna ali- quam erat volutpat. Ut wisi enim ad	Lorem ipsum dolor sit amet, consectetuer adipiscing elit, sed diam nonummy nibh euismod tincidunt ut laoreet dolore magna ali- quam erat volutpat. Ut wisi enim ad	Lorem ipsum dolor sit amet, consectetuer adipiscing elit, sed diam nonummy nibh euismod tincidunt ut laoreet dolore magna ali- quam erat volutpat. Ut wisi enim ad	Lorem ipsum dolor sit amet, consectetuer adipiscing elit, sed diam nonummy nibh euismod tincidunt ut laoreet dolore magna ali- quam erat volutpat. Ut wisi enim ad

Figure 10.17—Each text box displays a different type of text alignment: left, centered, right, and justified. Each text box is given a Text Inset value of 6 points, which puts an invisible border 6 points wide around the *four* sides of the text box.

VERTICAL ALIGNMENT

The four types of alignment displayed in Figure 10.17 apply to *horizontal* alignment of text, text running from the left to the right margin of a text box. XPress also supports vertical alignment or the alignment of text from the top to the bottom of the text box. Text can be vertically aligned from the top, the bottom, and the center of the text box. It can also be justified within the text box (Figure 10.18). Like horizontal alignment, vertical alignment observes any spacing limitations imposed by text inset or paragraph indent values.

Text can be vertically aligned from the first baseline, which is placed either from the top of the ascenders on letters like *d* and *l*; from the height of the capital letter plus any additional space needed to accommodate a punctuation mark; or from the height of the capital letters in the first line. These choices are made in the First Baseline field of the Text Box Specifications dialog box, where you can set the value and choose the minimum value (Figure 10.19).

<table>
<tr>
<td>Lorem ipsum dolor sit amet, consectetuer adipiscing elit, sed diam non-ummy nibh euis-mod tincidunt ut laoreet dolore</td>
<td>Lorem ipsum dolor sit amet, consectetuer adipiscing elit, sed diam non-ummy nibh euismod tin-cidunt ut laoreet</td>
<td>Lorem ipsum dolor sit amet, consectetuer adipiscing elit, sed diam non-ummy nibh euismod tin-cidunt ut laoreet</td>
<td>Lorem ipsum dolor sit amet, consectetuer adipiscing elit, sed diam non-ummy nibh euismod tin-cidunt ut laoreet</td>
</tr>
</table>

Ctrl+M Item/Modify

Figure 10.18—Each text box displays a different type of vertical alignment: top, centered, bottom, and justified. Each text box is given a Text Inset value of 1 point.

EXERCISE J

1. Select the text box you created earlier and choose Item/Modify (Ctrl+M). When the Text Box Specifications dialog box appears, locate the Vertical Alignment field on the right (Figure 10.19). Pull down the Type menu and notice that Top is checked. This means that the text is aligned, or starts to flow, from the top of the text box. Click on OK.

2. Click in the same text box to select it and choose Item/Modify (Ctrl+M) again. Use the Vertical Alignment drop-down menu to select Centered and click on OK. The text is now vertically aligned from the center of the text box with equal amounts of space between the text and the top and bottom edges of the text box.

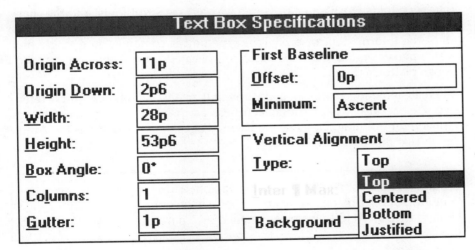

Figure 10.19—The Text Box Specifications dialog box defaults to vertical alignment from the top of the text box. The First Baseline is offset zero picas from the top of the ascenders (Ascent) in the first line of text in the text box.

FONT-HANDLING IN QUARKXPRESS FOR WINDOWS

One of the advantages of subscribing to technical support services is that you get on the mailing list for company literature, some of which provides information which is invaluable to making your use of the application more proficient and productive. The following material on font-handling in QuarkXPress for Windows is quoted from an article which appeared in *Expressions*, The Newsletter from Quark, Volume 4, Number 5, October, 1992. *Expressions* is produced by Quark Creative Services, Quark Inc., 1800 Grant St., Denver, Colorado.

POSTSCRIPT FONTS

A PostScript font for the PC is made up of a .PFB file which combines the screen and printer font files into one file, and a .PFM file which stores the "font metrics" for each font. With Windows 3.1, Adobe Type Manager assigns fonts to ports so that all printers connected to a single port have access to the font list. PostScript fonts and their path names are stored in the Windows startup file (WIN.INI), and when a document is sent to the printer, it downloads the fonts. You must use ATM Version 2.0 in order to run PostScript fonts in conjunction with Windows 3.1.

TRUETYPE FONTS

The PC supports TrueType fonts. TrueType is an electronic font format co-developed by Apple and Microsoft for use with Macintosh's System 7. Ironically, it is poised to find its best success on Windows.

TrueType fonts work much the same way as PostScript fonts, and the characters are scalable, so type is displayed smoothly at all sizes. Most notably, all of the information for each TrueType font is contained in a single file, which makes organizing fonts a less complicated process than on the Macintosh platform (Figure 10.20).

To create a menu, create a new document (Ctrl+N) and choose Edit/Preferences/General (Ctrl+Y) and select picas as the unit of measure. Choose Outside for Framing. Deselect the Facing Pages option as well as the Automatic Text Box option.

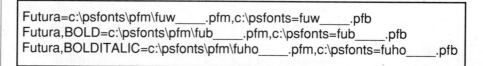

```
Futura=c:\psfonts\pfm\fuw____.pfm,c:\psfonts=fuw____.pfb
Futura,BOLD=c:\psfonts\pfm\fub____.pfm,c:\psfonts=fub____.pfb
Futura,BOLDITALIC=c:\psfonts\pfm\fuho____.pfm,c:\psfonts=fuho____.pfb
```

Figure 10.20—Windows' ATM.INI file lists each installed font in your system along with the paths to its .PFM and PFB font files.

REVIEW EXERCISE

1. Use the Text Box tool to draw a text box 30 picas wide and 45 picas high. This text box will eventually contain two other text boxes and a picture box. Choose Item/Frame (Ctrl+B) and type 2 in the Width field.

2. Draw another text box 30 picas wide and 43 picas high. With that text box still selected, choose Item/Modify (Ctrl+M) and on the right side of the Text Box Specifications dialog box, use the Color drop-down menu to choose None. This will make the text box transparent, so that the frame on the large text box will still be visible.

3. Use the Item tool to move this smaller text box inside the large one and place it directly under the top side of the large text box.

4. Use the Rectangle Picture Box tool to draw a picture box 2 picas wide and 7 picas high. Choose Item/Modify (Ctrl+M) and change its background color to None also. Place this box underneath the smaller text box.

5. Import a graphic into the picture box (Ctrl+E). Press Ctrl+Shift+F to fit it into the picture box.

6. Use the Text Box tool to draw another text box 30 picas wide and 35 picas high. Place this text box in the first text box you drew directly under the picture box.

7. Type in the menu items as they appear on the next page, being sure to press the Tab key after each item and its price and the Enter key after each of the headings. Feel free to change any of the items and/or the prices to reflect regional preferences.

8. Type "Gallagher's Grill" (no quotes) in the text box at the top of the large text box. Choose Edit/Select All (Ctrl+A) and use either the Style menu or the Measurements palette to format it in Helvetica, 36 point, Shadow.

9. Then choose Style/Alignment/Centered (Ctrl+Shift+C). With the text box still active, choose Item/Modify (Ctrl+M) and use the Vertical Alignment drop-down menu to choose Centered. Click on OK.

10. Select the headings and use either the Style menu or the Measurements palette to format them in Times New Roman, 18 point, Bold, Italic. Choose Style/Leading (Ctrl+Shift+E) and assign each heading 28 points of leading. Or click on "auto" in the Measurements palette and type in 28 after you have selected the text.

What you will need

A graphic file

Ctrl+N File/New
Ctrl+Y Edit/Preferences/ General
Ctrl+B Item/Frame
Ctrl+M Item/Modify
Ctrl+E File/Get Picture
Ctrl+A Edit/Select All
Ctrl+Shift+E Style/ Leading
Ctrl+Shift+C Style/ Alignment/ Centered

Big $ Tip

Once you get the hang of this menu, pick up menus from local restaurants and redo them for practice. If you like the way they come out, try and sell the mechanicals to the restaurants. Keep in mind that some menus may require that you create the file horizontally by choosing 11 x 8.5 in the New (document) dialog box and selecting Landscape Orientation from the Printer Setup dialog box.

Ctrl+Shift+I Style/Type
Style/Italic
Ctrl+Shift+T Style/Tabs
Ctrl+Shift+H Type/Type
Style/Small Caps
Ctrl+M Item/Modify

11. Select the six lines of sandwich listings and format them in Times New Roman, 12 point, Italic (Ctrl+Shift+I). Use the Leading field in the Measurements palette to assign them 15 points of leading. (Select "auto" and type 15, then press the Enter key.) With the six lines still selected, choose Style/Tabs (Ctrl+Shift+T) and in the Paragraph Tabs dialog box, click on the Right Alignment icon. Type 27p8 in the Position box and click on Apply. Click on OK. Repeat these steps to format the listings under "Side Dishes" and "Desserts."

12. Select the three lines under Beverages and choose Style/Tabs (Ctrl+Shift+T). Click on the Left Alignment icon and type 10p11 in the Position box. Click on Apply. Click on the Decimal Alignment icon and type 16p7 in the Position box. Click on Apply. Click on the Left Alignment icon and type 21p1 in the Position box. Click on Apply. Click on the Decimal Alignment icon and type 26p5 in the Position box. Click on Apply. Click on OK.

13. Triple-click to select the last line (Hours) in the text box and format it in Helvetica, 10 point Bold, Centered alignment with 25 points of leading. Select "am" and "pm" and choose Style/Type Style/Small Caps (Ctrl+Shift+H).

14. Then choose Item Modify (Ctrl+M) and use the Vertical Alignment drop-down menu to choose Justified. Click on OK. Your menu should resemble Figure 10.21.

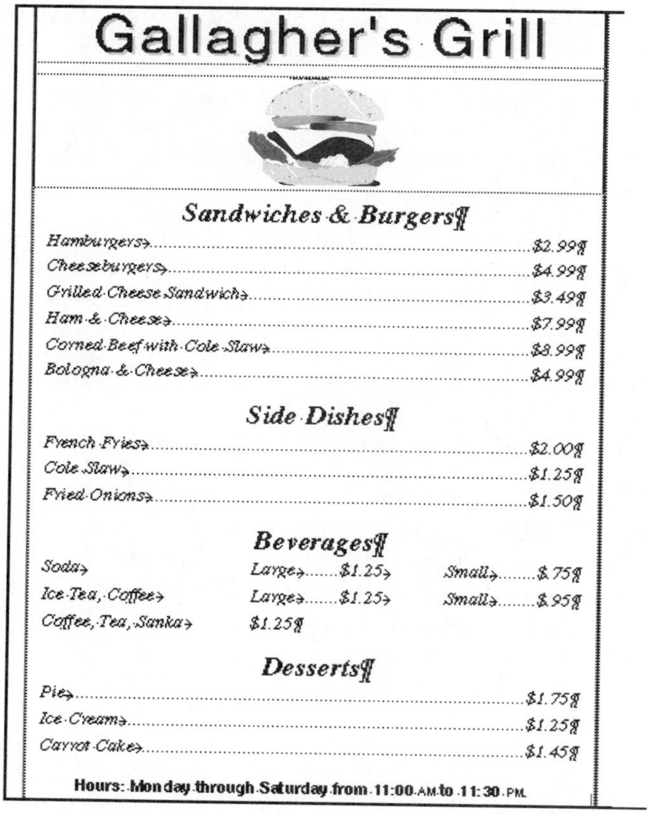

Figure 10.21—The finished menu.

REVIEW QUESTIONS

Read the following questions and choose the answer which best completes the statement.

1. Formatting text size, style, and leading are available from the _____.
   a. Style menu
   b. Text Box Specifications dialog box
   c. Measurements palette
   d. a and c

2. Before a tab stop can be applied, _____.
   a. text must be formatted
   b. text must be aligned
   c. text must be selected
   d. the rulers (Ctrl+R) must be visible

3. To set a tab in the document, click on _____.
   a. Apply in the Paragraph Formats dialog box
   b. OK in the Text Box Specifications dialog box
   c. the Position button in the Paragraph Tabs dialog box
   d. the vertical ruler

4. Invisibles are _____.
   a. accessed from the Style menu
   b. displayed in the Paragraph Formats dialog box
   c. non-printing characters
   d. little creatures who live in your document

5. Pressing Ctrl+Shift+F allows you to _____.
   a. access the Paragraph Formats dialog box
   b. make formatting selections which apply to an entire paragraph
   c. apply leading values and alignment commands
   d. all of the above

6. The "Keep Lines Together" command allows you to determine _____.
   a. a paragraph's distance from the page margins
   b. how many lines can appear at the end of the page or column
   c. how many lines must appear at the top of a page or column of text
   d. how many lines can appear on a page

7. The Vertical Alignment command _____.
   a. is available from the Style menu
   b. determines the placement of text relative to the baseline grid in a text box
   c. can be selected from the Measurements palette
   d. is an option in the Paragraph Formats dialog box

8. Text Inset refers to _____.
   a. the position of text relative to the left margin
   b. the distance between text and the inner edges of a text box
   c. the Left Indent and Right Indent values in the Paragraph Formats dialog box
   d. the First Line Indent value in the Paragraph Formats dialog box

9. Leading is measured from _____.
   a. one baseline to the top of the text box
   b. one baseline to the baseline below it
   c. one line to the next paragraph
   d. one paragraph to the next paragraph

10. (Horizontal) Justified alignment _____.
    a. places the same amount of space between text and the right and left indents of a text box
    b. places the same amount of space between text and the top of a text box
    c. reduces the indents to accommodate the text
    d. does not allow for first line indents

Answers: 1. d; 2. c; 3. a; 4. c; 5. d; 6. b; 7. b; 8. b; 9. a; 10. a

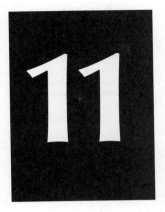

LESSON

11

Text Manipulation

OVERVIEW

In this lesson you will learn how to find and change text and text with specific attributes. You will also learn how to check the spelling of a word, a story, and an entire document, as well as how to create auxiliary dictionaries which contain words that you use frequently but are not found in the QuarkXPress dictionary. Finally, you will learn how to create and apply style sheets. As a review, you will import a text file, create style sheets for the document, and find and change text within the document. You will then create an auxiliary dictionary and spell check the document.

TOPICS

Finding and changing text
Finding and changing text with attributes
Spelling check
Creating an Auxiliary Dictionary
Editing an Auxiliary Dictionary
Creating style sheets
The Style Sheets palette
Applying No Style
Using style sheets
Appending style sheets
Review Exercise
Review Questions

TERMS

Auxiliary Dictionary
Find First
Find Next
Find/Change
Ignore Attributes
No Style
Style Sheets
Whole Word

Ctrl+F Edit/Find/Change
Ctrl+N File/New

Find First

Press the Alt key before clicking on the Find Next button to display Find First.

Tip

Press Ctrl+Alt+↑ to move quickly to the start of a story.

WARNING!

Find/Change begins searching at the insertion point (blinking cursor) and continues until it reaches the end of the story (linked chain of text boxes). Remember to click the cursor at the point in the story where you want to begin the search.

If you want to search the whole document, make sure that no text box is selected before selecting the Document option in the Find/Change dialog box. When Document is selected (and no text box is active), it doesn't make any difference where the insertion point is.

FINDING AND CHANGING TEXT

The word processor in XPress allows you to search for and change any character you type in the document. Choosing Edit/Find/Change (Ctrl+F) brings up the Find/Change dialog box (Figure 11.1).

Figure 11.1—The Find/Change dialog box.

Type the text you are searching for in the Find what field. Type the replacement text in the Change to field. If you want to search the entire document, then be sure that no text box is selected and click on the Document option to search and replace text throughout the entire document. Otherwise, XPress will search from the Insertion point to the end of the story.

Click on the Whole Word option to find a word preceded and followed by a space. For example, if you are searching for the word *break* and click on the Whole Word option, XPress will not flag words like *breakfast* and *breaking*. If you click on the Ignore Case option, XPress will find capitalized and uncapitalized versions of the word. If you leave Ignore Attributes selected, XPress will search for the text regardless of its typeface, size, and style. After typing in the original and/or replacement text, click on the Find Next button to begin the search.

When the master pages are selected, the Document option in the Find/Change dialog box changes to Masters. Click on this option to search only the master pages.

In Version 3.1, if you hold down the Alt key while clicking on the Find Next button, Find Next changes to Find First and allows you to find the first instance of that character(s) in the document.

EXERCISE A

1. Create a new document (File/New) with an automatic text box. Type the following sentences (no quotes): "Football is a sport that attracts many fans each season. It is a controversial sport which raises questions of promoting violence." Click to place the insertion bar before the word *Football*. This will begin the search from that point.

2. Choose Edit/Find/Change (Ctrl+F). Type "sport" in the Find what field. Type "gladiator sport" in the Change to field.

3. Click on the Whole Word option but leave the Document check box empty. Click on Find next. When the word *sport* is found and highlighted, click on the Change, then Find button. When the next occurrence of the word *sport* is found and highlighted, click on the

Find Next button (Figure 11.2). This will leave *sport* as is without changing it to *gladiator sport.*

4. Since there are only two occurrences of *sport* in this document, XPress beeps to let you know that it has finished its search and replace mission. Click on the Control Menu in the Find/Change window to return to the document.

5. Make sure that no text box is selected by clicking outside of the page. Choose Edit/Find/Change (Ctrl+F). Click in the Document check box to select it. Type "gladiator" in the Find what field. Leave the Change to field blank. Click on Find Next and when *gladiator* is found and highlighted, click on the Change All button. XPress will delete the one instance of *gladiator* and replace it with a space.

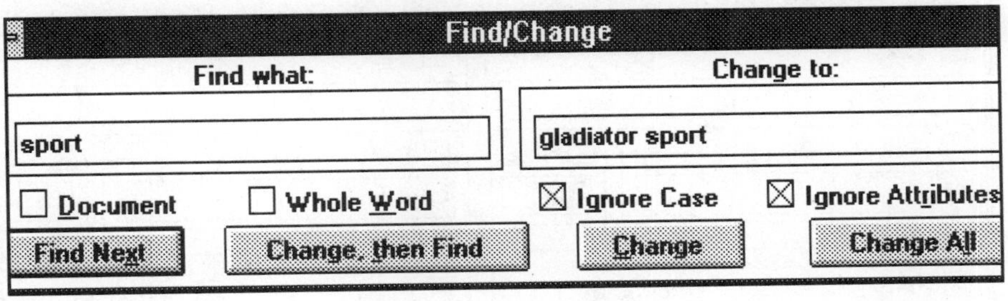

Figure 11.2—Click on the Find Next button to begin the search. If you hold down the Ctrl key when clicking on this button, Find Next becomes Find First and allows you to locate the first instance of the Find what text in the document.

FINDING AND CHANGING TEXT WITH ATTRIBUTES

You can also find text in a document based on its attributes—its typeface, size, and style.Then you can change those attributes globally in a document by clicking on the Change All button or change the text selectively by clicking on the Find Next or Change, then Find buttons.

EXERCISE B

1. Type the following sentence (no quotes): "The only thing we have to fear is fear itself." Use the Measurements palette to change the text to 10-point Arial.

2. Place the cursor at the beginning of the sentence and choose Edit/Find Change (Ctrl+F). When the Find/Change dialog box appears, click on the Ignore Attributes box to deselect it. This will display an expanded Find/Change dialog box (Figure 11.3).

3. Click on Text to activate the Find what text box. Type *thing* and make sure that the Font box is checked and displays Helvetica, the Size box is checked and displays 10 pt, and the Style box is checked and Plain is also checked.

Nothing but the word

If you select the Whole Word option in the Find/Change dialog box, XPress will find only instances of that word. If, for example, you are looking for the word *nation*, and you select Whole Word, XPress will ignore words like *national* and *destination.*

Play a wild card

To search for a word when you are not sure of its spelling, enter the wild card character in the Find what field by pressing Ctrl+? to display \? in the Find what field. For example, the Find what entry *ban\?s* would find both *banks* and *bands.*

FYI

Use the Find/Change dialog box to search for and replace many of the invisible, nonprinting characters, such as the Tab, Enter, and New Column characters by pressing the Ctrl key while pressing those keys in the Find what field. For example, to find a Tab key, press Ctrl+Tab in the Find what field. This displays \t and allows you to search for every tab in the story or document.

Make room for text

Click on the Control Menu of the expanded Find/ Change dialog box and select Condense. This will display only the selection buttons and allow you to see more of the text being checked.

4. Click on Text in the Change to area to activate the text box. Type "thing." Check the Font box and use the pull-down Font menu below it to select Times. Tab to the Size box, make sure it's checked, and type 18 in the box. Make sure Style is checked and click on Bold and Underline until an X appears in each box indicating that that style is selected.

5. Click on the Find Next button. When *thing* is found and highlighted, click on the Change All button. XPress will change the one instance of *thing* in the document and beep to tell you that 1 instance was changed. Click on the document page or close the Find/Change dialog box to return to the document. Your screen should resemble Figure 11.4.

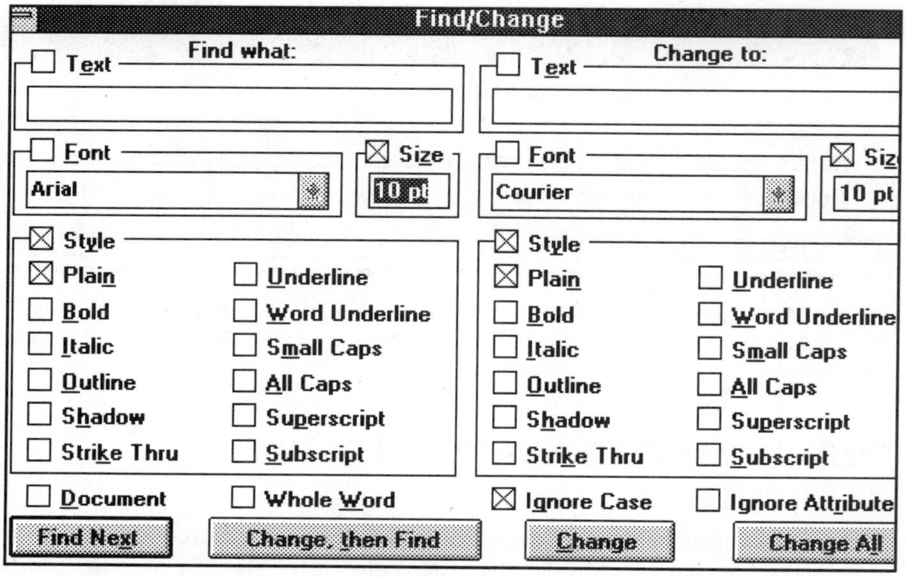

Figure 11.3—Displays the expanded Find/Change dialog box when the Ignore Attributes option is *deselected*.

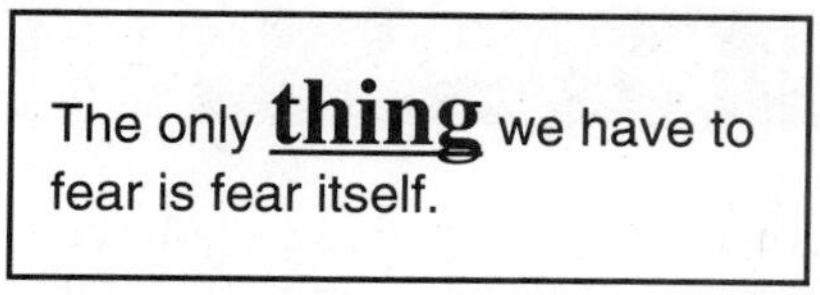

The only **thing** we have to fear is fear itself.

Figure 11.4—Choose Bold and Underline in the Change to fields of the expanded Find/Change dialog box.

SPELLING CHECK

You can check the words in your document against XPress's 120,000-word dictionary and you can create auxiliary dictionaries which contain words you use often but are not found in the program's main dictionary. XPress allows you to check the spelling of a single word, a chain of linked text, or the entire document with commands accessed from the Utilities menu.

EXERCISE C

Ctrl+W Utilities/Check
Spelling/Word
Ctrl+Alt+W Utilities/
Check Spelling/Story

1. Type the following sentence exactly as written (no quotes): "Hire a tenager wile he stil knoows evrything."

2. To check one word, double-click on *tenager* to select it. Choose Utilities/Check Spelling/Word (Ctrl+W). The Check Word dialog box (Figure 11.5) is displayed and two words are suggested as the correct spelling for *tenager*. Click on the second word, *teenager*, to highlight it and click on Replace. The dialog box disappears and the word is corrected in the document.

3. To spell check a single chain of linked text, choose Utilities/Check Spelling/Story. Place your cursor anywhere in the text box containing the *tenager* sentence. Choose Utilities/Check Spelling/Story (Ctrl+Alt-W). A Word Count box appears. Click on OK and the Check Story dialog box appears (Figure 11.6).

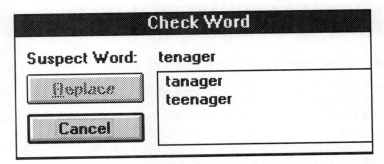

Figure 11.5—The Check Word dialog box allows you to double-click on a word in the list to place it in the document, or to click once on the word and click on Replace.

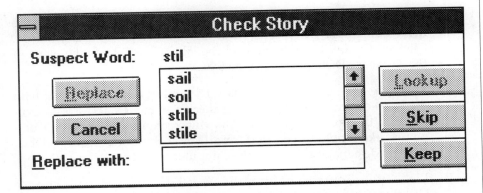

Figure 11.6—The Check Story dialog box allows you to Lookup words in the dictionary or to type in a replacement for the Suspect Word. When an Auxiliary Dictionary is open, the Keep function is available and allows you to save (Keep) words you commonly use in the Auxiliary Dictionary.

What you will need

A text file

Ctrl+E File/Get Text

WARNING!

Don't use the Lorem Ipsum file because XPress's dictionary will flag every Latin word in that file.

4. Click on the Lookup button to display suggested spellings for the Suspect Word. Either click on the correctly spelled word and click on the Replace button or double-click on the correctly spelled word. You can also type the correct spelling of a Suspect Word in the Replace with field. If you want to add the Suspect Word to an Auxiliary Dictionary, click on the Keep button and XPress will add the word, then display the next Suspect Word. When you have finished the spelling check, the Check Story dialog box disappears and you are back on the document page.

5. To spell check the entire document, choose File/Get Text (Ctrl+E) and import a text file that contains misspelled words.

6. Click anywhere in the document and choose Utilities/Check Spelling/Document. Click OK after the Word Count is completed and click on the Lookup, Replace, and Skip buttons until the spell checking is completed and you have been returned to the document screen.

CREATING AN AUXILIARY DICTIONARY

An Auxiliary Dictionary contains words you commonly use that are not found in XPress's dictionary. You can create more than one Auxiliary Dictionary, but you can have only one Auxiliary Dictionary open at one time.

Always open the Auxiliary Dictionary before you begin a spell check. If you do not open or create an Auxiliary Dictionary before you begin a spelling check, the Keep function will not be available (it will be dimmed) and you will not be able to add words to the Auxiliary Dictionary. Access the Auxiliary Dictionary or create a new one by choosing Utilities/Edit Auxiliary or Utilities/Auxiliary Dictionary.

EXERCISE D

1. Choose Utilities/Auxiliary Dictionary. Use the dialog box to locate the drive and folder where you want the Auxiliary Dictionary stored. Click on Create. Type "Names" in the File Name field as the name of the Auxiliary Dictionary. Click on Save.

2. You have now created an Auxiliary Dictionary and can access it with the Keep command in the spelling checker in any QuarkXPress document. In the text box, type the following sentence (no quotes): "Companies like Apple Corp., IBM, and Digital Equipment Corp. (DEC) have made a major impact on the computer industry."

3. Place your cursor before the word *Companies* and choose Utilities/Check Spelling/Document. After the number of Suspect Words is given, click on OK. When *IBM* is listed as a Suspect Word in the Check Document dialog box, click on the Keep button. This will add *IBM* to the Auxiliary Dictionary. Do the same when *DEC* is listed as the suspect word.

EDITING AN AUXILIARY DICTIONARY

You can also edit words in the Auxiliary Dictionary by adding and deleting words.

Ctrl+N File/New
Ctrl+Alt+W Utilities/
    Check Spelling/Story

1. Choose Utilities/Edit Auxiliary to display the list of words in the Names Auxiliary Dictionary. Notice that all words appear in lower-case letters. Click on *dec* and click on Delete. Then type your name in the box at the bottom of the dialog box and click on Add. Click on Save.

2. Close the document. Create a new document and type the following sentence (no quotes): "Thank you for your interest in Kitty Kat Corporation. We may not be IBM, but we are purrfect for you." Press Enter and type your name.

3. Choose Utilities/Auxiliary Dictionary and when the Auxiliary Dictionary "Names" is highlighted, click on Open. Nothing will appear to happen, but when you spell check this story, XPress will check the text against the words in both the main dictionary and the "Names" dictionary.

4. Choose Utilities, Check Spelling/Story (Ctrl+Alt-W). When *Kat*, *purrfect*, and your first and last names appear as suspect words, click on the Keep button to add them to the Auxiliary Dictionary. Notice that *IBM* is not flagged as a suspect word because it is already in the Auxiliary Dictionary.

5. Choose Utilities/Edit Auxiliary. When the "Names" Dictionary is displayed, click on your first name and click on the Delete button. Do the same for your last name. Your "Names" Auxiliary Dictionary should resemble Figure 11.7.

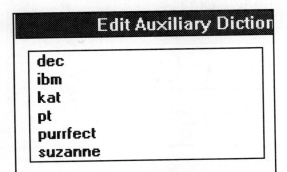

Figure 11.7—The Edit Auxiliary Dictionary dialog box allows you to add and delete words in a personal dictionary. Notice that capitalized words appear uncapitalized in the Auxiliary Dictionary.

CREATING STYLE SHEETS

A style sheet is the name of a group of commands to create paragraph attributes. For example, if a newsletter heading appears in 12-point Times bold, centered with 6 points of space between it and the first line of body copy, you could apply those five formatting commands with one keystroke if you create a style for that heading (paragraph).

Ctrl+N File/New
Ctrl+Alt+S File/Save as
Ctrl+Y Edit/Preferences/
   General
Ctrl+Alt+M View/Show
   Measurements
Ctrl+Shift+F Style/Formats

Take it easy

Formatting a paragraph, selecting it, and then choosing New in the Style Sheets for... dialog box is called creating a style sheet by example. This method saves you the trouble of invoking the several dialog boxes in the Style Sheets window to assign formatting effects.

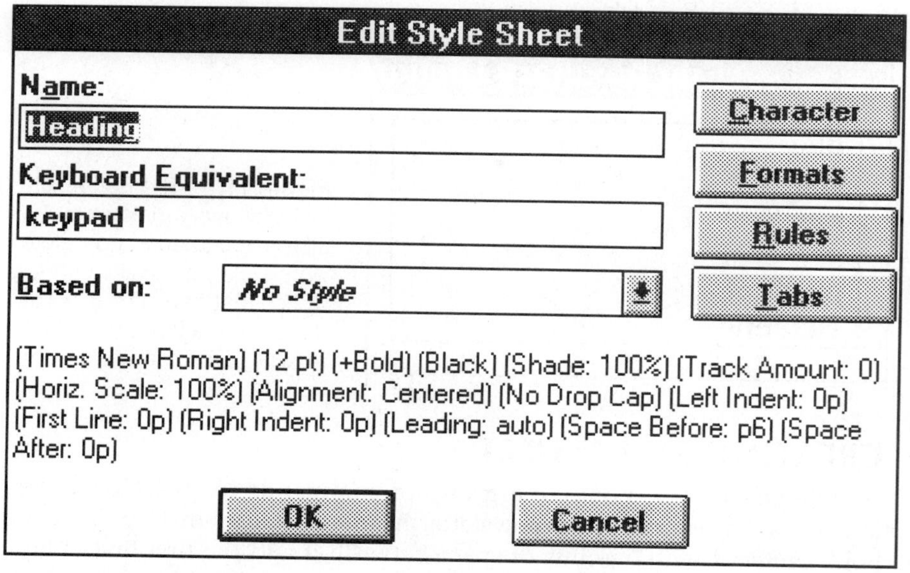

EXERCISE E

1. Create a new document (File/New) with an automatic text box and save it (File/Save as) under the name "Style Practice." Use the General Preferences dialog box (Ctrl+Y) to select picas as the unit of measure.

2. Type (no quotes): "This is a Heading" and triple-click to select the entire line. Use the Measurements palette (Ctrl+Alt-M) to format it in Times New Roman 12 point, bold, and center aligned.

3. Choose Style/Format (Ctrl+Shift+F) and in the Space After field on the right, type 0p6 (6 points). Click on OK. Press Enter after the formatted line, click on the Left Align icon in the Measurements palette, and type a few lines of text.

4. To define a style sheet for that paragraph, choose Edit/Style Sheets to display the Style Sheets for Style Practice dialog box. Click on New to display the Edit Style Sheet dialog box. In the Name field type "Heading."

5. Notice that because the text was selected before you created the style sheet, the Edit Style Sheet dialog box displays those formatting instructions already (Figure 11.8). Click on OK and click on Save in the Style Sheets for Style Practice dialog box.

6. In your document, press Enter a few times and type (no quotes): "This is Another Heading" and press Enter. Place your cursor anywhere in the paragraph and choose Style/Style Sheets/Heading. Your screen should resemble Figure 11.9.

Edit Style Sheet

N**a**me:

Heading

Keyboard **E**quivalent:

keypad 1

Based on: No Style

Character
Formats
Rules
Tabs

(Times New Roman) (12 pt) (+Bold) (Black) (Shade: 100%) (Track Amount: 0) (Horiz. Scale: 100%) (Alignment: Centered) (No Drop Cap) (Left Indent: 0p) (First Line: 0p) (Right Indent: 0p) (Leading: auto) (Space Before: p6) (Space After: 0p)

OK   Cancel

Figure 11.8—The lower part of the Edit Style Sheet dialog box indicates that the Heading style has 6 points of space after the paragraph, as well as other formatting information.

> **This is Another Heading**
>
> A style sheet is the name of a group of commands to create paragraph attributes. For example, if a

← 6 points of space after the paragraph

Figure 11.9—Displays the Heading style sheet as applied.

THE STYLE SHEETS PALETTE

Version 3.1 includes a Style palette which is accessed from the View menu (View/Show Style Sheets). Each time you create a new style or modify an existing style, that information is updated in the Style palette, whether or not the palette is displayed. When you place the cursor in a paragraph, instead of using the Style menu to apply a style, simply click on the style's name in the Style palette.

APPLYING NO STYLE

If you make formatting changes to a paragraph after a style has been applied, applying a second style to that same paragraph will not override local formatting like boldface and tabs. To apply a new style to a paragraph to which a style has already been applied, choose Style/Style Sheets/No Style. When No Style is applied to a paragraph, nothing appears to happen, but actually the paragraph has been stripped of any style information (including local formatting) and is ready to accept another style.

EXERCISE F

1. Type the following sentence (no quotes): "Mark Twain was opposed to millionaires but felt it would be dangerous to offer him the position."

2. Quadruple-click to select the paragraph and use the Measurements palette to format it in 12-point Times.

3. Choose View/Show Style Sheets to display the Style Sheets palette. It currently displays three styles, No Style, Normal, and Heading. Normal is the default style which is applied when you first install QuarkXPress. You can change these default settings by editing the Normal style sheet. No Style will strip a paragraph of any style previously applied to it.

4. Place the cursor anywhere in the Mark Twain paragraph and hold down the Ctrl key while you click on Normal in the Style Sheets palette. This is equivalent to choosing Edit/Style Sheets and will display the Style Sheets for (document name) dialog box.

5. Click on New to display the Edit Style Sheets dialog box. Type Name in the Name field. Tab to the Keyboard Equivalent field and, if you have an extended keyboard, press one of the Keypad keys. Notice that (Times), (12 pt), etc. is displayed at the bottom of the window.

6. Click on Character and when the Character dialog box is displayed, choose Helvetica, 14 point. Click on OK twice. Click on Save.

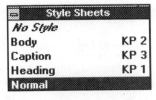

The Style Sheets palette includes three new styles with their keyboard equivalents.

No means NO!

No Style not only strips a paragraph of a style, it also strips it of any local formatting like bold and italic. You won't see the stripping effect (loss of local formatting like bold and italic) until you apply another style.

Sorry!

The keyboard equivalents for styles require the extended keyboard with its function keys and numeric keypad.

WARNING!

To edit a style sheet from the Style Sheets palette, always press the Ctrl key *before* clicking on the name of the style you want to edit. Unless you press the Ctrl key first, you will apply the style to the paragraph in which the I-beam is flashing.

Keyboard equivalents

You can apply a keyboard equivalent only from the function keys and keys on the numeric keyboard. You can also use the Ctrl, Shift, and Alt keys with the keypad keys to create additional keyboard equivalents.

The F1 function key is not available as a keyboard equivalent because it is the Help key. It's also a good idea to avoid using the Alt key as a modifier, because Windows uses it with digits for creating bullets and accented characters.

WARNING!

When you create a style by example by selecting a paragraph, that paragraph does not have the style applied to it. You must apply the style to that paragraph to ensure that any changes made to the style will also be made to that paragraph.

7. Notice that Name is now listed in the Style Sheets palette. Place your cursor anywhere in the paragraph and click on Name in the Style palette to apply the Name style to the paragraph.

8. Drag to select *Mark Twain* and use the Measurements palette (View/Show Measurements) to make it bold (B) and shadowed (S).

9. Ctrl-click on Name in the Style palette and in the Style Sheets for (document name) dialog box. Click on New.

10. In the Edit Style Sheets dialog box, type Body Style in the Name field and assign the style a Keyboard Equivalent.

11. Click on the Character button and select Times, 10 point, Italic. Click on OK twice. Click on Save.

12. Click in the Mark Twain paragraph again and click on Body Style in the Style Sheets palette. Notice that although the words *Mark Twain* became Times, 10-point italic, they retained their original bold and shadowed formatting, because you did not strip the local formatting by applying No Style to the paragraph.

13. Click anywhere again in the Mark Twain paragraph. Hold down the Ctrl key while you click on Body Style in the Style Sheets palette. This applies No Style before applying the new style. The paragraph is now stripped of its previous formatting and conforms to the Body Style characteristics.

USING STYLE SHEETS

Once a style sheet has been created and applied to a paragraph, any changes you make to the style sheet will also be made to any paragraphs in the document to which that style sheet has been applied.

EXERCISE G

1. Use the Document Layout palette (View/Show Document Layout) to add another page to the Style Practice document. Choose View/Show Style Sheets.

2. Type the following letter and format it in 10-point Helvetica, left aligned. Do not insert extra paragraph returns between paragraphs. (The lines have been numbered for ease of reference only; do not type the line numbers.)

1. Mr. Roland Sterner
2. 123 Linden Place
3. Waretown, MN 90875
4. January 5, 1993
5. Dear Mr. Sterner,
6. Thank you for your investment advice. I took it and am now worth several million dollars. On your recommendation I have purchased:

      7. 1. the White House, Washington D.C.

      8. 2. the Louvre, Paris

      9. 3. the Kremlin, Moscow

     10. Yours truly,

     11. Andy Brightboy

3. Place your cursor on line 1 and choose Edit/Style Sheets. Click on New and type Body in the Name field. Click on the Character button and when the Character Attributes dialog box appears, change the font to Times and the size to 12 point. Click on OK and click on Save.

4. Click on line 3. Choose Edit/Style Sheets. Click on New and type "Last Paragraph" in the Style Name dialog box. Pull down the Based on menu and select Body. This will base the Last Paragraph style on the 12-point Times formatting you used for the "Body" style sheet. Click on the Formats button and enter 0p6 in the Space After field to add 6 points of space after the paragraph return. Click on OK; click on OK again and click on Save.

5. Drag to select lines 7, 8, and 9. Choose Edit/Style Sheets and type Numbers in the Body field. Select Body from the Based on pull-down menu. Click on the Tabs button. In the Tabs dialog box type 5p. Click on OK. Click on OK again and click on Save.

6. Place your cursor before the numbers 1, 2, and 3 in lines 7, 8, and 9 and press the Tab key once before each number.

7. Drag to select lines 1 and 2 and choose Style/Style Sheets/Body or click on Body in the Style Sheets palette.

8. Drag to select lines 3, 4, and 5. Choose Style/Style Sheets/Last Paragraph or click on Last Paragraph in the Style Sheets palette

9. Select line 6 and apply the Body style sheet.

10. Drag to select lines 7, 8, and 9 and apply the Numbers style sheet to these three lines..

11. Apply the Last Paragraph style to line 10. Choose Edit/Style Sheets and click on Last Paragraph to select it (or Ctrl-click on Last Paragraph in the Style Sheets palette). Then click on the Duplicate button to make a copy of the Last Paragraph style sheet. In the Edit Style Sheet dialog box, type "Yours truly." Click on the Formats button, type 2p in the Space After field. Click on OK twice and click on Save. Select line 10 and apply the Yours truly style sheet to it.

12. Increase the space between *Yours truly* and the signature by choosing Edit/Style Sheets (or Ctrl-click on *Yours truly* in the Style Sheet palette). Click on *Yours truly*, click on Formats, and change the Space After value to 3p. Click on OK twice and click on Save. The new style is automatically applied to line 10.

Be selective

Because style sheets are paragraph formats, you do not have to drag to select the entire paragraph. Click anywhere in the paragraph and then apply the style sheet.

What you will need

A text file

Ctrl+N File/New
Ctrl+E File/Get Text
Ctrl+I View/Show Invisibles

APPENDING STYLE SHEETS

If you create a style in one document and want to use it in another document, import that style into the new document via the Style Sheets for... dialog box. With Document A open, Choose Edit/Styles and click on the Append button. When the Open dialog box appears, scroll through the folders and drives to find the document which contains the style sheets you want (Document B). Click on Open and the style sheets from Document B will be added to Document A. The new style sheets can be edited in Document A as if they had been created there.

If the style sheets in Document B have the same name as those in Document A, they will not overwrite the style sheets in Document A. Also, the *entire style sheet palette comes over.* You cannot pick and choose which style sheets you want to append.

REVIEW EXERCISE

In this exercise you will import a text file, apply style sheets, find and change text, and spell check the story. The contents of the text file are irrelevant.

1. Create a new document (File/New) with an automatic text box. Change the width of the text box to 15 picas and import a text file (Ctrl+E). Choose View/Invisibles (Ctrl+I).

2. Press the Enter key to place a paragraph return after the first line; after the next three or four lines; after the next line; after the next three or four lines; after the next line; and after the next three lines. Delete the rest of the file. Your screen should resemble Figure 11.10.

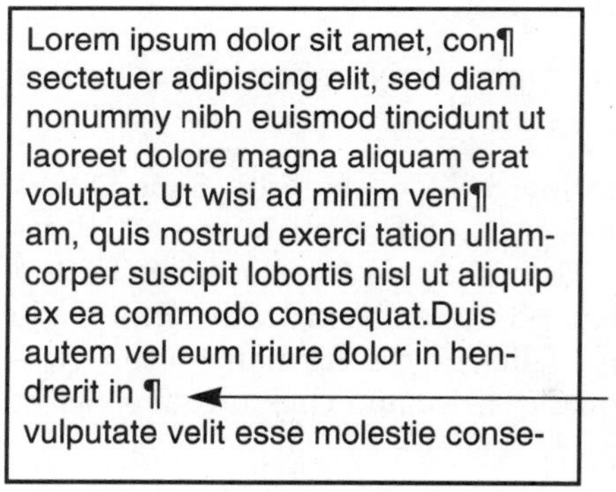

Lorem ipsum dolor sit amet, con¶
sectetuer adipiscing elit, sed diam
nonummy nibh euismod tincidunt ut
laoreet dolore magna aliquam erat
volutpat. Ut wisi ad minim veni¶
am, quis nostrud exerci tation ullam-
corper suscipit lobortis nisl ut aliquip
ex ea commodo consequat.Duis
autem vel eum iriure dolor in hen-
drerit in ¶
vulputate velit esse molestie conse-

Figure 11.10—Press Enter to place paragraph markers after lines. Choose View/Show Invisibles to display the markers.

3. Click on the first line and choose Edit/Style Sheets. Create a new style named Title. Click on Character and choose Times, 14 point, Bold. Click on OK.

4. While still in the Edit Style Sheets dialog box, click on the Formats button. Change Alignment from Left to Centered. Type 2p in the Space After field. Click on OK twice and click on Save.

5. Click on the first line and choose Style/Style Sheets/Title (or click on Title in the Style Sheets palette).

6. Click anywhere in the next paragraph to select it and choose Edit/Style Sheets. Click on New and type Body in the Name field. Click on the Character button and change the Font to Helvetica, the Size to 10 point and the Style to Italic. Click on OK.

7. In the Edit Styles dialog box, click on the Formats button. Make sure Alignment is set to Left and type 0p6 in the Space Before field. Click on OK twice and click on Save. Choose Style/Style Sheets/Body (or click on Body in the Style Sheets palette) to apply the style. Your Style Sheet menu should resemble Figure 11.11.

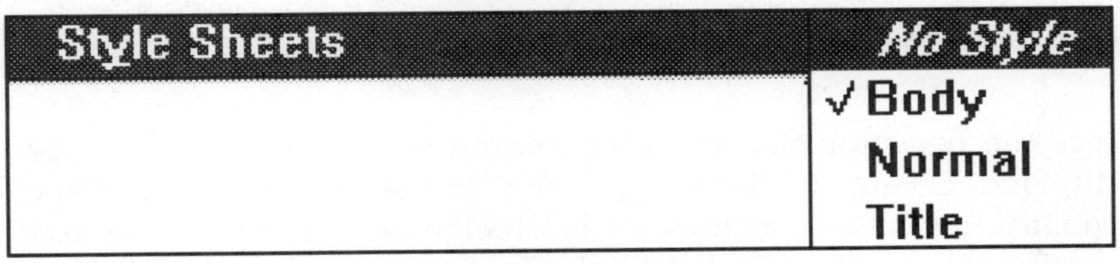

Style Sheets	No Style
	√ Body
	Normal
	Title

Figure 11.11—The Style Sheets menu for this document.

8. Click anywhere in the paragraph with the single line and choose Edit/Style Sheets. Click on New. Type "Heading" in the Name field.

9. Click on the Character button and assign that paragraph a Font of Times and a Size of 18 point. Click in the Underline and ALL CAPS check boxes. If necessary, deselect Italic. Click on OK to return to the Edit Style Sheets dialog box.

10. In the Edit Style Sheet dialog box, click on Formats. Type 1p6 in the Left Indent field. Type 1p in the Space After field. Click in the Keep with Next ¶ field to keep this heading on the same page with the paragraph that follows it. Click on OK twice. Click on Save.

11. With the single line still selected, choose Style/Style Sheets/Heading (or click on Heading in the Style Sheets palette) to apply that style to the paragraph. Click in the next paragraph and apply the Body style to it.

12. Click on the next line and choose Edit/Style Sheets (or Ctrl-click on Heading in the Style Sheets palette). Click on Heading to select it and click on the Duplicate button. In the Edit Style Sheet dialog box, change Copy of Heading to Heading.2. Choose Heading from the Based on pull-down menu (Figure 11.12). Click on the Character button and select the Strike Thru and All Caps options under Style. Click on OK twice and click on Save. Apply the Heading.2 style to the single line.

13. Click on the last paragraph and apply the Body style to it.

Shortcut

To apply the paragraph formatting from one paragraph to another, click in the paragraph whose format you want changed (target paragraph). Then Alt-Shift-click on the paragraph whose format you want to copy. This will copy the paragraph's style, margins, leading, and tabs to the target paragraph.

Edit Style Sheet

N̲ame:

Heading.2

Keyboard E̲quivalent:

B̲ased on: Heading

Heading

C̲haracter

F̲ormats

R̲ules

T̲abs

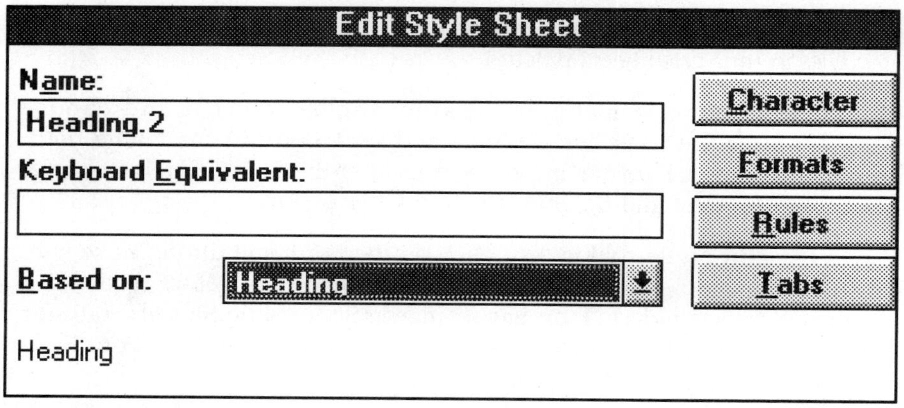

Figure 11.12—The Edit Style Sheet dialog box for Heading.2 is displayed when you check the Heading style and click on Duplicate.

FYI

When you select a style sheet from the Based on pull-down menu, any changes you make to the Based on Style sheet (Heading) will also be made to the Heading.2 style sheet.

14. Place the Insertion Bar at the beginning of the story and choose Edit/Find/Change (Ctrl+F). Type "the" in the Find what box. Type "Bananas" in the Change to box. Click on Ignore Attributes to deselect it and display the expanded Find/Change dialog box. In the Find what field, choose Text/Helvetica/10 pt/Italic. In the Change to field, select Times/14 pt/Bold/All Caps. Click on Whole Word. Click on Find Next. When the first occurrence of *the* is selected, click on the Change All button. When XPress beeps, click on the Find/Change Close box. Your screen should resemble Figure 11.13.

15. Choose Utilities/Check Spelling/Auxiliary Dictionary. Click on Create and type a name for the dictionary in the File Name field. Click on Save. Choose Utilities/Check Spelling/Document and Lookup and Replace any words flagged as a Suspect Word. Click on Keep to save some words in the Auxiliary Dictionary.

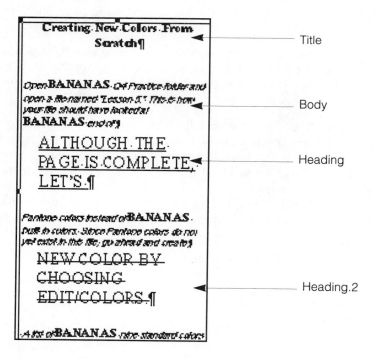

Title

Body

Heading

Heading.2

Figure 11.13—The completed document displays four different style sheets.

REVIEW QUESTIONS

Read the following questions and choose the answer which best completes the statement.

1. The Find/Change function starts _____.
    a. at the Insertion Point
    b. at the start of the first paragraph
    c. at the point you choose Edit/Find/Change
    d. a and c

2. Clicking on the Whole Word option in the Find/Change dialog box
    _____.
    a. finds a word with any suffix
    b. selects a word preceded and followed by a space
    c. finds a word with any prefix
    d. skips hyphenated words

3. Deselecting the Ignore Attributes check box in the Find/Change dialog box _____.
    a. finds a word based on the paragraph formats
    b. expands the dialog box to include formatting characteristics
    c. locates the document's Invisibles
    d. tags words that are all uppercase

4. Before clicking on the Document check box in the Find/Change dialog box, _____.
    a. click to place the Insertion Point
    b. open the Auxiliary Dictionary
    c. select the text box on the first page
    d. deselect all text boxes

5. Selecting Utilities/Check Spelling/Story _____.
    a. checks the spelling in a document
    b. checks the spelling in a text box
    c. checks the spelling in a chain of linked text
    d. a and c

6. Frequently used words can be stored _____.
    a. under the View menu
    b. in the Auxiliary Dictionary
    c. in the QuarkXPress Dictionary
    d. in the QuarkXPress application

7. Styles are _____.
    a. multiple commands executed with one keystroke
    b. formatting commands that are paragraph specific
    c. formatting combinations that are document specific
    d. a and b

8. Styles are created and accessed _____.
    a. from the Style Menu and Measurements palette
    b. from the Measurements palette
    c. from the Utilities menu
    d. from the Style menu and Style Sheets palette

9. Changes made to style sheets _____.
   a. are made to every paragraph
   b. are reflected in the selected paragraph
   c. are made to every paragraph based on that style
   d. are made throughout the document

10. Applying No Style to a paragraph _____.
    a. removes all formatting from the paragraph
    b. applies the default formatting characteristics
    c. removes all style and local formatting characteristics from the paragraph
    d. displays the paragraph's original formatting

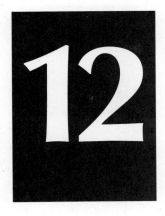

LESSON

12

Typography

OVERVIEW

In this lesson you will learn how to manipulate text by setting the first baseline of a line of text in a text box and shifting the baseline of any character in a line of text. You will expand and condense text characters by applying horizontal scaling values and learn how to add and delete space between characters by kerning and tracking. You will also learn how to apply hyphenation and justification commands to blocks of text. Finally, you will rotate text boxes, create drop caps, and generate special characters like accented letters. As a review, you will create an invitation, a logo, and a text block with custom spacing formatting.

TOPICS

Baseline grid	Justified text
Locking text to the baseline	Word spacing
Horizontal scale	Character spacing
Kerning letters	Rotating text
Tracking text	Drop caps
Baseline Shift	Special formatting characters
Hyphenation and Justification	Review Exercises
Applying H&J styles	Review Questions

TERMS

baseline	hyphenation
baseline grid	justification
baseline shift	kern
drop cap	letter spacing
en-space	track
horizontal scale	

WARNING!

It's a good idea to assign an increment value in the Baseline Grid area equal to your leading. If your Increment value is less than or equal to the specified leading, the lines of text will lock to every grid line. If you specify a grid Increment greater than the leading, the line of text will lock to the next grid line and create ugly gaps of space between lines.

BASELINE GRID

When you create a new document in QuarkXPress, the first line of text sits on an imaginary line called the baseline and all subsequent lines sit on their own baselines at specified increments from that first baseline. The position of the first baseline is determined in the Edit/Preferences/Typographic dialog box (Ctrl+Alt+Y). This feature allows you to line up the baseline of multiple columns on a page across the page, regardless of type size.

EXERCISE A

1. Create a new document (File/New) with 1-inch margins all around, 2 columns, and an automatic text box. Use the General Preferences dialog box (Ctrl+Y) to select inches as the unit of measure.

2. Display the Measurements Palette (Ctrl+Alt+M) and make the automatic text box 6.5 inches wide and 2 inches high. Choose File/Get Text (Ctrl+E) and import a file that fills both columns for at least half of the page.

3. Select all the text (Ctrl+A) and use the Measurements palette to format it in 10-point Helvetica on 12-point leading.

4. Below the first paragraph, type "Headline" (no quotes) and use the Measurements palette to assign it a type size of 14 point and a type style of Bold. Your screen should resemble Figure 12.1.

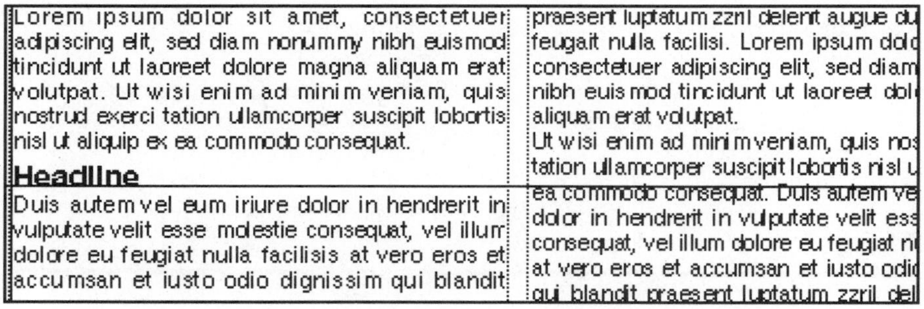

Figure 12.1—Notice that the baselines of the two columns do not align across the page.

To assign each paragraph an invisible grid, choose Edit/Preferences/Typographic (Ctrl+Alt+Y). In the Baseline Grid area (Figure 12.2), type 1, for example, in the Start field to place the first baseline grid 1 inch from the top of the page. In the Increment field, type 12. This will space the baseline of each line of text at 12-point intervals.

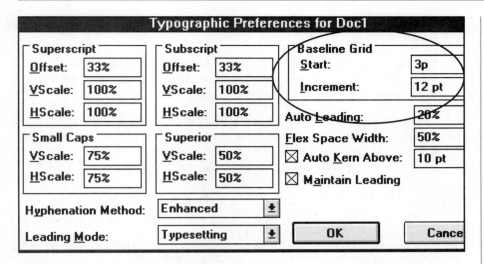

Figure 12.2—Displays a baseline grid placed 3 picas or ½ inch from the top of the page with each invisible grid line placed 12 points apart (Increment). The paragraph which is to be locked to this baseline grid should have a leading value that is equal to the Increment value.

LOCKING TEXT TO THE BASELINE

It's not enough to assign a Baseline Grid value in the Typographic Preferences dialog box. You have to *lock* each paragraph to that grid. This is done on a paragraph-by-paragraph basis. Version 3.1 allows you to view the baseline grid on the screen. This grid (View/Show Baseline Grid) is a non-printing grid.

EXERCISE B

1. In the current document, choose Edit/Select All (Ctrl+A).

2. Choose Style/Formats (Ctrl+Shift+F) to display the Paragraph Formats dialog box. Click in the Lock to Baseline Grid box on the left to select the locking option. Make sure that the selection has been assigned 12 points of leading. Click on OK (Figure 12.3). Your screen should resemble Figure 12.4.

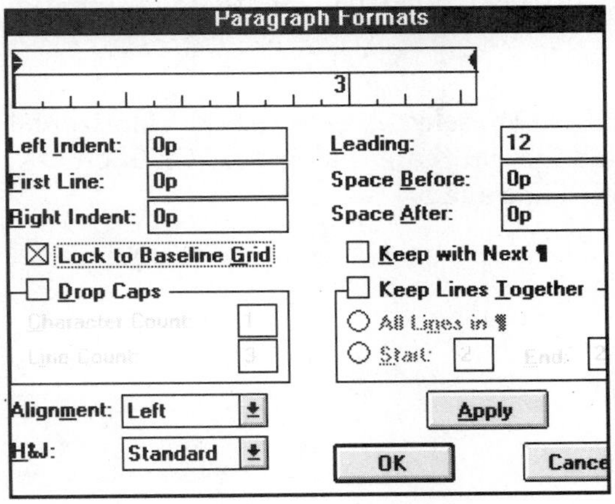

Figure 12.3—Click in the Lock to Baseline Grid check box to lock the selected paragraphs to the baseline grid established in the Typographic Preferences dialog box. The Leading value in the Paragraph Formats dialog box should equal the Increment value in the Typographic Specifications dialog box.

3. Choose View/Show Baseline Grid to see how each line sits on the baseline.

4. Choose View/Show Rulers (Ctrl+R) and pull down a horizontal ruler guide. Place the ruler guide on any baseline and notice how the text in both columns aligns on the ruler guide across the screen.

If you specify Justified as the vertical alignment for a text box in the Item/Modify dialog box and you select Lock to Baseline Grid in the Paragraph Formats dialog box, XPress will add small increments of space (not to exceed the Inter ¶ Max value) to justify the text vertically.

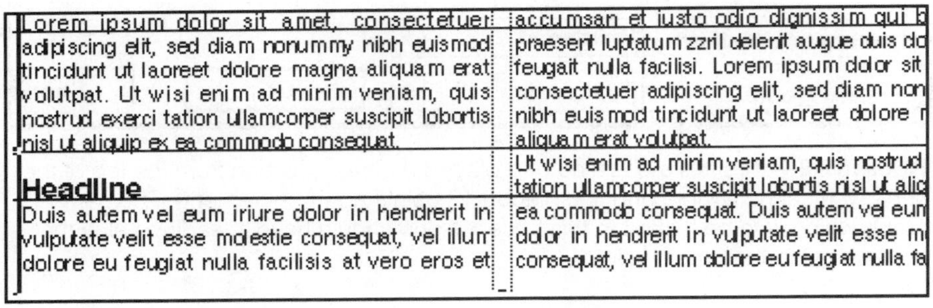

Figure 12.4—Notice that the baselines of the two columns now align across the page even though the word "Headline" is in a larger type size.

HORIZONTAL SCALE

The Horizontal Scale command, available from either the Style menu or the Character Attributes dialog box, allows you to expand or condense the width of characters. Be careful not to overdo horizontal scaling, lest you cross the fine line in typography between interesting and ugly.

EXERCISE C

1. In any text box, type the word "HELLO" (no quotes). Press Enter and type the word again. Repeat until you have three HELLO's on your screen. Format each word in 24-point Helvetica.

2. Double-click on the second HELLO to select it and choose Style/Horizontal Scale to display the Horizontal Scale dialog box.

3. In the Horizontal Scale dialog box, type 150%. Click on OK.

4. Double-click on the third HELLO to select it. Choose Style/Horizontal Scale. Type 400% in the Horizontal Scale dialog box. Click on OK. Your screen should resemble Figure 12.5.

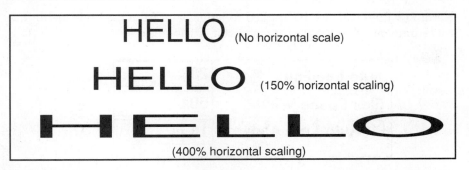

(No horizontal scale)

(150% horizontal scaling)

(400% horizontal scaling)

Figure 12.5—The first HELLO is set in Helvetica 24 pt. with a horizontal scaling value of 100% or no horizontal scaling. The second HELLO is set in Helvetica 24 pt. with 150% horizontal scaling applied. The third HELLO, also set in Helvetica 24 pt., displays 400% horizontal scaling.

Notice that the width of the letter expands when a value greater than 100% is entered in the horizontal scaling field. To condense the letters, apply a horizontal scaling value of less than 100%.

EXERCISE D

1. Double-click on the second HELLO to select it and choose Style/Character (Ctrl+Shift+D) to display the Character Attributes dialog box.

2. In the Horizontal Scale field on the left side of the Character Attributes dialog box, type 50% to condense each character 50% of its normal width. Click on OK.

3. Select the third HELLO and choose Style/Character (Ctrl+Shift+D). Type 25% in the Horizontal Scale field. Click on OK. Your screen should resemble Figure 12.6.

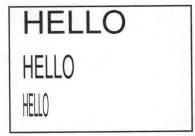

Figure 12.6—The first HELLO is set in Helvetica 24 pt. with no horizontal scaling applied. The second HELLO is set in Helvetica 24 pt. with 50% horizontal scaling applied. The third HELLO is set in Helvetica 24 pt. with 25% horizontal scaling applied.

KERNING LETTERS

Kerning, or letterspacing, is the process of adding or deleting space between letter pairs. XPress will automatically kern, or adjust the space between two adjacent letters, if the Auto Kern Above field in the Typographic Preferences dialog box is checked (Figure 12.7). With this option selected, XPress will adjust the spacing between characters using the values built into the program's kerning table.

Ctrl+Shift+D Style/
Character

Tip

When you type a character and assign it a particular typeface and a specific size, that character has a horizontal scale value of 100%. Increasing that 100% value expands the letter; decreasing that 100% value condenses the letter.

Ctrl+Alt+M View/Show
 Measurements
Ctrl+Alt+Shift { Style/
 Kern or Track
 (reduce space)
Ctrl+Alt+Shift } Style/
 Kern or Track
 (increase space)

FYI

In the Kern Amount dialog box, entering a positive number will increase the space between the character pair; entering a negative number will decrease the space between the character pair. You will usually have to kern type larger than 14 points.

An em-space is the width of two zeros in a given font. Enter a value of −1 to remove $\frac{1}{2,000}$-em space between character pairs; enter a value of −0.1 to remove $\frac{1}{20,000}$-em space.

Kerning values can also be applied to letter pairs from the Style menu, the Measurements palette, and the Character Attributes dialog box.

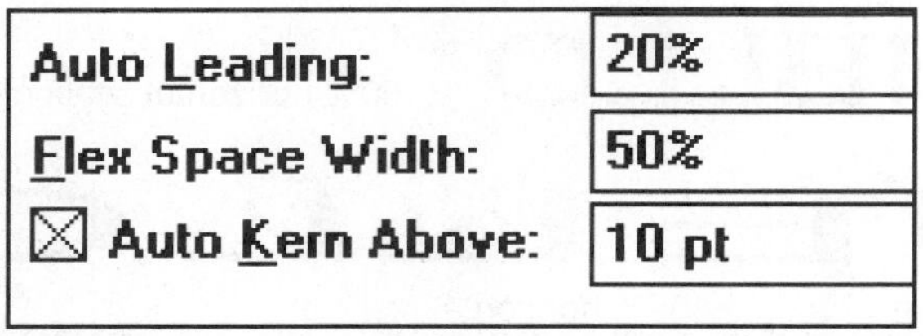

Figure 12.7—Displays the Auto Kern Above field in the Typographic Preferences dialog box. When this box is checked, XPress will automatically kern all text greater than 10 points.

EXERCISE E

1. Type the word "Today" (no quotes) and use the Measurements palette (Ctrl+Alt+M) to format it in 72-point Helvetica.

2. Select the Zoom tool and click on the *To* in the word. Notice that the *o* is too far away from the *T*. Place the I-beam between the *T* and the *o*. Choose Style/Kern and type −4 in the Kern Amount dialog box to remove $\frac{4}{200}$-em space from between those two letters.

3. Leave the I-beam between the two letters and notice that the kerning arrows in the Measurements palette now display −4 (Figure 12.8). Hold down the Ctrl key and click on the left pointing arrow to reduce the space between the two letters even more. Notice how the letters move closer together as you click on the arrow. Sometimes, because of low screen resolution, the letters will not always move on the screen, but they will kern properly in final output.

4. Drag the cursor over the value in the kerning arrows field and type −4 to return the spacing between the *T* and the *o* to the original value which you assigned it. Holding down the Ctrl key as you click on the left facing arrow (Ctrl+Alt+Shift {) decreases the kerning in .005-em ($\frac{1}{200}$) increments. Alt-clicking on the right facing arrow increases the kerning in $\frac{1}{200}$-em space increments.

5. Click between the *o* and the *d* in *Today*. Click on the left facing kerning arrow in the Measurements palette and notice that you have entered a value of −10, that is, you have reduced the space between the *0* and the *d* by $\frac{10}{200}$ of an em-space.

6. Continue to add negative kerning values to *Today* until your screen resembles Figure 12.9. Click or Alt-click on the kerning arrows in the Measurements palette or use the Style/Kern command to enter the kerning values displayed in Figure 12.9.

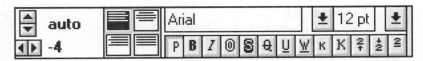

Figure 12.8—The kerning arrows display a –4 value. The space between the two letters has been reduced ⁴⁄₂₀₀ of an em-space.

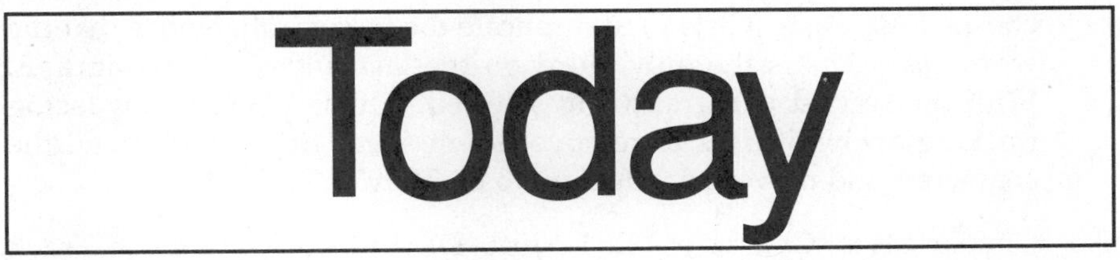

Today

Figure 12.9—Use the kerning arrows to delete excessive space between letters. The following kerning values were applied: Between *T* and *0*, –12; between *o* and *d*, –5; between *d* and *a*, –7; between *a* and *y*, –11.

TRACKING TEXT

Tracking, also called letterspacing, is the process of adding or deleting space between two or more selected adjacent characters. When two or more adjacent characters are selected, the Kern command in the Style menu becomes the Track command.

Just as kerning values can be added directly from the Style menu, in the Kern Amount field in the Character Attributes dialog box, and from the kerning arrows in the Measurements palette, so can tracking values also be applied. When one or more letters is selected, the Kern command under the Style menu becomes the Track command and the kerning arrows in the Measurements palette become the Tracking arrows.

EXERCISE F

1. In the same document, choose Page/Insert to add another page at the end of the document. Create a text box 3.5 inches wide by 4 inches high. Type "WELCOME HOME" (no quotes) and use the Measurements palette (Ctrl+Alt+M) to format both words in 24-point Helvetica, center aligned.

2. Select both words and choose Style/Track. In the Track Amount dialog box, type 30 to add ³⁰⁄₂₀₀-em space distributed evenly between the selected characters.

3. With the text box still selected, choose Item/Modify (Ctrl+M) and in the Vertical Alignment field, use the pull-down menu to choose Centered. The text is now centered horizontally and vertically in the text box and your screen should resemble Figure 12.10.

4. Choose Edit/Preferences (Ctrl+Y) and change the unit of measure from inches to picas. Then use the Document Layout palette (View/Show Document Layout) to add another page to the document.

Ctrl+Alt+M View/Show Measurements
Ctrl+M Item/Modify
Ctrl+Y Edit/Preferences/ General

More Info

Ctrl-clicking on the kerning arrows in the Measurements palette removes (left facing arrow) or adds (right facing arrow) space in ¹⁄₂₀₀-em increments.

Clicking on those same arrows increases and decreases space in ¹⁰⁄₂₀₀-em increments.

Ctrl+C Edit/Copy
Ctrl+V Edit/Paste
Ctrl+Shift+D Style/
    Character

Design Tip

Use tracking to make headlines fit in a particular column width. Tracking is also an effective method of getting rid of widows (short lines at the end of a paragraph) and orphans (single words at the end of a paragraph which appear on the following page).

5. Use the Text Box tool to create a text box 16 picas wide and 9 picas high. Type (no quotes): "The women in Shakespeare's plays like Lady Macbeth and Queen Gertrude tend to be unattractive characters." Press Enter after the last word and format the sentence in 12-point Times.

6. Quadruple-click on the paragraph to select the entire paragraph. Choose Edit/Copy (Ctrl+C). Click after the selected paragraph and choose Edit/Paste (Ctrl+V) to duplicate the paragraph. Notice that the word *characters* is the only word on the last line of the paragraph. With the second paragraph still selected, Alt-click on the left facing tracking arrow 5 times to remove ⁵⁄₂₀₀-em space from between all the characters and move characters up to the third line.

7. Choose Style/Character (Ctrl+Shift+D), and notice that the Track Amount dialog box also contains a value of –1. Your screen should resemble Figure 12.11.

WELCOME HOME

Figure 12.10—Text tracked to fit in the text box.

The women in Shakespeare's plays like Lady Macbeth and Queen Gertrude tend to be unattractive characters.

The women in Shakespeare's plays like Lady Macbeth and Queen Gertrude tend to be unattractive characters.

Figure 12.11—Tracking brings the word *characters* up to the previous line.

BASELINE SHIFT

Just because you establish a baseline doesn't mean that characters have to sit on it. The Baseline Shift command in XPress allows you to move text above or below its normal baseline position. Access the Baseline Shift command from the Style Menu (Style/Baseline Shift), from the Character Attributes box (Style/Character), or from the keyboard. Type a positive value in the Baseline Shift dialog box to move selected text above the baseline. Type a negative number to move selected text below the baseline.

If you have applied Baseline Shift commands that you want to remove, select the character or the block of text and choose Style/Baseline Grid and type 0 (zero) in the Baseline Shift dialog box to return the text to its original baseline.

Ctrl+Shift+D Style/
Character
Ctrl+Alt+Shift+ (+) or (−)
Style/Baseline

EXERCISE G

1. Type "Oopsie doosey" (no quotes) in any text box and format it in 14-point Helvetica, all caps, and left aligned.

2. Select the second *o* in *Oopsie* and choose Style/Baseline Shift. Type 3 in the Baseline Shift dialog box. Click on OK. Select the *p* in *Oopsie*, choose Style/Character (Ctrl+Shift+D), and type −4 in the Baseline Shift field in the Character Attributes dialog box. Click on OK.

3. Select the *s* in *Oopsie* and press Ctrl+Alt+Shift++ (plus sign) six times to move the letter 6 points above the baseline. Select the *i* and press Ctrl+Alt+Shift− (minus sign/hyphen) 3 times to move the letter 3 points below the baseline.

4. Select each letter in DOOSEY and use the Style menu, the Character Attributes dialog box, and the keyboard commands to apply positive and negative baseline shift values to each letter in the word. Your screen should resemble Figure 12.12.

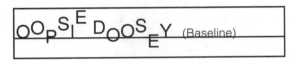

Figure 12.12—Using the Baseline Shift command can achieve interesting typographic effects.

HYPHENATION AND JUSTIFICATION

The Hyphenation and Justification commands in XPress allow you to hyphenate words, to increase and decrease the white space between characters and between words to create text that is visually correct, and to force text to fit a specified space. You can create different hyphenation and justification values and apply them to different paragraphs as well as include specific H&J styles in a style sheet (Figure 12.13).

FYI

Version 3.1 allows you to choose between Standard and Enhanced Hyphenation. Standard applies the hyphenation method used in earlier versions of XPress. Enhanced Hyphenation will hyphenate more words more conventionally. Access the H&J commands by choosing Edit/H&Js.

☒ **Auto Hyphenation**

Enables hyphenation

Smallest Word: 6

Number of characters word must contain to be hyphenated

Minimum Before: 3

Number of characters that fall before and after a hyphen

Edit Hyphenation & Justification

Name:
Standard

☒ **Auto Hyphenation**

Smallest **W**ord: 6

Minimum **B**efore: 3

Minimum **A**fter: 2

☐ **B**reak Capitalized Words

Hyphens in a **R**ow: unlimited

Hyphenation **Z**one: 0p

Justification Method

	Minimum	Optimum	Maximum
Space:	100%	100%	150%
Char.:	0%	0%	15%

Flush Zone: 0p

☒ **Single Word Justify**

OK   Cancel

Figure 12.13—Displays the Edit Hyphenation & Justification dialog box in Version 3.1.

Ctrl+Alt+M View/Show
Measurements
Ctrl+D Item/Duplicate

EXERCISE H

1. Use the Document Layout palette (View/Show Document Layout) to add another page to your document. Use the Text Box tool to create a text box 13 picas wide (13p) by 11½ picas high (11p5).

2. Type the following paragraph in the text box: "I am pleased to inform you that SuperStar pictures has chosen your home as the locale for its next blockbuster movie, "Heartbreak Hunger." SuperStar studio will pay you $200 for the use of your home for six months and requests that you sign a waiver allowing us to make any necessary structural changes to your house."

3. Quadruple-click to select the paragraph and use the Measurements palette (Ctrl+Alt+M) to format it in 10-point Helvetica, 12-point leading, and alignment justified. Your screen should resemble the left text box in Figure 12.14.

4. Click on the Item tool, click on the text box, and choose Item/Duplicate (Ctrl+D). Move the duplicate next to the original text box.

5. Click to place the Insertion Point in the second (duplicate) text box. Choose Edit/H&Js. Click on Standard, click on Edit, and notice that the Auto Hyphenation box defaults to selected, which means that hyphenation is enabled. Leave the Smallest Word value at 6. XPress will not hyphenate a word with fewer than 6 letters. Leave the Minimum Before and Minimum After values at 3 and 2. XPress will now require at least 3 letters to come before a hyphen and at least 2 letters to come after a hyphen before hyphenating a word.

6. Click in the Break Capitalized Words check box to select it. Type 2 in the Hyphens in a Row field. XPress will allow only two lines in a row to end with a hyphenated word. The Hyphenation Zone specifies how far from the right edge of a column XPress will place a hyphen. Your screen should resemble Figure 12.15. Click on OK.

I am pleased to inform you that SuperStar pictures has chosen your home as the locale for its next blockbuster movie, "Heartbreak Hunger." SuperStar studio will pay you $200 for the use of your home for six months and requests that you sign a waiver allowing us to make any necessary structural changes to your house.	I am pleased to inform you that SuperStar pictures has chosen your home as the locale for its next blockbuster movie, "Heartbreak Hunger." SuperStar studio will pay you $200 for the use of your home for six months and requests that you sign a waiver allowing us to make any necessary structural changes to your house.

Figure 12.14—The left text box displays justified text which has not been hyphenated. The right text box displays a paragraph to which the Standard H&J values (Figure 12.15) have been applied.

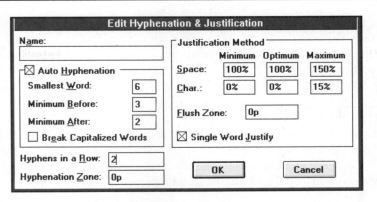

Figure 12.15—The Standard H&J style displays enabled hyphenation (Auto Hyphenation is checked) and instructions to break capitalized words.

APPLYING H&J STYLES

If you want to apply different hyphenation values to a paragraph in the same document, create another H&J style. This new style will be available under the H&J pull-down menu in the Paragraph Formats dialog box. You have already created an H&J style, Standard.

EXERCISE I

1. To apply the Standard H&J style which you just created, click anywhere in the second (duplicate) text box and choose Style/Formats (Ctrl+Shift+F).

2. Use the H&J pull-down menu to select the H&J style sheet named Standard. Click on Apply.

3. Notice that the extra space between the words of justified type has been removed because hyphenation was enabled. Click on OK. Your screen should resemble the right text box in Figure 12.14.

EXERCISE J

1. On another page create a text box, import text (Ctrl+E), and choose Style/Edit H&Js. Activate hyphenation by clicking in the Auto Hyphenation check box and enter different values in the various fields on the left side of the Edit Hyphenation & Justification dialog box.

2. Apply these various values to justified and unjustified text. Notice how the absence of hyphenation creates uneven right edges in text that is left aligned and how it leaves excessive white space between words in justified text.

3. Choose Edit/H&Js, click on Standard to select it, and click on New. Change the H&J specifications and give these new specifications a name in the Name field. Click on Save.

What you will need

A text file

Ctrl+Shift+F Style/Formats
Ctrl+E File/Get Text

Justified type

Justified type is text that extends from the left indent of a column or text box to the right indent of that column or text box. It is a paragraph alignment command accessed from either the Paragraph Formats dialog box or from the Measurements palette. Clicking on the Justified alignment icon will justify the text in a paragraph.

Ctrl+Shift+F Style/Formats

Minimum (least) amount of space XPress will place between words to justify text. This minimum value is expressed in terms of the percentage of the normal word space in a font.

This is the normal space between words as defined by a particular font. This value applies to both justified and non-justified text.

How it works

Word Spacing values are based on a percentage of the normal word spacing built into the font. Character spacing values are based on a percentage of the size of a font's en-space.

An en-space is a square of white space equal to half the point size of an em-space in a given font. An en-space is created by typing Alt+Space.

Figure 12.17—Displays an H&J dialog box where values have been entered for word spacing justified text. These values (1) tell XPress that it can reduce a font's normal word space by no more than 90%; (2) define the Optimum word spacing as 90% of what the typeface calls for; (3) indicate that XPress will increase the space between words no more than 90% of the normal word spacing as defined by the font.

4. Click in any paragraph and choose Style/Formats (Ctrl+Shift+F). Use the H&J pull-down menu to select your new H&J style sheet. Click on Apply and notice how the word spacing and character spacing in your text changes.

JUSTIFIED TEXT

On the right side of the Edit H&J dialog box are located the options for determining word spacing and character spacing of justified text (Figure 12.16). Only the Optimum values for word spacing and character spacing apply to both justified and non-justified text.

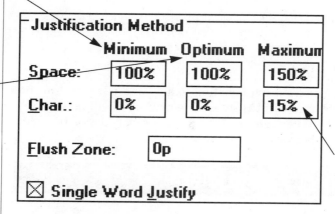

The maximum space between characters of justified paragraphs. This value is expressed as a percentage of the normal space between words which is built into the particular font.

Figure 12.16—The Word Spacing values for justified text are based on a percentage of the normal width built into the font.

WORD SPACING

The Minimum Word Spacing value defaults to 100%, which means that XPress will insert all of the space (100%) between words which the typeface calls for. If this value were 50%, XPress would insert only half (50%) of the space between words which the typeface calls for.

The Optimum value is the percentage of the word space built into a particular typeface. Reducing this value reduces the space between words.

The Maximum word spacing value defaults to 150%, which means that XPress will increase the space between words in justified text by 50% more than the Optimum value—that value defined by the typeface's designer. Figure 12.17 displays an Edit Hyphenation & Justification dialog box where word and character spacing have been reduced to tighten the spacing.

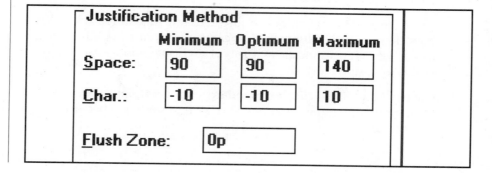

CHARACTER SPACING

The Character Spacing fields in the Edit H&J Specification dialog box apply to increasing or reducing space between individual characters in a line of text.

The Optimum value defaults to 0%, which means that the best intercharacter spacing in a line of text does not add or remove any (0%) percentage of a font's en-space. XPress will attempt to set a line of justified and non-justified text based on the normal character spacing built into a font.

The Minimum value indicates the least amount of space which XPress will remove or insert between characters of justified paragraphs. This value is expressed in terms of a percentage of the width of the font's en-space.

The Maximum value indicates the most space, expressed in a percentage of the width of a font's en-space, which XPress will insert or delete between characters in a justified line of text.

EXERCISE K

1. Press Ctrl+Y and, in the General Preferences dialog box, make sure the unit of measure for the document is picas. Choose Page/Insert and insert another page in the document. Create a text box on that page that is 30 picas wide and 20 picas high with 4 columns. Display the Measurements palette (Ctrl+Alt+M).

2. Type the following paragraph in the first column (no quotes): "This is a paragraph that has tremendously long words which have successfully or unsuccessfully been manipulated so that they fit into the ridiculously inadequate space of this text box."

3. After the last word, choose Edit/Select All (Ctrl+A), then choose Edit/Copy (Ctrl+C). Press the Enter key *on the numeric keypad* to move the cursor to the top of the next column and choose Edit/Paste (Ctrl+V). Press the Enter key after the last word and Paste the same paragraph in the third column and again in the fourth column.

4. Click anywhere in the first column and click on the Justified alignment icon in the Measurements palette. Notice that since neither hyphenation nor justification values were applied, the paragraph displays excessive white space between words and characters (Figure 12.18).

5. Choose Edit/H&Js. Click on New and type Column 2 in the Name field. Click on Auto Hyphenation to activate it, but leave the default values in the other fields. Click on OK. Click on Save.

6. Click anywhere in Column 2 and choose Style/Formats (Ctrl+Shift+F). In the Paragraph Formats dialog box, use the pull-down menus on the left to select Justified from the Alignment field and Column 2 from the H&J field. Your screen should resemble the Column 2 screen in Figure 12.18. Because Hyphenation and Justification values were applied to the paragraph, much of the white space between characters and between words has been reduced.

Ctrl+Y Edit/Preferences/ General
Ctrl+A Edit/Select All
Ctrl+C Edit/Copy
Ctrl+V Edit/Paste
Ctrl+Shift+F Style/Formats
Ctrl+ M Item/Modify
Ctrl+Alt+M View/Show Measurements

Enter here

When you	appears
press the	and text
Enter	moves to
key, *on the*	the next
numeric	column or
keypad,	to the next
this sym-	text box.
bol called	
the New	
Column	
marker ↓	

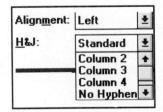

The H&J pop-up menu in the Paragraph Formats dialog box

7. Click anywhere in Column 3. Click on the Alignment Justified icon in the Measurements palette to justify the paragraph. Choose Edit/H&Js. Type Column 3 in the Name field and change the Hyphenation, Word Spacing, and Character Spacing values to match those in Figure 12.19. Click on OK. Click on Save.

8. With the cursor still in Column 3, choose Style/Formats (Ctrl+Shift+F) and use the H&J pull-down menu to select the Column 3 H&J style. Click on OK.

| This is a paragraph that has a few really long words which have successfully or unsuccessfull y been manipulated to fit into the ridiculously inadequate space of this text box. | This is a paragraph that has a few really long words which have successfully or unsuc- cessfully been manipu- lated to fit into the ridiculously inadequate space of this text box. | This is a para- graph that has a few re- ally long words which have suc- cessfully or unsuccessful- ly been ma- nipulated to fit into the ridicu- lously inade- quate space of this text box. | This is a paragraph that has a few really long words which have successfully or unsuc- cessfully been manip- ulated so that they fit into the ridiculously inadequate space of this |

Figure 12.18—Column 1 text has no H&J values applied; Column 2 text has only Hyphenation values and no Justification values applied; Column 3 text has Hyphenation, tight word spacing, and tight character spacing values applied; Column 4 has Hyphenation, loose word spacing, and loose character spacing values applied.

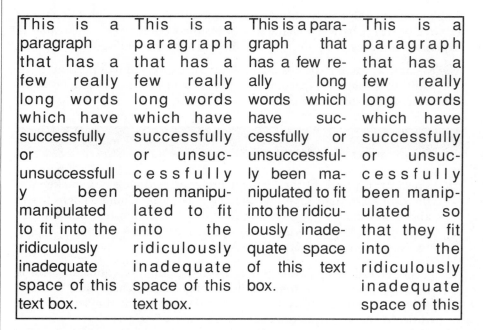

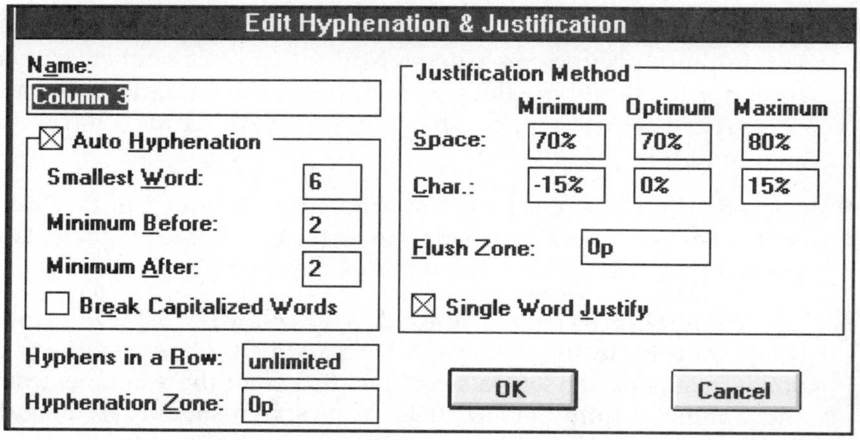

Figure 12.19—The Edit Hyphenation & Justification dialog box for Column 3. This H&J style calls for tighter word spacing and tighter character spacing than the program's default values.

In this paragraph you have applied hyphenation, tight word spacing, and tight character spacing controls. In the Word Spacing field, you specified a Minimum of 60%, which means that justification will reduce the space between words on each line by at most 60% and and leave a space 80% of its original size. An Optimum value of 80% applies spacing between words at 80% of the spacing built into the font by the fontographer. A Maximum value of 80% tells XPress that the most space it can place between words to justify text cannot exceed 80% of the normal word space built into the font.

Under Character Spacing, a Minimum value of –15 tells XPress to reduce the space between each character in a line of text by no more than 15%, while a Maximum value of 0% tells XPress not to exceed by any percentage the character spacing built into the font. The Optimum value of –5% makes XPress attempt to justify text by reducing the font's normal en-space width by 5%.

Setting values in the H&J dialog box does not affect text until that new H&J style is applied via the H&J pull-down menu in the Paragraph Formats dialog box. The only H&J style that is applied to a document is Standard—the program's default style.

If you check the Single Word Justify check box in the H&J dialog box, XPress will hyphenate a single word in a line, as long as it isn't the last line in a paragraph.

EXERCISE L

1. Click anywhere in Column 4. Click on the Alignment Justified icon to justify the paragraph. Choose Edit/H&Js. Type Column 4 in the Name field and change the Hyphenation, Word Spacing, and Character Spacing values to match the values in Figure 12.20. Click on OK. Click on Save.

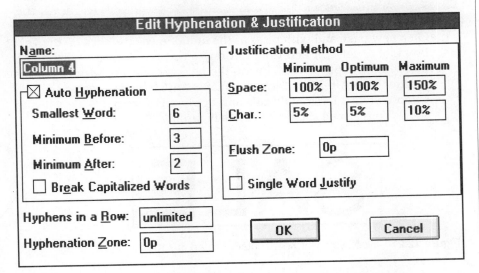

Figure 12.20—Displays the Edit Hyphenation & Justification dialog box for the paragraph in Column 4. The values create a looser letter and word spacing than the program's default values.

Design Tip

Create a H&J style with Auto Hyphenation turned off and select it in the Paragraph Formats dialog box when creating paragraph formats for a style to be applied to headlines, which you would never want hyphenated.

Ctrl+Shift+F Style/Formats
Ctrl+Alt+M View/Show
    Measurements

Arrowhead Pointer

Rotation field in the Measurements palette

Design Tip

The "color" of a page refers to the density of text on a page. A "darker" page results if lower values for character and word spacing are used. A "lighter" page results when higher word spacing values are used.

2. With the cursor still in Column 4, choose Style/Formats (Ctrl+Shift+F) and use the H&J pull-down menu to select the Column 4 H&J style. Click on OK. Click on Save.

3. The Column 4 H&J style applies values that create loose letter spacing and loose word spacing. The 100% Minimum Word Spacing value means that justification will not reduce the space between words beyond the value built into the font. Optimum Word Spacing means that XPress will set justified and non-justified text with the full percentage of interword space built into the font. The 130% Maximum Word Spacing value means that XPress will increase interword space by no more than 130% of its normal (built-in) interword spacing.

4. Under Character Spacing, the 5% Minimum value means that XPress will reduce intercharacter spacing in justified text by 5% of the width of that font's en-space. It considers the Optimum character spacing to be 5% of the font's en-space and the Maximum character spacing not to exceed 10% of the font's en-space.

ROTATING TEXT

Many layouts call for text that is rotated or positioned at an angle. All rotated text in XPress is rotated within a text box; it's actually the text *box* that's rotated, not the text.

XPress allows you to (1) rotate text boxes manually around a rotation point which you establish by using the Rotation tool from the Tool palette; (2) rotate an item around its center by entering the numeric values in the Rotation field in the Measurements palette; (3) rotate an item around its center by entering a value in the Box Angle field of the Text Box Specifications dialog box.

EXERCISE M

1. On a new page and with picas as the unit of measure, click on the Text Box tool to select it and drag to draw a text box 15 picas wide and 5 picas high. Type "SALE" inside the box and use the Measurements palette (Ctrl+Alt+M) to format it in 60-point Helvetica, center aligned. Choose Style/Horizontal Scale and apply a Horizontal Scale value of 110%. Your screen should resemble Figure 12.21.

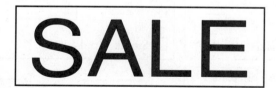

Figure 12.21—Displays a word horizontally scaled at 110%.

2. With the text box still selected, click on the Rotation tool in the Tool palette to select it. The Rotation Pointer is displayed. To rotate the text box around the crossbar in the letter *A*, click on the crossbar with the Rotation pointer; the Arrowhead Pointer is displayed. Rotate the box around the crossbar until 90° is displayed in the Rotation field of the Measurements palette. Your screen should resemble Figure 12.22.

3. With the text box still selected, type 0 (zero) in the Rotation field of the Measurements palette. The Text box will return to its normal horizontal position.

4. With the text box still selected, choose Item/Modify (Ctrl+M) and type –36 in the Box Angle field on the left side of the Text Box Specifications dialog box. Doing this will rotate the text box 36° to the right from the center of the text box. Your screen should now resemble Figure 12.23.

Ctrl+M Item/Modify

Rotation Pointer

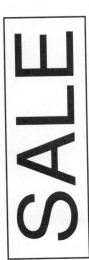

Figure 12.22—Displays a word rotated 90° around the crossbar of the letter A.

Tip

Double-click on a text box with the Item tool to display the Text Box Specifications dialog box. Double-clicking with the Item tool on a picture box, group, or line also displays their specifications dialog boxes. This saves you the trouble of choosing Ctrl/Modify.

Related Tip

If you have the Content tool selected, change it temporarily to the Item tool by holding down the Ctrl key.

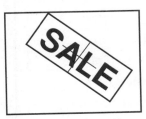

Figure 12.23—This text box has been rotated 36° to the right by typing –36 in the Box Angle field of the Text Box Specifications dialog box. You could also type –36 in the Rotation field of the Measurements palette. The lines cross at the center of the text box from which the box was rotated.

Rotating text boxes with the Rotation Pointer is easier if you draw out a long handle from the point of rotation. It's easier still to rotate items by typing values in the Specifications dialog box or in the Measurements palette.

Remember, XPress always rotates items starting from a value of zero. If you rotate an item 10° and then rotate that same item 90°, the item will rotate 90°, not 100°.

Ctrl+Alt+M View/Show
Measurements
Ctrl+Shift+F Style/Formats

DROP CAPS

A drop cap is the first letter of a paragraph which has been enlarged and which "drops" down into the paragraph. The letter *A* in this paragraph is an example of a drop cap. Drop Caps controls are accessed from the Paragraph Formats dialog box. (This text is 10-point Palatino on 12-point leading.)

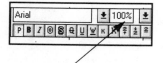

When a drop cap is selected, the Type Size field in the Measurements palette displays a percentage value which can be increased as well as decreased.

EXERCISE N

1. Use the Document Layout palette to add another page to the current document. Create a text box and use the Measurements palette (Ctrl+Alt+M) to make sure it is 30p6 wide and 10p high. Type the paragraph above (the one with the drop cap) in the text box.

2. Click anywhere in the paragraph and choose Style/Formats (Ctrl+Shift+F) to display the Paragraph Formats dialog box. Click in the Drop Caps check box on the left side of the dialog box to display the Drop Caps options. Select Justified from the Alignment pull-down menu.

3. In the Character Count field, type 1. This will drop 1 character, although you can drop as many as 8 characters.

4. In the Line Count field, type 2. This will drop that 1 character 2 lines into the paragraph. Your dialog box should resemble Figure 12.24. Click on OK. Your screen should resemble the first paragraph on this page.

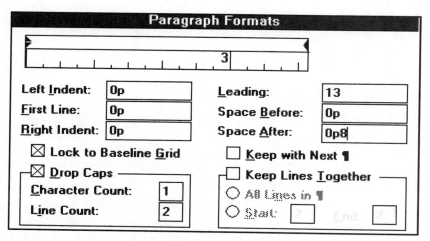

Figure 12.24—The Paragraph Formats dialog box, which displays a Drop Caps command to drop 1 character 2 lines into the paragraph.

A drop cap can be treated much like any other text character. You can change its typeface, type size, and type style, as well as apply scaling values to it.

Ctrl+Shift+F Style/Formats
Ctrl+Alt+M View/Show
 Measurements
Ctrl+\ [backslash] Indent
 Here

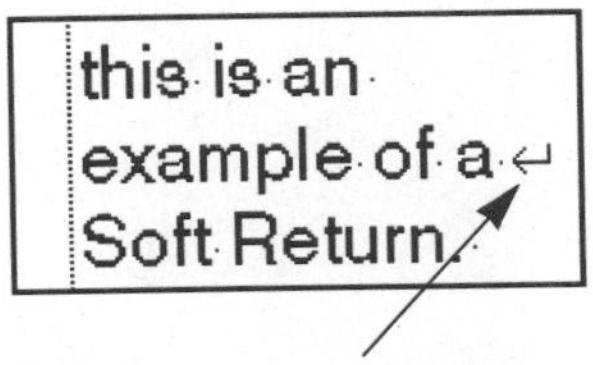

EXERCISE O

1. Create a text box 10 picas wide and 5 picas high. Type about 5 lines in the text box and format them in 10-point Helvetica.

2. Click anywhere in the paragraph and choose Style/Formats (Ctrl+Shift+F). Click on Drop Caps. Type 1 in the Character Count field to drop 1 character; type 3 in the Line Count field to drop that character 3 lines. Click on OK.

3. Select the drop cap and use the Measurements palette (Ctrl+Alt+M) to format it in Times italic.

4. In the Type Size field of the Measurements palette, select 100% and change it to 150%. Your screen should resemble Figure 12.25.

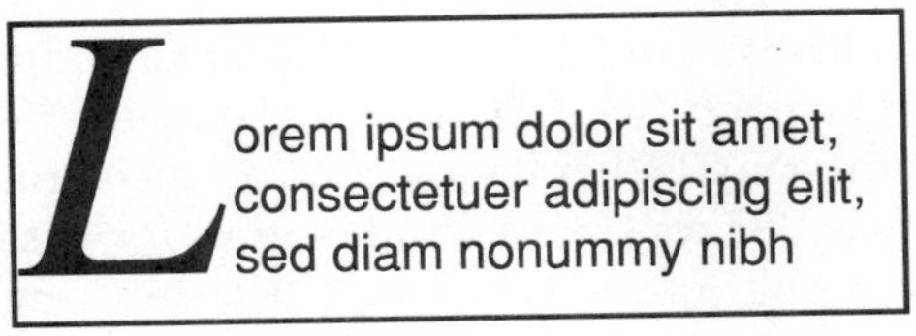

*L*orem ipsum dolor sit amet, consectetuer adipiscing elit, sed diam nonummy nibh

Figure 12.25—Displays a single drop cap which has been dropped 3 lines into the paragraph, then selected and increased in size by 50%.

this is an
example of a ↵
Soft Return

When you type Shift+ Enter to create a Soft Return, this marker is displayed if Show Invisibles is selected from the View menu.

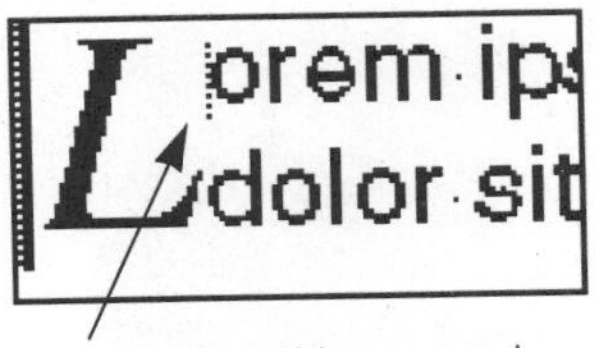

SPECIAL FORMATTING CHARACTERS

XPress allows you to generate other special characters used for formatting text, as well as accessing the punctuation marks and symbols built into the Macintosh. Many of them are necessary to reproduce foreign words and symbols, while others allow you greater control over text flow in the document. You will find all the special formatting characters listed with their keyboard commands in the QuarkXPress documentation. The most commonly used ones are described below.

1. Soft Return (Shift+Enter). A Soft Return forces a new line in the same paragraph without starting a new paragraph. A soft return keeps all the paragraph attributes like leading, indents, etc. while allowing you to place text from one paragraph at the start of another line.

2. Indent Here (Ctrl+\ (backslash)). This character forces the rest of the lines in a paragraph to indent over to that character. This is an especially useful command to use with drop caps (Figure 12.26).

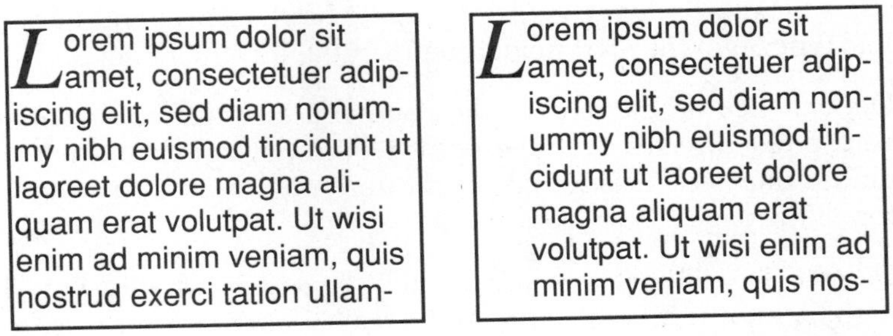

*L*orem ips
*L*dolor sit

The Indent Here marker results at the insertion point when Ctrl+\ (backslash) is pressed.

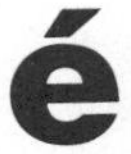

*L*orem ipsum dolor sit amet, consectetuer adipiscing elit, sed diam nonummy nibh euismod tincidunt ut laoreet dolore magna aliquam erat volutpat. Ut wisi enim ad minim veniam, quis nostrud exerci tation ullam-

*L*orem ipsum dolor sit amet, consectetuer adipiscing elit, sed diam nonummy nibh euismod tincidunt ut laoreet dolore magna aliquam erat volutpat. Ut wisi enim ad minim veniam, quis nos-

Figure 12.26—The first text box displays a 2-line drop cap. The second text box displays the same drop cap with the Indent Here command applied between the initial *L* and the letter *o*.

é The acute e (é) is generated by typing Alt+0233 on the numeric keypad.

Ctrl+Y Edit/Preferences/
    General
Ctrl+Alt+Y Edit/
    Preferences/
    Typographic

1. Open double quote	Alt+Shift+[	"
2. Close double quote	Alt+Shift+]	"
3. Open single quote	Alt+[	'
4. Close single quote	Alt+]	'
5. Nonbreaking em dash	Ctrl+Alt+Shift+=	—
6. Nonbreaking en dash	Ctrl+=	–
7. Round bullet	Alt+Shift+8	•
8. Ellipse	Alt+0133 (keypad)	...
9. E acute	Alt+0233 (keypad)	é

You have access to the special formatting characters like foreign symbols and accented characters in many fonts via the Character Map accessory which is part of the Windows environment. To display the Character Map, double-click on the Character Map icon in the Accessories group in the Windows Program Manager. When the map is displayed, click on the symbol or character you want. Notice that the keystroke combination for that character appears in the lower right corner of the window. Click on Copy to copy the selected character to the Clipboard. Return to the document and choose Edit/Paste to paste the character into the document.

If you want to generate the character or symbol from the keyboard, *use the numeric keypad* to press the combination for the character which appeared in the lower right corner of the Character Map. To generate the ellipse, for example, in the Times font, hold down the Alt key while typing the numbers 0133 on the numeric keypad.

REVIEW EXERCISE #1

In this exercise you will use formatting commands to create an invitational flyer.

1. Choose View/Show Document Layout. Drag the Master Page A icon down to add another page to your document. Choose Edit/Preferences/General (Ctrl+Y) and assign picas as the unit of measure. Choose Edit/Preferences/Typographic (Ctrl+Alt+Y) and under Baseline type 6p in the Start field; type 16 in the Increment field.

2. Double-click on the icon of the page you just created and move the zero point directly over the point where the upper and left margin guides intersect. This will place the zero point 6 picas down from the top of the page.

3. Use the Text Box tool to draw a text box 17 picas wide by 14 picas high. Assign it a 0p X value and a 0p Y value in the Measurements palette. Type the following announcement with a paragraph return where indicated by the ¶ mark:

Parlez-vous?

QuarkXPress for Windows will soon be available in several different language versions.

Introducing ¶ Katie's Custom Earrings ¶ Indian Melodies ¶ Earrings made of carved wooden beads ¶ strung on silver wire ¶ 13 Totem Place ¶ Wakanada, NP ¶ Tuesday, February 1 ¶ 9:00 am to 9:00 pm

Ctrl+Alt+M View/Show
Measurements
Ctrl+A Edit/Select All
Ctrl+Shift+F Style/Formats
Ctrl+Shift/H Style/Type
Style/Small Caps

4. Choose Edit/Select All (Ctrl+A) and use the Measurements palette to format the text in Times, 12/16 (12-point type on 16-point leading).

5. Click on the first line (the first paragraph) and choose Style/Formats (Ctrl+Shift+F). Click in the Lock to Baseline Grid check box to lock that first line to the baseline grid established in the Typographic Preferences dialog box. Because 6 picas with an increment of 16 points was established as the start of the baseline, *Introducing* will sit on a baseline 7 picas and 4 points from the top of the page. Click on OK.

6. Triple-click on the first line to select the word *Introducing*. Choose Style/Horizontal Scale. In the Horizontal Scale dialog box, type 300. Click on OK.

7. Select the Zoom tool and draw a marquee around *Introducing* to magnify it. Place the Insertion Bar between the *n* and the *t*. Alt-click 4 times on the left kerning arrow in the Measurements palette to apply a value of –4, that is, to remove $\frac{4}{200}$-em space from between those two letters. Place the Insertion Bar between the *n* and *g*. Double-click on the –4 value in the Kerning field and type –5. Press Enter.

8. Triple-click on the third line, *Indian Melodies,* to select it. Click on the right tracking arrow in the Measurements palette three times to add $\frac{30}{200}$-em space evenly between all the selected letters and words.

9. Triple-click on the fifth line to select it. Choose Style/Baseline Shift. Type 5 in the Baseline Shift dialog box to move the *strung on silver wire* line up 5 points. Click on OK. Select *to* in the last line. Press Alt+Hyphen to change it to an en-dash.

10. Select *am* and choose Style/Type Style/Small Caps (Ctrl+Shift+H). Do the same with *pm.* Your screen should resemble Figure 12.27.

> **Introducing**
> Katie's Custom Earrings
> Indian Melodies
> Earrings made of carved wooden beads
> strung on silver wire
>
> 13 Totem Place
> Wakanada, NP
> Tuesday, February 1
> 9:00 AM–9:00 PM

Figure 12.27—Displays horizontal scaling, tracking, and kerning values applied to text.

What you will need

A text file

Ctrl+Shift–C Style/
    Alignment/Centered
Ctrl+M Item/Modify
Ctrl+A Edit/Select All
Ctrl+E File/Get Text
Ctrl+Shift–J/Style/
    Alignment/Justified
Ctrl+D Item/Duplicate

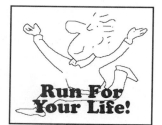

Peek-a-boo!

When you choose None as
the background color for a
text box or picture box, it
becomes transparent and
will reveal the text or items
behind it. In this illustration, the text box was
assigned a Background
Color of None and placed
on top of the picture box to
display the entire picture
behind the text.

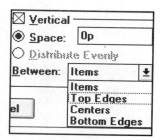

Use the Vertical field to
align items across. It
doesn't make sense, but it
works. The idea behind it
is to place the items at the
same point on the vertical
ruler.

REVIEW EXERCISE #2

In this exercise you will use formatting commands to create a logo.

1. Use the Text Box tool to create a text box 10p5 wide by 3p high. Type
"LANDSLIDE" and format it in 18-point Helvetica bold, center
aligned (Ctrl+Shift+C). With the text box still selected, choose
Item/Modify (Ctrl+M) and assign it a Box Angle of –20 and a Background Color of 100% Black. Click on OK.

2. Choose Edit/Select All (Ctrl+A) to select *LANDSLIDE*. Click 3 times
on the right tracking arrow in the Measurements palette to apply a
value of $\frac{3}{200}$-em space evenly between the letters. Choose
Style/Color/White to create reverse type. Choose Style/Baseline Shift
and type –4 in the Baseline Shift dialog box. Click on OK.

3. Draw another text box 11p8 wide by 1p8 high. Type "Graphics."
Double-click on the word to select it and format it in Helvetica 12-
point, Bold. Select the first four letters of the word and choose
Style/Color/White. Choose Item/Modify (Ctrl+M) and use the Background Color pull-down menu to select None. This will make the box
transparent and allow the "Landslide" box to show through it.

4. Click on the Item tool to select it; click on the "Graphics" text box and
move it so that the first four letters are positioned on the black part of
the "LANDSLIDE" text box. Your screen should resemble Figure
12.28.

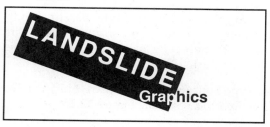

Figure 12.28—Displays a
rotated text box with tracked
and reverse text.

REVIEW EXERCISE #3

In this exercise you will edit Hyphenation and Justification values in a
paragraph with a drop cap.

1. Use the Text Box tool to draw a text box 18 picas wide by 16 picas
high. Import a text file into the box (Ctrl+E) and justify it
(Ctrl+Shift+J). Choose Item/Duplicate (Ctrl+D) and use the Item tool
to place the text boxes side by side.

2. Shift-select the three boxes and choose Item/Space Align. Click in the
Vertical field and use the Between pop-up menu to select Top Edges.
Click on OK.

Ctrl+Shift+F Style/Formats
Ctrl+\ Indent Here

3. Choose Edit/H&Js. Click on New to create a new H&J style. Type "Loose Text" in the Name field. Activate Auto Hyphenation and change the Word Spacing and Character Spacing values to match those in Figure 12.29. Click on OK.

4. Click in the second text box. Choose Style/Formats (Ctrl+Shift+F) and use the pull-down H&J menu to select Loose Text. Click on OK. Notice the difference in word and character spacing between the first and second text boxes.

5. Click in the first paragraph of the first text box and choose Paragraph/Formats (Ctrl+Shift+F). Click in the Drop Caps check box. Type 3 in the Character Count field. Type 3 in the Line Count field. Click on OK.

6. Place the cursor between the third drop character and the following character. Press Ctrl+\ (backslash) to insert the invisible Indent Here character and indent the entire paragraph under that fourth character. Select any letter *e* and change it to an e-acute by pressing Alt+0233 on the numeric keypad. Your screen should resemble Figure 12.30.

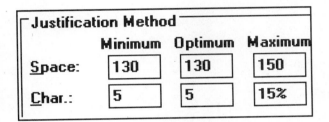

Figure 12.29—The H&J values for the "Loose Text" H&J style.

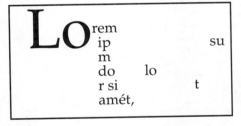

Figure 12.30—Text box displaying a 3-character drop cap, Indent Here formatting, and e-acute (é) in the second line.

FYI

When you place a cursor between a drop cap and another character, be sure that the blinking cursor runs the full length of the drop cap. The long cursor controls the relationship between the drop cap character and the regular paragraph character.

REVIEW QUESTIONS

Read the following questions and choose the answer which best completes the statement.

1. The leading value of a paragraph that is locked to the baseline grid should be _____.
    a. greater than the Increment value in the Typographic Preferences dialog box
    b. less than the Increment value in the Typographic Preferences dialog box
    c. equal to the Increment value in the Typographic Preferences dialog box
    d. irrelevant; it doesn't make any difference what the paragraph's leading is

2. Paragraphs are locked to the baseline grid via the _____.
   a. Edit menu
   b. General Preferences dialog box
   c. Paragraph Formats dialog box
   d. Item menu

3. Adding or deleting space between character pairs is called _____.
   a. tracking
   b. scaling
   c. kerning
   d. justifying

4. Adding or deleting space between two or more selected adjacent characters is called _____.
   a. tracking
   b. scaling
   c. kerning
   d. justifying

5. Hyphenation and Justification values are _____.
   a. application-specific
   b. document-specific
   c. text box-specific
   d. paragraph-specific

6. Horizontal scaling _____.
   a. expands and condenses text
   b. distorts text
   c. reduces type size
   d. a and b

7. The Optimum value for justifying characters in the H&J dialog box defaults to _____.
   a. 100% of a font's size
   b. 0% of a font's en-space
   c. 15% of a character's width
   d. 100% of a font's en-space

8. Drop caps are applied via the _____.
   a. Paragraph Formats dialog box
   b. Text Box Specifications dialog box
   c. H&J dialog box
   d. Measurements palette

9. Rotating text in XPress is achieved by _____.
   a. applying rotation values to the text
   b. using the Paragraph Formats dialog box
   c. rotating the text box
   d. accessing the Style menu

10. The command to force the rest of the lines in a paragraph to indent over to an invisible character is _____.
    a. Ctrl+Backslash
    b. Shift+Enter
    c. Alt+Shift+Hyphen
    d. Alt+8

Answers: 1. c; 2. c; 3. c; 4. a; 5. a; 6. d; 7. b; 8. a; 9. c; 10. a

13

Modifying

Text Boxes

OVERVIEW

In this lesson you will learn how to determine the origins of a text box, modify and move a text box, and navigate among multi-column text boxes. You will also change the Text Inset value and vertical alignment of text within a text box. You will learn how to group and ungroup items and multiple groups and apply background color to text boxes in a group. Finally, you will learn how to suppress the printout of a group. As a review, you will create a two-page catalog spread. Although you have used many of these functions in earlier lessons, you will fine tune your skills so that you can work more easily and efficiently.

TOPICS

Text box origins
Constraining boxes
Resizing text boxes
Columns
Text Inset
Vertical alignment
Inter ¶ Max
Grouping items
Modifying groups
Group Specifications dialog box
Suppress Printout
Grouping and ungrouping groups
Review Exercise
Review Questions

TERMS

Background Color
cap height
Group
Inter ¶ Max
justified vertically aligned
New Column marker
Origin Across

Origin Down
Resizing Pointer
Suppress Printout
text inset
Ungroup
vertical alignment

Ctrl+N File/New
Ctrl+Y Edit/Preferences/
  General
Ctrl+R View/Show Rulers
Ctrl+Alt+M View/Show
  Measurements
Ctrl+M Item/Modify

The Item tool is used for moving items. To temporarily turn any cursor into the Item tool, hold down the Ctrl key.

TEXT BOX ORIGINS

A text box's point of origin or the horizontal and vertical position of its top left corner on the page is reflected in the X and Y values in the Measurements palette and by the Origin Across and Origin Down values in the Text Box Specifications dialog box.

The X value (Origin Across) indicates the box's horizontal distance *from the zero point*. The Y value (Origin Down) indicates its position above or below the zero point.

If a text box's point of origin is to the left of the zero point on the horizontal ruler, its X value will be a negative number. If the box's point of origin is above the zero point on the vertical ruler, then its Y value will be a negative number.

CONSTRAINING BOXES

If you press the Shift key while moving boxes, you can constrain their movement horizontally or vertically. If you hold down the Shift key while you are resizing a box, the box is constrained to a square. Likewise, if you hold down the Shift key while resizing a picture box created with the Oval Picture Box tool, this will constrain the box to a circle. This type of constraining is a different constraining function from the Constrain command under the Item menu, which constrains or keeps items inside a box with which they are grouped.

EXERCISE A

1. Choose File/New (Ctrl+N) and create a new document with 1-inch margins all around, an automatic text box, and 1 column. Use the General Preferences dialog box (Ctrl+Y) to select inches as the unit of measure. Choose View/Show Rulers (Ctrl+R) and display the Measurements palette (Ctrl+Alt+M).

2. Click on the Text Box tool to select it and drag to create a text box 3 inches wide and 4 inches high. Use the Measurements palette to adjust the size of the text box.

3. Notice the X and Y values in the Measurements palette. Choose Item/Modify (Ctrl+M) to display the Text Box Specifications dialog box and notice that the same X value on the Measurements palette appears in the Origin Across field of the dialog box. Notice also that the Y value on the Measurements palette appears in the Origin Down field of the dialog box. Click on OK.

4. Click on the Content tool to select it and hold down the Ctrl key to temporarily turn the I-beam into the Item tool. Click on the text box with the temporary item tool to select it and drag it around the screen. Notice how the X and Y values in the Measurements palette change to reflect the box's movement to the right and left and up and down.

5. Now hold down the Shift key while you drag and notice that the box will move only horizontally, not vertically.

6. Hold down the Shift key while you drag the box up and down and notice that it is constrained to vertical movement.

7. Leave the box anywhere on the page and type 1 in the X and Y fields of the Measurements palette to position the box at the 1-inch mark on the horizontal and vertical rulers.

8. With the Item tool selected (or "transformed" from the Content tool), drag the box to the 2-inch mark on the horizontal ruler. Notice the dotted line which appears on the ruler and indicates the position of the box on the page (Figure 13.1). When the dotted guideline is over the 2-inch mark on both the horizontal and vertical rulers, release the mouse button.

9. Choose Item/Modify (Ctrl+M) and make sure the Origin Across and Origin Down fields display 2 inches. Click on OK.

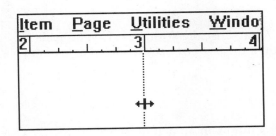

Figure 13.1—Guides appear along the ruler to indicate an item's position on the page.

RESIZING TEXT BOXES

A text box can be sized and resized from both the Measurements palette and the Text Box Specifications dialog box. It can also be resized using the Resizing Pointer (Figure 13.2). The Resizing Pointer appears whenever you move the cursor onto one of the eight handles of a text box. Dragging the handle with the Resizing Pointer allows you to resize the text box or constrain it to a square by holding down the Shift key as you drag.

As you drag to resize the text box, the dotted gray bar moves horizontally or vertically along the ruler (depending on whether you're dragging across or down) and lets you see height and width of the newly sized box.

If you drag one of the side handles, you will resize the box in one direction, either horizontally or vertically. Dragging one of the corner handles resizes the box both horizontally and vertically.

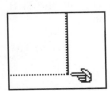

Figure 13.2—The Resizing Pointer is one of three ways XPress allows you to resize a text box.

Ctrl+M Item/Modify

FYI

You can change the Content tool temporarily to the Item tool by pressing the Ctrl key when the Content tool is active.

FYI

When a text box is selected, it displays 8 handles. It will stay selected while you click on a tool.

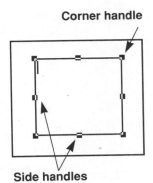

Corner handle

Side handles

What you will need

A text file

Ctrl+Alt+M View/Show
     Measurements
Ctrl+M Item/Modify
Ctrl+E File/Get Text

EXERCISE B

1. Click on the 3 x 4-inch text box you just created to select it. In the Measurements palette (Ctrl+Alt+M), change the W (Width) value to 2 and the H (Height) value to 3. Press Return or Enter to apply the new values.

2. With the text box still selected, choose Item/Modify (Ctrl+M). Type 4.5 in the Width field. Press Tab to move the cursor into the Height field. Type 3.7 in the Height field. Click on OK.

3. With the text box still selected, click on any one of the eight handles to display the Resizing Pointer. Drag the Pointer to resize the box horizontally and vertically.

4. Hold down the Shift key while resizing with the Resizing Pointer and notice that the text box is constrained to a square. The size of the square changes as you drag with the Resizing Pointer, but it remains a square.

5. Choose Item/Modify (Ctrl+M) and use the Width and Height fields to change the height and width of the text box back to a rectangle of any size. Click on OK.

COLUMNS

You can change the number of columns in an active (selected) text box from the Measurements palette by changing the value in the Cols (Columns) field. The number of columns can also be changed in the Text Box Specifications dialog box by typing a new number in the Columns field on the left side of the dialog box.

EXERCISE C

1. Choose View/Show Document Layout to display the Document Layout palette. Insert another document page and go to that page.

2. Select the Content tool and click inside the text box to select it. Use the Measurements palette (Ctrl+Alt+M) to change the Cols (Columns) value to 3.

3. With the text box still selected, choose Item/Modify (Ctrl+M) and change the Columns value to 6. Your screen should resemble the Text Box Specifications dialog box in Figure 13.3. Click on OK.

4. Choose File/Get Text (Ctrl+E) and import a text file into the 6-column text box.

5. Scroll to the bottom of the first column and click to place the insertion point after the last word in the first column. Press the Enter key *on the numeric keypad*. This displays the New Column marker (Figure 13.4) and forces all the text after that marker to move to the next column.

6. Click before the first word in the second column. Press the Enter key *on the numeric keypad*. This shifts all the text after the marker to the third column. Your screen should resemble Figure 13.5. You can reposition the text by selecting the New Column marker and deleting it.

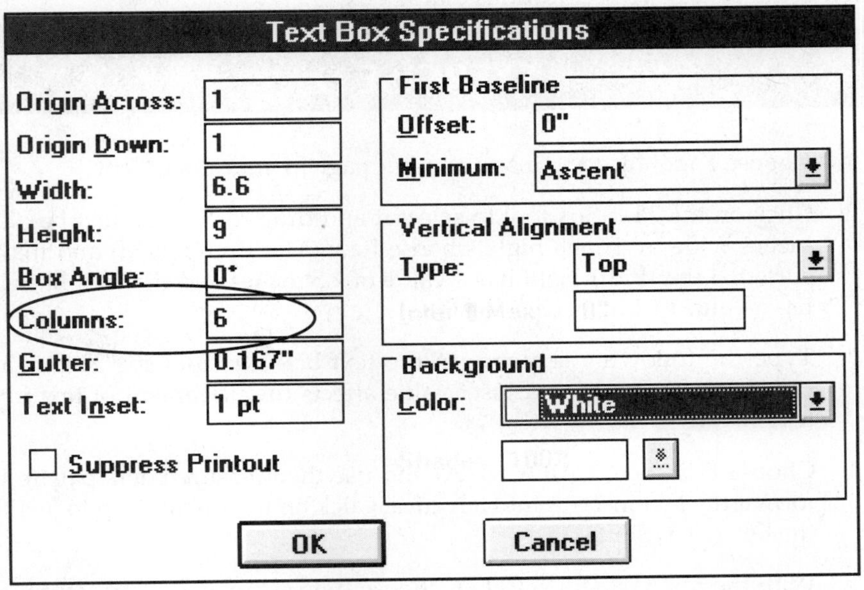

Text Box Specifications

Origin Across:	1	First Baseline	
Origin Down:	1	Offset:	0"
Width:	6.6	Minimum:	Ascent
Height:	9		
Box Angle:	0°	Vertical Alignment	
Columns:	6	Type:	Top
Gutter:	0.167"		
Text Inset:	1 pt	Background	
☐ Suppress Printout		Color:	White

[OK]   [Cancel]

Figure 13.3—Displays the Text Box Specifications dialog box for a 6-column text box that is 6.5 inches wide and 9 inches high.

Vale et vade.   ↓

Figure 13.4—The New Column marker is displayed when you press Enter after a character.

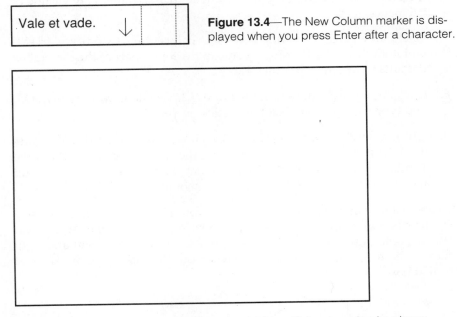

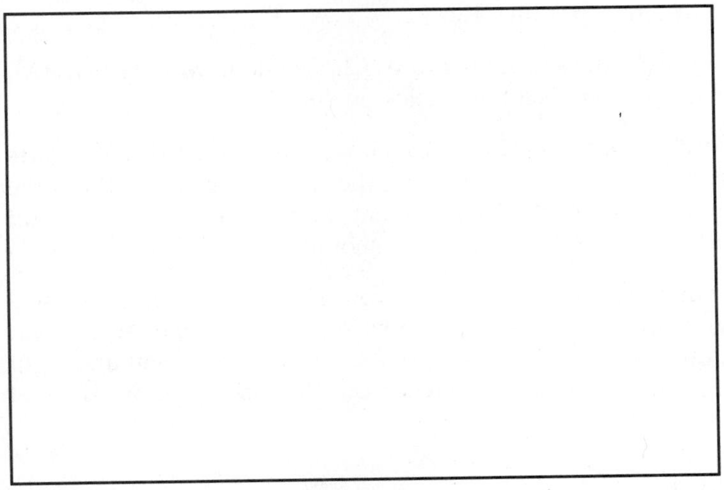

Figure 13.5—Displays a 6-column text box. A New Column marker has been placed before the first word in column 2 which moved the text to the next column, column 3.

FYI

If you press Enter (on the numeric keypad) anywhere in a single column text box, all subsequent text will be shifted to the next text box in a chain of linked text.

Ctrl+M Item/Modify

Ctrl+A Edit/Select All

Ctrl+Shift+J Style/
    Alignment/Justified

Ctrl+D Item/Duplicate

Ctrl+Shift+F Style/Formats

It all adds up

If you apply a left or right indent value to a paragraph from the Paragraph Formats dialog box, that value will be added to the Text Inset value in the Text Box Specifications dialog box. So if you indicated an 8-point Left Indent value for the paragraph in the second text box to which you already applied an 8-point Text Inset value, the text would be inset 16 points from the left side of the text box and 8 points from the top, right, and bottom sides of the text box.

TEXT INSET

The Text Inset value in the Text Box Specifications dialog box determines the space between the four inner edges of the text box and the text in that text box. XPress defaults to a 1-point text inset value, but you can change this in the Text Box Specifications dialog box.

EXERCISE D

1. Choose Page/Insert to insert another page in your document.

2. Click on the Text Box tool to select it and drag to create a text box 2.5 inches wide by 1 inch high. Choose Item/Modify (Ctrl+M) and make sure that the Width field has a value of 2.5 inches and the Height field has a value of 1 inch. Click on OK.

3. Type the following sentence in the text box (no quotes): "This is an example of how the text inset value affects the placement of text in a text box."

4. Choose Edit/Select All (Ctrl+A) and use the Measurements palette to format the text in 14-point Helvetica. Click on the Justify icon to justify the text (Ctrl+Shift+J).

5. With the text box still selected, choose Item/Duplicate (Ctrl+D) twice to make two duplicates of the original text box.

6. Click on the Item tool to select it and move the text boxes one under the other. Use the Measurements palette to assign them an X value of 2.5 inches.

7. Click anywhere in the first text box. Choose Item/Modify (Ctrl+M) and notice that the Text Inset value in the lower part of the dialog box defaults to 1 point. Click on OK.

8. Click anywhere in the second text box. Choose Item/Modify (Ctrl+M) and type 8 in the Text Inset field. Click on OK.

9. Click anywhere in the third text box. Choose Style/Formats (Ctrl+Shift+F). Type 0p8 (8 points) in the Left Indent field. Press the Tab key twice to select the Right Indent field. Type 0p8 in the Right Indent field. Click on OK. Your screen should resemble Figure 13.6.

Notice that 8 points of space surround the four sides of the text in the second text box and, in doing so, cause a text overflow marker to appear. Although the third text box displays 8 points of space on the left and right sides of the text, it does not inset the text from the top or bottom sides of the text box.

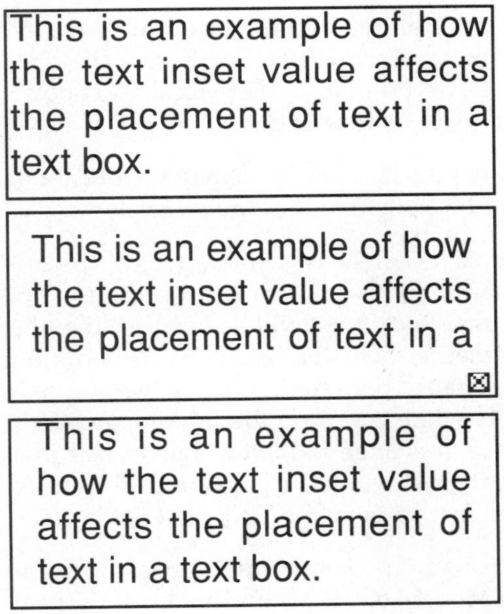

This is an example of how the text inset value affects the placement of text in a text box.

This is an example of how the text inset value affects the placement of text in a ⊠

This is an example of how the text inset value affects the placement of text in a text box.

Figure 13.6—Displays three text boxes with different Text Inset values. The top box displays a Text Inset value of 1 pt. The middle text box displays a Text Inset value of 8 pts. The bottom text box displays a Text Inset value of 1 point and a right and left indent of 8 points.

WARNING!

XPress has to get the space it needs to vertically align lines from someplace—and it gets it from the space between lines (leading) and paragraphs. Whenever you apply vertical spacing values, you risk changing leading and paragraph values.

VERTICAL ALIGNMENT

Vertical alignment is positioning text vertically within a text box. Text can be positioned to flow from the top or bottom of the text box or it can be centered at equidistant points within the text box. Text can also be justified vertically in a text box. The Vertical Alignment commands are accessed from the Text Box Specifications dialog box (Figure 13.7).

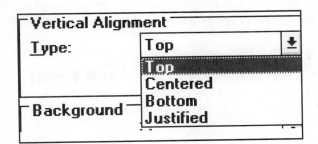

Figure 13.7—The Vertical Alignment options in the Text Box Specifications dialog box.

EXERCISE E

1. Use the Document Layout palette (View/Show Document Layout) to add another page to your document.

2. Click on the Text Box tool to select it and hold down the Shift key while you drag to create a text box that is a 2-inch square. Use the Measurements palette (Ctrl+Alt+M) to make sure that the W and H values of the selected text box are 2 inches.

3. Type the following sentence in the text box (no quotes): "This is an example of the different kinds of vertical alignment formatting commands which can be applied to text in a document."

Ctrl+Shift–J Style/
    Alignment/Justified
Ctrl+D Item/Duplicate
Ctrl+M Item/Modify

4. Format it in Helvetica 12/14 (12-point type on 14-point leading). Choose Style/Alignment/Justified (Ctrl+Shift+J) to justify the text. Choose Item/Duplicate (Ctrl+D) and duplicate the selected text box 3 times. You now have four text boxes on the page.

5. Select the Item tool or hold down the Ctrl key to change the I-beam to the Item tool and move the text boxes so that they are all easily visible.

6. Click inside the first text box to select it; choose Item/Modify (Ctrl+M). Notice that the default Vertical Alignment option is Top. This means that the top of the first line of text will be positioned at the point specified in the First Baseline field (Figure 13.8). This option defaults to 0 (zero) with the distance between the top edge of a text box (Text Inset) and the first baseline based on the tallest character's cap height (Ascent). So unless you change it, the top line of text in a text box that is Top vertically aligned will fall 1 point from the top of the text box (unless you change that value in the Text Inset field).

7. Click inside the second text box and type *Bottom* after the last word in the paragraph. Choose Item/Modify (Ctrl+M) and use the Vertical Alignment drop-down menu to select Bottom. Click on OK.

8. The text is now positioned in the text box with the last line 1 point (as per the Text Inset value) from the bottom of the text box (Figure 13.9). Text will flow upward as it is entered. Click on OK.

9. Type a few words after *Bottom* and notice how the text moves upward from the bottom of the box.

10. Click inside the third text box and type *Center* after the last word in the paragraph. Use the Text Box Specifications dialog box (Ctrl+M) to select Centered from the Vertical Alignment drop-down menu. Click on OK. The text is now positioned in the center of the box with equal space above the first line and below the last line of text (Figure 13.9).

11. Click inside the fourth text box and type *Justified* after the last word in the paragraph. Use the Text Box Specifications dialog box (Ctrl+M) to select Justified from the Vertical Alignment drop-down menu. Click on OK. The text now fills the box evenly between the top and bottom lines (Figure 13.9).

Tip

To keep a tool selected after using it once, press the Alt key when first selecting that tool.

INTER ¶ MAX

When you select Justified from the Vertical Alignment drop-down menu, the Inter ¶ Max field becomes active. This option allows you to indicate the maximum amount of space that XPress will place between paragraphs before adding or deleting space between lines in order to vertically justify the paragraph. If you type .5" in the Inter ¶ Max field, for example, XPress will place no more than a half-inch of space between the paragraphs and then adjust the space evenly between lines in a text box to vertically justify the text (Figure 13.10).

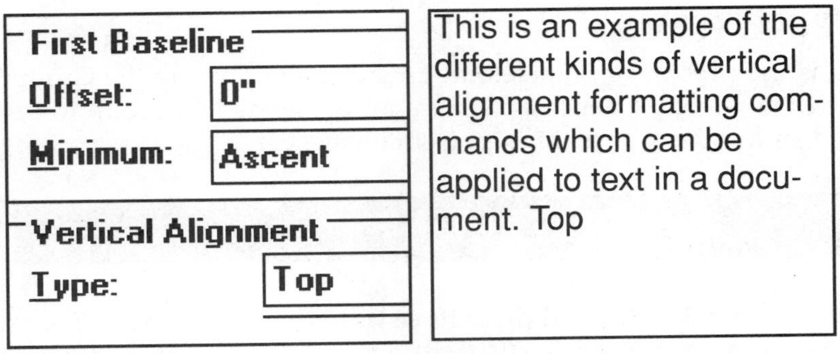

First Baseline

Offset: 0"

Minimum: Ascent

Vertical Alignment

Type: Top

This is an example of the different kinds of vertical alignment formatting commands which can be applied to text in a document. Top

Figure 13.8—A text box that is Top vertically aligned. The first line sits on a baseline which is offset 0 (zero) points from the top edge of the text box.

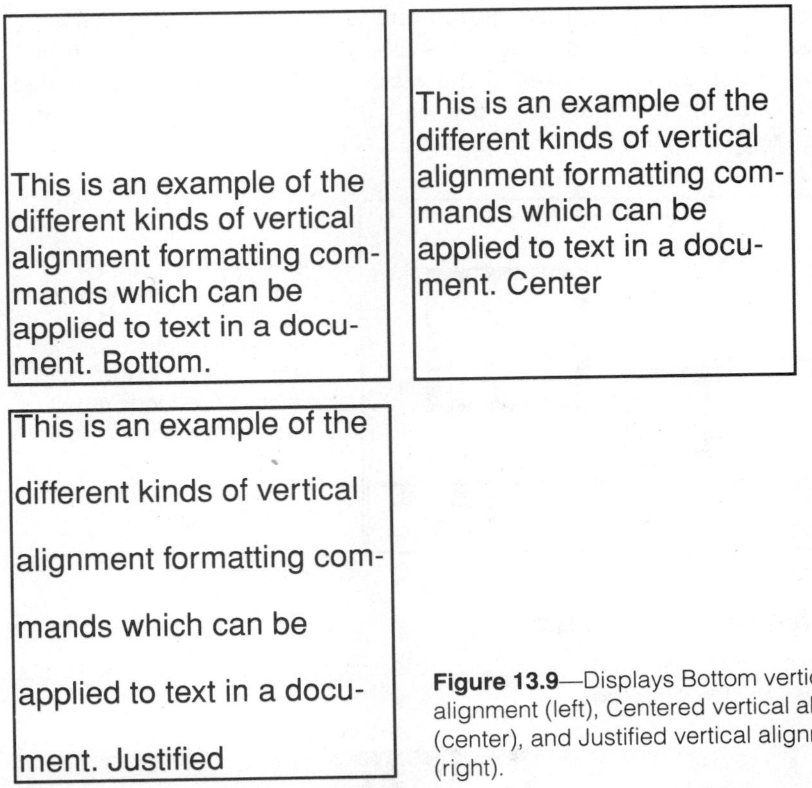

This is an example of the different kinds of vertical alignment formatting commands which can be applied to text in a document. Bottom.

This is an example of the different kinds of vertical alignment formatting commands which can be applied to text in a document. Center

This is an example of the different kinds of vertical alignment formatting commands which can be applied to text in a document. Justified

Figure 13.9—Displays Bottom vertical alignment (left), Centered vertical alignment (center), and Justified vertical alignment (right).

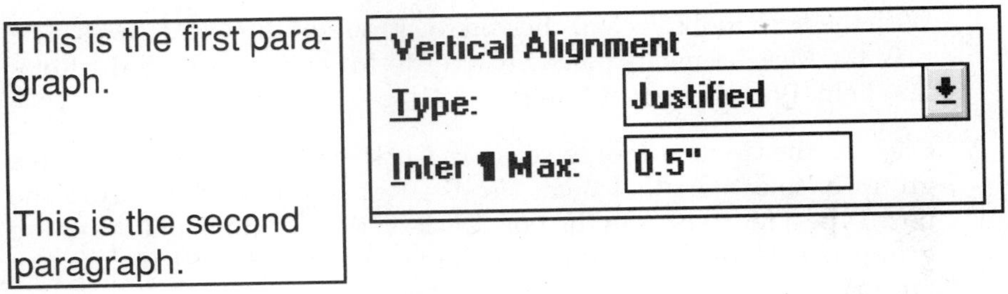

This is the first paragraph.

This is the second paragraph.

Vertical Alignment

Type: Justified

Inter ¶ **Max:**   0.5"

Figure 13.10—The Inter ¶ Max value of .5 inches places a half inch of space between the two paragraphs before adjusting the space needed to vertically justify the text.

Tip

You can first Shift-select text boxes with the Item tool, then choose Item/ Modify to apply the same vertical alignment command to all the selected boxes.

How it does it

When justified vertical alignment is applied to a text box, XPress positions the *first* line as specified in the First Baseline field of the Text Box Specifications dialog box and the *last* line in the text box flush with the text inset at the bottom of the box. The rest of the lines in the text box are justified between those two lines.

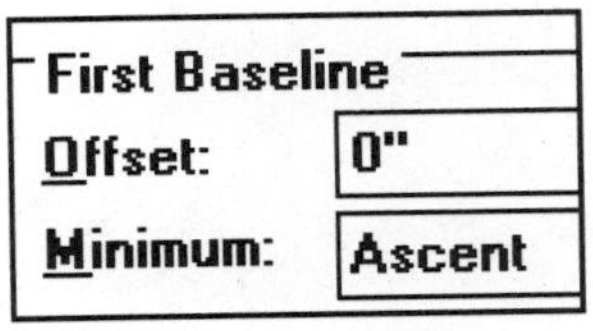

First Baseline

Offset: 0"

Minimum: Ascent

The minimum distance between the baseline of the first line of text and the Text Inset value is set to Ascent. The distance is equal to the height of ascenders in the font of the largest character on the first line of text in that text box.

Ctrl+B Item/Frame
Ctrl+G Item/Group
Ctrl+Alt+M View/Show
        Measurements

Item tool selects a group
and is used to move it.

Content tool selects an
item within a group.

GROUPING ITEMS

Grouping is the process of Shift-selecting items and applying the Group
command (Item/Group), which will cause all the items in a group to be
moved and/or in some way manipulated simultaneously.

EXERCISE F

1. Select the Text Box tool and draw three text boxes on the page. Select
    each box, choose Item/Frame (Ctrl+B), and assign each box a different
    frame.

2. Click on the Item tool to select it and hold down the Shift key while
    you click on each box. When the three boxes display their selection
    handles, release the mouse button and choose Item/Group (Ctrl+G).
    This will designate the three boxes as a group and place a bounding
    box around all three boxes. If the Measurements palette is displayed
    (Ctrl+Alt+M), it will display only the X and Y origins of the group and
    the group's angle of rotation (Figure 13.11).

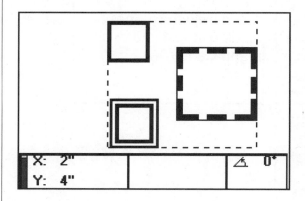

Figure 13.11—A group of
items surrounded by its
bounding box. The Mea-
surements palette displays
the group's position from
the left (X) and top (Y)
margins measured from
the upper left corner of
the bounding box and the
angle of rotation for the
entire group.

MODIFYING GROUPS

To move a group, use the Item tool. To edit or modify any element within a
group, use the Content tool.

EXERCISE G

1. With the Item tool selected, click on the group of three text boxes. Dis-
    play the Measurements palette (Ctrl+Alt+M) and type 45 in the Rota-
    tion field. Press Return or Enter.

2. Click on the Content tool to select it. Click on one of the boxes in the
    group to select just that item. Use the Resizing Pointer to resize the
    box. Type a few words in the box. Click on the Item tool and the entire
    group is selected, displaying the enlarged box as still part of the
    group.

3. With the group still selected (use the Item tool), choose Item/Modify (Ctrl+M) or double-click on the group with the Item tool. Because all the items in this group are text boxes, the Text Box Specifications dialog box is displayed.

4. Use the Vertical Alignment drop-down menu to select Bottom. This will vertically justify the words you just typed in the text box from the bottom to the top of the text box. Click on OK. Your screen should resemble Figure 13.12.

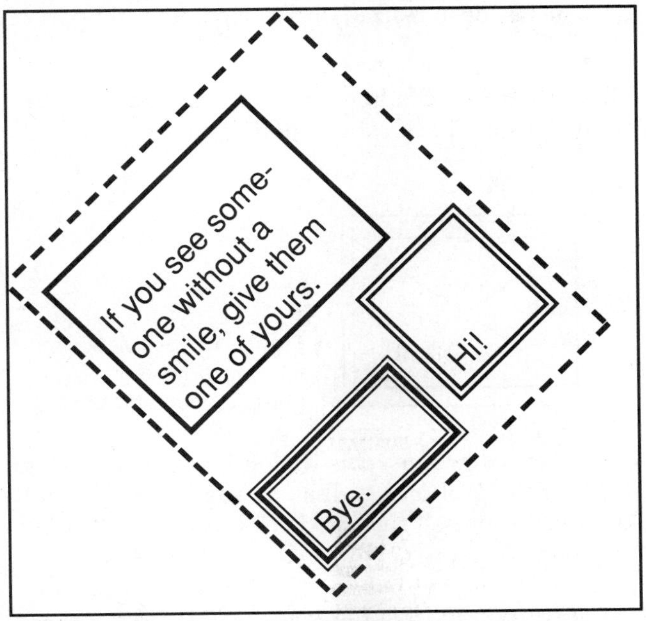

Ctrl+M Item/Modify

Figure 13.12—A group of text boxes which has been rotated 45° and to which a Bottom Vertical Alignment command was applied.

Angle of Rotation field in the group's Measurements palette

GROUP SPECIFICATIONS DIALOG BOX

If a group consists of different kinds of items—text boxes, picture boxes, or lines—the Group Specifications dialog box is displayed when you choose Item/Modify (Ctrl+M).

Sorry!

The Group Specifications dialog box is not available when one group is grouped with another group.

EXERCISE H

1. Use the Document Layout palette (View/Show Document Layout) to create another page in your document by using the Insert command onto the palette.

2. Select the Text Box tool and draw a small text box. Select the Picture Box tool and draw a small picture box. Select the Orthogonal Line tool and draw a horizontal line connecting the two boxes.

3. Click on the Item tool to select it. Press the Shift key, then click on the text box, the picture box, and the line to select all three items. Release the Shift key.

Ctrl+G Item/Group
Ctrl+M Item/Modify

4. Choose Item/Group (Ctrl+G) to group the items. With the Item tool selected, click on the group. Notice the bounding box that encloses the three items (Figure 13.13). Drag the group around the page with the Item tool and notice that when you move a grouped item, all the items within that group move together.

5. Click on the Content tool to select it. Now click on the line in the group. The arrow changes into the Mover tool and allows you to move and resize the line anywhere on the page. Lengthen the line and move it. Then click on the Item tool and click on the group. Notice that even though the line has been resized and moved, it is still part of the group.

6. With the group still selected (use the Item tool), choose Item/Modify (Ctrl+M) to display the Group Specifications dialog box, as displayed in Figure 13.14.

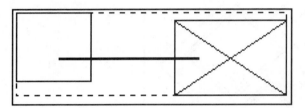

Figure 13.13—Displays the dashed line of a group's bounding box.

Like the Measurements palette for groups, this dialog box allows you to change the X and Y origins of the group as well as its angle of rotation. It also allows you to click in the Suppress Printout check box and to assign a Background Color to the group.

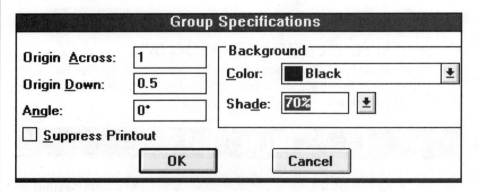

Figure 13.14—The Group Specifications dialog box is displayed when a group which contains different kinds of items is selected with the Item tool.

EXERCISE I

What you will need

A graphic file

Ctrl+M Item/Modify
Ctrl+B Item/Frame
Ctrl+E File/Get Picture
Ctrl+Alt+Shift+F Propor-
    tionally fits a picture
    in the box
Ctrl+P FIle/Print

1. Select the group with the Item tool and choose Item/Modify. Pull down the Shade menu under the Background Color menu and choose 50% Black. Click on OK. Notice that both boxes and the line in the group now contain a background color of 50% Black, because a Background Color command applied to a group affects every box, text, picture, or line in the group. Your screen should resemble Figure 13.15.

2. Click on the Content tool to select it and click on the picture box in the group. Choose Item/Modify (Ctrl+M) to display the Picture Box Specifications dialog box. Because you selected a specific item in the group, the Specifications dialog box for that *item* appears, not the group's Specifications dialog box.

3. Use the Shade drop-down menu to assign that picture box a shade of 0% Black. Click on OK. With the picture box still selected, choose Item/Frame (Ctrl+B). Scroll to select any frame and assign it a Weight of 4 points. Click on OK. Notice that only the picture box which you selected with the Content tool reflects the changes you made.

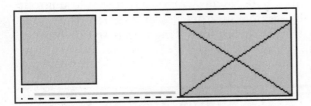

Figure 13.15—A group with a Background Color of 50% Black applied to all the boxes and the line in the group.

SUPPRESS PRINTOUT

The Suppress Printout command in the Specifications dialog box allows you to suppress the printout of that selected item—a line, box, or a group of items.

Save time!

Use the Suppress Printout command to speed up printing. If you Suppress Printout of pictures, for example, a page of text will print much more quickly.

EXERCISE J

1. Select the Item tool and click on the picture box in the group. Choose File/Get Picture (Ctrl+E) to import a picture into the box. Press Ctrl+Alt+Shift+F to fit the picture in the box.

2. Use the Item tool to select the group. Choose Item/Modify (Ctrl+M) to display the Group Specifications dialog box. Click in the Suppress Printout check box. Then click on OK. Print the page (Ctrl+P) and notice that no item in the group printed.

3. Click on one of the picture boxes with the Content tool and choose Item/Modify (Ctrl+M) to edit just that item, not the group.

Ctrl+P File/Print
Ctrl+G Item/Group
Ctrl+U Item/Ungroup
Ctrl+N File/New
Ctrl+Y Edit/Preferences/
    General
Ctrl+Alt+M View/Show
    Measurements
Ctrl+B Item/Frame
Ctrl+M Item/Modify
Ctrl+A Edit/Select All

4. Because you selected an individual item, the picture box, the Picture Box Specifications dialog box is displayed. Click in the Suppress Printout check box to deselect that option and allow the picture box to be printed. Click on OK.

5. Print this page (Ctrl+P) and notice that now the one picture box for which you deselected the Suppress Printout command has printed.

GROUPING AND UNGROUPING GROUPS

You can group groups by Shift-selecting groups and items and/or other groups. You can also ungroup a group.

EXERCISE K

1. Use the Line tool to draw two lines near your original group. Use the Item tool to Shift-select both lines. Choose Item/Group (Ctrl+G) to group the lines. With the line group selected, click on the original group with the Item tool. Choose Item/Group (Ctrl+G) to join both groups into one group.

2. Click on the new group. Choose Item/Ungroup (Ctrl+U) to ungroup the line group from the original group. Click anywhere off the page. Click on the original group. Choose Item/Ungroup (Ctrl+U). Now all items are ungrouped.

REVIEW EXERCISE

In this exercise you will create a two-page spread for a catalog.

1. Choose File/New (Ctrl+N) to create a new document with 1-inch margins all around, an automatic text box, and facing pages. Choose Edit/Preferences/General (Ctrl+Y) to select inches as the unit of measure and the Delete Changes option after Master Page items.

2. Display the Measurements palette (Ctrl+Alt+M). Choose Page/Display/A Master A. On the left Master A page, draw a text box .5 inches high and 6.5 inches wide. Choose Item/Frame (Ctrl+B), scroll to select a frame, and assign it a Weight of 4 points. Click on OK. Position the box at the 1-inch X and 1-inch Y points of origin.

3. In that box type (no quotes): "TO ORDER CALL 800-967-1234" and format it in Helvetica, 24 points. Click on the Center Alignment icon to center the text.

4. With the text box still selected, choose Item Modify (Ctrl+M) and use the Vertical Alignment menu to select Centered.

5. Choose Edit/Select All (Ctrl+A) and click on the right tracking arrow in the Measurements palette 3 times to assign it a tracking value of 30.

6. Choose Page/Insert to display the Insert Pages dialog box. Insert 2 pages after page 1 based on M1 Master 1. Choose Document/Show Master Pages. Double-click on the M1 icon and scroll to the left master page.

7. Draw a picture box; use the Measurements palette to assign it the values in Figure 13.16. Draw a text box and assign it the values in Figure 13.17.

8. With the Item tool selected, Shift-select both boxes. Choose Item/Group (Ctrl+G). Choose Item/Modify (Ctrl+M) to display the Group Specifications dialog box. Use the Shade drop-down menu to assign the boxes a shade of 30% Black. Click on OK.

9. With the Item tool and the group still selected, choose Item/Duplicate (Ctrl+D) and use the Measurements palette to position the duplicate group as indicated in Figure 13.18.

10. Choose Item/Modify (Ctrl+M) and in the Group Specifications dialog box assign the boxes a shade of 40% Black.

11. With the Content tool, click on each text box, choose Item/Modify (Ctrl+M), and assign it a Background color of 0% Black. Click on OK and type (no quotes) "Caption" in each text box.

12. With the Item tool, Shift-select the two groups and the text box at the top of the page. Choose Item/Group (Ctrl+G) to add the horizontal text box to the group. Choose Item/Duplicate (Ctrl+D) to duplicate the group which now consists of two groups and a text box.

13. Drag that new group from the left to the right page. Choose Item/Ungroup (Ctrl+U) and click anywhere off the page. Your screen should resemble Figure 13.19.

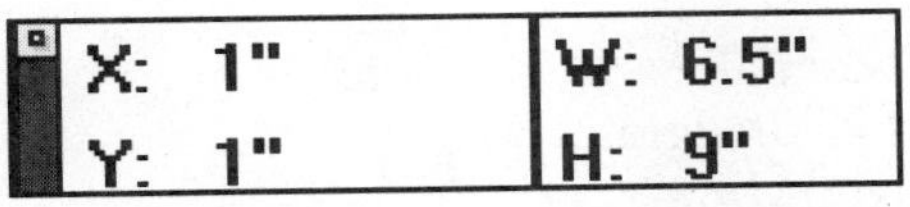

Ctrl+G Item/Group
Ctrl+M Item/Modify
Ctrl+D Item/Duplicate
Ctrl+U Item/Ungroup

| X: 1" | W: 6.5" |
| Y: 1" | H: 9" |

Figure 13.16—Dimensions for the picture box.

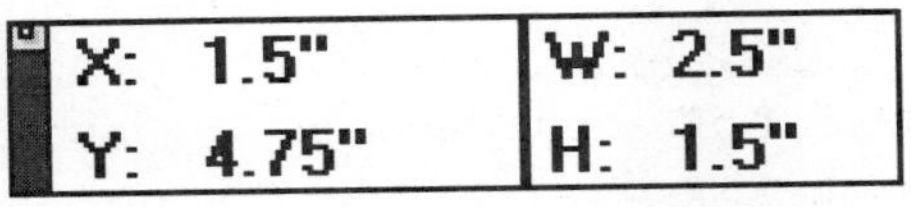

| X: 1.5" | W: 2.5" |
| Y: 4.75" | H: 1.5" |

Figure 13.17—Dimensions for the text box.

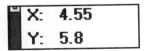

Figure 13.18—Dimensions for the duplicate group.

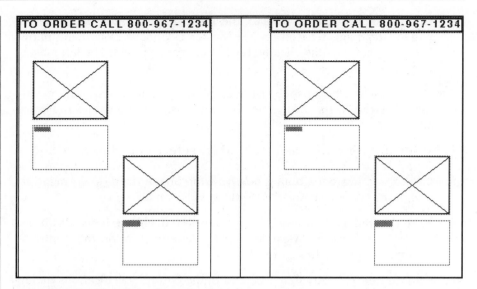

| Figure 13.19—The finished two-page spread.

REVIEW QUESTIONS

Read the following questions and choose the answer which best completes the statement.

1. A text box's origins are determined from its position relative to _____.
   a. the top and left margins
   b. the top and bottom margins
   c. the right and left margins
   d. the top and right margins

2. Text boxes can be constrained horizontally and/or vertically by _____.
   a. holding down the Shift key while dragging
   b. pressing the Alt key while dragging
   c. dragging with the Item tool
   d. dragging with the Content tool

3. The number of columns in a text box _____.
   a. is set in the General Preferences dialog box
   b. can be changed via the Text Box Specifications dialog box
   c. cannot be changed once the box is resized
   d. can be changed via the Measurements palette and the Text Box Specifications dialog box

4. Vertical alignment is _____.
   a. fitting text in a text box
   b. aligning text from the right and left margins
   c. hanging tight
   d. centering text at equidistant points from the top and bottom of a text box

5. A group can be comprised of _____.
    a. text boxes and picture boxes
    b. picture boxes and lines
    c. boxes and lines
    d. boxes, lines, and groups

6. Groups can be modified _____.
    a. with the Content tool
    b. when items are selected with the Item tool
    c. from the Item menu
    d. by dragging on the bounding box

7. Items within a group can be modified _____.
    a. from the Item menu
    b. when selected with the Content tool
    c. with the Item tool
    d. a and b

8. The Measurements palette for a group _____.
    a. is displayed when an item in a group is selected
    b. allows you to resize the group
    c. allows you to reposition the group
    d. includes the same fields as the Group Specifications dialog box

9. When all the items in a group are the same, _____.
    a. the Measurements palette for a group allows you to apply
        scaling values to pictures
    b. the Specifications dialog box for the item is displayed
    c. no Measurements palette is displayed
    d. the group can be resized from the Measurements palette

10. To suppress the printout of an item in a group, _____.
    a. use the Measurements palette
    b. select Suppress Printout in a Specifications dialog box
    c. use the Print dialog box
    d. select Suppress Printout in the Group Specifications dialog box

Answers: 1. a; 2. a; 3. d; 4. d; 5. d; 6. c; 7. b; 8. c; 9. b; 10.

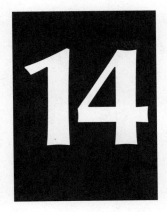

LESSON

14

Lines
and
Rules

OVERVIEW

In this lesson you will learn how to use the Orthogonal Line tool to draw horizontal and vertical lines and the Line tool to draw lines at any angle. You will learn how to modify lines from their endpoints, right points, left points, and midpoints. You will also learn how to create rules, anchor them to text, and save the rule as part of a paragraph's style sheet. As a review, you will create an announcement incorporating lines and anchored rules.

TOPICS

Orthogonal and diagonal lines
Line Modes
Endpoints Mode
Left Point Mode
Line Style menu
Right Point Mode
Midpoint Mode
Anchored rules
Overriding the unit of measure
Rules as styles
Review Exercise
Review Questions

TERMS

angle of rotation
endcaps
endpoints
indents
left point
midpoint

right point
rule
rule above
rule below
X and Y values
XC and YC values

ORTHOGONAL AND DIAGONAL LINES

Unlike picture boxes and text boxes, a line does not contain anything. It's an item that can be created, resized, and repositioned. Because it is an item, it can be locked, constrained, and grouped with other items.

In XPress an orthogonal line, a line which is drawn either horizontally or vertically, is created with the Orthogonal Line tool. A diagonal line is drawn with the Line tool. You can draw a horizontal or vertical line with the Line tool by holding down the Shift key before releasing the mouse button to constrain the line to a horizontal or vertical position. Choose Item/Modify (Ctrl+M) when a line is selected to display the Line Specifications dialog box (Figure 14.1).

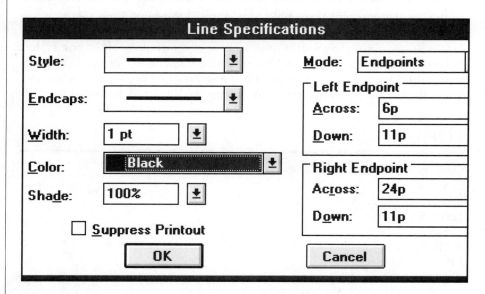

Figure 14.1—The Line Specifications dialog box for an active (selected) line.

LINE MODES

Regardless of whether a line is vertical, horizontal, or diagonal, it has four modes: Endpoints Mode, Left Point Mode, Right Point Mode, and Midpoint Mode. These modes are accessed from the Mode drop-down menu in the Line Specifications dialog box (Figure 14.2).

A line that is created in one mode can be modified in another. You could, for example, create a line with certain Endpoints values. To reposition one of those Endpoints, you could change one of its right or left points.

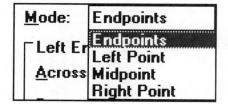

Figure 14.2—The four different line modes in the Line Specifications dialog box. These modes are also available from the Style menu when a line is active.

ENDPOINTS MODE

Endpoints Mode refers to the line's left point and right point as they are positioned on a coordinate of X and Y (Figure 14.3). The line specified in Figure 14.1 has an X1 (Left Endpoint) value of 6 picas, that is, its left endpoint starts 6 picas from the left margin on the page. It has an X2 value of 24 picas, which means it extends to the 24-pica mark on the horizontal ruler, the position of the right endpoint. It has a Y1 value of 11 picas, meaning that its left endpoint starts 11 picas down from the top margin. It has a Y2 value of 11 picas, meaning that the line's left endpoint ends at the 11-pica mark on the vertical ruler.

Since both the Y1 and Y2 values are the same, this is a horizontal line. If the X1 and X2 values were the same, it would be a vertical line. If all four X and Y values were different, it would be a diagonal line.

| X1 : 2" | X2 : 4" | Endpoints |
| Y1 : 3" | Y2 : 3" | |

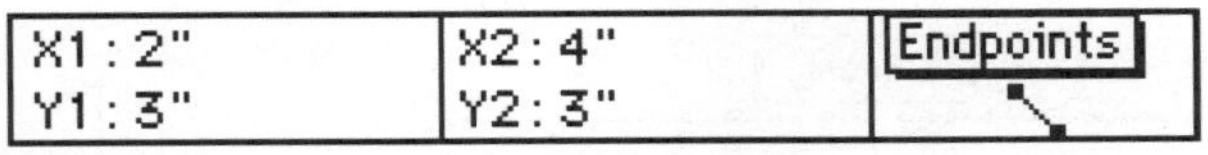

Figure 14.3—X and Y coordinates for a horizontal line.

EXERCISE A

1. Create a new document (Ctrl+N) with 1-inch margins all around and an automatic text box. Use the General Preferences dialog box (Ctrl+Y) to select picas as the unit of measure. Display the Measurements palette (Ctrl+Alt+M).

2. Click on the Orthogonal Line tool to select it and draw a horizontal line anywhere on the page. With the line selected, use the Measurements palette to assign it the X and Y values for Endpoints mode as displayed in Figure 14.3.

3. With the Orthogonal Line tool still selected, draw a vertical line anywhere on the page. Using the Measurements palette, assign it the Endpoints values displayed in Figure 14.4.

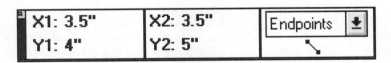

| X1: 3.5" | X2: 3.5" | Endpoints |
| Y1: 4" | Y2: 5" | |

Figure 14.4—X and Y coordinates for a vertical line.

Orthogonal Line tool used to draw horizontal and vertical lines

Line tool used to draw lines of any angle

Ctrl+N File/New
Ctrl+Y Edit/Preferences/
General
Ctrl+Alt+M View/Show
Measurements

Ctrl+M Item/Modify
Ctrl+Alt+M View/Show
    Measurements

4. Draw another vertical line with the Orthogonal Line tool anywhere on the page. With the line still selected, choose Item/Modify (Ctrl+M) and assign the line the specifications in Figure 14.5. Click on OK. Your screen should resemble Figure 14.6.

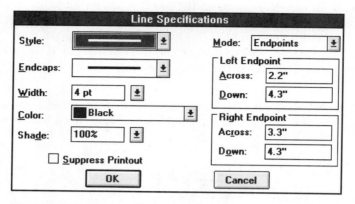

Figure 14.5—The Line Specifications dialog box for a vertical line.

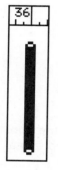

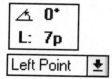

This line displays an X1 value of 36 picas, indicating that it is at the 36-pica marker on the horizontal (X axis) ruler.

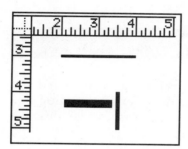

The same line extends 7 picas (L value) from its left point.

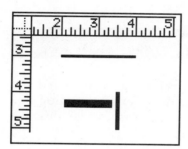

Figure 14.6—Horizontal and vertical lines drawn with the Orthogonal Line tool.

LEFT POINT MODE

The Left Point Mode specifies a line's position in terms of its left endpoint (X1 value), its bottom endpoint (Y2 value) (its length), and its angle.

EXERCISE B

1. Click on the first horizontal line you drew (with either the Item tool or the Content tool) and in the Measurements palette, use the Endpoints drop-down menu to select Left Point. Notice that the X1 value is 2 inches, indicating that the line begins at the 2-inch mark on the horizontal ruler or 2 inches from the left margin. The Y1 value is now 3 inches, indicating that the left point of the line is at the 3-inch mark on the vertical ruler or starts 3 inches down from the top margin. It has a 0 (zero) angle of rotation and is 2 inches long.

2. With the line still selected, use the Measurements palette (Ctrl+Alt+M) to assign it the values in Figure 14.7. Remember to press Enter to accept the values.

3. Click on the second horizontal line to select it. Choose Left Point from the Mode drop-down menu in the Measurements palette and change its Y1 value to 2.3 inches and its length to 2 inches.

4. Click on the vertical line to select it. Choose Item/Modify (Ctrl+M) to display the Line Specifications dialog box. Assign the line a Left Point X1 value of 1.5 inches, a Y1 value of 2 inches, an angle of rotation of 10°, and a length of 2 inches. Click on OK. Your screen should resemble Figure 14.8. Notice that when you applied an angle of rotation value, the line rotated from its left point, because that was the mode selected.

5. Click on the Line tool to select it and draw a diagonal line anywhere on the page. Use the Measurements palette to assign it a width of 6 points and Left Point mode.

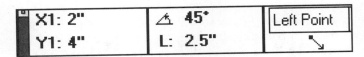

Figure 14.7— Values for a line's left point.

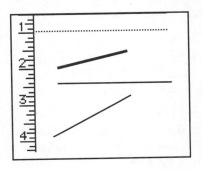

Figure 14.8—Displays lines with different Left Point values.

LINE STYLE MENU

When a line is active, the Style menu for lines allows you to modify a line's style, width, endcaps, color, and shade.

EXERCISE C

1. Use the Line tool to draw a diagonal line. With the line still selected, choose Style/Line Style. Use the Line Style drop-down menu in the Measurements palette to select a dashed line.

2. With the line still selected, choose Style/Endcaps and use the drop-down menu to select the double pointed arrow, the last option in the menu. Then choose Style/Shade and assign that line a Shade of 40% Black.

3. Choose Item/Modify (Ctrl+M) and change the line's Width to 8 points and its Angle to –10. Click on OK. Your screen (depending on the line's angle of rotation) should resemble Figure 14.9.

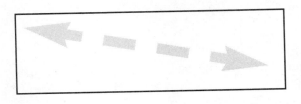

Figure 14.9—Displays a line rotated at –10° or 10° to the right from its left point.

Ctrl+Y Edit/Preferences/
   General
Ctrl+D Item/Duplicate
Ctrl+M Item/Modify

RIGHT POINT MODE

So far you have manipulated lines from their endpoints and from their left points. You can also manipulate them from their right points and from their midpoints. The right point of a line specifies a line's position in terms of its right endpoint (X2 value), its bottom endpoint (Y2 value), its length, and its angle.

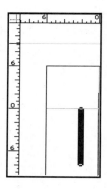

EXERCISE D

1. Choose Ctrl+Y and select inches as the unit of measure.

2. Click on the Line tool to select it. Draw a line and hold down the Shift key while you draw to constrain the line to a 45° angle and create a diagonal line. With the line selected, choose Item/Modify (Ctrl+M) and choose Right Point from the Mode drop-down menu on the right side of the Line Specifications dialog box. Type 1.5 in the Length field. Click on OK.

3. With the line still selected, choose Style/Endcaps and select the fourth endcap style, a right arrow with a tailfeather. Then choose Style/Width/8 pt. Your screen should resemble Figure 14.10.

4. With the line still selected, choose Item/Duplicate (Ctrl+D). Choose Item/Modify (Ctrl+M) and type 75 in the Angle field and 2 in the Length field. This will rotate the line 75° from the right endpoint (tip of the arrow) and change its length to 2 inches. Click on OK. Your screen should resemble Figure 14.11. Notice how the line rotates to the left from its right point, because that was the mode selected when the Angle value was applied.

Right Point This line displays an X2 value of –2p, which means that the right endpoint extends 2 picas beyond the left margin.

X2: -2p
Y2: 8p Its Y2 value indicates that its bottom endpoint is at the 8-pica mark on the vertical (Y axis) ruler.

∡ 0°
L: 8p The L value indicates that the line's length is 8 picas.

Figure 14.10—A line rotated 45° to the left and displaying an endcap style.

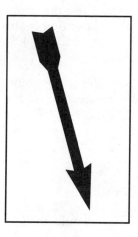

Figure 14.11—A line rotated 75° to the left from its right point.

MIDPOINT MODE

The midpoint of a line specifies its position in terms of its center point (XC value), its bottom endpoint (YC value), its length, and its angle.

EXERCISE E

1. Use the Line tool to draw a line in any direction.

2. Choose Item/Modify (Ctrl+M) and choose Midpoint from the Mode drop-down menu. Type 2 in the Length field. Select an endcap style from the Endcaps drop-down menu.

3. Assign it a Weight of 8 points and a Shade of 30% Black.

4. Type –20 in the Angle field on the right to rotate the line 20° to the right from the midpoint of the line. Since this is a 2-inch line, it will rotate from the 1-inch point on the line. Click on OK.

5. With the line still selected, choose Item/Step and Repeat (Ctrl+Alt+D). Type 1 in the Repeat Count field; 0 (zero) in the Horizontal Offset field; and –p3 in the Vertical Offset field to position one duplicate of the line 3 points below the original. Click on OK.

6. With the duplicate still selected, choose Style/Shade/100% to create an outlined arrow.

7. Click on the lighter arrow in front and choose Item/Send Backward. Your screen should resemble Figure 14.12.

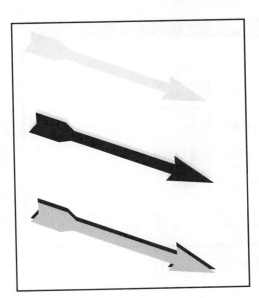

Figure 14.12—A line rotated 20° to the right from its midpoint. The line was styled and given a Shade value of 50% Black, then duplicated and positioned to create a drop shadow effect.

Ctrl+Shift+E Style/Leading
Ctrl+Shift+N Style/Rules

ANCHORED RULES

An item drawn with the Orthogonal Line tool or with the Line tool is called a line. A line placed above or below a paragraph for emphasis or embellishment is called a rule. XPress allows you to anchor rules to text as part of that text's paragraph format so that when the text moves, the rule moves with it.

When the Content tool is selected, the Rules formatting option is available from the Style menu. It is also accessed from the the Edit/Style Sheets dialog box. However, the best way to format paragraphs with rules is from the Style menu, because the Paragraph Rules dialog box contains an Apply button which allows you to see how the rule looks and to make changes before closing the dialog box.

EXERCISE F

1. Use the Document Layout palette (View/Show Document Layout) and drag to create a new page. Type (no quotes): "THIS IS A HEADING." Press the Enter key and type "THIS IS ANOTHER HEADING." Format both lines in 18-point Times.

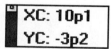

2. Click anywhere in the second paragraph and choose Style/Leading (Ctrl+Shift+E). Type 36 in the Leading dialog box to apply 36 points of leading between the second line and the line above it. Click on OK.

The Midpoint XC value (X axis) of this line is 10p1.

3. With the cursor anywhere in the first paragraph, choose Style/Rules (Ctrl+Shift+N) to display the Paragraph Rules dialog box. Click in the Rule Below check box to display the expanded Paragraph Rules dialog box (Figure 14.13).

Its YC (Y axis) value is −3p2 because it is 3 picas and 2 points up from or above the top margin.

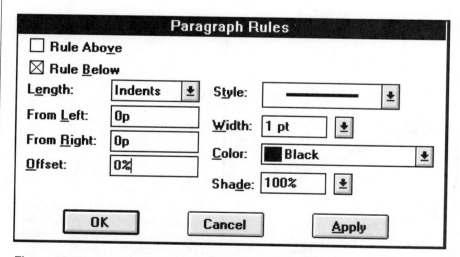

Figure 14.13—The expanded Paragraph Rules dialog box.

4. Use the Length drop-down menu to choose Text, which will limit the length of the rule to the length of the line of text. Type 30% in the Offset box. When you specify a percentage as an offset value, XPress will place the rule between two paragraphs based on the value in this field. Entering a 30% Offset value specifies that 30% of the total space is between the top paragraph and the rule and the remaining 70% of the space is between the rule and the following paragraph.

5. Use the Width drop-down menu to select Hairline and the Shade drop-down menu to select 60% Black. Click on Apply to see the effect of those values.

6. Change the 30% Offset value to 10%. Change the Width to 4 point and click on OK. Notice that the line moves up closer to the top paragraph. Your screen should resemble Figure 14.14.

7. Click immediately before the first letter in the first paragraph and press Enter a few times. Notice that the rule moves with the paragraph and maintains its position in relation to the paragraph. Notice also that the second paragraph also displays the same Rule Below format as the first paragraph. This is because the Rule Below command is embedded in the paragraph return marker, which is repeated each time you press Enter.

8. To remove the Rule Below command from all lines following the first paragraph, choose View/Show Invisibles (Ctrl+I). Drag the cursor to select all the paragraph return markers below the first one, including the one at the end of the second paragraph.

9. Choose Style/Rules (Ctrl+Shift+N) and click in the Rule Below check box to deselect it and remove the Rule Below formatting from the selected text. Click on OK twice.

10. Press Enter a few times after the second paragraph and type (all caps, no quotes) "THIS IS THE THIRD PARAGRAPH." Use the Measurements palette (Ctrl+Alt+M) to format it in 18-point Times. With the cursor anywhere in the line, choose Style/Rules (Ctrl+Shift+N) to display the Paragraph Rules dialog box. Click in the Rule Above check box to display the expanded Paragraph Rules dialog box.

11. Use the drop-down menu in the Length field to select Indents. This will place a rule above the text and extend it from the paragraph's left and right indents as indicated in the From Left and From Right fields.

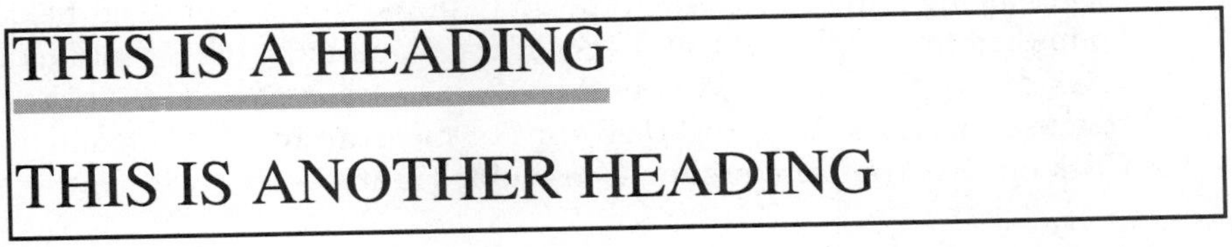

THIS IS A HEADING
THIS IS ANOTHER HEADING

Figure 14.14–A 4-point rule anchored below the first paragraph.

Ctrl+I View/Show Invisibles
Ctrl+Shift+N Style/Rules
Ctrl+Alt+M View/Show
 Measurements

Ctrl+Shift+N Style/Rules

12. With the cursor any place in the third paragraph, apply the values displayed in Figure 14.15 and click on Apply. Click on OK.

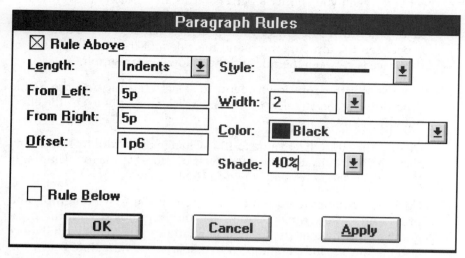

Figure 14.15—The expanded Paragraph Rules dialog box displays formatting for a rule to be placed above a paragraph indented a half-inch from each side of the text box and offset a quarter-inch from the baseline of the first line of the paragraph.

Big Tip

When assigning a Rule Above command to the first paragraph in a text box, use picas as the unit of measurements in the Offset field of the Paragraph Rules dialog box. If you use a percentage value, the line will not be displayed.

OVERRIDING THE UNIT OF MEASURE

You can always override the unit of measure established in the General Preferences dialog box. Since this document calls for inches as the unit of measurements, any value you type in a dialog box or in the Measurements palette will be converted to inches once you press the Apply or OK buttons. To input a value in another unit of measure, picas for instance, type *p* after the number.

EXERCISE G

1. Click anywhere inside the "THIS IS THE THIRD HEADING" paragraph and choose Style/Rules (Ctrl+Shift+N).

2. In the expanded Paragraph Rules dialog box for your document, with inches as the unit of measure, type 5p (5 picas) in the From Left field, 5p in the From Right field, and 1p6 (1pica, 6 points) in the Offset field. Click on Apply and notice how those values are converted to inches, because inches is the designated unit of measure for this document. Click on OK. Your screen should resemble Figure 14.16.

THIS IS THE THIRD PARAGRAPH.

Paragraph Rules

☒ **Rule Above**

Length: [Indents ▼] **Style:** [▬▬▬▬▬ ▼]

From Left: [5p] **Width:** [2 ▼]

From Right: [5p] **Color:** [■ Black ▼]

Offset: [1p6] **Shade:** [40% ▼]

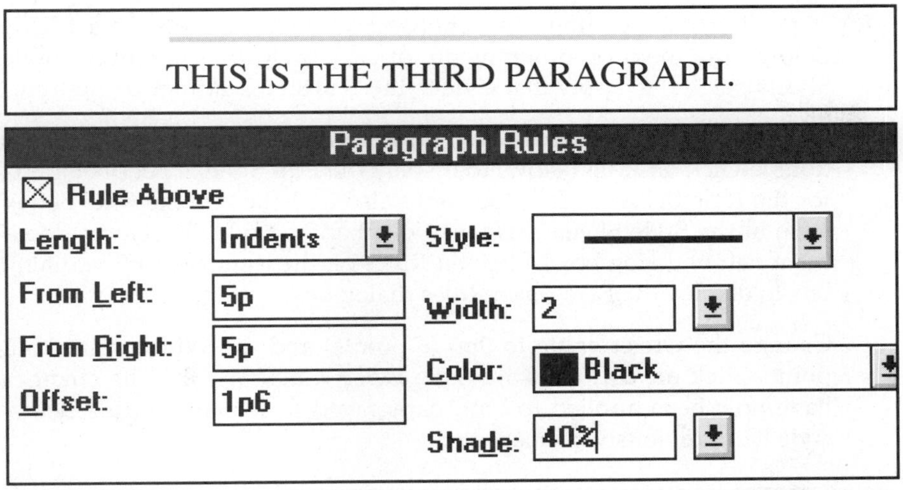

Figure 14.16—A paragraph formatted with the Rule Above command using the values in the Paragraph Rules dialog box. These values are input using picas as the unit of measure by typing *p* after the value, even though the document's unit of measure is inches.

RULES AS STYLES

It's always a good idea to include the rule as part of a style sheet. This way, if you ever have to make a change to the rules in a document, you can do it globally.

EXERCISE H

1. Choose View/Show Style Sheets to display the Style Sheet palette. Type "Assignments" anywhere on the page and format it in Helvetica, 14 point, Bold.

2. Choose Style/Rules (Ctrl+Shift+N). Click in the Rule Below check box.

3. Choose Text from the Length drop-down menu. Type 1p (1 pica) in the Offset field. Choose 4 point from the Width drop-down menu. Click on Apply to view the rule. Click on OK.

4. Place the cursor anywhere in the "Assignments" paragraph. Choose Edit/Style Sheets to display the document's Style Sheets dialog box. Click on New.

5. Type Rule Below in the Name field. Click on Rules on the right side of the dialog box. Notice that it reflects the rule below the "Assignments" paragraph which you just created. Click on OK. Click on Save.

6. Click anywhere in the "Assignments" paragraph and choose Style/Style Sheets. Use the Style Sheets submenu to select Rule Below and assign it to the Assignments paragraph. You could also click on Rule Below in the Style Sheets palette. Although nothing appears to happen, the style has been applied to the paragraph.

FYI

Lines disappear when you select the Content tool and reappear when you select the Item tool or either of the line tools. This is why it's a good idea to anchor rules to text instead of just drawing them on the screen.

Ctrl+Y Edit/Preferences/
    General
Ctrl+Alt+M View/Show
    Measurements
Ctrl+M Item/Modify
Ctrl+B Item/Frame
Ctrl+A Edit/Select All
Ctrl+Shift+F Style/Formats
Ctrl+Shift+N Style/Rules

7. Type "Further Reading" and choose Style/Style Sheets. Select Rule Below from the drop-down menu (or click on Rule Below in the Style Sheets palette) to apply that style to the "Further Reading" paragraph.

8. Choose Edit/Style Sheets. Click on Rule Below and click on Edit (or double-click on Rule Below) to display the Edit Style Sheet dialog box for the Rule Below style. (You could also Ctrl-click on the Rule Below style in the Style Sheets palette to display the Style Sheets for (document name) dialog box.) Click on Rules on the right side of the dialog box to display the Paragraph Rules dialog box.

9. Change the Offset value to 0p6 (6 points) and the Width value to 2 point. Click on OK. Click on Save twice. Click on OK. The changes have now been applied to both paragraphs to which the Rule Below style had previously been applied.

REVIEW EXERCISE

In this Review Exercise you will create a layout for an announcement.

1. Create a new document (File/New). Use the General Preferences dialog box (Ctrl+Y) to select picas as the unit of measure. Create a text box 30 inches wide by 36 inches high. Choose View/Show Measurements (Ctrl+Alt+M) to display the Measurements palette.

2. Inside the box, type the following words (no quotes) and press the Enter key to create a paragraph return where indicated: "Announcing ¶ Marty's Miracle Maps ¶ Find your way to any place on earth. ¶ These indispensable directional guides are available at your local book store." Format the text in 36-point Times.

3. Choose Item/Modify (Ctrl+M) and use the Vertical Alignment menu to select Centered from the Type drop-down menu. Click on OK.

4. With the text box still selected, choose Item/Frame (Ctrl+B). Select a frame and assign it a width of 4 points. Click on OK.

5. Choose Edit/Select All (Ctrl+A) and click on the Center Alignment icon to center the text horizontally in the text box.

6. Place the cursor anywhere in the second line and choose Style/Formats (Ctrl+Shift+F). Type 2p in both the Space Before and Space After fields. Click on OK.

7. With the cursor still in the second line, choose Style/Rules (Ctrl+Shift+N) to display the Paragraph Rules dialog box. Click in the Rule Above check box to display the expanded Paragraph Rules dialog box. Format the paragraph with a rule above and rule below using the values in Figure 14.17.

8. Click on the Orthogonal Line tool to select it and draw a line about 4 inches long. Use the Measurements palette to assign it a width of 4 points.

WARNING!

When typing indent values in the Paragraph Rules dialog box, be sure to type either " for inches or p for picas after the number—8" or 8p. Type the p for points before the number—p8.

9. Drag the line and position it in the center of the top line of the text box. With the line still selected, choose Item/Step and Repeat (Ctrl+Alt+D). Type 1 in the Repeat Count field; type 0 in the Horizontal Offset field; type 6.125 in the Vertical Offset field. Click on OK. Your screen should resemble Figure 14.18.

Ctrl+Alt+D Item/Step and Repeat

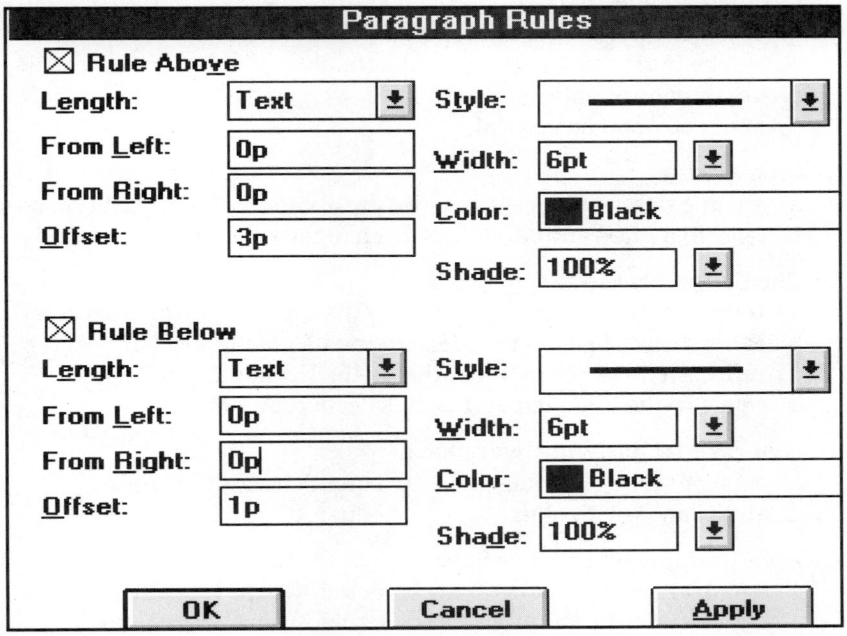

Figure 14.17—The expanded Paragraph Rules dialog box.

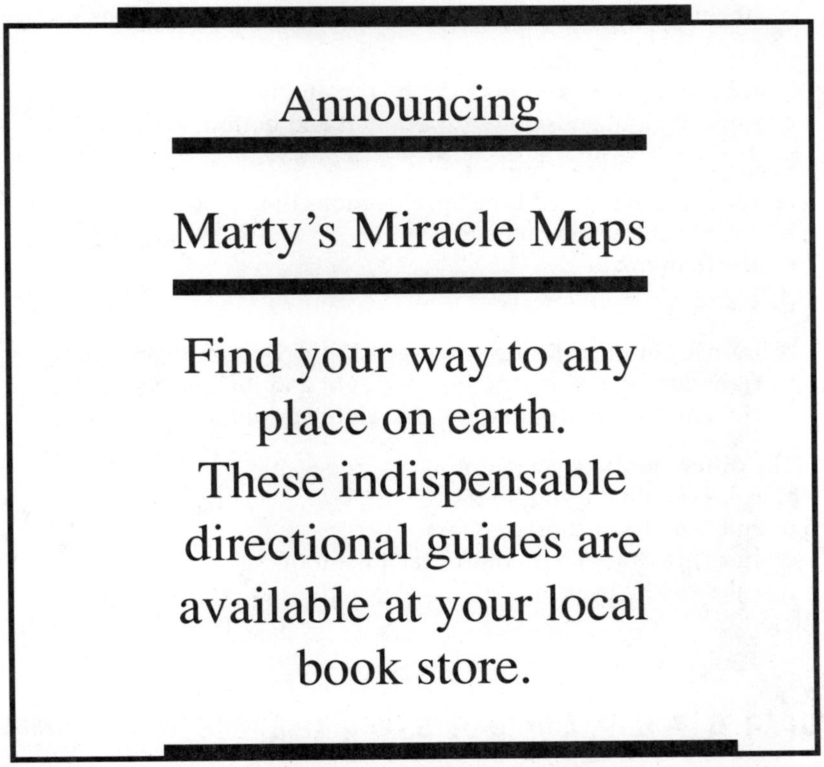

Figure 14.18—The finished advertisement displays horizontal and vertical lines on the text box itself, as well as a rule above and a rule below the second paragraph.

REVIEW QUESTIONS

Read the following questions and choose the answer which best completes the statement.

1. Orthogonal lines _____.
   a. are either horizontal or diagonal
   b. can be horizontal, vertical, or diagonal
   c. are only horizontal
   d. are horizontal or vertical

2. Line Modes _____.
   a. are line descriptions   b. are accessible from the Style menu
   c. refer to a line's endpoints   d. change as the line is modified

3. The Endpoints Mode _____.
   a. reflects a line's position relative to the top and bottom margins
   b. is not available from the Measurements palette
   c. reflects a line's position relative to the left and top margins
   d. refers to the line's left and right selection points

4. A horizontal line will always have _____.
   a. equal Y1 and Y2 values   b. equal X1 and X2 values
   c. an XC and a Y2 value   d. equal XC and YC values

5. A vertical line will always have _____.
   a. equal Y1 and Y2 values   b. equal X1 and X2 values
   c. an XC and a Y2 value   d. equal XC and YC values

6. A diagonal line will always have _____.
   a. equal Y1 and Y2 values   b. equal X1 and X2 values
   c. unequal X and Y values   d. equal XC and YC values

7. A line's Left Point Mode specifies its position in terms of its _____.
   a. left and right endpoints   b. top and left endpoints
   c. top and right endpoints   d. left and bottom endpoints

8. Shade is applied to a line via _____.
   a. the Style menu and Line Specifications dialog box
   b. the Measurements palette
   c. the Item menu
   d. b and c

9. A line's Right Point Mode specifies a line's position in terms of _____.
   a. right and bottom endpoints b. right and top endpoints
   c. right and left endpoints   d. right endpoint

10. The difference between a line and a rule is that _____.
    a. rules can't have endpoints
    b. rules can be anchored to text
    c. lines are drawn with one of the Line tools
    d. rules can be broken

Answers: 1. d; 2. a; 3. c; 4. a; 5. b; 6. c; 7. d; 8. a; 9. b; 10. b

LESSON

15

Graphics and Text Together

OVERVIEW

In this lesson you will learn how to anchor picture boxes and text boxes to a paragraph. You will also learn how to use the Runaround command to run text around an item and around the picture in a picture box. As a review, you will create a business card and a page from a newspaper.

TOPICS

Anchored picture boxes
Anchored Picture Box Specifications dialog box
Aligning the anchored picture box
Anchored text boxes
Text runaround
None Mode
Item Mode
Auto Image Mode
Manual Image Mode
Adding and deleting handles
Review Exercises
Review Questions

TERMS

anchored boxes
Ascent icon
Baseline icon
reverse text
Text Outset
Text Runaround

What you will need

Several text and graphic files

Ctrl+N File/New

Ctrl+Y Edit/Preferences/ General

Ctrl+Alt+M View/Show Measurements

Ctrl+E File/Get Picture

Ctrl+Alt+Shift+F Proportionally fits a picture in the box

Ctrl+X Edit/Cut

Ctrl+V Edit/Paste

FYI

You can also use the Edit/Copy command to copy a text box or a picture box before anchoring it to text. This, however, leaves the box on the screen and may disrupt the flow of text.

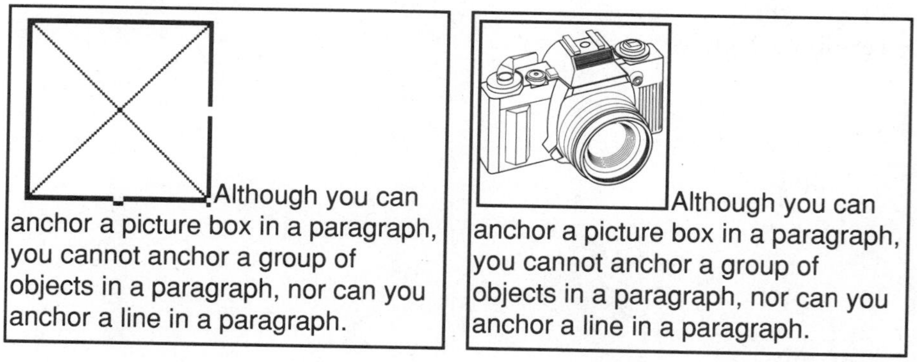

ANCHORED PICTURE BOXES

Just as you are able to anchor rules to text, you can also anchor picture boxes and text boxes to text. Anchored boxes move with the paragraph and allow you to create interesting visual effects on a page.

Because boxes are anchored to text, they are treated in some ways like text characters. The only way to delete an anchored picture box or an anchored text box is to select it with the Content tool and press the Backspace key

EXERCISE A

1. Choose File/New (Ctrl+N) to create a new document with 1-inch margins all around, 1 column, and facing pages. Choose Edit/Preferences/General (Ctrl+Y) to select picas as the unit of measure.

2. Type the following paragraph (no quotes): "Although you can anchor a picture box in a paragraph, you cannot anchor a group of objects in a paragraph, nor can you anchor a line in a paragraph."

3. Click on the Picture Box tool to select it and hold down the Shift key while dragging to create a 6-pica square. Use the Measurements palette (Ctrl+Alt+M), if necessary, to make sure that both the W and H values are 6p (6 picas).

4. With the picture box selected and the Content tool active, choose File/Get Picture (Ctrl+E) and import a picture into the box. Press Ctrl+Alt+Shift+F to fit the picture proportionally into the picture box.

5. Click on the Item tool to select it, click on the picture box to select it, and choose Edit/Cut (Ctrl+X).

6. Click on the Content tool to select it and click before the *A* in *Although* to place the insertion point there. Choose Edit/Paste (Ctrl+V). The picture box appears as the first item in the paragraph. Your screen should resemble Figure 15.1.

7. Click to place the insertion point in the paragraph directly above the one with the anchored graphic. Press Enter a few times and notice that the graphic is truly anchored to the paragraph and moves with the text.

Figure 15.1—A picture box anchored to a paragraph. Notice the anchored picture's bounding box displaying three resizing handles. At the right, a picture has been imported into the picture box.

ANCHORED PICTURE BOX SPECIFICATIONS DIALOG BOX

Once a picture box is anchored to a paragraph, that paragraph contains both anchored picture box specifications and text box specifications. A Specifications dialog box is available depending on whether the anchored picture box or the text box containing the anchored picture box is selected.

If you select the anchored picture box, the Anchored Picture Box Specifications dialog box is displayed. This contains the same fields as does the Measurements palette for an anchored picture box, but also includes commands for applying color to the background of the picture box and suppressing printout for the picture and for the picture box.

Remember that a box must be cut (or copied) with the Item tool and then pasted with the Content tool in order to anchor it to a paragraph. Always place the I-beam at the position in the paragraph where you want the box anchored.

Ctrl+Alt+M View/Show
 Measurements
Ctrl+M Item/Modify

Remember

Anchoring picture boxes to text is a two-step process involving two tools. *Cut* (or copy) the picture with the *Item tool.* *Paste* the picture at the desired location in the paragraph with the *Content tool.*

When an anchored picture box is active, the Measurements palette displays the Ascent icon (top) and the Baseline icon for aligning the picture box to the text.

You can also select Ascent or Baseline from the Anchored Picture Box Specifications dialog box.

EXERCISE B

1. With either the Item tool or the Content tool selected, click on the anchored picture box to select it. The picture box displays three handles which allow you to resize the box. Click on one of the handles to make the Resizing Pointer appear and drag the box's handle to resize the picture box.

2. Use the Measurements palette (Ctrl+Alt+M) to resize the picture box with a width of 8 picas and a height of 6p5.

3. With the anchored picture box still selected, choose Item/Modify (Ctrl+M) to display the Anchored Picture Box Specifications dialog box (Figure 15.2).

Anchored Picture Box Specifications

Align with Text		
○ Ascent ● Baseline	Scale Across:	13.5%
	Scale Down:	13.5%
Width: 8p	Offset Across:	-p.002
Height: 6p5	Offset Down:	1p10.481
	Picture Angle:	0°
	Picture Skew:	0°
☐ Suppress Picture Printout	**Background**	
☐ Suppress Printout	Color: ■ Red	
	Shade: 50%	

OK   Cancel

Figure 15.2—The Anchored Picture Box Specifications dialog box contains fields for aligning and resizing the picture box; scaling, offsetting, and rotating the picture; applying background color; and suppressing printout.

4. Use the Color drop-down menu and in the Background field, choose Red. Use the Shade drop-down menu and choose 50% to apply a 50% shade of Red to the background of the picture box. Click on OK.

5. With the Content tool selected, click on the picture box and notice that the Measurements palette displays some of the values for a regular picture box: width and height of the picture box, as well as scaling, offset, picture rotation, and skewing values for the picture.

6. With the anchored picture box still selected, choose Item/Modify (Ctrl+M) to display the Anchored Picture Box Specifications dialog box again.

7. Notice that the left side of the Anchored Picture Box Specifications dialog box deals with the box itself and the right side deals with the picture in the box. Change some of the scaling, offset, and angle of rotation values of the picture *only*. Click on OK and see how the new values affect the image but not the anchored picture box. Notice also how your new values are reflected in the Measurements palette.

ALIGNING THE ANCHORED PICTURE BOX

The Measurements palette for an anchored picture box displays two icons on the left when the anchored box is selected. The top icon is the Ascent icon; the lower icon is the Baseline icon.

Because an anchored picture box flows with the text to which it is anchored, you cannot change its X and Y points of origin. However, you can align the top of the anchored picture box with the top of the character on its right by clicking on the Ascent icon in the Measurements palette, or you can align the bottom of the anchored picture box with the baseline of the line of text to which it is anchored by clicking on the Baseline icon.

EXERCISE C

1. Select the anchored picture box you just created with either the Item tool or the Content tool. Notice the two alignment icons on the left side of the Measurements palette. These allow you to align the anchored picture box either by the Ascent or the Baseline (Figure 15.3).

2. Click on the picture box in the anchored paragraph and choose Item/Frame (Ctrl+B). Assign it a weight of 1 point. Click on OK.

3. Click on the Ascent icon in the Measurements palette. Notice how the top of the box aligns with the top of the *A* in *Although* (Figure 15.4).

4. With the anchored picture box still selected, click on the Baseline icon in the Measurements palette. Notice how the bottom of the box aligns with the baseline of the first line of text (Figure 15.4).

Figure 15.3—The Measurements palette which is displayed when an anchored picture box is selected. Clicking on the top icon to select it allows you to align an anchored picture box by the Ascent, where the top of the picture box aligns with the ascender of the tallest letter in that line of text. The icon below it allows you to align the picture box by Baseline, where the bottom of the picture box aligns with the baseline of the line of text it's sitting on.

▥	W: 8p		X%: 15%
▦	H: 6p5		Y%: 15%

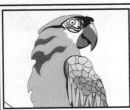 Although you can anchor a picture box in a paragraph, you cannot anchor a group of objects in a paragraph nor can you anchor a line in a paragraph. However, there is an XTension which allows you to anchor groups within lines of text.

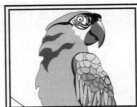 Although you can anchor a picture box in a paragraph, you cannot anchor a group of objects in a paragraph nor can you anchor a line in a paragraph. However, there is an XTension

Ctrl+M Item/Modify

Figure 15.4—An anchored picture box aligned by Ascent (left) where the top of the anchored picture box is flush with the top of the first line, and anchored by Baseline (right) where the anchored picture box is anchored with the baseline of the first line. Notice that it is the picture *box* which is aligned, not the picture itself.

ANCHORED TEXT BOXES

Thus far you have worked only with the anchored picture box and the picture within it. You can also anchor a text box to a paragraph using the same Cut and Paste commands (Cut with the Item tool; Paste with the Content tool) used to anchor picture boxes.

When an anchored text box is selected, choose Item/Modify (Ctrl+M), which will display the Anchored Text Box Specifications dialog box (Figure 15.5).

Anchored Text Box Specifications

Align with Text
○ Ascent   ● Baseline

Width: 2p
Height: 4p

Columns: 1
Gutter: 1p.024
Text Inset: 1 pt

☐ Suppress Printout

First Baseline
Offset: 0p
Minimum: Ascent ⬍

Vertical Alignment
Type: Top ⬍
Inter ¶ Max.   0p

Background
Color: White ⬍
Shade: 100%

OK   Cancel

Figure 15.5—Displays the Anchored Text Box Specifications dialog box. The values on the left side of the box affect the text box itself; the values on the right side affect the text.

Ctrl+A Edit/Select All
Ctrl+Shift+D Style/
    Character
Ctrl+M Item/Modify
Ctrl+X Edit/Cut
Ctrl+V Edit/Paste

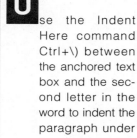
se the Indent Here command Ctrl+\) between the anchored text box and the second letter in the word to indent the paragraph under the second letter in the first word.

EXERCISE D

1. Use the Text Box tool to create a text box 1p10 wide and 1p6 high. Type "W" in that box. Select the letter (Ctrl+A), choose Style/Character (Ctrl+Shift+D), and select Times, 24 pt. White, and Italic.

2. Select the text box and choose Item/Modify (Ctrl+M). Use the Shade drop-down menu to select 100% Black. Click on OK. You have now created reverse text. Reverse text is white text on a black background.

3. In the automatic text box on the same page (not the anchored text box), type the following paragraph (no quotes): "Whenever an anchored text box is selected, the Anchored Text Box Specifications dialog box is displayed."

4. With the Item tool selected, click on the reverse text box to select it. Choose Edit/Cut (Ctrl+X).

5. Click on the Content tool to select it and click immediately *before* the letter *W* in *Whenever* in the paragraph. Then choose Edit/Paste (Ctrl+V).

6. Press the right arrow key once to move the cursor between the *W* and the *h* in *Whenever*. Press the Backspace key to delete the *W* in *Whenever*. Your screen should resemble Figure 15.6.

7. Click on the anchored text box with either the Item tool or the Content tool and notice that the three resizing handles appear.

8. Choose Item/Modify (Ctrl+M) to display the Anchored Text Box Specifications dialog box. Notice that it displays the values in Figure 15.5. Many of these fields are also available when a non-anchored text box is selected. Notice also that the same values are displayed in the Measurements palette. Click on OK.

*W*henever an anchored text box is selected, the Anchored Text Box Specifications dialog box is displayed.

Figure 15.6—An anchored text box with reverse text as an anchored text box for the initial cap.

TEXT RUNAROUND

Text runaround defines text that flows around an item (box or line) in its text column. The Runaround Specifications dialog box is accessed from the Item menu whenever an item is active.

If, for example, you draw a line in a column of text, the text must deal with that line by either repelling it, covering it, or flowing around it. It has two Runaround Mode options available to it from the Runaround Specifications

Ctrl+T Item/Runaround

dialog box (Ctrl+T): Item Mode and None Mode. However, when the active (selected) item is a picture box, there are four Runaround modes available from the Runaround Specifications dialog box: None Mode, Item Mode, Auto Image Mode, and Manual Image Mode.

NONE MODE

Figure 15.7 displays an item (arrowhead line) placed directly on top of text. Because the Mode value in the Runaround Specifications dialog box (Ctrl+T) is set to None, the line has no Runaround value and text cannot run around it (Figure 15.7). The item, in this case the line, will intrude on the text and cover it, but it will not repel it.

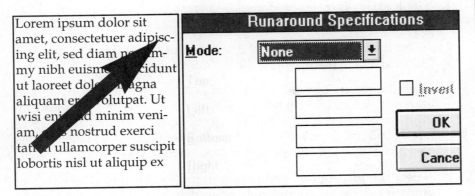

Figure 15.7—A text box with an item assigned no Runaround values in the Runaround Specifications dialog box. The None Mode dims all Text Outset values.

ITEM MODE

In Figure 15.8, because the Mode value is set to Item, the item (line) has a default Runaround value of 1 point and the text can run around it. Here the item repels the text. Notice that no Text Outset option is available in this mode.

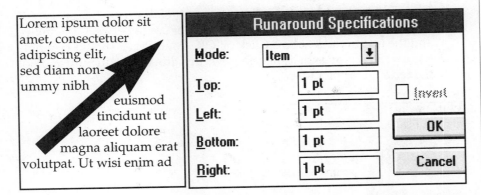

Figure 15.8—A text box on which an item has been placed and assigned the Item Mode in the Runaround Specifications dialog box.

Ctrl+T Item/Runaround

Ctrl+E File/Get Text/
      Picture

Ctrl+E File/Get Picture

Ctrl+Alt+Shift+F Propor-
      tionally fits a picture
      in the box

FYI

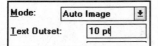

Text Outset refers to the amount of space between a picture and the text which is being forced to run around it when either Auto Image or Manual Image is selected from the Mode drop-down menu in the Runaround Specifications dialog box.

AUTO IMAGE MODE

When a picture box is active and Item/Runaround (Ctrl+T) is selected, Manual Image Mode and Auto Image Mode are available. If a picture box containing a picture is selected with the Content Tool and Auto Image Mode is selected from the Runaround Specifications dialog box, then the Text Outset field becomes active and you can specify how far from the picture (not the picture box) you want the text.

EXERCISE E

1. Use the Text Box tool to draw a 1-column text box. Choose File/Get Text (Ctrl+E) and import enough text to fill the box.

2. Select the Picture Box tool and draw a picture box in the text box. Use the Item tool to place it along the left side of the text box.

3. With the picture box still active, choose File/Get Picture (Ctrl+E) and import a picture into the box. Press Ctrl+Alt+Shift+F to proportionally fit the picture into the picture box. Your screen should resemble Figure 15.9. Since there are no Runaround specifications assigned to this text box, notice how the picture box sits on top of the text.

4. Select the picture box and choose Item/Runaround (Ctrl+T). The Runaround Specifications dialog box is displayed (Figure 15.10).

5. Use the Mode drop-down menu to select Item. Type 6 in the Top, Right, and Bottom fields to place 6 points of space between the top, right, and bottom edges of the picture box and the text. In other words, you are specifying 6 points of text runaround. Click on OK. Your screen should resemble Figure 15.11.

6. When you choose the Item mode, text runs around the item, in this case, the picture *box.* To force the text to run around the *picture,* select the picture box (with the Content tool) and choose Item/Runaround (Ctrl+T). Use the Mode drop-down menu to select Auto Image. Type 6 in the Text Outset field to place 6 points of space between the image and the text in the text box. Click on OK. Your screen should resemble Figure 15.12. Notice that the text now runs around the picture and not the rectangular picture box.

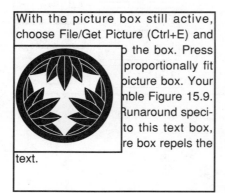

Figure 15.9—A text box containing a picture box. No Runaround values have been assigned to the text box or to the picture box.

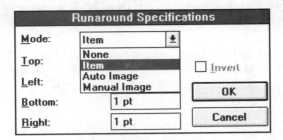

Figure 15.10—The Runaround Specifications dialog box for an active picture box. Selecting the Item option will force the text to run around the picture box. Selecting the Auto Image option will force the text around the *picture*, not the box. Selecting the Manual Image option will create a polygon around the image (picture) and allow you to manipulate the polygon's handles.

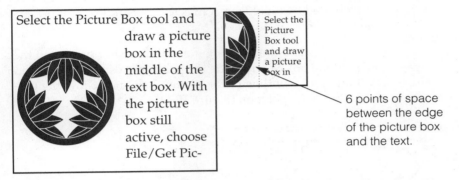

6 points of space between the edge of the picture box and the text.

Figure 15.11—A picture box with Runaround set to Item and 6 points of Runaround space assigned to the top, right, and bottom edges of the picture box. (See inset.)

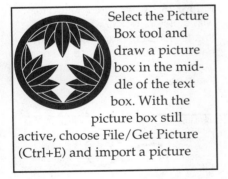

Figure 15.12—A picture box with Auto Image selected as the Runaround mode and with 6 points of Runaround space assigned in the Text Outset field. Auto Image Mode runs text around the *picture* (image), not the picture box. If the graphic were placed on the right side of the picture box, the text would run around the left side of the picture.

FYI

Runaround occurs around the four sides of a box only when the item is placed between two columns. If the item is placed in a one-column text box, text will run around only three sides of the item.

MANUAL IMAGE MODE

The fourth Runaround option available in XPress is Manual Image Runaround. When this option is selected in the Runaround Specifications dialog box, the image is surrounded by a polygon with editable handles. This allows you to run the text in almost any position around the image.

Ctrl+Alt+M View/Show
    Measurements
Ctrl+E File/Get Text/
    Picture
Ctrl+Alt+Shift+F Propor-
    tionally fits a picture
    in the box
Ctrl+T Item/Runaround

If you Ctrl-click on a polygon segment, the crosshair changes to the Handle Creation Pointer and creates another handle on the polygon.

The Handle Delete Pointer appears when you Ctrl-click on a polygon's handle, and deletes that handle.

EXERCISE F

1. Use the Text Box tool to create a text box. Use the Measurements palette (Ctrl+Alt+M) to format it in 2 columns. Choose File/Get Text (Ctrl+E) and import text into the box. Use the Measurements palette to justify the text.

2. Use the Picture Box tool to create a picture box and place it in the text box between the two columns. Choose File/Get Picture (Ctrl+E) to import a picture into the box. Press Ctrl+Alt+Shift+F to proportionally fit the picture into the picture box.

3. Select the picture box with either the Item tool or the Content tool. Choose Item/Runaround (Ctrl+T) and use the Mode drop-down menu to select Manual Image. Click on OK. Notice that now the entire image is surrounded by a polygon connected by handles. Your screen should resemble Figure 15.13.

4. Click on the handles and drag them to force the text to run around the image. The polygon box can override the picture box's boundaries and the text will ignore the outline of the picture box and follow the outline you create with the polygon (Figure 15.14).

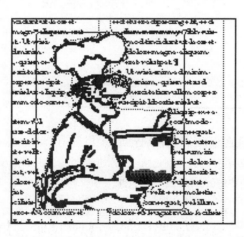

Figure 15.13—A 2-column text box with a picture box to which Manual Image Runaround specifications have been applied. Notice the polygon with handles which surrounds the image.

Figure 15.14—A picture box displaying the default position of Manual Image Runaround; with the handles pulled out beyond the picture box (left); and the resulting text runaround (right).

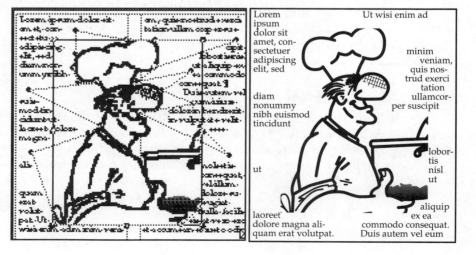

ADDING AND DELETING HANDLES

You can add handles to and delete them from the runaround polygon just as you can to a polygon picture box. To add handles to the polygon, hold down the Ctrl-key and click on one of the polygon's segments. To delete a handle, Ctrl-click on the handle.

Ctrl+Y Edit/Preferences/
   General
Ctrl+M Item/Modify
Ctrl+Alt+M View/Show
   Measurements
Ctrl+B Item/Frame
Ctrl+A Edit/Select All
Ctrl+Shift+D Style/
   Character
Ctrl+X Edit/Cut
Ctrl+V Edit/Paste

REVIEW EXERCISE #1

In these exercises you will create a business card and a page from a newspaper.

1. Use the Document Layout palette to add another page to your document. Choose Edit/Preferences/General (Ctrl+Y) and make sure that picas is the unit of measure.

2. Use the Text Box tool to draw a text box 3.5 inches wide by 2 inches high. Type (no quotes) "Quilting Supplies" inside the text box.

3. With the text box selected, choose Item/Modify (Ctrl+M). Type 2p in the Offset box of the First Baseline field in the Text Box Specifications dialog box to drop the first line of text in the text box 2 picas from the top of the text box.

4. Create another text box, a 3-pica square, and use the Measurements palette (Ctrl+Alt+M) to adjust its size.

5. Choose Item/Frame (Ctrl+B). Assign it the first frame with a width of 2 points. Click on OK.

6. Type "Q" in the box and select it (Ctrl+A). Choose Style/Character (Ctrl+Shift+D) and format it in Times, 36 points, Bold, and Shadow. Click on OK.

7. Select the small text box with the Item tool. Choose Edit/Cut (Ctrl+X). Select the Item tool and click to place the insertion point before the Q in *Quilting*. Choose Edit/Paste (Ctrl+V). Delete the original Q.

8. Select the anchored text box and click on the Ascent alignment icon in the Measurements palette (Ctrl+Alt+M). Add other information to the card. Your screen might resemble Figure 15.15.

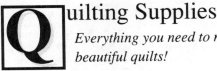

ulting Supplies
Everything you need to make beautiful quilts!

Lynn Stitch
West End Fabrics
Shore Road • Brooklyn, New York 11217
718-123-4567

Figure 15.15— The finished business card displays an anchored text box.

What you will need

Three graphic files
A text file

Ctrl+E File/Get Text/
Picture
Ctrl+T Item/Runaround

REVIEW EXERCISE #2

1. Use the Page Insert command to add another page to your document. Use the Text Box tool to create a large text box and use the Measurements palette to assign it 3 columns. Import a text file into that box (Ctrl+E).

2. Place a picture box in the upper left corner, another picture box in the center between the two columns, and a third picture box in the lower right corner. Choose File/Get Picture (Ctrl+E) and import a picture into each box.

3. Select each picture box and choose Item/Runaround (Ctrl+T). Choose Item from the Mode menu for the first picture box; choose Mode/Auto Image for the second picture box; and choose Mode/Manual Image for the third picture box.

4. Move the handles in Auto Image to change the text runaround. Your screen should resemble Figure 15.16.

Figure 15.16—A 3-column text box with picture boxes displaying different Runaround values. The picture in the first column displays Item Runaround where the text runs around the three sides of the item (picture box) at the specified text outset distance. The middle picture between the two columns displays Auto Image runaround with a Text Outset value of 8 points. Because the picture is set between the two columns, text will run around all four sides. Notice how the text conforms to the shape of the *picture,* not the box. The third picture displays Manual Image runaround with a Text Outset value of 1 point. Notice how the handles have been pulled away from the picture (image) and how the text follows the outline of the handles.

These picture boxes are framed to better display the Runaround effect.

History of Color
20,000 BC Paleolithic Era
Cave Paintings:
1 . Clay: stained dull yellow or rusty red by iron-bearing impurities.
2. Black: charred wood or oily soot scraped from a cave roof
3. White: from chalk chipped from an eroded cliff face.
Minerals: 1. Malachite: green tints
2. azurite: blue tints

Egyptians:1. sulfides of mercury and lead to create vermilion
2. galea, a mineral lead sulfide, the principal ore of lead, (powered) to create rouge
Romans   1. White and green pigments: lead and copper corroded in sour wine (poisonous eyeliner)
2. dull red: extract of madder root to dye fabrics and leather
3. yellow-orange: from the saffron crocus
4. blue- from the indigo shrub of the West Indies

1856   W.H. Perkin chemistry student; class project to analyze black sludge

left over when coal is roasted in the absence of air. Isolated a dark purple compound and created aniline dyes for fabrics which were obtained from coal tar which revolutionized the fashion industry.

Color Theory
1. Plato: light was such a pure, elevated thing that it was nobody's business but God's.
Aristotle: Color was the result of light being polluted by its interaction with matter: "Whatever is visible is color and color is what lies on what is in its own nature visible."

2. 1666 (plague) Isaac Newton poked a hole in a blanket, nailed it to a sunny window and experimented with what happened to sunbeams passing through a pair of triangular glass prisms. He demonstrated that white light didn't need to interact with matter to acquire color; white light already had all the colors in it. He coined the word spectrum: a beam of light split into its component colors. Newton demonstrated that

two beams of pure color falling on the same spot combine to produce a third color. This is the "additive" theory of color mixing that governs how we perceive color on a video screen. Pigments of nature and art result from a "subtractive" process, absorbing part of the spectrum and reflecting the diminished remains. Newton also invented the color wheel and concept of complementary colors.

3. Late 19th century Theoreticians and experimenters showed that visible light is just a narrow subset of an infinite spectrum of waves otherwise invisible to us, all of which are related in frequency, wavelength, and energy by simple formulas and are transformable into each other in predictable ways.

Human Eye
The human eye has three kinds of color-sensitive cells: each "tuned" to respond preferentially to different wavelengths centered in the red, green, and blue sectors of the spectrum. Stimulate any one and a sensation of the corresponding color reaches the

REVIEW QUESTIONS

Read the following questions and choose the answer which best completes
the statement.

1. Anchoring boxes to text _____.
   a. is done through the Item menu
   b. is available from the Measurements palette
   c. requires cutting and pasting
   d. b and c

2. Selecting a text box with an anchored picture box displays the _____.
   a. Anchored Picture Box Specifications dialog box
   b. Text Box Specifications dialog box
   c. Anchored Text Box Specifications dialog box
   d. a and b

3. Resizing can be applied to _____.
   a. an anchored text box
   b. an anchored picture box
   c. an automatic text box
   d. all of the above

4. If a line in a text box is assigned Item Mode in the Runaround
   Specifications dialog box, _____.
   a. the line will repel the text
   b. the Text Outset options become available
   c. the line covers the text
   d. the text covers the line

5. When Auto Image Runaround Mode is applied to a picture box,
   _____.
   a. the picture box covers the text
   b. a polygon surrounds the picture
   c. the Text Outset option is available
   d. Text Outset options apply to the picture box, not to the picture

6. Polygon handles _____.
   a. surround a picture when Auto Image Runaround is applied
   b. surround a picture box when Manual Image Runaround is
      applied
   c. surround a text box when Manual Image Runaround is
      applied
   d. b and c

7. When an anchored picture box is selected, _____.
   a. the Picture Box Specifications dialog box is not available
   b. the Measurements palette is not available
   c. the picture must be resized before selection
   d. the picture can be resized using the Measurements palette

8. The polygon picture box which appears when Manual Image Runaround Mode is applied to a picture box _____.
   a. can have handles added to it
   b. can have handles deleted from it
   c. can be resized from the Measurements palette
   d. a and b

9. A picture box _____.
   a. that is anchored has four Runaround Image options
   b. cannot be anchored once it has been resized
   c. that is not anchored can be anchored to the ascent or baseline of the line of text
   d. that is not anchored has two Runaround Image options

10. Text Outset applies to _____.
    a. unanchored picture boxes
    b. anchored text boxes
    c. an item with None Runaround options
    d. an anchored text box

OVERVIEW

In this lesson you will learn how QuarkXPress 3.1 handles color. You will learn about color models and how to specify color for text and for items. You will also learn how to create, edit, append, duplicate, and delete colors. Finally, you will learn how to avoid problems when printing color documents by applying trapping values. As a review, you will create a flyer with assorted colored elements.

Working

with

Color

TOPICS

The complexities of color
Process color
Spot color
Color models
Pantone Matching System®
TRUMATCH Swatching System®
FOCOLTONE Color System
Specifying color for text
Specifying color for items
Specifying colors for graphic files

Adding colors
Duplicating colors
Appending colors
Deleting colors
The Colors palette
Linear blends
Color trapping
Foreground and background
Trapping mechanisms in QuarkXPress 3.1
Application Preferences trap settings
Auto Method
Absolute trapping
Proportional trapping
Auto Amount

Indeterminate field
Overprint Limit
Ignore White
Process Trap
Trap Specifications dialog box
Automatic trapping
Overprinting
Trap field
Indeterminate trapping
Trap Information palette
Review Exercises
Review Questions

TERMS

append
background
choke
CMYK
color separations
Edit Color
FOCOLTONE System
foreground object
HSB
knockout

misregistration
overprint
Pantone Matching System®
process color (4-color)
RGB
shade
spot color
spread
trapping
TRUMATCH Swatching System®

+ and –

Additive color adds color to an object to make it whiter; subtractive colors become whiter as you subtract color from them and get darker as you increase color.

```
HSB
RGB
CMYK
PANTONE✦
TRUMATCH
FOCOLTONE
```

The six color models in QuarkXPress

THE COMPLEXITIES OF COLOR

There is no way that any book is going to make you an expert on color—and if you're not an expert, pay an expert to produce color output until you become one yourself. Factors which affect color output include the chemistry of the ink colors, the settings on the imagesetter, the variables of the film processor, the room temperature, condition of the press, weather, and the expertise of the pressperson—over which you have very little control.

In this lesson you will learn how to use the sophisticated color controls in QuarkXPress 3.1 to create, edit, and apply colors to items and text in a document. However, your correct use of the color manipulation commands built into XPress will come only after much practice and interaction with an experienced color printer.

PROCESS COLOR

Color comes in two flavors: process and spot. The process of blending percentages of four colors, Cyan, Magenta, Yellow, and Black (CMYK), to form a new color which is printed on four separate plates is called process color or color separations or 4-color process. Any color can be separated into percentages of Cyan, Magenta, Yellow, and Black (CMYK). In XPress, the Print dialog box offers the option of automatically separating a document's colors. Click in the Make Separations check box in the Print dialog box and any colors which you have specified as process colors will print out on four separate plates.

SPOT COLOR

Spot color, on the other hand, is created by using a *single ink* of one solid color instead of the four colors (inks) used to create process colors. All of the Pantone Matching System® colors can be designated as spot colors. Designating a color as a spot color means that a separate plate on the printing press will be used just for that color. This is fine for a color job of one to three spot colors, but can become very expensive if you are using more than four colors in a document. This is where 4-color separations can be more economical.

COLOR MODELS

To view the color models available in XPress, choose Edit/Colors. Click on Blue and click on Edit to display the Edit Color dialog box. Under the color's name (Blue) is the Model drop-down menu which lists the six models available in QuarkXPress 3.1.

The program defaults to RGB (Red, Green, Blue), an additive color model which displays color the way the eye views color. The computer monitor generates colors and images by mixing different intensities of red, green, and blue phosphors and displaying them on the screen.

HSB (Hue, Saturation, and Brightness) describes color by hue (a color's position on the color wheel or its name, like Blue); saturation or the amount of white in a color; and its brightness, the amount of black in a color.

These two models are useful in the video and multimedia fields, but have little value for producing printed materials unless you use the TRUMATCH Swatching System®, which has applied the concept of HSB to process color, producing a logical and organized approach to the 4-color process. The CMYK model is the standard color format in the printing industry, and the Pantone Matching System® and the TRUMATCH Swatching System® are the two standards for selecting inks for color production from the Pantone and TRUMATCH libraries in QuarkXPress 3.1.

PANTONE MATCHING SYSTEM®

The Pantone Matching System® (PMS) consists of a swatch book from which you pick a color, apply it to an item in your document, then give that color's number to the printer, who mixes the color using Pantone's formula. The simplicity and consistency of this model (a printer in Tennessee is using the same formula for a Pantone color as a printer in Montreal) has made it a favorite with designers. Although the Pantone library is displayed in XPress, what you see is on the screen is not usually what you will get, so always use a Pantone swatch book when specifying Pantone colors and hope for the best.

TRUMATCH SWATCHING SYSTEM®

The TRUMATCH Swatching System® is a digital four-color matching system which allows you to specify proportional gradations of process colors (Cyan, Magenta, Yellow, and Black) using the imagesetter's ability to electronically produce process colors in increments of 1%. It is the best system to use when you are specifying process color on a computer because TRUMATCH is as close to WYSIWYG color as you can get in this life.

For example, TRUMATCH color #28c3 describes a shade of turquoise blue. The number, 28, refers to the color's hue. The Tint Code, "c", indicates the tint or value strength of the hue gradated from "a", which is 100% value strength, to "h", which is a 5% value strength. The Shade Code is 3, indicating an 18% Black (3 x 6%=18%) in that color. This number following the letter indicating tint value identifies the percentage of Black in 6% increments, from 0% if there is no number, to 42% Black for the number 7. TRUMATCH color #35a7, then, is a Blue—Blue or Hue #35 with 100% Tint value (the letter "a") and 42% Black (the number "7").

A TRUMATCH color selector, called the Colorfinder, contains evenly gradated colors (tints) arranged according to the colors of the spectrum. You choose a color like 43-f1, which is a pale violet color, and then use the Colorfinder to locate a darker tint or lighter shade of that color. An imagesetter like the Linotronic can produce screen percentages in 1% increments so you can select from over 2,000 TRUMATCH colors which give the equivalent CMYK percentages used to create that color.

EXERCISE A

1. Create a new document (File/New) with any specifications. Draw a text box.

2. Choose Edit/Colors to display the document's color palette. Click on New to display the Edit Color dialog box. Use the Model drop-down menu to select TRUMATCH. When the TRUMATCH library is displayed, click on Color 1–a, a warm red. Click on OK. Click on Save.

Ctrl+N File/New
Ctrl+M Item/Modify

In the old days

Before the days of electronic imagesetters like the Linotronic, screen tints were available in 5% increments, frequently too large a jump to maintain correct proportions when selecting lighter or darker colors in the 4-color process.

FYI

The Shade menu allows you to select a percentage of a color's saturation. As colors darken, they lose intensity and are called shades. When colors become lighter, they are called tints.

Ctrl+M Item/Modify

You have now added the color TRUMATCH 1-a to your document's color palette and that color is now available under the Style menu (Figure 16.1).

3. With the text box selected, choose Item/Modify (Ctrl+M). Use the Background Color drop-down menu to select TRUMATCH 1-a. Use the Shade menu to select 100%. Never indicate a Shade value less than 100% for a TRUMATCH color because the Colorfinder gives you the increasing and decreasing tint values in their accurate proportions. If you want a darker shade or lighter tint, choose another TRUMATCH color and assign it a Shade of 100%. Click on OK.

4. Choose Edit/Colors. Click on New. The Model menu should still display TRUMATCH. Click on Color 1–d1, a lighter tint of red. Click on OK. Click on Save.

5. Create another text box. Choose Item/Modify (Ctrl+M) and use the Color drop-down menu to select TRUMATCH 1-d1. Click on OK. You have now applied the same color, red, in a lighter shade without changing the color's hue.

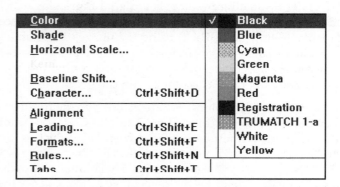

Figure 16.1—The color palette for this document now displays the new color, TRU-MATCH 1-a, which was created via the Edit/Colors menu.

FYI

When applying color to text from the Colors palette, be sure to click on the *name* of the color, not on the color swatch in the palette. And as always, be sure that text has been selected before applying color—or any other formatting, for that matter.

FOCOLTONE COLOR SYSTEM

The FOCOLTONE system is used primarily in Europe. It's a complicated system of swatch books which allows you to mix percentages of CMYK to produce a spot color and thus reduce trapping problems.

SPECIFYING COLOR FOR TEXT

XPress allows you to specify color for text, for the background of text boxes and picture boxes, and for box frames, as well as for lines and rules. It also allows you to specify a shade of the color for these elements. You can also create colors and add them to the Color submenu and to the Colors palette.

Specifying color for text is as easy as selecting the text and then choosing a color from the Color submenu under the Style menu.

Ctrl+N File/New
Ctrl+Alt+M View/Show
  Measurements
Ctrl+M Item/Modify

EXERCISE B

1. Create a new document (File/New) with an automatic text box. Type a few words in the box and triple-click to select the whole line of text.

2. Choose Style/Color. The submenu defaults to Black. Select Magenta from the Color submenu (Figure 16.2). Any text you selected is now Magenta.

Color		√	Black
Sha**d**e			Blue
Horizontal Scale...			Cyan
Trac**k**...			Green
Baseline Shift...			Magenta
C**h**aracter...	Ctrl+Shift+D		Red
Alignment			Registration
Leading...	Ctrl+Shift+E		White
Formats	Ctrl+Shift+F		Yellow

Figure 16.2—The default color palette in XPress includes the four process colors (Cyan, Magenta, Yellow, and Black), White, and Registration, as well as three spot colors, Blue, Green, and Red.

SPECIFYING COLOR FOR ITEMS

Applying color to box frames is done through the Frame Specifications dialog box. Specifying color for the background of text boxes and picture boxes is done through their Specifications dialog boxes.

EXERCISE C

1. Use the Measurements palette (Ctrl+Alt+M) to add another page to the current document. Click on the Text Box tool and drag to create a small text box. Click on the Picture Box tool and drag to create a small picture box.

2. Select the text box and choose Item/Modify (Ctrl+M) to display the Text Box Specifications dialog box. In the Background field (Figure 16.3), use the Color drop-down menu to select Green. Use the Shade drop-down menu to select 30%. Click on OK.

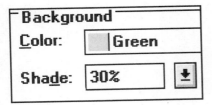

Figure 16.3—The Text Box Specifications dialog box allows you to apply color to the box's background by using the Color and Shade drop-down menus.

The Color Wheel

Although you could click on the Color Wheel (also called the Color Picker) until the color you like appears in the New Field of the Edit Color dialog box, remember that the screen does not display an accurate representation of how that color will print. The best way to match the color in XPress with the final printout is to use a TRUMATCH Colorfinder or a Pantone swatch book to create and name screen colors in a document.

Ctrl+B Item/Frame

3. With the text box still selected, choose Item/Frame (Ctrl+B) to display the Frame Specifications dialog box. Scroll to select any frame, assign it a Width of 8 points, and use the Color drop-down menu to select Red. Click on OK.

4. Follow similar steps to color both the background and the frame of the picture box.

5. Click on the Line tool to select it and drag to create a line on the page. Choose Style/Color and use the Color submenu to select Blue. Use the Shade submenu to select 50%.

SPECIFYING COLORS FOR GRAPHIC FILES

QuarkXPress applies color differently to different types of graphic files which you import into the program. You can specify color for line art and grayscale Bitmap, Metafile, and TIFF files. Color bitmaps, Metafiles, TIFFs, and EPS (Encapsulated PostScript) files cannot be colorized. However, the background color of any picture box, regardless of the kind of picture file it contains, can be colorized.

Line art and grayscale Bitmap, Metafile, and TIFF files can be colored from the Style menu where you apply a color and/or a shade of that color from the color palette. You can also specify a background color for the picture box into which you imported the file.

EPS images, however, are imported with the color information specified in the original program like Adobe Illustrator. If you have specified a spot color in Illustrator and named it, you must (1) export the file as an EPS file; (2) use the Get Picture command in XPress to import the picture into a picture box; and (3) add that spot color's name *exactly as it appears in Illustrator* to the QuarkXPress Color menu in your document. If you apply a Pantone or TRU-MATCH color to an illustration from Illustrator, you must (1) export the file as an EPS file; (2) use the Get Picture command in XPress to import the picture into a picture box; and (3) add that Pantone color *exactly as it is named in the graphic application* to the QuarkXPress Color menu in your document.

If you apply process colors from CMYK (Cyan, Magenta, Yellow, and Black) percentages to the EPS graphics, XPress will separate those colors automatically when you print the graphic if you choose the Make Separations option in the Print dialog box..

ADDING COLORS

The default color palette in XPress includes the four process colors (Cyan, Magenta, Yellow, and Black), White, and Registration, as well as three spot colors, Blue, Green, and Red. You can, however, add other colors to this menu. Unless a color is on the Color menu, even though it is present in the Pantone and TRUMATCH libraries, it is not available to be applied to text or to items.

FYI

If you import grayscale TIFF images and single-color bitmap images, you can convert them to a one-color image and separate them in XPress. However, any *color* TIFF images cannot be separated, but they can be printed to a color PostScript printer from XPress.

EXERCISE D

1. Choose Edit/Colors. The Colors for (document name) dialog box appears (Figure 16.4). Click on New to display the Edit/Color dialog box (Figure 16.5).

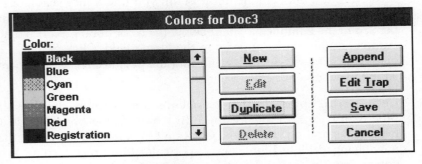

Figure 16.4—Displays the current Color palette for the document. From this dialog box you can choose to create a new color, edit or duplicate an existing color, append the color palette from another document, or edit the trapping values of a color.

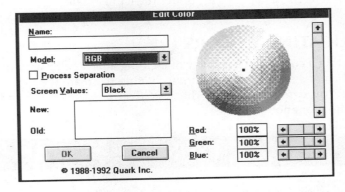

Figure 16.5—The Edit Color dialog box in Version 3.1 is where you create a new color to be added to the color palette.

2. Notice that the default model is RGB. Use the Model drop-down menu to select CMYK.

3. Type "Light Blue" in the Name field. Assign percentages of the four process colors (CYMK) by typing values in their percentage fields in the lower right side of the dialog box until you have an attractive shade of light blue. Selecting 5% Cyan, 15% Magenta, 0% Yellow, and 5% black gives a nice, uninspiring color.

4. Leave the Process Separation check box empty to define Light Blue as a spot color. Click on OK. Click on Save.

5. Select some text and choose Style/Color and notice that Light Blue now appears in the Color submenu and is available for use in your document. Because you designated Light Blue as a spot color, when

Registration color

Registration defaults to Black, but you can change it to any color for screen display only. Apply the Registration color to items and these items will print on every separation plate when you choose the Make Separations option in the Print dialog box.

Apply Registration to guide lines you may want on a page or to text which will eventually be trimmed after printing.

Ctrl+Alt+S File/Save as

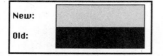

FYI

As you make changes to the duplicate color, those changes are reflected in the upper bar (New) of the swatch box in the Edit Color dialog box.

you assign this color to text or to an item and print this file, only one plate will print for Light Blue.

6. Choose Edit/Colors. Click on New in the document's color dialog box to display the Edit/Color dialog box (Figure 16.5). Use the Model drop-down menu to select Pantone.

7. Scroll through the Pantone library until you find a nice shade of purple (I like #233). Click on the color bar for that color or type the number 233 in the Pantone No. field below the color library. Notice that its Pantone number now appears in the Name field. Click on OK. Click on Save. Choose Style/Color and find the purple color you just created in the document's color palette.

8. Choose Edit/Colors. In the document's color palette, click on Light Blue. Click on Edit and in the Edit Color dialog box, click in the Process Separation check box. Click on OK. Click on Save. You have now changed Light Blue from a spot color to a process color. When you assign this color to an element and print this file, four pages will print, each with the correct percentage of Cyan, Magenta, Yellow, and Black needed to produce the color you called Light Blue. Those four separations will be used to make four plates for printing the final page on which Light Blue appears.

9. Save this file (File/Save as) under the name "Blue."

DUPLICATING COLORS

Duplicating a color is an easy way of creating a new color with many of the original color's specifications without having to create the new color from scratch. You can change only the specifications you want and give the duplicate color another name.

EXERCISE E

1. In the "Blue" file, choose Edit/Colors. In the document's color palette, click on Light Blue. Click on Duplicate. The Edit Color dialog box is displayed with "Copy of Light Blue" in the Name field (Figure 16.6).

2. Type "Medium Blue" in the Name field and adjust the CMYK percentages until you have an attractive shade of medium blue. Click in the Process Separation box to deselect it so Medium Blue will print on only one plate as a spot color. Click on OK. Click on Save.

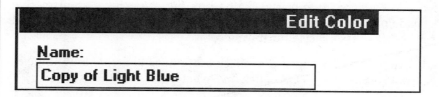

Figure 16.6—Clicking on Duplicate in the Edit Color dialog box places a copy of the selected color in the Name field of the Edit Color dialog box.

Ctrl+N File/New

APPENDING COLORS

Sometimes you will want to create a new document but use the color palette from another document. The Append option in the document's color dialog box allows you to do this.

EXERCISE F

1. Choose File/New (Ctrl+N) to create a new document. Choose Edit/Colors. In the document's color palette dialog box, click on Append, which will display the Append Colors dialog box. Scroll through the directories until you find the document you saved as "Blue."

2. Click on OK. Click on Save. Type a few words in the new document and choose Style/Color. The color palette from the "Blue" file now appears in the color palette for Document 1 (Figure 16.7). Click on Save.

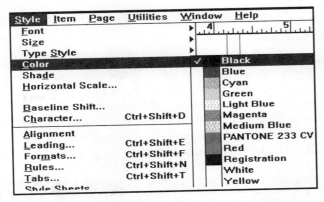

Figure 16.7—When the Append option is selected, XPress allows you to locate a previously saved file and append its color palette into the current document.

DELETING COLORS

It's easy to delete a color from a document's color palette. However, the four process colors, as well as Black, White, and Registration, cannot be deleted. If you delete a color that has already been applied to an element, XPress will ask if you really want to delete it. If you click on OK, XPress will replace every instance of the deleted color with Black. To delete a color, click on the Delete button in the document's color dialog box. Click on Save.

THE COLORS PALETTE

QuarkXPress includes a Colors palette (Figure 16.8) which works much like the Style palette. The top part of the palette contains three icons and a drop-down menu for selecting percentages of a color.

What's in a name?

When appending colors from Document A to Document B, if the colors in Document A have the exact same names as the colors in Document B, XPress will not overwrite the colors in Document B with the colors from Document A.

FYI

Most of the dialog boxes for manipulating color require you to click on Save instead of on OK. Unless you click on the Save button, any changes you made will not be applied.

Ctrl+N File/New
Ctrl+Y Edit/Preferences/
General

Click on the framed rectangle icon on the left to apply color to a frame around a picture box or text box. Click on the rectangle icon with an A to apply color to selected text. Click on the rectangle icon on the right to apply color to the background of a box.

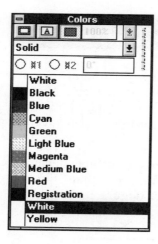

Figure 16.8—The Colors palette for the "Blue" file. Click on the icons in the top row to apply colors to a selected box's frame and background as well as to selected text.

Box Background icon

Text
icon

Frame
icon

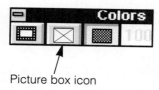

The Colors palette contains three icons used to apply color: the Frame icon on the left, the Text icon (center); and the Background icon (text or picture) on the right.
If a picture box is active, the middle icon changes to a picture box icon.

Picture box icon

LINEAR BLENDS

When you click on the solid rectangle icon, two other information bars are displayed (Figure 16.9).The Solid drop-down menu allows you to apply a percentage of a solid color to the background of a selected box. The Linear Blend option allows you to create a blend of two colors and apply that blend to the background of the box. The information bar below the drop-down menu allows you to designate the two colors which will be blended, as well as the angle of the blend's rotation.

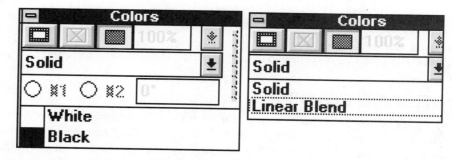

Figure 16.9—When the solid rectangle icon is selected, two more information bars appear below the icons (above), allowing you to create a solid or linear blend fill.

EXERCISE G

1. Create a new document (File/New) and use the General Preferences dialog box (Ctrl+Y) to select picas as the unit of measure.

2. Use the Text Box tool while holding down the Shift key to create a text box that is a 15-pica square. Use the Measurements palette (Ctrl+Alt+M) to adjust the size of the square.

3. Type (no quotes) "This text is placed in a box which contains a linear blend." Format the text in 12-point Helvetica bold.

4. Choose Item/Modify (Ctrl+M) to display the Text Box Specifications dialog box. Choose Centered under the Vertical Alignment drop-down menu.

5. Choose View/Show Colors to display the Colors palette. Click on the solid rectangle icon to display the two extra information bars.

6. With the text box selected, use the Solid drop-down menu to select Linear Blend.

7. Click on circle #1 and click on Yellow in the Colors palette. Use the percentage drop-down menu at the top of the Colors palette to select 100%.

8. Click on circle #2 and click on Red. Use the percentage drop-down menu at the top of the Colors palette again to select 100%.

9. Type 75 in the blend angle field (next to the numbered circles) to set the blend at a 75° angle.

10. Click on the Item tool or deselect the text box. This is important because XPress will not display the blend while the Content tool is active. This control mechanism allows you to edit the text in a box to which a blended background has been applied. Your screen should resemble Figure 16.10.

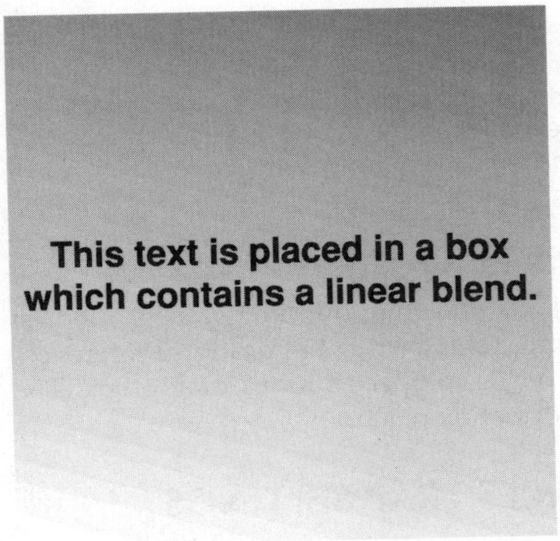

Ctrl+Alt+M View/Show Measurements
Ctrl+M Item/Modify
Ctrl+B Item/Frame

This text is placed in a box which contains a linear blend.

Figure 16.10—A text box to which a linear blend has been applied. Since the foreground object, the text, is a darker color (Black) than the Background colors, Overprint the text when applying trapping values.

To apply color to text from the Colors palette, *select the text*, click on the text icon (the middle icon) in the Colors palette, and click on a color's name in the Colors palette. To apply color to a box's frame, first use the Frame command (Ctrl+B) to apply the frame. Next, click on the frame icon in the Colors palette (the first icon), and click on a percentage value and also on a color's name in the Colors palette.

COLOR TRAPPING

If you are printing a piece in which elements of different colors do not overlap or touch each other, you have no problem. But in those documents where one color is adjacent to another, the movement of paper and plates through the printing press can cause misregistration—gaps between colors or overlapping and blending of colors. This can cause lines and/or white space to appear between an object color and its background color. To compensate for misregistration, XPress provides powerful trapping controls.

Trapping is the process of either "stretching" an object color or "shrinking" a background color to avoid gaps and lines between colored items and between colored text and a colored background. When you "stretch" an object color, you create a spread; when you "shrink" a background color, you create a choke.

FOREGROUND AND BACKGROUND

In an XPress document, the term *object* refers to any foreground element, while the term *background* refers to an item that is positioned behind a foreground object (Figure 16.11).

Because the object (Z) overlaps the background (30% Black color), when this text box is printed, should either the paper or the plate move even a fraction of a decimal of an inch, a dark line could appear where the background and text overlap, or white space might appear where the elements do not meet precisely. To avoid this problem, apply trapping values to the elements.

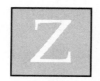

Figure 16.11—This text has a background of 30% Black. The letter Z is the foreground object and has been colored 100% Yellow. Because the foreground object is the lighter color, spread the Yellow on the darker background.

TRAPPING MECHANISMS IN QUARKXPRESS 3.1

Quark XPress 3.1 offers three methods of setting trapping values. The first is to set trapping values in the Trap fields of the Application Preferences dialog box. The second is to use the Trap Specifications dialog box. The third method is to use the Trap Information palette.

APPLICATION PREFERENCES TRAP SETTINGS

The Application Preferences dialog box contains a Trap field (Figure 16.12) where you can specify how XPress will apply automatic trapping values, that is, how XPress will trap elements when you do not specify other trap settings in either the Trap Specifications dialog box or in the Trap Information palette. These are the automatic trapping settings built into the program and they are very conservative.

AUTO METHOD

The Auto Method field has a drop-down menu which allows you to select either Absolute or Proportional. Both of these default to very conservative trapping values.

ABSOLUTE TRAPPING

Absolute will use the Auto Amount (next field) value to apply trapping to an element based on which of the two colors, the background color or foreground object color, is darker. If the background is darker, the foreground object color will spread the amount specified in the Auto Amount field. If the foreground object is darker, the background color will choke the amount specified in the Auto Amount field.

PROPORTIONAL TRAPPING

The Proportional setting will use a fraction (proportion) of the amount specified in the Auto Amount field when choking and spreading colors. XPress uses a formula based on the differences in the level of darkness (luminescence) in each color to arrive at the fractional (proportional) value that is applied to color.

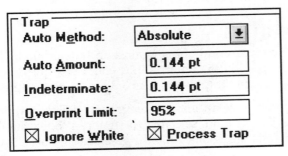

Figure 16.12—The Trap fields in the Application Preferences dialog box. The values in these fields affect the way all elements in the document are trapped unless you specify other values in the Trap Specifications dialog box or in the Trap Information palette.

AUTO AMOUNT

The value in the Auto Amount field determines the amount of trapping that XPress applies to colors. It is also the figure that the Auto Amount + and Auto Amount – commands in the Trap Information palette will use. You can enter an amount between 0 and 36 points in .001-point increments. If you type "Overprint" in this field, all objects to which you apply automatic trapping will overprint each other.

The default setting, 0.144 points, is a very conservative trapping value and may not provide enough trapping for large objects. There's a lot of voodoo in color work, so experiment with it. Trade standards, however, often "hover" around a quarter point (0.25) of trapping.

INDETERMINATE FIELD

If a background consists of more than one color, or if a foreground object only partially touches a background color, XPress can get confused. Against which background color should it trap the foreground color? This is called an Indeterminate background and the trapping values for an Indeterminate background default to the Indeterminate setting unless you input other values in the Trap Information palette.

The Auto Method drop-down menu in the Trap field of the Application Preferences dialog box

Overprint

When Overprint is selected as a trapping mechanism in either the Application Preferences dialog box or in the Trap Specification dialog box, the object color prints without knocking out the background color on the separation plates. The object prints on top of the background color when the plate goes to press.

Ctrl+N File/New

Because the foreground object (the Q) only partially touches the background, that background color is called Indeterminate. In this case, overprint the Q on the lighter background

You can specify any value from 0 to 36 points in .001-point increments in this field. You can also type "Overprint," which will cause all foreground elements to overprint on any Indeterminate background.

OVERPRINT LIMIT

An object to which Overprint trapping has been applied prints over the background. True—only if the background color's tint (Shade) level is greater than the value specified in the Overprint Limit field. For example, you set the Overprint Limit in the Trap field of the Application Preferences dialog box to 95%, its default value. Then you create red text on a black background and you apply a Shade value of 40% to the red. Because the 40% red is not greater than the 95% Overprint Limit value, XPress will not overprint the red on the black background; rather, it will knock out the red.

XPress always overprints Black if it is set to Automatic, as long as the Shade value of Black is greater than the Overprint Limit.

IGNORE WHITE

When you have a foreground object against an Indeterminate background that includes white, select the Ignore White check box (the default setting). This tells XPress to apply trapping values only to the non-white colors.

If, for example, you have an orange foreground object printing against a green and white background, selecting the Ignore White option will cause XPress to trap the orange against only the green and ignore the white.

PROCESS TRAP

When the Process Trap option is checked (its default status), XPress will trap the process separation plates on an individual basis whenever one process color overlaps another process color on the same page. XPress does this by comparing the darkness of each color. If the process color in the foreground object has a greater percentage of that color than the same color in the background, the process color in the foreground object is spread by half the amount specified in the Auto Amount field or half of any trapping value specified in the Edit Trap dialog box or in the Trap Information palette. If the process color in the foreground object is lighter (has a lower percentage) than the same process color in the background, that foreground object is choked by half of the same trapping values.

It's a good idea to keep this option checked to ensure a smoother trap while maintaining the same amount of overlap.

EXERCISE H

1. Create a new file (File/New) with an automatic text box. Choose Edit/Preferences/General and select picas as the unit of measure.

2. Choose Edit/Preferences/Application and make sure Auto Method is set to Absolute; Auto Amount is set to 0.144 points; Indeterminate is also set to 0.144 points; the Overprint Limit is 95%; and the Ignore White and Process Trap check boxes are selected. Click on OK.

3. Create a text box 15 picas wide by 5 picas high. Use the Text Box Specifications dialog box (Ctrl+M) to apply a background color of 40% Black to the text box.

4. Type "This text is considered a foreground object." Select the text (Ctrl+A), and format it in Helvetica, 18 point, Bold. Choose Style/Color and choose 100% Yellow. The shaded text box is the background. The yellow text is the foreground object.

5. Choose Edit/Colors to display the document's color palette dialog box. Scroll to find Yellow in the Color field and click on it to select it. Click on Edit Trap to display the Trap Specifications for Yellow dialog box (Figure 16.13). The scroll box on the left lists all the other colors in the document. Because Yellow is the color of the foreground object, the other colors appear under the Background heading.

6. Click on Black, the background color for the Yellow text. The Default column on the right of that heading displays the trapping values for these background colors and defaults to Automatic. Click on OK. Click on Save. You have applied 0.144 points of trapping to the yellow text. The yellow text will now spread on the darker background.

Ctrl+M Item/Modify
Ctrl+A Edit/Select All

TRAP SPECIFICATIONS DIALOG BOX

When you click on a Background Color in the Trap Specifications dialog box, three buttons on the right are activated: the Automatic button, the Overprint button, and the Trap field button.

AUTOMATIC TRAPPING

Automatic is just that—automatic. XPress applies trapping values to either spread ("stretch") the object color (Yellow) or choke ("shrink") the background color (Black) based on the options you select in the Application Preferences dialog box. With Automatic trapping, the object color "knocks out" the background color.

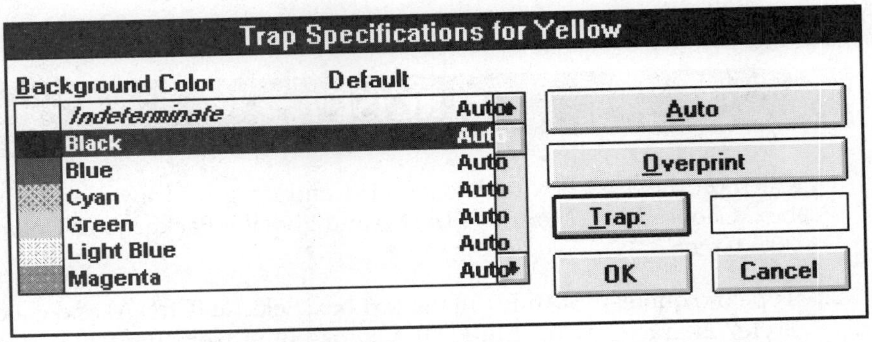

Tip

It's a good idea to use Select All (Ctrl+A) whenever you are selecting all the contents of a text box, even if it's just one letter.

FYI

XPress assumes that an item (box or line) against the page or the first item in the stacking order is being trapped against a white background.

Figure 16.13—The Trap Specifications for Yellow dialog box allows you to specify trapping values for the object color (Yellow).

Ctrl+M Item/Modify
Ctrl+A Edit/Select All
Ctrl+Shift+D Style/
    Character

WARNING!

Always check with your printer before applying trapping values. The type of press, ink, and paper all affect trapping values.

OVERPRINTING

Overprint will cause the object color (Yellow) to be printed without "knocking out" the background color (Black) in the color separations. The Yellow object will print over or on top of the Black background. This trapping option is available only when the object color has a Shade value greater than that specified in the Overprint Limit field of the Application Preferences dialog box. Because you specified a 95% Overprint Limit, you could have clicked on the Overprint button, because the 100% Yellow is greater than 95%.

TRAP FIELD

The Trap field allows you to enter your own value for trapping the object color and the background color. You can enter a value between −36 points and +36 points in .001 increments. Once you enter a value, click the Trap button to apply and save that value.

INDETERMINATE TRAPPING

Sometimes an object will only partially touch a background color, or touch a colored picture (text superimposed on a color halftone), or touch more than one colored object. XPress treats such a background as an Indeterminate color (Figure 16.14).

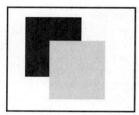 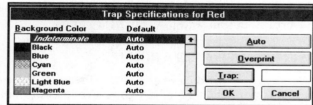

Figure 16.14—The background box is 100% Blue. The foreground object is 40% Red. Because the foreground object (Red) is not totally contained by the background object (Blue), the background color is called Indeterminate.

WARNING!

You must click on the Trap button to apply the trap values. Clicking on Save without clicking on Trap will not apply the trap values.

EXERCISE I

1. Click on the Text Box tool to select it and drag to draw a small text box. Choose Item/Modify (Ctrl+M) and give it a Background Color of 30% Green.

2. Type (no quotes) "SMILE!" in the text box. Select it (Ctrl+A) and choose Style/Character (Ctrl+Shift+D). Choose Blue from the Color drop-down menu and 100% from the Shade drop-down menu. Click on OK.

3. Choose Edit/Colors. Click on Blue to select it and click on Edit Trap to display the Trap Specifications dialog box for Blue. In the dialog box, click on Green to select it as the background color. Type −0.5 in the Trap field to choke or "shrink" the Green background by five-tenths of a point. *Click on the Trap button to apply the trap* (Figure 16.15). Click on OK. Click on Save.

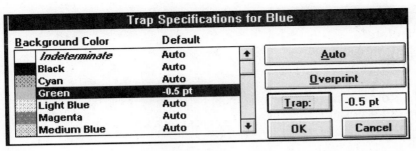

Figure 16.15—The –0.5 trap value for Blue will choke ("shrink") the Green background by five tenths of a point.

TRAP INFORMATION PALETTE

Setting trapping values in the Application Preferences and Edit Trap dialog boxes applies those values based on the relationship of one color to another throughout the document. In other words, if you specify trapping for Blue, that color will be trapped throughout the document, regardless of where it is used in the document. Version 3.1 includes object-by-object trapping which allows you to apply custom trapping values to individual objects.

This type of custom trapping permits you to trap one object color differently from the way that same color traps against another background. This is an important feature when trapping text against a background. Smaller letters or letters with serifs may need less trapping than larger objects.

Custom trapping is available by choosing View/Show Trap Information, which displays the Trap Information palette (Figure 16.16). When this palette is displayed, you can click on an object to select it and apply trapping values directly from the palette.

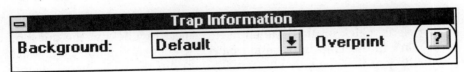

Figure 16.16—The Trap Information palette. When the question mark is visible, click on it and hold the mouse button down to display an information box which gives you the reason the selected item is trapped the way it is.

The Trap Information palette gives you the default trap information for a selected object and reason why those trapping values are in effect. You then apply your custom trapping values based on the selected object.

The Default drop-down menu (Figure 16.17) lets you select from Default, Overprint, Knockout, Auto Amount (+), Auto Amount (–), and Custom. The Auto Amount values allow you to increase (+) or decrease (–) the trapping value stated in the Auto Amount field of the Application Preferences dialog box.

If you select Default, a question mark is displayed in the right corner of the palette. Click on the question mark to display the info box which gives the reason for the Default trapping value.

Ctrl+Y Edit/Preferences/
  General
Ctrl+M Item/Modify

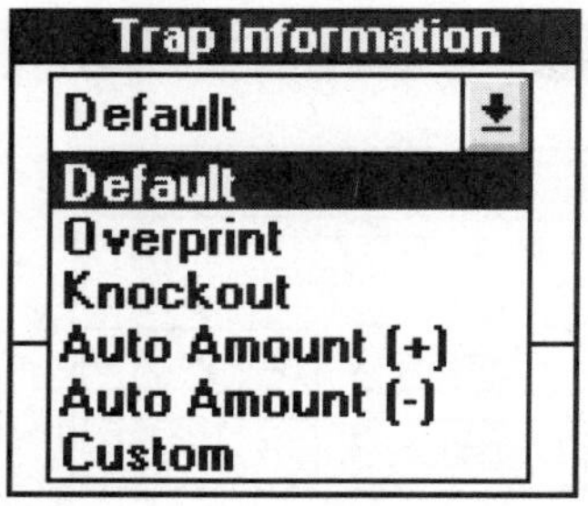

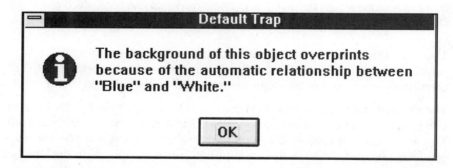

Figure 16.17—The Default drop-down menu in the Trap Information palette displays other trapping options for an individual object or background.

Knockout

A knockout is part of the background color that is not printed on that background color's separation plate.

EXERCISE J

1. Use the Document Layout palette (View/Show Document Layout) to add another page to your document. Choose Edit/Preferences/General (Ctrl+Y) and make sure that Framing is Outside.

2. Use the Oval Picture Box tool to draw an oval about 2 inches wide. Choose Item/Modify (Ctrl+M) to give it a background of 100% Blue. Click on OK.

3. Use the Text Box tool to create a text box about 3 picas wide and 2 picas high. Choose Item/Modify (Ctrl+M) to give it a Background color of None. This will make the box transparent. Click on OK. Use the Item tool to position the text box on top of the blue ellipse so that the text sits on top of the blue ellipse. Choose Item/Bring to Front to bring the text to the front.

4. Type the letter X in the text box. Choose Style/Color and use the Color submenu to select Magenta. Use the Shade menu to select 80%.

5. Choose View/Show Trap Information to display the Trap Information palette. Click on the blue ellipse to select it. Click on the question mark in the Trap Information palette to display the info box, which tells you that the blue ellipse will overprint the white paper (Figure 16.18). Release the mouse button.

Default Trap

> The background of this object overprints because of the automatic relationship between "Blue" and "White."

OK

Figure 16.18—The Trap Information palette for an ellipse colored 100% Blue.

6. Click on the text box to select it and choose Edit/Select All (Ctrl+A) to select the letter A. Click on the question mark in the Trap Information palette. The info box tells you that the text traps by 0.144 points (the value stated in the Auto Amount field of the Application Preferences dialog box) or that the Magenta A will spread by 0.144 points (Figure 16.19).

Ctrl+A Edit/Select All
Ctrl+B Item/Frame
Ctrl+Y Edit/Preferences/
General

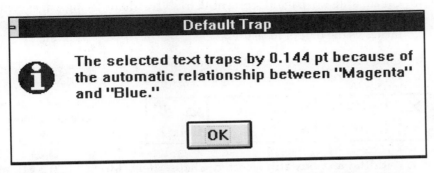

Figure 16.19—The Trap Information palette for the selected Magenta text traps with the default values.

FYI

The Trap Information palette is the only way that you can apply object-by-object trapping. All trapping values applied via the Edit Trap dialog box affect every object in the document to which that color has been applied.

7. Click on the blue ellipse and choose Item/Frame (Ctrl+B) and assign the picture box a 4-point frame. Use the Color and Shade drop-down menus to make it 100% Yellow. Click on OK.

8. With the ellipse still selected, look at the Trap Information palette. The display tells you that the frame outside the blue ellipse will overprint the white paper (Figure 16.20). Click on the question mark and read the message.

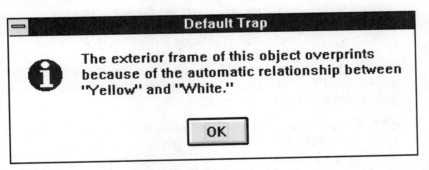

Figure 16.20—The Trap Information palette for an outside frame.

9. Choose Edit/Preferences/General (Ctrl+Y) and change Framing to Inside. Click on OK.

10. With the blue ellipse still selected, look at the Trap Information palette. The default trapping value of 0.144 (the amount specified in the Auto Amount field of the Application Preferences dialog box) is applied to the Yellow frame, which will cause it to spread that amount onto the Blue.

Ctrl+Y Edit/Preferences/
   General
Ctrl+N File/New
Ctrl+M Item/Modify
Ctrl+B Item/Frame
Ctrl+Shift+F Style/Formats
Ctrl+A Edit/Select All
Ctrl+Shift+E Style/Lead-
ing

REVIEW EXERCISE #1

In this exercise you will create a flyer incorporating spot colors, process colors, and color trapping.

1. Create a new 1-page document (Ctrl+N) without facing pages, without an automatic text box, with 1-inch margins all around, and with inches as the unit of measure.

2. Click on the Text Box tool to select it and drag to create a text box. Use the Measurements palette to apply the values in Figure 16.21.

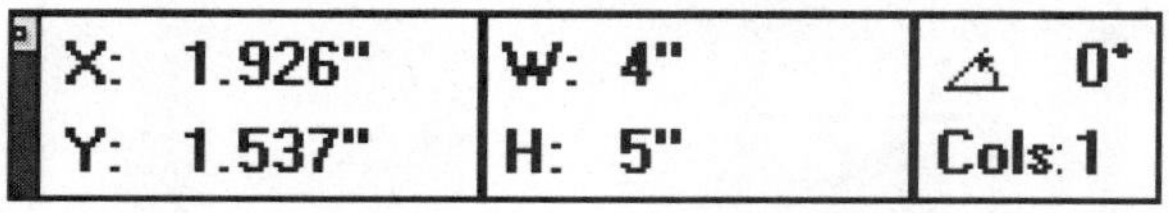

| X: 1.926" | W: 4" | △ 0° |
| Y: 1.537" | H: 5" | Cols: 1 |

Figure 16.21—Measurements palette for the text box.

3. With the text box still selected, choose Item/Modify (Ctrl+M) and assign the text box a Background color of 50% Blue. Click on OK.

4. Choose Item/Frame (Ctrl+B) and scroll to select a frame. Assign it a Width value of 4 point.

5. Type the following in the text box, pressing the Enter key where indicated by the ¶ mark: "ALPHABET SALE! ¶ ALL UPPER-CASE LETTERS ON SALE AT ¶ GREATLY REDUCED PRICES ¶ Choose from serif and sans serif letters in a variety ¶ of typefaces and type styles. ¶ Call 800-123-ABCD for pricing information."

6. Click in the "Alphabet Sale!" paragraph and format it in 18-point Helvetica with 24 points of leading (18/24). Choose Edit/Preferences/Typographic and type 24 in the Increment field under Baseline Grid. Type .5 in the Start field. Click on OK.

7. With the first line still selected, choose Style/Formats (Ctrl+Shift+F) to display the Paragraph Formats dialog box. Click in the Lock to Baseline Grid check box. Click on OK.

8. Click in the "Choose from serif..." paragraph, and choose Style/Formats (Ctrl+Shift+F). Type 3 in the Space Before field. Click on OK. This places 3 inches of space between the first 3 and the last 3 lines.

9. Select all the text (Ctrl+A) and click on the Center alignment icon in the Measurements palette.

10. Format the next two lines beginning with "All Upper-case..." in 12-point Helvetica.

11. Select the 3 lines on the bottom. Format them in 10-point Helvetica. Choose Style/Leading (Ctrl+Shift+E) and type 12 in the Leading dialog box.

12. Choose File/Save as (Ctrl+Alt+S). Save this file under the name "Trap."

CREATING COLORS

1. Now you will create custom colors for this document. Choose Edit/Colors. Click on New. Click on Pantone and scroll to find Pantone 192 or type 192 in the Pantone No. field. Be sure that the Process Separation check box is deselected (empty). This will print Pantone 192 as a spot color. Click on OK. Click on Save.

2. Repeat this process to create Pantone colors 333 and 581. But this time click on the Process Separation button in the Edit Color dialog box to print Pantone 333 and 581 as process colors.

3. Choose Edit/Colors again and click on New to display the Edit Color dialog box. Choose the CMYK model. Type Orange in the Name field. Type 10 in the Cyan field; 75 in the Magenta field; 100 in the Yellow field; and 0 in the Black field. Leave Process Separation deselected to print Orange as a spot color. Click on OK. Click on Save.

You have assigned a shade of 50% Blue as a spot color to the background of the box. You have created Pantone 192 as a spot color and created Orange as a spot color. You have created Pantone 333 and Pantone 581 as process colors. Now apply those colors to items. Before continuing, save this document (Ctrl+Alt+S) with the name "Trap".

Ctrl+Alt+S File/Save as
Ctrl+M Item/Modify
Ctrl+B Item/Frame

FYI

You don't have to click on Save in the Edit Colors dialog box until you have completed creating, editing, etc. colors from this dialog box.

REVIEW EXERCISE #2

1. In the "Trap" file, use the Text Box tool to draw three text boxes on the same page, each 1 inch square. Type a capital letter in each box. Select each letter and format it in any typeface at 60 points. Choose Item/Modify (Ctrl+M) and select Centered from the Vertical Alignment drop-down menu. Click on the Center alignment icon in the Measurements palette.

2. Select the original large text box and choose Item/Frame (Ctrl+B). Pull down the Color menu and select Pantone 192. Click on OK.

3. Triple-click to select the first line of text. Choose Style/Color and select Orange.

4. Select the second and third lines. Choose Style/Color and select Pantone 192.

5. Select the last three lines at the bottom of the text box and choose Style/Color and choose Pantone 333.

6. Select the first 1-inch text box and choose Item/Modify. Use the Background drop-down menu to select Pantone 581. Assign it a Shade value of 100%. Click on OK. Select the letter in the box and choose Style/Color/Red.

7. Select the second 1-inch text box and choose Item/Modify. Use the Background drop-down menu to select Pantone 192. Assign it a Shade value of 100%. Click on OK. Select the letter in the box, choose Style/Color, and choose Black.

Ctrl+M Item/Modify
Ctrl+S File/Save

8. Select the third 1-inch text box and choose Item/Modify again. Use the Background drop-down menu to select Yellow. Assign it a Shade value of 100%. Click on OK. Select the letter in the box and choose Style/Color/Orange. Save your file (Ctrl+S).

REVIEW EXERCISE #3

Now that you have created and applied colors, you will apply trapping values to elements in your document.

1. Choose Edit/Colors. Click on Pantone 192. Click on Edit Trap to display the Trap Specifications dialog box for Pantone 192. Click on Blue. Click on Overprint. Click on Save twice (Figure 16.22).

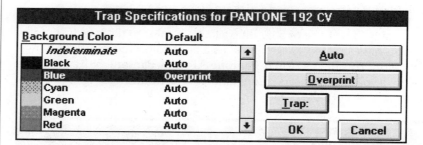

Figure 16.22—Trap Specifications for Pantone 192 overprints on the Blue background throughout the document.

2. Choose View/Show Trap Information to display the Trap Information palette. Click on the text box with the letter A and use the Content tool to select the letter. Click on the question mark in the Trap Information palette to learn how XPress traps the red A against the Pantone 581 background.

3. Choose Edit/Colors. Click on Orange. Click on Edit Trap to display the Trap Specifications dialog box for Orange. Click on Blue. Click on Overprint. Click on Save twice. Repeat this process to trap Orange on the Yellow background.

4. Choose Edit/Colors. Click on Pantone 333. Click on Edit Trap to display the Trap Specifications dialog box for Pantone 192. Click on Blue in the Background field. Type .75 in the Trap field to spread ("stretch") Pantone 192 three-quarters of a point against the Blue background. Click on the Trap button to apply the trapping value. Click on Save twice.

5. Repeat this process to trap Red against the Pantone 581 background and the Orange against the Yellow background. Although you will not be able to view the results of the trapping values you applied, your screen should resemble Figure 16.23.

6. Save this file (File/Save). When you complete the next lesson, you'll print this "Trap" file and see how the spot colors and color separations print on separate pages.

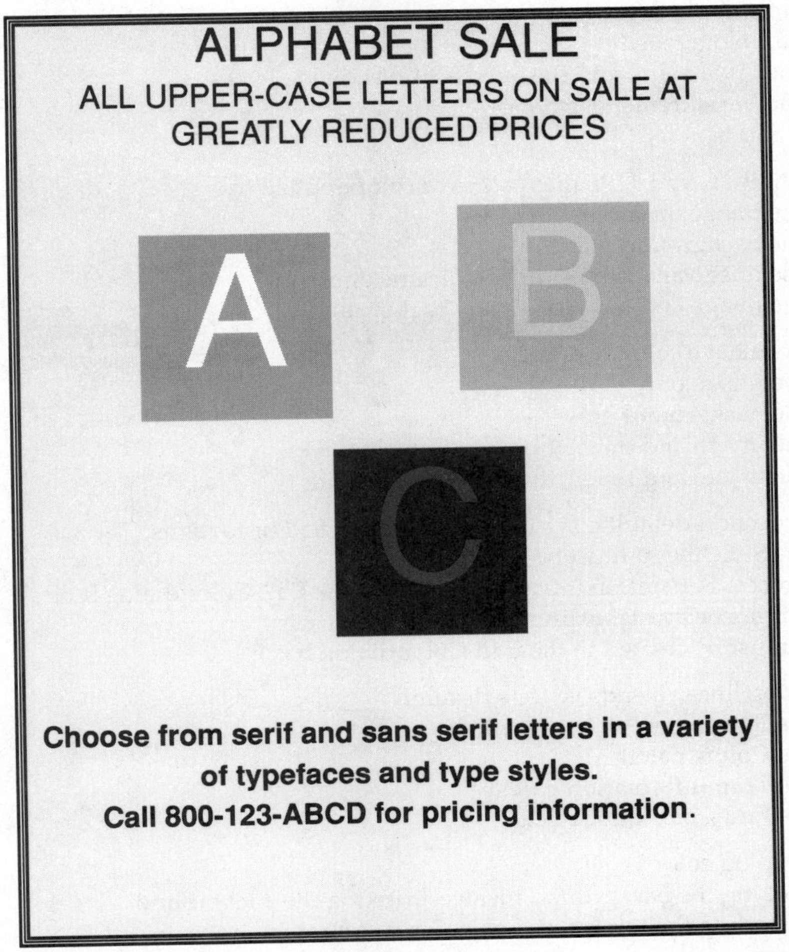

Figure 16.23—The finished flyer, which incorporates several trapping values.

REVIEW QUESTIONS

Read the following questions and choose the answer which best completes the statement.

1. Color that is created using one ink is called _____
   a. Pantone color
   b. 4-process color
   c. spot color
   d. RGB color

2. A color comprised of the percentages of CMYK colors is a _____.
   a. Pantone color
   b. 4-process color
   c. spot color
   d. RGB color

3. Color is applied from _____.
   a. the Colors palette
   b. the Style menu and the Specifications dialog boxes
   c. the Measurements palette
   d. a and b

4. Paint, PICT, and TIFF files can have color applied to _____.
   a. the image only
   b. the background only
   c. the image and the picture box frame only
   d. the image and the picture box background

5. EPS can have color applied to _____.
   a. the image only
   b. the background only
   c. the image and the picture box frame only
   d. the image and the picture box background

6. Before a non-default color can be applied to text or to items, _____.
   a. the Style menu must be active
   b. Process Separation must be checked in the Edit Color dialog box
   c. it must be available under the Item menu
   d. it must be created in the Edit Color dialog box

7. Creating linear blends is done through _____.
   a. the Style menu
   b. the Colors palette
   c. the Trap Information palette
   d. the Edit Color dialog box

8. In trapping colors, _____.
   a. choking the background means shrinking the background
   b. spreading the foreground object means stretching the object
   c. overprinting the foreground object means knocking out the
      background
   d. a and b

9. Automatic trapping values are specified in _____.
   a. the General Preferences dialog box
   b. the Colors palette
   c. the Trap Information palette
   d. the Application Preferences dialog box

10. To specify custom trapping for an object, use the _____.
    a. Style menu
    b. Trap Information palette
    c. Colors palette
    d. Edit Color dialog box

Answers: 1. c; 2. b; 3. d; 4. d; 5. b; 6. d; 7. b; 8. d; 9. d; 10. b

LESSON

17

Printing

OVERVIEW

In this lesson you will learn how to print your files to a laser printer and how to prepare files for output to an imagesetter at a service bureau. You will examine the Printer Setup dialog box as well as options in the Print dialog box. In the course of the lesson, you will print the "Trap" file you created in the last lesson.

TOPICS

Preparation for printing
Printing to a laser printer
Activating the printer
Printer Setup
Print dialog box
Tiling
Printing to an imagesetter
Sending files to a service bureau
Review Exercise
Review Questions

TERMS

Font Usage
Halftone Screen
Orientation
Page Gap
Paper Offset
paper size
Reduce/Enlarge
Resolution
Windows Control Panel

Ctrl+O File/Open

PREPARATION FOR PRINTING

Ultimately, anything that you generate in a page layout program like QuarkXPress is destined to be printed, either on a laser printer like the LaserJet II/III or an imagesetter like the Linotronic. Getting all your text and graphic elements from screen to print, however, is a little more complicated than choosing Command/Print.

PRINTING TO A LASER PRINTER

Before printing to a laser printer, you must first activate and then configure the printer driver in the Windows Control Panel. Here you will specify the printer type and output port to which you will be printing. Then you must use the Printer Setup dialog box in QuarkXPress to specify the way you want the document printed.

ACTIVATING THE PRINTER

These instructions for designating a target printer are for Windows Version 3.0. Under Windows 3.1, all installed printers are automatically active. If you are using another version of Windows, consult your Windows manual for information. Activating the printer is done through the Windows Program Manager, where clicking on the Main window group should display the Windows Control Panel. Your setup may be different, but if you pull down enough windows you will locate the Windows Control panel.

Tip

For proofing purposes *only*, reduce an oversized page so that it will print on one letter size page.

EXERCISE A

1. Begin by activating the printer by double-clicking on the Windows Control Panel in the Windows Program Manager (Figure 17.1).

2. Use the Installed printers scroll list to select the printer driver for your printer. If you are using a PostScript printer, choose the PostScript Printer driver.

FYI

If you are printing to a roll-fed printer, the Paper Size option is not available.

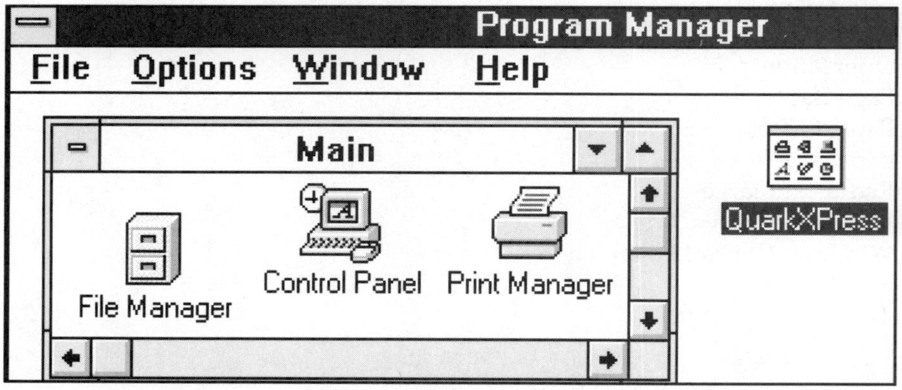

Figure 17.1—Double-clicking on the Windows Control Panel displays the Printers dialog box where you scroll to select a printer from the Installed Printers list. Under Windows 3.1, because all of the installed printers are automatically active, you can choose one printer to be the default printer (the first printer QuarkXPress will choose when you create a new document).

3. Click on Active in the Status area to make the printer driver you selected active. Then click Configure to display the Printers/Configure dialog box. Select a port from the Ports scroll list, and click Setup to display the Printer on [Port] dialog box. When you have completed all the entries, click on OK.

PRINTER SETUP

Now that you have *designated* a target printer, you must *configure* it to the document you are printing. This is done in QuarkXPress from the Printer Setup dialog box.

1. Launch QuarkXPress and open the file you saved as "Blue." Choose File/Printer Setup (Ctrl+Alt+P) to display the Printer Setup dialog box (Figure 17.2). If you are not printing to the Default Printer, click on Specific Printer and scroll to display the printer you will be using.

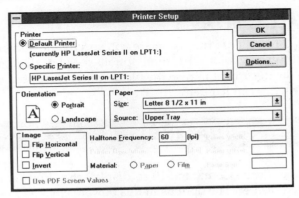

Figure 17.2—The Printer Setup dialog box.

2. The Orientation field allows you to specify whether the document will print horizontally (Landscape mode) or vertically (Portrait mode). Select Portrait mode to print this document to a laser printer.

3. The Paper Size option refers to the size of the paper which will be fed into the paper, not to the page size you specified in the New (document) dialog box. The Source option allows you to choose Upper Tray (automatic feed) or Manual Feed. Select Manual Feed only if you are inserting single sheets of paper into the printer manually.

4. The options in the Image field allow you to reverse the printing of page images from left to right (Flip Horizontal), or to print the images upside down (Flip Vertical).

5. The Halftone Screen field is where you to specify the default line screen value at which XPress prints halftone pictures (photographs that have been prepared for printing by being photographed through a screen) and for EPS graphic files. You can enter a value from 15 to 400, but your halftone lpi value should match the selected printer's resolution capability. For PostScript printers, this value defaults to 60 lpi.

What you will need

A text file
A graphic file

Ctrl+P File/Print
Ctrl+N File/New

WARNING!

If you used 11 x 8.5 for the Width and Height fields in the New (document) dialog box, you must select Landscape Orientation in the Printer Setup dialog box.

Ctrl+P File/Print

6. Click on the Options button to display the Printer on [Port] dialog box. Here you can enter a value in the Scaling field to print a document's pages scaled from 25% to 400% in 1% increments. You may not have this feature unless your printer supports it. Keep in mind that the values you selected will not affect the contents of the document, only the way the document is printed.

7. If you have selected a PostScript printer, the Options dialog box allows you to print either to the printer or to an Encapsulated Post-Script file. You can also specify the print area margins with reference to the printer (not relative to the document itself), and to specify whether each job will print with a header, general PostScript printing information not related to any specific document. Click on OK until you have closed all of the dialog boxes and returned to the document. Now that you have activated and configured the printer, you are ready to make the necessary selections in the Print dialog box.

Tidy up!

If you should change the Halftone Screen value in a document and save the document, when you open a new document, the Screen Frequency value of the previously saved document may be in effect. Always check the Printer Setup dialog box before printing any document.

PRINT DIALOG BOX

The Print dialog box (File/Print) is where you specify the number of pages, the type of output, and color separation options for your document. Before printing, save the document in case the file becomes corrupted in the printing process. Yes, this can happen!

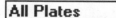

The All Plate drop-down menu in the Print dialog box lists all the colors used in the document.

EXERCISE B

1. Choose File/Print (Command-P) to display the Print dialog box for the selected printer. The options in this box are covered in more detail in Lesson 7.

2. Click on the Make Separations button in the Color field and leave All Plates displayed in the Plate field to print 7 plates for the file named "Trap". Click on OK. XPress displays a Print Status box (Figure 17.3).

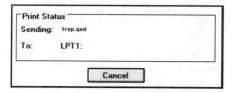

Figure 17.3—The Print Status box displays the name of the file and the printer. Click on the Cancel button to end the printing process.

3. The "Trap" file contains 3 spot colors, Blue, Pantone 192, and Orange, as well as 2 process colors, Pantone 333 and Pantone 581. This means that 7 plates will print—Cyan, Magenta, Yellow, Black (for the process colors) and Blue, Pantone 192, and Orange (for the spot colors). This is an expensive way to print, however, and we are doing so for demonstration purposes only. On a real job, all the spot colors would be designated as process colors, which means that only four plates would be printed.

TILING

If we all lived in a letter size world, it would be easy but boring. You may find yourself printing oversized documents like tabloids and multiple-page spreads that won't fit on a letter size page. An imagesetter with a larger paper size can take care of that, but for proofing purposes you may need to tile, that is, to print sections of the large page on many smaller pages.

Selecting the Tiling feature allows you to print large documents in sections (tiles) which XPress prints with tick marks to help you reassemble the tile into the larger page(s).

EXERCISE C

1. Create a new file (File/New) and in the New dialog box select Other for Page Size and type 24" by 24" in the Width and Height fields. Select the Automatic Text Box option and allow a 1-inch margin all around. Click on OK.

2. Import text and graphics into the one-page file so that you have pretty much filled the entire page.

3. Choose File/Printer Setup and make the appropriate selections.

4. Choose File/Print and locate the Tiling section in the lower part of the Print dialog box (Figure 17.4). Notice that you have three options: Off, Manual, and Auto. The default is Off, which means that unless you select another option, printing will begin from the upper left corner of the page and print only what fits on the paper in your printer.

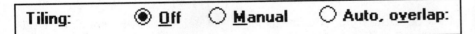

Figure 17.4—The Tiling option in the Print dialog box defaults to Off.

5. If you select Auto, XPress determines how much of your document to fit on each page that is printed. It defaults to a 3-inch overlap between pages, but you can type in another value. Leave the default value at 3 inches.

6. If you want more control over how XPress prints the tiles, click on Manual. Now XPress will print only what will fit on the selected page starting with ruler coordinates of X=0 and Y=0. It will then keep printing pages until the entire document is printed. Once the first page is printed, move the ruler origin and print the page again from the new origin. XPress will continue printing the document from the new location each time you move the ruler origin. Continue to move the zero point and print until the document is completed. For now, click on Auto and click on Print.

7. When all the tiles are printed, get your tape and scissors. Cut, align, and tape the pages together using the tile location information in the upper left corner of each tile to create the large-page document.

Sorry!

Tick marks are printed only on tiles generated with the Auto option.

FYI

The numbers at the top of a tile refer to the page number, column number, and row number.

Move the ruler origin to another position before printing each tile.

Ctrl+O File/Open
Ctrl+P File/Print

PostScript dumps

A PostScript dump is a print-to-disk file which you create that includes all the printer and Printer Setup settings; all the screen fonts used in the document; and all the pictures (even the high resolution graphics) imported into that file—"dumped" into *one file* which the service bureau runs out on the imagesetter.

The advantage of using a PostScript dump is that any information necessary for outputting the file is embedded in that file; the disadvantage is that that the service bureau is not responsible for any settings in the Printer Setup or Print dialog boxes.

PRINTING TO AN IMAGESETTER

When you select an imagesetter in the Windows Control Panel, other options are available in the Printer Setup dialog box. Because high resolution imagesetters print finer line screens than ordinary laser printers, you can specify a higher value for the Halftone Screen value. Generally, 133 is a line screen used in printing to an imagesetter.

Other options are also available in the Printer Setup dialog box. The Resolution field allows you to enter a value that does not determine the resolution at which your document will print, but rather how XPress will handle black and white bitmapped and TIFF images. This value, however, should match the printer's resolution. So if you're printing to a Linotronic 300 imagesetter, type in 1270 or 2400, depending on the resolution you indicate on your service bureau's worksheet.

A roll-fed imagesetter usually supports multiple paper widths. Enter the Paper Width value supported by the imagesetter to which you are printing.

The Paper Offset field allows you to shift the image of the printed page to the right on the paper or film. Paper Offset is measured from the left edge of the paper or film. You would normally leave this value at 0 (zero).

If you don't specify a value in the Page Gap field, pages will print on a roll-fed imagesetter with no space between them, making it difficult to cut the printed pages before printing. A value of 1 pica is usually enough.

SENDING FILES TO A SERVICE BUREAU

Regardless of how knowledgeable and helpful your service bureau is, whenever you send a file for output on an imagesetter, you are responsible for the preparation of that file. There are several important steps you must take to ensure that your document will print properly on an imagesetter.

1. Check the fonts you are using in your document by choosing Utilities/Font Usage. Use the drop-down menu under Find what to make sure that no fonts labeled Unknown are listed (Figure 17.5). If they are, that means that XPress is substituting fonts in your document and will do the same when printed to an imagesetter. Either install the fonts that are missing or install other fonts and make any necessary formatting changes in your document.

2. Then make copies on a disk of all the screen fonts used in your document. Make a list of the fonts by name and manufacturer. Adobe typefaces will print differently from Bitstream typefaces, so be sure to list the font's manufacturer. Figure 17.6 displays a standard work order which the service bureau will ask you to fill out. Notice that it requires specific information about your file.

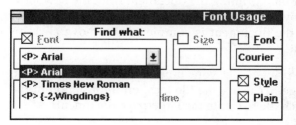

Figure 17.5—The {-2) symbol in the Font Usage dialog box indicates that the Wingdings font was used in this file, but it is not currently installed in the system.

Riverside Imagesetters
Linotronic Output Center

(908) 758-1133
FAX (908) 741-4129 • MODEM (908) 530-4594
225 Hwy. 35 • Middletown Twp., NJ 07701
OUTSIDE LOCAL AREA CALL 1-800-783-7474

№ 11505

POSTSCRIPT OUTPUT WORK ORDER

Bill to _____

Complete Address _____

Contact _____ Phone No. (___) _____

P.O. No. _____ Job No. _____

Ship to _____

Address _____

_____

Date _____ Due Date _____

SERVICES DESIRED: *(Please check appropriate boxes)*
☐ Standard 24-Hour Service
☐ Same Day Service (50% Surcharge) in by 12 noon, out before 8 pm.
☐ **RUSH:** While-U-Wait (100% Surcharge, 200% after 8 pm.)

☐ Special Instructions _____

_____

_____

_____

FOR OFFICE USE ONLY	
Date Received _____ Date Out _____	
Time ___:___ _M Time ___:___ _M	
Job handled by _____	
Total No. Pgs. _____	
Output/Other info. _____	
Extra process time _____	
Problems _____	

Subtotal	Credit Invoice No.
Tax	Amount
Total	New Balance
Invoice No.	Reason
Date	Initial	Date

Please list EVERY font family used in pages to be output

_____
_____
_____
_____
_____
_____

☐ Paste-up   ☐ No. Scans ___
☐ Conversion ☐ Editing
☐ Pick-up by Riverside ☐ Call when ready. We will pick up.

Desktop business hours are: Monday-Friday: 8 am-8 pm. Files submitted after 8 pm will be considered in-house the next business day. Weekend hours available by special arrangement only.

Deliver by:
☐ Riverside Messenger
☐ Federal Express
   Your Account # _____
☐ UPS Ground/Priority Mail
☐ Special Courier (Call for price)

PROGRAM USED/VERSION	FILE NAME	Specify Pages or ALL	No. of Copies	Total Pages Expctd	OPTIONS				PAGE SIZE		PAGE ORIENTATION			TYPE OF OUTPUT						
					Crop marks	Negative	Emulsion Down	Color Seps	Letter	Other Please fill in page size	Ver-tical	Hori-zontal	LW 300 DPI	COLOR		L-300/500				add $2 per pg.
														Paper	Film	RC Paper	Film	1693	1270	2540

TOTAL PAGES EXPECTED _____

PLEASE NOTE: 1. Furnish a laser print-out or photocopy along with all text and/or graphic files on a **BACKUP** disk—**NEVER** send us the only copy in existence. **2.** All information requested on this Work Order form **MUST** be provided before your files can be typeset. **3.** The program and fonts used to generate your files must be compatible with the Linotronic. **4.** Riverside Imagesetters is **NOT** responsible for any errors resident in files submitted for output. **5.** All files are output as received unless you specifically request special handling. **6.** Any incorrect information may delay completion of your job. **7.** All requested changes to your files, before or after submission, are subject to our regular hourly rates—minimum $15. Standard processing time per page is 15 minutes. Additional processing time will be billed at $1 per minute. **9.** The authorized signature below denotes acceptance of the above conditions.

If you have any questions regarding this Work Order, please call us for clarification.

_____
Authorized Signature

H 90 F68-73 6/30/92 95%

WHITE COPY FOR RIVERSIDE   YELLOW COPY FOR INVOICE   PINK COPY FOR CUSTOMER

Notice that the output work order asks you for information about the application in which you created the file(s) and the version number of that application. This is critical because earlier versions of a program do not always handle color functions in the same way as later versions do.

You must also specify the number of pages to be output from each file; the orientation of those pages; and the type of output you want. Pricing for RC (resin coated) paper will differ from the cost of negatives. Likewise, outputting at 1693 dpi, 1240 dpi, or 2540 dpi will affect the cost of a job. This information is required for each *file*, not just for each job.

Figure 17.6—A sample work order for files to be output at a service bureau. *(Courtesy of Riverside Imagesetters, Red Bank, New Jersey.)*

Ctrl+P File/Print

3. Use the Picture Usage dialog box to list all the pictures in your document (Utilities/Picture Usage). Pictures are listed by name and location. Copy any high resolution pictures like EPS and TIFF files to the same folder as the document on the floppy disk you are taking to the service bureau. XPress displays only a screen representation of high resolution files and needs the original file to print the picture at the higher resolution.

4. QuarkXPress has a Complete Save feature which will incorporate any changes you made to the Application Preferences, default General Preferences, Typographic Preferences, and Hyphenation and Justification Preferences. However, if you are printing a document with color and you made changes in the Trap fields of the Application Preferences dialog box, be sure to make a copy of those settings when a file is being printed to any kind of color printer.

5. Print your file and give the service bureau hard copy of the file they are outputting for you. If they have questions about how a page should look, it is easier for them to check the hard copy than to either guess or get in touch with you.

Troubleshooting

When you print a document and only the bitmapped fonts appear instead of the smoother PostScript printer fonts, you have to make the printer fonts accessible to the system. Use the Windows Control Panel to get to Fonts where you can install the necessary fonts.

If your document uses downloadable or soft fonts, check the WIN.INI file and make sure the soft fonts list for the active printer is configured correctly.

REVIEW QUESTIONS

Read the following questions and choose the answer which best completes the statement.

1. Activate a printer _____.
    a. in the Windows Control Panel
    b. in the Printer Setup dialog box
    c. in the Print dialog box
    d. a and c

2. Specifications for paper size and page orientation are made in the _____.
    a. Printer Setup dialog box
    b. Print dialog box
    c. Windows Control Panel
    d. a and c

3. When a black and white file is being printed to an imagesetter, _____.
    a. click in the Print Colors as Grays check box
    b. increase the Halftone Screen (lpi) value
    c. leave the Halftone Screen (lpi) value at the default value
    d. check the All Plates option in the Print dialog box

4. The Page Gap and Paper options are available _____.
    a. in the Print dialog box
    b. when a laser printer is selected in the Windows Control Panel
    c. in the Document Setup dialog box
    d. when an imagesetter is selected in the Printer Setup dialog box

5. When printing process colors, _____.
   a. select the Print Colors as Grays check box
   b. make the necessary changes in the Application Preferences dialog box
   c. check the Make Separations check box in the Print dialog box
   d. make sure All Plates is displayed in the Printer Setup dialog box

6. When printing files with color information to a black and white printer, it's a good idea to _____.
   a. make sure All Plates is displayed in the Printer Setup dialog box
   b. click in the Print Colors as Grays check box in the Print dialog box
   c. make the necessary changes in the Application Preferences dialog box
   d. a and b

7. In order for high resolution files to print at the higher resolution, they must be _____.
   a. listed in the Picture Usage dialog box
   b. available to QuarkXPress when the file is printing
   c. listed in the Windows Control Panel
   d. a and c

8. You should give the imagesetter _____.
   a. hard copy of your QuarkXPress file
   b. a copy of your version of QuarkXPress
   c. copies of the screen fonts used in your document
   d. a and c

9. If your file contains color information and you have made changes to the default trapping values, _____.
   a. make the necessary changes in the Printer Setup dialog box
   b. select Color in the Document Setup dialog box
   c. give the service bureau a printed copy of your Application Preferences dialog box
   d. choose Print Colors as Grays in the Print dialog box

10. Registration marks are specified in the _____.
    a. Print dialog box
    b. Printer Setup dialog box
    c. Document Setup dialog box
    d. Chooser

Answers: 1. a; 2. a; 3. b; 4. d; 5. c; 6. b; 7. b; 8. d; 9. d; 10. a

GLOSSARY

ABSOLUTE PAGE NUMBER is a page's position relative to the first page of the document, regardless of the actual folio (page) number.

ALIGNMENT is both paragraph specific (left, right, centered, and justified) and text box specific (top, bottom, centered, and justified). See Vertical Alignment.

ANCHORED BOX is a text box or picture box set in a paragraph which moves with that paragraph.

ANCHORED RULE is a line set above or below a paragraph which moves with that paragraph.

ANGLE OF ROTATION is the value entered in the Box Angle field of the Picture Box or Text Box Specifications dialog box; or in the Angle field of the Line Specifications dialog box; or in the Angle of Rotation field of the Measurements palette for those items.

APPEND command allows you to add to the current document the color palette, style sheet, or H&J specifications from another document.

ASCENT ICON is selected to align anchored boxes with the top of the first line of text in the paragraph to which it is anchored.

ASPECT RATIO is the ratio or proportion of an element's width and height. Maintaining aspect ratio when resizing an element does not distort the element.

AUTO LIBRARY SAVE check box in the Application Preferences dialog box allows you to automatically save changes to a library each time an entry is added.

AUTO PAGE INSERTION pop-up menu in the General Preferences dialog box allows you to specify whether pages will be inserted and where they will be placed when you enter or import more text than a text box can display.

AUTOMATIC TEXT BOX is a text box that appears on a master page and on its corresponding document pages when you check the Automatic Text Box option in the New (document) dialog box.

AUTOMATIC TEXT CHAIN is a text chain that is defined by the automatic text box on a master page. An automatic text chain is created when text overflow causes pages to be automatically inserted. See Story.

AUXILIARY DICTIONARY is a dictionary of user-defined words used in conjunction with the main QuarkXPress dictionary. There can be more than one Auxiliary Dictionary.

BACKGROUND is that part of a text box or picture box within the border of the box and behind the contents of the box.

BACKGROUND COLOR is the color applied to the background of a text box or picture box.

BASELINE is the invisible horizontal line upon which characters are placed.

BASELINE GRID is the invisible horizontal grid on which text is set.

BASELINE ICON is selected to align anchored boxes with the baseline of the first line of text in the paragraph to which it is anchored.

BASELINE SHIFT command is applied to single or multiple characters and to drop caps to raise or lower the text relative to its normal baseline position.

BOUNDING BOX is a non-printing box which appears around all the items in a group and around a polygon picture box.

BROKEN CHAIN ICON is displayed in the upper left corner of a master page when that master page does not contain an automatic text box.

CAP HEIGHT is the distance from the baseline to the top of an uppercase letter. This value is always measured in points.

CHOKE is a color trapping command in which the knockout area of the background color is reduced and which causes the object in front to print over the background.

CLOSE command closes a saved document.

CMYK (Cyan, Magenta, Yellow, Black), ink colors used in 4-color or process color printing.

COLOR PALETTE contains the colors available to be applied to text and items in a document.

COLOR SEPARATIONS for spot or process colors are the separation plates for the colors used on each page of a document.

CONSTRAIN under the Item menu allows you to prevent grouped items contained entirely within the constraining box from being moved or enlarged beyond the sides of the constraining text box or picture box. Items can also be constrained to 45° and 90° angles when being drawn or resized.

CONTENT TOOL is used to select and manipulate the contents of text boxes and picture boxes.

CONTRAST is the relationship between light areas, midtones, and shadows (dark areas) of a picture.

COPY command copies the selected item or text to the Clipboard.

CORNER RADIUS is the value for the radius of a corner of a rectangle and rounded corner picture box which is entered in the Corner Radius field of the Measurements palette or in the Picture Box Specifications dialog box.

CROP MARKS are short horizontal and vertical lines which are printed on a page and indicate the trim area of a page or where the page is to be cut before binding.

CURRENT PAGE NUMBER SYMBOL (#) appears when you type Ctrl-3 in a text box on the master page. The current page number itself is displayed on the document page(s).

CUT command deletes an item (when the Item tool is selected) or text (when the Content tool is selected) and places it on the Clipboard. It can then be pasted at another location in the document.

DEFAULT SETTING is a program setting which stays in effect until you change it. When you first launch the program and open dialog boxes, the values you see displayed are the default settings.

DELETE CHANGES specified in the General Preferences dialog box means that both modified and unmodified master page items on the document pages will be deleted if you apply a new master page format or reapply the same master page format to those pages.

DELETE PAGES command allows you to delete a single page or a range of pages from the document.

DOCUMENT LAYOUT PALETTE allows you to create new master pages, to delete master pages, to insert and delete document pages, to create spreads, and to apply master page formats to document pages.

DOCUMENT PAGE ICON appears in the Document Layout palette and allows you to position document pages.

DRAG-COPYING copies an item, group, or page from one document to another or from a document to a library without deleting the selected item from the document.

DROP CAP is an initial letter that is positioned below the first line in a paragraph and extends (drops) vertically more than one line into the paragraph.

EDIT COLOR dialog box is where you access one of the six color models available in QuarkXPress, create new colors to add to the Color palette, and edit existing colors.

EM DASH (—) is the width of two zeros in a font. Generate an em dash by pressing Ctrl+Alt+ Shift+=.

EM-SPACE is the width of two zeros in a font. See Flex Space.

EN DASH (–) is wider than a hyphen and half the width of an em dash. Generate an en dash by typing Ctrl+=.

EN-SPACE is a space that is half the width of an em-space. Generate an en-space by typing Ctrl+Alt+Shift+6.

ENDCAPS are straight, arrow, or tail feather cap styles applied to the beginning or end of a line.

ENDPOINTS describes a line by its two ends relative to the horizontal and vertical rulers.

Facing master page icon on the Document Layout palette displays "dog ears" indicating that all pages based on that master page will be facing pages.

FACING PAGES are right and left pages with a gutter between them. Documents with facing pages have inside and outside margins instead of left and right margins.

FILL CHARACTER is any character that appears before a Tab stop.

FILTERS are import and export translators which allow programs to share text.

FIND/CHANGE dialog box allows you to search and replace text in a story or a document.

FIND FIRST command finds the first instance of selected text in the Find/Change dialog box.

FIND NEXT command finds the next instance of selected text in the Find/Change dialog box.

FIRST LINE INDENT is the distance between the first character in a paragraph and the Left Indent value specified in the Paragraph Formats dialog box.

FLEX SPACE is a user-defined variation of an en-space. Flex Space Width is specified in the Typographic Preferences dialog box. QuarkXPress defaults to a Flex Space Width value of 50%. Generate a flex space by pressing Ctrl+Alt+Shift+5.

FOCOLTONE SYSTEM is a color system used mainly in Europe.

FONT USAGE dialog box lists all the fonts used in the active document and allows you to change any font, including its style and/or size.

FOREGROUND OBJECT is a colored item or text placed in front of or on top of a background color.

FRAMING places a border of a specified width around a box. Framing is accessed from the Item menu.

GET PICTURE command displays the Get Picture dialog box from which you can select a picture (graphic file) to place in an active picture box.

GET TEXT displays the Get Text dialog box from which you can select a text file to place in an active text box.

GREEKING refers to text and pictures that are displayed as gray bars (text) or boxes (pictures) to speed screen redraw.

GROUP command combines items which can be moved together as one unit.

GUTTER WIDTH is the vertical space between two adjacent columns. It is also the area between the inside margins in facing page documents.

H&J refers to establishing Hyphenation and Justification rules to be applied to text.

HALFTONE is a photograph which has been reproduced by photographing the picture through a screen.

HALFTONE SCREEN is a screen made up of many dots, ellipses, squares, or lines of various sizes through which a continuous tone image like a photograph is reproduced.

HORIZONTAL AND VERTICAL OFFSET terms describe a picture's distance from the left side of a picture box (horizontal offset) and from the top of the picture box (vertical offset).

HORIZONTAL SCALE is a command applied to text which expands (positive value) or condenses (negative value) the width of the character(s).

HSB is an acronym for Hue, Saturation, and Brightness in color.

HYPHENATION is the division of a word into syllables at the end of a line of text. QuarkXPress defaults to hyphenation enabled.

IGNORE ATTRIBUTES is checked in the Find/Change dialog box and limits the search criteria to text, not to style and size attributes.

INDENTS refer to the distance of text in a paragraph from the left side (Left Indent) or right side (Right Indent) of the text box, as well as the distance from the left side of the text box of the first line of text in a paragraph (First Line Indent).

INTACT CHAIN ICON is displayed in the upper left corner of a master page when that master page contains an active text box.

INTER ¶ MAX value specifies the maximum amount of space which can be placed between paragraphs when Justified Vertical Alignment is selected.

ITEM COORDINATES pop-up menu in the General Preferences dialog box allows you to specify whether the horizontal ruler displays values continuously across multiple pages in a spread or if it starts from zero at each new page.

ITEM TOOL is used to move, edit, and group text boxes, picture boxes, and lines.

JUSTIFICATION expands or condenses the space between characters and words in a line of text to fill the width of the column.

JUSTIFIED VERTICALLY ALIGNED applies to text which has space added between the lines of text so that it fits the column from top to bottom.

KEEP CHANGES specified in the General Preferences dialog box means that both modified and unmodified master page items on the document pages will not be deleted if you apply a new master page format or reapply the same master page format to those pages.

KERNING is adding or deleting white space between two characters by using the Kerning dialog box under the Style menu or the kerning arrows in the Measurements palette. A positive value adds space between letters. A negative value deletes space.

KNOCKOUT is created in color work when an object is placed in front of a background area. The background area "knocked out" by the foreground object is not printed on the color separation plate.

Labels menu in the Library palette displays the library entries—all entries or only the ones you wish to be displayed.

LEADING is the amount of space between baselines. In QuarkXPress, the leading value includes the font size plus the space between the lines.

LEFT INDENT is the distance between the left edge of a text box or a column of text and the left edge of the text in that box or column.

LEFT POINT describes the position of a line's left endpoint relative to the horizontal and vertical rulers.

LETTER SPACING (CHARACTER SPACING) is the amount of space between characters, especially when dealing with justified text.

LIBRARY ENTRY dialog box allows you to name items which are stored in the Library palette.

LIBRARY PALETTE is a floating palette which allows you to store and access items by drag-copying. You can add and delete items from the library via the Library palette.

LINE SCREEN refers to the screen angle, pattern, and number of lines per inch used to reproduce an image.

LINE tool draws lines at any angle.

LINKING is a way of joining text boxes so that text will automatically flow from one linked box to another.

LOCK TO BASELINE GRID is to horizontally align the lines of text from column to column and from text box to text box. See Baseline Grid.

MARGIN GUIDES are four non-printing guides which appear around the page and define the printing area.

MASTER GUIDES are the margin and column guides as they are defined on the master page.

MASTER PAGE is a non-printing page with formatting that is automatically applied to document pages.

MASTER PAGE ICON is used to position master pages.

MASTER PAGE ITEMS are formatting items placed on a master page which repeat on all document pages based on that master page.

MEASUREMENTS PALETTE is a floating palette where you can make formatting changes to text and items.

MENU BAR is the menu which runs along the top of the page from which you select program commands and functions.

MIDPOINT describes the position, angle, and length of an active line relative to its center point.

MISREGISTRATION occurs when the movement of paper through the printing press causes colors to be printed inaccurately.

NEW command displays the New (document) dialog box.

NEW COLUMN MARKER is displayed when the keypad Enter is pressed in a text box. Text then moves to the next column or linked text box.

NO STYLE is applied to a paragraph and strips it of any style sheet attributes while leaving local formatting intact.

NON-FACING MASTER PAGE ICON allows you to create non-facing master pages and non-facing document pages in a document.

OPEN displays the Open dialog box from which you select a drive and a document to open.

ORIENTATION icons for the printed page in the Printer Setup dialog box refer to vertical (portrait) and horizontal (landscape).

ORIGIN ACROSS refers to an item's position relative to the zero point on the horizontal ruler.

ORIGIN DOWN refers to an item's position relative to the the zero point on the horizontal ruler.

Orphan is a short line of type that falls at the top of a column or page.

ORTHOGONAL LINE TOOL draws either horizontal or vertical lines only. See Line Tool.

Oval Picture Box TOOL creates circles and ellipses.

OVERFLOW INDICATOR appears in the lower right corner of a text box when more text than can fit into the text box is entered or imported into that text box.

OVERPRINT indicates that a colored object is not knocked out of the background's color separation plate, but instead prints over the background color.

PAGE GAP value specifies the amount of space to be inserted between pages when printing to an imagesetter.

PANTONE MATCHING SYSTEM® lists pre-mixed ink colors.

PAPER OFFSET field in the Printer Setup dialog box is active when an imagesetter is the selected printer and allows you to specify the distance a printed page image is moved from the left edge of the paper or film.

PAPER SIZE field in the Printer Setup dialog box is active when certain printers are selected and allows you to specify a paper size for that printer.

PASTE command places the contents of the Clipboard at the insertion point on the page.

PASTEBOARD is the non-printing area outside of the margin guides.

PICTURE ANGLE command in the Picture Box Specifications dialog box or in the Measurements palette allows you to specify the angle of a picture in a picture box from −360° to 360°.

PICTURE BOX COORDINATES describe the position of a picture box relative to the horizontal (X value) and vertical rulers (Y value).

PICTURE SKEW slants a picture at a specified angle.

PICTURE USAGE Dialog box displays a list of the pictures in a document and their status as either modified, missing, or OK, and allows you to update the status of missing or modified pictures.

POLYGON PICTURE BOX TOOL is used to draw polygon picture boxes of at least three sides.

PRINT command displays the Print dialog box.

printer SETUP dialog box is where you specify printing information such as the specific printer, paper and page size, and page orientation.

PROCESS COLOR (4-COLOR) is a color composed of percentages of Cyan, Magenta, Yellow, and Black. Each of these four colors is printed on a separate separation plate. Overlaying these four plates in the printing process creates 4-color art.

RECTANGLE PICTURE BOX TOOL is used to draw rectangle picture boxes and square picture boxes.

REDUCE/ENLARGE field under Options in the Printer Setup dialog box allows you to reduce or enlarge a printed page between 25% and 400%.

REGISTRATION MARKS are symbols which print on camera-ready pages and are used to align plates which overlay one another.

RESHAPE POLYGON command allows you to add and delete handles from a polygon picture box in order to reshape it.

RESIZING POINTER appears when you click on a box or line handle and is used to resize the item.

RESOLUTION refers to a printer's level of clarity. A laser printer can have a resolution of 300 dots per inch while an imagesetter can have a resolution of 2400 dots per inch. The higher the resolution of the output device, the greater the clarity of detail on the printed page.

REVERSE TEXT (REVERSE TYPE) is light type (usually white type) set against a dark background.

REVERT TO SAVED command closes the current document and opens the most recently saved version of that same document.

RGB is an acronym for Red, Green, and Blue. It defines the way a computer monitor displays color.

RIGHT INDENT is the distance between the right edge of a text box or column and the right edge of the text in that box or column.

RIGHT POINT describes the right endpoint of a line relative to the zero point on the horizontal and vertical rulers.

ROTATION TOOL is used to rotate boxes, groups, and lines.

ROUNDED CORNER PICTURE BOX TOOL creates picture boxes with round corners.

RULE is a line placed above or below a paragraph.

RULE ABOVE is a line placed above a paragraph. It can be anchored to the paragraph.

RULE BELOW is a line placed below a paragraph. It can be anchored to the paragraph.

RULER GUIDES are non-printing guides pulled down and across from the horizontal and vertical rulers. They are used to align items on a page.

RULER ORIGIN is the zero point at which the horizontal and vertical rulers intersect.

RULERS are horizontal and vertical units of measure displayed on the page.

SAVE command saves a previously named document under the name it was assigned when it was first saved.

SAVE AS command allows you to name or rename a document and save it.

SAVE PAGE AS EPS saves the entire active page as an Encapsulated PostScript picture file.

SAVE TEXT displays the Save Text dialog box and allows you to export the text in a variety of formats.

SCALE values allow you to reduce or enlarge pictures and boxes.

SECTION START dialog box is where you specify a new section with new page numbers.

SHADE value makes the selected text or item darker (higher value) or lighter (lower value).

SHIFT-DRAGGING constrains a box to a square or circle.

SNAP TO GUIDES under the View menu causes items to align with guides when they are positioned in the Snap Distance as specified in the General Preferences dialog box.

SPECIFICATIONS DIALOG BOXES allow you to input values for items.

SPOT COLOR is a color printed with one ink and which produces a separation plate for that color.

SPREAD (pages) is comprised of two or more adjacent pages. In color trapping, applying a spread means to enlarge a foreground object.

STORY is the text in a linked chain of text boxes.

STYLE SHEET is a group of paragraph and character attributes that can be applied simultaneously to selected text.

SUPPRESS PICTURE PRINTOUT command is applied to a picture box which prevents the picture in the box from printing. The box frame and background color, however, will be printed.

SUPPRESS PRINTOUT command is applied to a box which prevents the frame or background color from printing. Any picture in the picture box will also not print. When applied to a text box, that text box will not print.

TAB STOP moves the Text Insertion bar a distance specified in the Paragraph Tabs dialog box when you press the Tab key.

TEMPLATE is a file that cannot be saved under the same name. A template is used as a basis or grid for other documents.

TEXT BOX COORDINATES refer to the text box's position from the horizontal ruler (X value) and from the vertical ruler (Y value).

TEXT BOX TOOL is used to create text boxes.

TEXT INSET is the distance between the text and the left edge of the text box as specified in the Text Inset field in the Text Specifications dialog box.

TEXT OUTSET value in the Runaround Specifications dialog box specifies the amount of space between a picture and the text that is running around it. Auto Image or Manual Image must be selected to enable the Text Outset field.

TEXT RUNAROUND command allows you to specify the way in which text flows around, behind, or in front of pictures and items.

THUMBNAILS view displays a miniature view of document pages and allows you to drag-copy pages between documents and to move pages within a document.

TOOL PALETTE is a moveable palette which displays the tools available in QuarkXPress used to generate and manipulate text and items.

TRACKING is adding or deleting white space between selected words and characters via the Tracking dialog box or the tracking arrows in the Measurements palette. A positive value adds space; a negative value deletes space.

TRAPPING is compensating for printing misregistration by increasing the foreground object (spread) or reducing the background color (choke).

TRUMATCH SWATCHING SYSTEM® is a color system which allows to you specify lighter or darker colors with digital precision.

TYPE SIZE is the size of a selected character (in points).

TYPE STYLE refers to any of the thirteen default styles (Bold, Italic, etc.) available under the Style submenu.

UNCONSTRAIN command removes the Constrain attribute from a group without ungrouping it.The group can now be moved outside the boundary of the holding box with which it was originally grouped.

UNGROUP separates items in a group so they can be manipulated individually without reference to other items.

UNLINKING tool allows you to break links between text boxes. Shift-click with the Unlinking tool on a linked text box to remove that text box from the chain.

VERTEX is the point where a line and a corner meet in a polygon picture box.

VERTICAL ALIGNMENT determines the vertical alignment (top, bottom, centered, or justified) of text in a text box. See Horizontal and Vertical Alignment.

WHOLE WORD is checked in the Find/ Change dialog box when the Find what text should match only a whole word (like break), not the word or words embedded in other text (like breakfast).

WIDOW is the last line in a paragraph which falls at the top of a column. An **ORPHAN** is the first line of a paragraph that falls at the bottom of a column of text.

XAND Y VALUES indicate an item's position from the zero point on the horizontal ruler (X value) and from the zero point on the vertical ruler (Y value).

XC AND YC VALUES indicate the midpoint or center of a line from the zero point on the horizontal ruler (XC value) and from the zero point on the vertical ruler (YC value).

ZERO POINT or ruler origin is the point on the ruler where the horizontal and vertical rulers intersect. Item positions are measured from the zero point.

ZOOM TOOL is used to magnify (click) or demagnify (Alt-click) the screen display. Pressing the Control key temporarily changes the cursor to the Zoom tool.

INDEX

NOTES

NOTES

NOTES

NOTES

NOTES

NOTES

NOTES

NOTES

NOTES

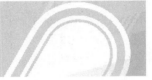

NOTES

NOTES

NOTES